The Economics of Corporate Enterprise

NORMAN S. BUCHANAN

Associate Professor of Economics
University of California

NEW YORK
HENRY HOLT AND COMPANY

PRINTED IN THE
UNITED STATES OF AMERICA

To My Grandmother

MARY JANE MC KENZIE

with Respect and Admiration

PREFACE

Some explanation is perhaps necessary for offering yet another volume to the already long list of books dealing with the
corporation. Whatever justification there is for the present effort
lies in its somewhat different treatment of familiar problems; with
respect to the chosen title, *The Economics of Corporate Enterprise*, the emphasis falls upon the word economics.

One of the virtues of modern economic analysis is that the consequences of any change in the economic data can be traced
through to show their impact upon the output, prices, profits, and
general behavior of the individual firms that compose the economic system. And an important group of writers has developed
the economic theory of the single enterprise to an incisiveness
not known a few years ago. Presumably these latter-day achievements in the economic theory of the enterprise and in economic
theory in general have some relevance to business enterprises in
the real world; if not, they are no more useful than other harmless
forms of mental gymnastics. So far as I am aware, however, there
has been no thorough-going attempt to apply them to the corporation as the characteristic form of business enterprise in the real
world. This seems unfortunate insofar as it is true. Descriptive
material on how corporations are organized, how they raise funds
by the sale of security contracts, the provisions of such contracts,
corporate expansion, reorganization, etc., are all very well. But
unless such descriptions are draped over a firm theoretical skeleton
so that they form a recognizable and logical body of thought they
are likely to remain unassorted and unrelated piles of gaudy and
drab materials. Moreover, there is the ever-present risk that the
materials will be rendered styleless and obsolete by a new act of
Congress, the establishment of a new regulatory commission, or a
judicial decision in an important case. In other words, there is the
very real danger of a person having his useful knowledge decreed
away or suddenly relegated to the attic. As a consequence it is

my own view that in offering courses of instruction to university students there should be a constant effort to emphasize the theory and logic underlying outwardly different forms and factual situations. While the latter are in a state of continuous flux and change, the former seem to have a surprising permanence and durability. The present work endeavors throughout to maintain the emphasis on general principles and to develop a more or less integrated body of theory of the corporate enterprise possessing general applicability. In the pursuit of this goal, however, there is no claim to having developed new doctrines; rather the aim has been to tie together the work of earlier writers into a useful pattern and to employ the tools they have fashioned in the treatment of important problems. The degree to which success has attended the effort is for the reader to judge.

A more descriptive title for the volume would have been *Some Aspects of the Economics of Corporate Enterprise*, since not all the economic problems of corporate enterprise in the modern world are here treated. In fact, the scope of the work has been deliberately narrowed down to include certain problems which, it seems to me, constitute an integrated unity. Consequently, and despite their importance, the broad problems growing out of the dispersion of corporate ownership and its counterpart, the separation of ownership and control, are scarcely considered except for a few general comments in the final chapter. Similarly, the whole problem of public control and regulation of corporate enterprise is accorded no explicit and organized analysis. These and other omissions were deliberate because to have discussed such questions properly would have overbalanced the treatment of those other problems I particularly wished to consider. An added reason for their omission was that other and better-qualified writers have already dealt, or will shortly deal, with these problems effectively and at length.

Because of its unwonted emphasis on economic analysis it may be that students will find that the book reads less rapidly than some other volumes of a closely related character. On the other hand its relatively shorter length and the summaries at the end of each chapter may serve to offset the difficulty. In preparing the volume I have assumed throughout that the reader is not wholly unacquainted with economics but that he has had at least an introductory course in the field.

Since many instructors will, I am sure, wish to supplement the present volume with additional reading assignments, numerous references are appended to each chapter. While these doubtless exceed the number it will be possible to assign, there is, I think, a virtue in indicating to ambitious and curious students where they may find scope for their energies. Those instructors who find the "problem" or "case" method of instruction a helpful supplement to more formal pedagogy will discover, I hope, that the present volume integrates well with the more widely used case books. Indeed, it is my own intention to use the book along with case materials.

My indebtedness to the work of others is but inadequately revealed by the acknowledgments in the text. The willingness of departmental colleagues past and present to discuss controversial issues and common problems has been of enormous assistance. Likewise their kindness in reading and criticizing all or certain parts of the manuscript at various stages of its development in spite of the pressure of their own activities has placed me heavily in their debt. I should especially like to mention in this connection my obligations to R. D. Calkins, William Fellner, E. T. Grether, Henry Rand Hatfield, Oscar Lange, A. P. Lerner, Earl Rolph, C. C. Staehling, and Elliott Swan. Professor E. G. Nelson of Stanford University contributed helpful suggestions for the improvement of several chapters. Two of my students, Sheridan Atkinson and William Poggetto, have given me the benefit of their criticisms based upon a careful reading of the manuscript. Miss Fern Peterson patiently and carefully typed through several drafts of the various chapters, and in general served as a capable research assistant for a period of more than two years. The arduous tasks of preparing the final draft for the printer have been enormously lightened by Miss Constance Hagan whose intelligence and judgment have saved me many worries. To all the aforementioned and to the various economists with whom it has been my privilege to discuss common problems from time to time I am sincerely grateful for assistance and enlightenment. For the errors that remain of course I am alone responsible.

The Editors of the *Quarterly Journal of Economics* have kindly permitted me to reproduce in Chapters IX, XII, XIII, and XIV material that first appeared in their pages in substantially its present form.

N. S. B.

Berkeley, California
June, 1939

ANALYTICAL TABLE OF CONTENTS

Part One

LEGAL ASPECTS OF CORPORATE ENTERPRISE

Chapter 1

INTRODUCTION: CORPORATE ENTERPRISE AND ECONOMIC ANALYSIS

Although there are available many excellent volumes dealing with corporations, not all of them, by any means, spring from a common point of view. Some stress the importance of the corporation as the dominant or typical form of business ownership organization in the occidental world. Others, obversely, are concerned more to emphasize the growing dangers of the corporate form as a vehicle for the exercise of important powers by a few persons. Some authors, again, aim to point out the relationship between the growth of the corporate form and the rapidity of the rate of real capital accumulation which, in many ways, is the most important single characteristic of economic development in the period since the industrial revolution and a fruitful source of contentious problems plaguing the present era. Alternately, certain writers are no little concerned with the urgent necessity of developing ways and means of bending the corporation as an economic institution, that is to say as a way of organizing economic activity, more in the service of general welfare. There can be no question whatever as to the vital importance of all these topics and many more besides on which volumes are already extant. For the most part these are not the main theme of the present work and they enter the discussion and analysis only incidentally. Our task here is to formulate the underlying principles and logic that are applicable to the formation, operation, expansion, reorganization, and dissolution of corporate enterprises organized for purposes of private profit and carrying on their activities in an economic system characterized by production for sale in a market. At least this does well enough at the present juncture as a first approximation in few words.

Historically and practically, however, the corporation is a legal institution, a convenient device by which economic activities are organized and carried on. For our purposes it is insufficient merely

3

to postulate the existence of private property and free contract in general terms as is so frequently done in general economic theory. The legal rules surrounding the organization and operations of corporations are frequently quite important because they modify and set the limits to corporate action. This is particularly the case with respect to the procurement of capital by the sale of security contracts, the relations between shareholders and creditors, dividend payments, and the failure and dissolution of corporations. Here the legal rules are distinctly important and no inkling of their importance and meaning is supplied by simply stating that private property and free contract are assumed. Freedom of contract is responsible for an enormous number of variations in the kind of ownership rights and creditors' rights that persons may hold against the corporation, but the many different types of security contracts offered to investors by the modern business corporation are not easily comprehended by simply stating that free contract is assumed. Hence in what follows we shall find it necessary at various points to deal with such legal matters as seem to impinge upon the economic analysis of the corporation with especial force. Indeed, the whole of Part Two is an attempt to clarify the nature of the corporation and of creditors' and shareholders' rights and duties therein.[1]

Our discussion of the economics of corporate enterprise will also have to take into consideration at various points certain related problems of accounting. Economic theory often has a good deal to say about such concepts as income and cost and profits, and there is frequently a detailed analysis of the meaning of maximizing income and minimizing cost. In formal economic theory such questions are dealt with conceptually rather than statistically; that is, the aim throughout is to formulate the meaning and connotation of such terms precisely rather than to measure cost, income, or profit in a particular case. In economic theory it is very unusual to attempt a quantitative measure of, say, the amount of net income in a given instance, or the degree to which income had been maximized. Yet in the real world, and especially in corporations where there are various parties in interest, these prob-

---

[1] Readers who are already familiar with these matters may prefer to omit Part Two entirely and pass directly to the economic analysis of Part Three.

lems must somehow be met and an answer supplied. It is of little assistance to shrug one's shoulders or throw up one's hands in the face of the real difficulties such computations present. As a practical matter a corporation must make some "report" concerning its income and financial condition at regular and frequent intervals. As a consequence we have the very widespread use of accounting records and accounting techniques. Moreover, these accounting reports and data have a very general currency and they often become the basis for inferences and conclusions that lead on to actions by persons both within the corporation and without it. And the actions taken have important repercussions. In view of these facts it behooves us to inquire rather closely into the relationship between such concepts as income, cost, value, etc., as employed in accounting and the meaning of the same terms as used in economic analysis. One cannot blithely assume that they are identical and proceed to draw deductions on this basis. It is imperative that they be examined and compared with one another on important points. Hence in what follows we shall at times (especially in Chapter VIII) find it necessary to deal with accounting theory and accounting problems of a practical sort.

While the strands of our discussion on some occasions will lead us into certain branches of legal theory and in others towards some phases of accounting, nevertheless the main thread of our analysis will run along the paths of economic theory. And before passing directly to our main task it may not be out of place to say a word or two on the nature of that discipline.

Formal economics, the science that concerns itself with the problem of the allocation of scarce resources capable of alternative uses between competing ends, has sought to formulate the solutions of partial and complete equilibrium. An equilibrium adjustment in economic theory is simply such a balancing of opposing tendencies that no further changes in prices, products, the volume or scale of production, the distribution of the factors of production between employments, etc., need occur so long as the conditions postulated remain unaltered. Of course not all problems of interest to economists lend themselves to such solutions. For instance, no sensible person would care to argue that the historical process of progressive technological change tended to gravitate towards any position of equilibrium; nor, on the other hand, that the continual alterations in consumers' tastes move towards any definable equilibrium. But it is quite possible to define theoretically the nature of an equilibrium adjustment to a given technological innovation within a particular firm where the degree of competition is given. Such a theoretical exposition of the character of the equilibrium may be of great service in predicting the probable results of the introduction of a given invention into a particular industry. In postulating an equilibrium to a given invention the economist will do so with full awareness that this will probably not be the invention to end inventions. In the real world, of course, such positions of final adjustment, even within comparatively small sectors of the economic system, are unlikely to be precisely attained; or, if achieved, in the typical instance they do not long persist. Usually before one position of final equilibrium is reached the economic data have so changed that the gravitation is towards a somewhat different equilibrium. And depending upon the impinging variations in the economic data the new equilibrium will be different from the old in a greater or smaller degree. Notwithstanding the imperfect realization of these changing equilibria, there is quite obviously a continuous adaptation and movement in the direction of them. It is doubtless true, for example, that under competitive conditions product prices almost never attain a precise equality with their costs of production, except by a momentary accident. But it is certainly *not* true that product prices tend to move indefinitely farther and farther away from costs of production.[2] Any such contention is plainly false. Consequently there is merit in seeking to define equilibria because our comprehension of the economic process is enhanced thereby.

These movements towards positions of partial or complete equilibrium that are so much the concern of the economic theorist are in the main brought about through the medium of business enterprises; and this holds true both of the theory and of the real world. It is individual enterprises that marshal resources and re-

[2] It may be thought that the now familiar "cobweb" theorem constitutes an exception to the above; but I have tried to show elsewhere that this theorem is wrong even on its own assumptions. See "A Reconsideration of the Cobweb Theorem," *Journal of Political Economy*, Vol. 47 (1939), pp. 67-81.

allocate them in consideration of changes in the economic data; it is they who bid productive resources away from one use and into another. The realignment of production in response to demand shifts, changes in technology, the opening of new markets, variations in relative prices, etc., is achieved through the efforts of the many individual enterprises to maximize their profits. The business enterprise and its operations are therefore especially important in an economic system that relies upon the principles of free enterprise and the institution of the price system for the control of economic activity. Indeed it is a virtue of contemporary economic theory that it can trace down the effects of any change in the economic data to its repercussions on the activities of the individual enterprises; it can be shown just how a shift in demand, an increase in the cost of a factor of production, etc., will cause business enterprises to vary their prices, their rates of output, or their scale of production.

This virtue of modern economic theory that consists in its ability to show the impact of economic change upon particular firms from which the adjustments towards equilibrium emanate has been acquired only in comparatively recent times. But within the past few years a number of writers have succeeded in broadening our knowledge and understanding of the individual firm by their original and stimulating contributions. So great have been these advances that one might venture the assertion that if in 1926 [3] an economist versed in the economic literature up to that time had turned into a Rip Van Winkle and reawakened a dozen years later he would have been greatly mystified and confounded by the strange language, formulations, and constructions then employed by his fellow economists. He would learn too that during his slumbers the change had been more than terminological; new problems, he would discover, had sprung from what he had regarded as settled solutions; and he would see likewise that there

[3] We cite the year 1926 because in that year Mr. P. Sraffa published his paper "The Laws of Return Under Competitive Conditions" in the *Economic Journal* (Vol. 36, p. 535), and that paper more or less unleashed the whole flood of literature on monopolistic and imperfect competition. Despite the advances in economic theory, however, it still has to resort to simplified models to make its problems tractable. But nowadays the models are much better.

were sharp, new tools available for the treatment of problems of long standing.

In no small measure these advances in economic theory just mentioned have consisted in the fuller application of the principles of marginal analysis to a great variety of problems that had long staved off successful attack. This has been particularly true of the economic theory of the individual business enterprise which is of most immediate interest to us in the present volume. Now in its basic logic the marginal principle is quite simple: it merely aims to show what allocation of given scarce resources must obtain if the returns from those resources are to be a maximum with respect to the given ends. Yet while the underlying idea of the marginal principle is easy enough, it cannot be said that its full implications are at once obvious in the resolution of particular problems. It is the opinion of the writer that many important economic problems connected with the promotion, operation, expansion, failure, and reorganization of business enterprises become tractable with the marginal technique where other modes of treatment yield unsatisfactory results. A considerable portion of our efforts in the succeeding pages will be directed towards an attempted demonstration of the usefulness of marginal analysis in the handling of these questions. How far we succeed is of course for others to judge.

In the formal development of the marginal analysis, and in formal economic theory generally, it has been customary to define the problems posed and the solutions reached in rather rigorous terms. In this way the reasoning is made sharp and incisive. This common practice has led some persons to the conclusion that the rather austere formulations employed in economic theory have no relevance or application to the economic world as we encounter it in day-to-day life. The writer finds it hard to concur in this view, although he would freely admit that the transition from "theory" to "practice" is not always as easy as might appear at first glance. Despite the difficulties of transition, however, the human intellect is simply incapable of reasoning about the real world at all without employing simplifying assumptions and without coralling some of the many variables in a given problem into the pound of *ceteris paribus*. We do this continually in planning our daily affairs and give it no thought at all. When I say, "Tomorrow morning I shall go to the bank," I assume that between now and then I will not be murdered in my bed, maimed by a motorist, mangled by a train, or find twenty dollars in the street. One cannot make even the simplest predictive statement without employing certain assumptions that explicitly or tacitly set certain possible variables at rest. So it is with economic reasoning. From one point of view economic theory or analysis is only a method of treating problems by which the relevant factors therein are explicitly recognized and given formal statement. And the ensuing reasoning is valid only within the limits of the assumptions. But this is true of all reasoning: it is valid and accurate only within the bounds of the assumptions. Hence while economic analysis falls far short of what we would really like it to be, and while its predictive powers are sadly limited, it is, none the less, superior to vague intuitions, shadowy surmises, or personal hunches which seem to be the available alternatives to the reasoning process.

Chapter II

THE INDIVIDUAL ENTERPRISE IN
A CAPITALISTIC ECONOMY

*I. The Price System in a Capitalistic Economy. II. The Individual
Enterprise and the Price System. III. Capital Concepts as Applied
to the Business Enterprise. IV. Summary.*

〰〰〰〰〰

I. THE PRICE SYSTEM IN A CAPITALISTIC
ECONOMY

*1. The price system as the arbiter of production and consumption
in a capitalistic economy. 2. The organization of production within
the price system now on the basis of firms or enterprises. Alternative
of organizing production through the price system without the use of
business enterprises; and wholly without the use of the price system.*

*1. The price system as the arbiter of production and consump-
tion in a capitalistic economy.* Anyone who has read a book on
general economics or reflected on the economic world in which he
lives has had emphasized to him how, in capitalistic economies, the
institution of the price system organizes and controls production
through the medium of markets. And usually there is much stress
placed upon the "automatic" character of this regulation of production and consumption through changes in prices. It is pointed
out, for instance, that in an economy such as that which prevails
in the United States and other countries which have not yet gone
over to a comprehensive system of economic planning there is no
central authority that decides what commodities will be produced,
in what amounts, by what methods, in what places, etc. Instead
of these vitally important questions being determined by an authoritative body, they are the result of countless decisions on the
part of a multitude of persons each acting largely without knowledge of the others. The thing that co-ordinates their activities is

10

the institution of the price system. Within any industry it is probably more often true than not that those in charge of the particular
enterprises that compose it have little knowledge of how much of
the product each of the others is planning to produce or how much
consumers in the aggregate are likely to want. Each enterprise,
however, finds itself confronted with a framework of prices within
which it must carry on its activities; and it is the relationship between certain of these prices and the changes in these relationships
that indicate to the individual enterprise what action it ought to
take. In the first place, there are the prices for the commodities or
services that the business enterprise sells; or, if the firm has the
power to determine the price at which it sells, there are changes in
the rate at which purchasers absorb the product at that price. On
the other hand, there are the prices at which the enterprise buys
commodities and services that it needs in order to produce whatever
it sells. Each business concern decides to produce more or less, to
expand or to contract the scale of its operations, largely on the
basis of present or prospective changes in the relationships between
the prices of the things it buys and those it sells. But what we have
just said about any particular business enterprise operating within
a framework of prices is also true of business enterprises in general.
Each concern finds itself within a "price system" where the alterations of certain relative prices are, to it, of peculiar importance and
significance.

While in a capitalistic economy each individual firm quite
properly regards the vast multitude of prices which directly or
indirectly impinge upon it as a *datum* over which it has practically no control or influence, the same cannot be said with respect
to the price system from the point of view of the whole economy.
For the economy as a whole the system of related and interrelated
prices is clearly not a given, but is itself the resultant of the decisions and actions of individuals and enterprises confronted with
price relationships that appear to them as beyond their sphere of
influence. For example, the Acme Corporation would regard the
wage rates that it has to pay its employees as determined by factors
over which it had little or no control; its problem is to decide how
many persons it ought to employ at these rates. On the other hand,

the aggregate weekly, monthly, or yearly wage bill of the Acme Corporation is not without its effect upon other business enterprises for whose products and services the employees of the Acme Corporation are accustomed to spend their wages and salaries. To be sure, the employees of the Acme Corporation are but a minute fraction of the total body of consumers making purchases from business enterprises as a whole. But, with a few unimportant exceptions, persons in a capitalistic economy receive money incomes because they and/or their property are employed by business enterprises that, directly or indirectly, are engaged in selling commodities or services to income receivers for a money price. Consequently, from the point of view of the whole economy, the price system—the system of consumers' goods prices, the prices of agents or factors of production, etc.—is a system of mutual determination. Consumers' outlay reacts upon the prices and quantities sold of consumers' goods, which, in turn, react upon the quantities produced and the number of persons hired and paid incomes; on the other hand, the total salaries and wages paid, the total interest, dividends, and rents distributed, become the source from which consumers' outlay is derived. What we have in reality is a system of mutual price determination in which the prices of the factors of production and the aggregate incomes paid out thereto are closely interrelated with the prices of finished goods offered for sale and the quantities bought. It is this whole complicated arrangement, in which the power of individual persons and particular business enterprises is patently very limited, that we have in mind when we say that, in capitalistic economies, the control of production —what is to be produced, in what amounts, by what methods, in what places, etc.—is cared for by the institution of the price system.[1] That some persons hold to the view that the price system performs its functions very poorly is common knowledge; but at present we are not concerned with these criticisms. Our only interest here is to point out what we mean by saying that in capitalistic economies the control of production is vested in the price system.

[1] In many respects perhaps the most lucid and non-mathematical account of the operations of this price system is to be found in Wootton, Barbara, *Plan or No Plan*, London (Gollancz), 1934, Chs. I, III.

2. *The organization of production within the price system now on the basis of firms or enterprises. Alternative of organizing production through the price system without the use of business enterprises; and wholly without the use of the price system.* A characteristic thing about the organization of production in capitalistic economies through the price system is that while the price system is the primary regulator of production the process itself is typically undertaken by productive combinations or entities called "firms" or "enterprises." [2] That is, when we examine the structural organization of production in capitalistic economies we observe at once that it is business enterprises that hire labor, that undertake the production of new commodities, that introduce technological changes, that invest funds in real capital goods, etc. The way in which production is in fact organized is typically not on a human individualistic basis but rather in somewhat larger producing units, called firms, within which economic resources are applied in the production of products for sale in more or less well-organized markets. Yet control of production by the price system does not logically necessitate or require the existence of business enterprises.

It is at least theoretically conceivable that all production might be organized entirely through the medium of the price system and firms or enterprises as we know them could be quite absent. Individuals as real persons could specialize in producing particular commodities or rendering particular services and be guided in their activities simply and solely by relative prices and the changes therein. In such a system the production unit would be the individual, and would be identical with the consuming unit (except insofar as the consuming unit is usually the family). Each person (in his economic capacity) would presumably endeavor to maximize his net satisfactions, that is, he would try to extend his working hours up to that point at which the value of what he produced in the last "hour" of his work just balanced what it cost him. And

---

[2] The latter terms do not here imply any particular legal form of business entity such as the corporation, the partnership, the single proprietorship, etc., but merely refer to all such forms of business ownership organization. In the succeeding pages we shall use the words "firm," "enterprise," "business enterprise" as synonyms.

presumably it would be relatively easy for him to translate money costs and receipts into real terms. Each individual would be a producing unit and a consuming unit; and the activities of all of them would be co-ordinated and controlled by the institution of the price system. A comparatively simple society might very well be organized in this manner with good results. Indeed in certain countries even now the organization of production corresponds to this pattern fairly well, while during pioneer days in the United States the system was not greatly dissimilar.[3]

Conversely we can easily imagine an organization of the production of goods and services along entirely different lines in which the existing price system, if any, did not regulate output at all. All productive resources, the factors of production if we will, might be regarded as belonging to the community as a whole (the State) and their allocation between alternative uses might be planned or dictated from above by persons democratically selected or by an autocrat, benevolent or otherwise. Here the application of resources in production would not necessarily have any definable connection with consumers' preferences between various types of consumption goods or between consumption and saving. To be sure, some kind of a system of consumers' goods prices would be of almost indispensable assistance in distributing the final products between persons. But the organization and composition of production would be determined by a planning authority, and industry as a whole would probably be broken up into gigantic "trusts." Firms or enterprises, as we know them, would probably not exist at all, but production would be organized and controlled more on the authoritarian principles of an army. Regarded solely from the point of view of mere technological efficiency such a system perhaps has much to recommend it, although the sacrifices in other directions seem more than to outweigh these achievements.[4]

Our concern here, however, is not with any of these alterna-

[3] See Dobb, Maurice, *Capitalist Enterprise and Social Progress*, London (Routledge), 1925, especially Ch. IV.

[4] It is doubtless unnecessary to point out that the number of countries in which economic activity is approximately so organized has increased greatly in recent years. For an interesting account of one such, see Balogh, T., "The National Economy of Germany," *Economic Journal*, Vol. 48 (1938), pp. 461-497.

tive systems by which production might be organized without the use of business enterprises, but rather with a capitalistic system wherein firms or enterprises, notably corporate enterprises, are characteristic. Indeed our primary interest is precisely in the individual business enterprise as such. Consequently it may be worth while to pause a moment and inquire why in capitalistic economies production should be organized on the basis of firms. Moreover, in the process, we may derive a somewhat clearer idea of the economic characteristics of the business enterprise or firm in a capitalistic economy.

II. THE INDIVIDUAL ENTERPRISE AND THE PRICE SYSTEM

1. The business enterprise as a unit of ownership in pursuit of profits. 2. The difficulties and costs of organizing production entirely through the price system where the technology of production is highly developed. 3. The need for business enterprises accentuated in a dynamic as opposed to a static economy; the problem of co-ordination and adaptation to economic change. 4. The enterprise as a unit for the computation of costs and income. 5. The differentiation of types of business enterprises on the basis of the kind of competitive situation within which they operate: pure competition, monopolistic competition, monopoly.

1. *The business enterprise as a unit of ownership in pursuit of profits.* Doubtless the most common and obvious implication of the term "business enterprise" is that of an aggregation of assets devoted to the earning of profits in which certain individuals possess rather well-defined rights. That is, we think of the enterprise as owning certain assets which it uses in various ways to make a profit for the benefit of its owners. What the enterprise owns is thought to be clearly distinguishable from things that it does not own; furthermore, certain persons are regarded as possessing definable rights in the things owned by the firm, its assets, and these rights are considered to have a value. At any instant of time it is theoretically possible to define precisely what the firm owns and explicitly what persons hold valuable rights against

it.[5] While these rights and the assets to which they relate are fixed and given at any point in time, they are not constant through historical time but alter and are redefined as a consequence of the operations of the enterprise. Indeed, from one point of view, the operations of the enterprise during any period of time are evidenced by the changes wrought in its assets and the resulting changes in the valuable rights therein. In general, it can be said that desirable changes in the assets and the rights therein, that is, those changes that the enterprise plans to achieve, are changes which, on net balance, result in an increase in the total of the proprietors' claims. This last is essentially what we mean when we say that in a capitalistic economy the aim and objective of business enterprises is to make profits.

While the ultimate objective of a business enterprise, as a business enterprise, is to maximize profits to the owners, the acquisition of profits may be achieved by applying the assets in various alternative directions. The phrase alternative directions has here both a wide and a narrow sense. In the wide sense, there is a choice between, say, making household furniture and office furniture, that is, a choice as to the kind of product to be made.[6] In the narrow sense, there is a choice between various ways and means of maximizing profits once the decision has been reached to produce a given product, say, to manufacture office furniture. Consequently within the individual enterprise there must be some means (commonly contractual) of determining (1) those persons or parties in interest entitled to formulate matters of policy, and (2) the method of selecting those individuals who will be charged with attaining the ends so formulated. At the time of its organization there will probably be little doubt on these points, since the business enterprise will have been formed expressly to under-

[5] We do not mean here, of course, that various fact situations may not arise that elicit disputes between the parties in interest as to their respective rights. This is an everyday occurrence. All we mean is that at any point in time the valuable rights of the parties have been predetermined and there is an established procedure for resolving disputes; the law on any particular point, in a given jurisdiction, is precisely definable. Through the years, of course, the law changes and develops in the sense that the answer to particular questions alters.

[6] As we shall see more clearly later, after an enterprise has once made a decision as to the kind of product it will manufacture it is not always easy to change over to another if the original choice proves to have been a mistake.

take some particular activity; but subsequently a change may be necessary, the original activity ought to be abandoned and profits sought elsewhere, and therefore it is essential to designate those persons who have the power to change the direction of the enterprise.[7]

Such a general concept of the business enterprise, i.e., an aggregation of assets that is directed towards the making of profits, is what we usually have in mind when we use the term. But the individual firm has certain other economic attributes that will bear further comment.

2. *The difficulties and costs of organizing production entirely through the price system where the technology of production is highly developed.* We have already alluded to the organization of production in capitalistic economies by means of the institution of the price system: the relationship between various prices causes output to be expanded or contracted, and the agents or factors of production to be shifted from one employment to another. Now, although a business enterprise is a production unit operating within the framework of the price system, it is noteworthy that within the production unit (the firm) the application and utilization of economic resources are not controlled by the price system, but rather some individual determines what uses and applications of the available resources are to be made and issues orders to that effect. That is, within the business enterprise, economic resources are shifted about, are employed here rather than there, because some person has given an order to do so, doubtless on the belief that returns will be maximized as a consequence. As Mr. D. H. Robertson once wrote, there are "islands of conscious power in this ocean of unconscious co-operation, like lumps of butter coagulating in a pail of buttermilk."[8]

---

[7] In a corporation the charter will typically delimit the scope of its activities, although usually the limits are quite broad. Within the bounds set by the charter the power to determine the general direction in which the assets shall be applied rests with the board of directors. The function of the board of directors, however, must be distinguished from that of the management. The former is concerned primarily with policy formation while the latter is chiefly occupied with the execution of those policies. The shareholders elect the directors, the directors appoint the managers, and the managers select their subordinates. And speaking broadly the tasks and functions of each become more specific and less discretionary as we move down the hierarchy.

[8] *The Control of Industry*, New York (Harcourt), 1923, p. 84.

If we ask why, within business enterprises, the factors of production are directed and co-ordinated by an "orderer" instead of directly through the price system, the answer is, probably, that it can be done more economically in this fashion.[9] A very simple economy using only simple capital instruments and small-scale production methods would have little need for the existence of firms or business enterprises as we know them. But as the scale of production increases and becomes more "capitalistic," and the economy becomes more complex in a variety of ways, there is an advantage in organizing production into firms instead of leaving all co-ordination entirely to the price system.

Where the agents of production necessary for efficient operations are numerous, varied, and often highly specialized, the arrangement of leaving the organization of production entirely to the price system would involve the negotiation of many separate contracts in the market and for that reason would be both costly and clumsy. For, if only the market mechanism were used to organize production and there were no business enterprises as such, a host of market transactions would be necessary; and the costs of actually knowing at all times all the prices relevant to the efficient negotiation of these transactions would be considerable. But by purchasing some agents of production and renting others for relatively long periods the number of transactions required is greatly reduced with resulting economies.[10] The application of these hired and rented resources in the production process is then left to whoever is placed in charge of the enterprise; having fewer transactions to negotiate, he can presumably carry them out with greater efficiency. Furthermore, by having a legal entity such as the firm larger productive organizations are possible because several, or even a large number of persons, can pool their resources in a common venture. The corporation especially facilitates these associations. It is difficult to imagine the large productive combinations that are now so common being organized on an individualistic basis with the co-ordination of the factors being achieved

---

[9] In section I (2) of this chapter we tried to show that production could conceivably be organized entirely by the price system.

[10] See Coase, R. H., "The Nature of the Firm," *Economica*, August, 1937, upon which this account is partly based.

entirely through the market mechanism. Reflection suggests that the existence of business enterprises is an indispensable counterpart to large-scale production in the technological sense.

3. *The need for business enterprises accentuated in a dynamic as opposed to a static economy; the problem of co-ordination and adaptation to economic change.* The advantages of organizing production on the basis of individual enterprises or firms are undoubtedly accentuated when the economic system is characterized by uncertainties and progressive change. In a *completely* "static" economy (in the theoretical sense) the prices of all commodities and all agents of production would be the same yesterday, today, and tomorrow; and the results in terms of product of any given input of economic resources could be predicted with absolute accuracy. In such an economy the price system would be quite sufficient to organize production without the necessity for firms at all. As already suggested, one of the difficulties of organizing production directly through the market mechanism of the price system is the cost of knowing all the relevant prices all the while. In the static economy no such problem would arise because there would be no changes in the economic data that would cause price changes. But, in the real world, changes in the economic data are many and frequent and, as a result, price changes are forever occurring. Thus, in an unstable world, the problem of knowing all the relevant prices really reduces to the problem of keeping informed on the changes in such prices. By organizing production on the basis of individual firms, which own some productive resources and rent others on long-term, the currently relevant price changes are reduced in number and the task of carrying on production is consequently made easier and more efficient. If we can imagine, for example, that our Acme Corporation had each day to negotiate a separate transaction for the services of each and every tool, machine, plot of land, laborer, piece of material, item of supplies, etc., that it would use each day, we can visualize at once the additional problems that would arise in keeping abreast of all the many price changes and making the necessary adaptations to them. By having many of the productive resources owned by the business enterprise a whole host

of otherwise necessary market transactions is done away with. And this is particularly true of productive operations in a dynamic economy.

In a dynamic world, moreover, not all persons are equally well qualified either by training or aptitude to see the consequences and implications of various changes in the economic data and to recognize the appropriate adaptations to them. Some individuals do these things much better than others and the latter recognize the fact. Consequently, they are willing to entrust the readaptation and recombination of the factors of production required to meet changing conditions to those with special abilities.[11] What this means in practice is that some persons allow their property and their services to be directed by others whose judgment and competence they believe to be superior to their own.[12] In this way productive economic resources are likely to be organized on the basis of business enterprises in which those who are especially competent to make the necessary decisions are given a chance to do so. It is to be emphasized, however, that the basic difficulties in the adaptation to changing conditions, the thing that makes decisions unavoidable, is the fact of uncertainty and continual change itself.[13] As someone has observed, "the successful conduct of business operations consists in making correct decisions on the basis of inadequate information."

The exact nature of the tasks of co-ordination and adaptation that have to be performed within the business enterprise perhaps deserves a further word. More specifically: What do we mean by

[11] See Knight, F. H., *Risk, Uncertainty, and Profit,* Boston (Houghton Mifflin), 1921, pp. 241-242.

[12] "The responsible decision is not the concrete ordering of policy, but ordering an orderer as a 'laborer' to order it . . . the crucial decision is the selection of men to make decisions." *Ibid.,* p. 297.

[13] As Mr. Kaldor has expressed it, ". . . the function which lends uniqueness and determinateness to the firm—the ability to adjust, to co-ordinate—is an *essentially dynamic function;* it is only required so long as adjustments are required; and the extent to which it is required (which, as its supply is 'fixed,' governs the amount of other factors which can be most advantageously combined with it) depends on the frequency and the magnitude of the adjustments to be undertaken." Kaldor, N., "The Equilibrium of the Firm," *Economic Journal,* Vol. 44 (1934), pp. 60-76. Mr. Kaldor would make the "unit of co-ordinating ability" the distinguishing mark of individual firms. (See pp. 69-70.) Although this has some advantages for certain problems it is not altogether satisfactory for our purposes.

co-ordination as applied to the business enterprise? Certainly we mean that someone somewhere is charged with the job of seeing to it that the actions and behavior of the different individuals within the enterprise are working towards a common end; that the amount of working at cross purposes is reduced to a practicable minimum. Another aspect of this co-ordination is that of synchronizing and integrating the different branches or phases of the firm's activities: production schedules must somehow be carefully co-ordinated with sales of finished product and the purchase of materials and supplies; and all these must be synchronized with the flow of cash receipts and outlays at the same time that the latter are co-ordinated with each other. In the nature of the case these problems do not solve themselves; they require careful thought and planning. With respect to the problem of "adaptation" the essential difficulty, as we have already indicated, is to know what changes in the firm's plans and operations are called for in view of changes in the economic data with which the firm operates: the prices of the things it buys and sells, the rate of absorption of the product by purchasers, the technological conditions of production, etc. Certain it is that these do not remain constant in the course of time; and, therefore, having achieved an "ideal" solution for one set of data, the problem is not solved for all time because these data themselves change. Whatever the change, however, someone has to decide what adaptation the enterprise ought to make to it, and how the change should be carried through in order that profits will be maximized. Indeed, it can be urged that the success of the business enterprise in its search for profits is in no small measure a function of its ability to make self-consistent adaptations in its business plans quickly and easily in response to changes in the economic data with which it has to work.[14]

---

[14] As Professor A. G. Hart has emphasized, this is essentially a problem in "anticipations" since the business enterprise in the real world is never in the position of knowing exactly if the production plans, selling plans, etc., will prove to be correct until it is too late to change them completely. See his excellent paper, "Anticipations, Planning and the Business Cycle," *Quarterly Journal of Economics,* Vol. 51 (1937), pp. 273-297. The present writer has drawn many valuable suggestions from this article and from conversations with Professor Hart which are here gratefully acknowledged.

4. *The enterprise as a unit for the computation of costs and income*. From several points of view it is important to observe that in a capitalistic economy the individual business enterprise is perhaps the most important type of entity for the calculation of costs and incomes. It is axiomatic that the terms "cost" and "income" have no meaning unless they relate to some unit or entity from which the rest of the universe is set apart for the purpose in hand. Thus, I can speak of costs to me and income to myself in a meaningful manner only on the assumption that I regard myself as a unit distinguishable from the whole social and economic environment in which I am located. On no other basis do the words cost or income have any meaning in this connection. Now in a capitalistic economy the individual business enterprises constitute such units: they are entities from the point of view of which costs and incomes get computed. It is from the point of view of the business enterprise that we speak of a tendency for the prices of products to reach an equality with their costs of production under competitive conditions. And furthermore, when we say that, during a business depression, the prices of many products are below their costs of production so that business enterprises are making losses we must always keep in mind that the terms cost and loss refer to individual firms as units or entities for the computation of expense and income. As a consequence it is quite important to inquire just what items are deemed to be costs from this point of view and what are not; and the same applies to income. For example, it is quite true that during a depression period a business corporation can reduce its costs by dropping persons from the payroll and thereby minimize its losses or show even a net profit for the accounting period; but, from the point of view of the economy as a whole, it cannot be assumed at all that there has been an equivalent reduction in costs; in all probability there has been nothing more than a shifting of costs from one type of unit to another. This fact that business enterprises are units for the computation of expense and income tends to have important repercussions upon the general level of total output in the economy (including fluctuations therein) and the composition of that output between goods and services of various kinds. For

instance, where the organization of production is on the basis of individual business enterprises, only those commodities and services will be produced which give promise of selling for a price above their costs of production where costs are reckoned *from the point of view of the business enterprise.*[15]

We are not here concerned with the question of whether or not the determination of costs and incomes in this manner is desirable or the reverse; that raises issues of great breadth which lie beyond the scope of the present volume. We are only concerned to emphasize the fact that the organization of production by individual enterprises which serve as the basis for the determination of income and expense carries with it important consequences.

5. *The differentiation of types of business enterprises on the basis of the kind of competitive situation within which they operate: pure competition, monopolistic competition, monopoly.* For purposes of economic analysis it is often useful to differentiate business enterprises on the basis of the type of competitive situation within which they operate. There are essentially three types: pure competition, monopolistic competition, and monopoly.

A firm is said to be selling under conditions of pure competition when the price at which it may sell its product is determined by market forces wholly beyond its control: it has no degree of price control at all. Each individual seller is so small relative to the total sources of supply that his influence on the price of the product is infinitesimal. The action of one seller will, of course, have some (very small) effect upon the price, but the point is that it is so small that he does not take it into account in determining how much he will produce. For instance, no wheat farmer considers it worth while to contemplate the probable effect that his producing more or less wheat is likely to have upon its price: output will be so small a portion of the total that he can afford to

[15] It is partly for this reason that certain services that are generally acknowledged as worth more than their costs have to be undertaken by the State rather than by private business enterprises. For example, it is doubtful if a private corporation could show a net return from the business of vaccinating people for smallpox; but few would deny that the returns to the community at large far outweigh the costs.

disregard its influence on the price.[16] For such conditions to prevail the products of the individual sellers must be regarded as
absolutely identical from the point of view of every buyer.[17]
Neither product differentiation, nor locational differences, nor
anything else is present to induce any buyer to prefer one seller
rather than another. In the circumstances the price and the quantity sold will be determined by all the factors that go together
to make up the demand and supply situation. In a competitive
situation of this kind the demand curve for the product of the
individual firm will be portrayed by a horizontal straight line extending to the right from the vertical (price) axis at the level
of the ruling price.[18]

Once the conditions of pure competition are stated for the individual firm it is obvious that very few enterprises in the real world
operate in a competitive milieu of this kind. Producers of certain
agricultural staples are very nearly in this situation: each seller
regards the price as being determined by factors entirely beyond
his control. But clearly there are very few business enterprises
that operate under conditions of pure competition; for most firms
a slight rise in price will not cause the amount sold to drop to
zero, nor a slight decrease cause it to rise indefinitely far. Pure
competition is definitely a special limiting case.

If the demand curve for the product of the individual enterprise
is not a horizontal straight line (at the level of the price fixed by
the whole demand and supply situation), it must slope downwards from left to right to indicate that the quantity sold varies
inversely with price. Over a certain range the business enterprise
can alter its price without the quantity sold either dropping to
zero or rising to infinity. The reasons why this is likely to be
true are many and mostly obvious: there may be slight differences
between the product this firm sells and those that its competitors
sell, and these differences may be real or imaginary in the minds

[16] Another reason for the wheat producer taking such a view is that the total
crop available for harvesting will be partly determined by factors beyond his
control, e.g., weather factors such as the amount and distribution of rainfall.

[17] In technical language the elasticity of substitution between his product and
that of others is infinite.

[18] Since the firm prefers to receive as high a price as possible for its product,
and since it can sell its whole output at the ruling price, it has no incentive to
offer to sell at a price lower than that ruling in the market.

of the buyers; again the particular firm may be so situated geographically that some purchasers will continue to buy from it even at a slightly higher price simply because of the time and trouble (and therefore cost) of going elsewhere; also, the particular enterprise may be so important within its industry that its price policies influence the prices of its immediate competitors. When, for these or other reasons, the demand curve for the product sold by the business enterprise shows some inverse relationship between the price and the quantity sold [19] the firm either operates in a monopoly situation or under conditions of monopolistic competition.[20] It should be obvious that most business enterprises in the world as we know it are in this kind of situation: 'they have some smaller or larger degree of price control over the commodity or service they offer for sale.

These then are the kind of competitive conditions under which the business enterprises we shall be dealing with are assumed to operate: either conditions of monopolistic competition or conditions of monopoly where they possess various degrees of mo-

[19] For many problems it is convenient to have a short-hand expression to describe accurately the proportional relationship between changes in price and the resulting variations in the quantity sold with respect to demand curves. A demand curve is said to have an elasticity of *unity* when the *product* of the number of units sold and the price, the aggregate expenditure on the commodity, is a constant for all points on the curve. If this product increases as the price becomes smaller, the demand curve is said to have an elasticity *greater than unity*, or briefly, the curve is said to be an elastic demand curve. Conversely, if the product of the price and the quantity sold decrease as the price becomes less, the demand curve is said to have an elasticity *less than unity*, or shortly, it is said to be inelastic. Any demand curve is, of course, almost certain to have different degrees of elasticity in its different segments. Moreover, for the individual enterprise, the demand curve for the product it sells is likely to have an elasticity greater than unity under ordinary conditions. It is worth noting here, however, although the point will come in for discussion later, that the elasticities of the demand curves of business enterprises are likely to undergo important changes from prosperity through depression.

[20] It is not easy to formulate a satisfactory definition of monopoly. Certainly the notion of simply *one seller* of the particular product in question is not particularly helpful since under modern conditions where individual business enterprises all tend to sell slightly differentiated products this definition would make them all a "monopoly." Perhaps the simplest concept of monopoly is that which would make its existence turn upon the presence or absence of rates of net return in excess of the ruling rate. Yet this too is not without difficulties. For a provocative discussion of the problem in its theoretical aspects see Lerner, A. P., "The Concept of Monopoly and the Measurement of Monopoly Power," *Review of Economic Studies*, Vol. 1 (1934), p. 157.

nopoly power. The instance of pure competition will only be of interest as a limiting case. Most business enterprises have some control over the prices at which they can sell their product.

For some purposes it is useful to distinguish business enterprises from one another on the basis of the market situation under which they buy or hire agents of production for use within the firm. Although one advantage of having business enterprises is to reduce the number of market transactions necessary to organize production, this does not mean that market transactions can be done away with entirely.[21] Consequently, the kind of market situation which the business enterprise encounters when it comes to purchase or hire agents of production is of some interest.

The usual assumption in this connection is that the supply curve of all agents of production to the individual firm is completely elastic at the prevailing market price.[22] Undoubtedly this is a proper assumption in many cases. For, if the firm constitutes but a small fraction of the total demand for any factor, it may buy more or less over a considerable range without appreciably affecting price: the supply curve of the agent to the enterprise is (almost) completely elastic at the ruling price. For relatively small firms this is approximately the position in which they find them-

[21] It is quite clear also that there are limits to how far it is appropriate to organize additional transactions within the firm. Depending, of course, upon the industry of which the enterprise is a part, the costs of organizing more and more of the productive process within the firm will tend to rise relatively to the costs of using the market organization and will at some point come to exceed the latter. In other words there are economic limits to the size business enterprises can profitably attain in the real world. See Coase, *op. cit.*, p. 395.

For instance, some years ago in the United States a then prominent motor manufacturer outlined his scheme for a complete vertical integration of his enterprise. The plan as described embraced rubber plantations, tire factories, glass plants, steel mills, and many other intermediate products all integrated into the production of automobiles. Unfortunately he undertook to realize this grandiose dream with disastrous results. The costs of organizing additional transactions within the business enterprise were much greater than achieving the same result through using the price system, i.e., buying products and services from other firms.

[22] Symmetrically with a demand curve a supply curve relates prices and quantities. A demand curve shows the price necessary if a given quantity is to be sold or the amount which would be sold at a given price under the conditions assumed; so on the other hand a supply curve indicates (again for *given* conditions) what quantities will be offered at various prices or, conversely, what price must be offered if a given quantity is to be forthcoming.

selves with respect to most of the things they buy. Typically, for example, a firm will be able to hire additional men without raising the wage rate.[23] But this does not hold in all cases nor for all types of labor; nor is it equally true for any particular firm in all phases of the business cycle, being most likely during a slump and least probable as the boom gathers strength. At the height of prosperity it is quite improbable that the firm can secure additional labor without directly or indirectly offering a higher wage.[24]

Apart from cyclical factors, however, other conditions may cause the supply curve to the firm of an agent of production to be less than completely elastic at the ruling price, i.e., not horizontal. If, for example, the firm constitutes a relatively large fraction of the total demand for the agent, then its purchasing or hiring more or less will have an important influence on the price. But whether larger purchases will raise or lower price will depend upon the other attendant circumstances. If, for instance, the firm is almost the sole employer in the local market and the opportunities for self-employment by the laborers are very slight, the supply curve of labor may conceivably be negatively inclined over a certain range: more persons offer themselves for jobs at starvation wages than at higher rates. On the other hand, if there are alternative opportunities for employment and yet the firm normally hires a large proportion of the local labor supply, higher wages may be necessary to attract more persons from other occupations.

The same kind of analysis, *mutatis mutandis*, will apply to agents of production other than labor under certain circumstances. A firm may purchase certain of its materials and supplies under

[23] The assumption that the supply curve for a particular kind of labor is completely elastic at the prevailing price implies the further assumption that either competition is not sufficiently keen to reduce wages to a level at which all persons seeking employment find jobs; or that the wage rate is fixed by an authority at a level which leaves some members unemployed.

Sometimes a firm may be able to hire more persons at the ruling rate yet encounter really rising labor costs since the additional men hired are less efficient than those already employed. It seems reasonable to suppose that the workers last hired are likely to be those least desirable from point of view of the firm.

[24] Indirectly, for instance, in the form of more attractive working conditions or other factors which lead a worker to prefer one firm to another at the same money wage.

conditions of monopsony or oligopsony, although such situations are perhaps relatively uncommon.[25]

The conditions under which the firm hires or purchases agents of production may therefore diverge from pure competition. And as we shall have occasion to note subsequently this may have important consequences.

III. CAPITAL CONCEPTS AS APPLIED TO THE BUSINESS ENTERPRISE

1. Capital in the sense of capital goods: assets and capital goods; subdivisions thereof. 2. The capitalized value of capital goods: capital in the sense of the value of the claims against assets; the concept capitalization as applied to a corporation; the concept capital as meaning the value of the proprietors' claims. 3. Capital in the sense of free or disposable capital.

There are very few terms in the English language that have a wider variety of meanings and connotations than the word "capital." According to the context or the whim of the user, the word is made to mean wealth, a factor of production, produced means of production, the value of these means of production, money, the money value of assets, the net worth of a business enterprise, anything that yields an income, and possibly other things as well. Capital is thought of in physical terms, in value terms, and in money terms. To be sure, these different senses are often qualified by an adjective or explanatory phrase; but none the less the term capital yet retains a certain ambiguity that the efforts of many writers have not yet dispelled.[26]

Fortunately our interests in the present volume do not require us to consider all these various uses of the word capital because in large part the necessity for them grows out of the complex prob-

[25] Monopsony is the term for single buyer but many sellers; oligopsony where there are a few buyers and many sellers.

[26] For a good account of the various senses of the term capital, together with an attempt to show their various interrelations and implications, see Fraser, L. M., *Economic Thought and Language*, London (Black), 1937, Ch. 14. See also Marshall, Alfred, *Principles of Economics*, 8th ed., London (Macmillan), 1920, Appendix E.

lem of capital accumulation and utilization in the economy as a whole: a problem we do not need to deal with. What we are interested in, however, is the different senses in which the term capital is used with reference to the individual enterprise—a much narrower problem.

1. *Capital in the sense of capital goods: assets and capital goods; subdivisions thereof.* We have already suggested that the business enterprise is a unit of productive organization within which the agents of production are consciously co-ordinated and directed by some individual or group rather than by the price system.[27] Now in the economic sense, production requires the co-operation of the three factors of production—land, labor, and "capital"— towards the objective of turning out a salable product or service. But it must be pointed out that the business enterprise as such, in the legal and accounting sense, consists entirely in "owned" things like land, buildings, machines, inventories, receivables, cash, and rights to receive valuable services from things or real persons.[28] The enterprise never owns any of the factor of production labor, although, of course, it typically exchanges cash for labor services in functioning as a unit of production. The items of productive resources that the business enterprise does own are typically referred to individually and collectively as its "assets." And an asset, in the broadest sense, is a source of a valuable service flow. What the business enterprise needs in its operations is not the assets as concrete items *per se*, but the services that these items are capable of rendering: not machines, but the particular service operations that the machines are able to perform; not cash, but the valuable services that cash is in a position to command. So, for example, a business enterprise often has the choice between owning the agent that is capable of rendering the particular serv-

---

[27] Cf. Hart (*op. cit.*, p. 277), where the firm is defined as "*a complex of productive resources*—persons and things yielding useful services—whose *services are directed under a common plan and authority to the maximization of profit* for the owners of the enterprise. . . ."

[28] The reason why in its accounting and legal aspects the business enterprise does not include labor is probably twofold: first, it is legally impossible to own labor anyway; second, accounting, which is built around the balance sheet which has meaning only at an instant of time, would not find it possible to give meaning to "labor" which cannot be owned because the idea of labor service relates only to a period of time.

ice needed and simply buying the services from some other enterprise without bothering to own the source: one can buy heat, or one can buy coal and manufacture his own heat.

As soon as we recognize that assets are sources from which valuable services can be derived, the relation between assets and the concept of capital goods becomes much clearer.

The concept of capital in the sense of "capital goods" is one of the commonest in the whole of economic literature. Capital goods, or what is sometimes called "real" capital, means simply (man-made) instruments used for further production. It is at once obvious, however, that what items are to be included in this category turns upon the definition of the term production, i.e., where it is convenient to regard production as completed and consumption ready to commence. In strict logic it must be admitted that in the last analysis all income consists of "services" and is psychic in character. And on this basis all sources of these services are instrumental in character, and one might regard them all as capital. Yet such a broad view, although logically unassailable, is open to some practical objections because it lumps together too many things that are usefully distinguishable: while an ice cream cone and a hydro-electric power dam are both capital because they yield valuable services, there are important differences between them notwithstanding. As a consequence many writers have found it convenient, either when discussing the individual enterprise or the whole economy, to differentiate between longer and shorter time intervals over which different kinds of capital goods (in the broadest sense) yield valuable services, or between capital goods which are capable of rendering consumption services themselves and those which are only capable of turning out goods that are able to yield consumption services. The first distinction would be that, for instance, between a machine and the lubricating oil used in its operation; the second would be the distinction, say, between a machine used to make electric refrigerators and the electric refrigerator itself. Hence we have "durable" and "non-durable" capital goods; and "consumers' capital goods" and "producers' capital goods." And both distinctions are useful but not co-extensive.

If we refer to the "capital" of a business enterprise and mean the real things it has to work with, such as buildings, machines, tools, dies, materials, semi-finished goods, completed product, etc., we had best call them its "real" capital. This real capital will consist partly of "durable" capital goods which only yield up their services gradually, such as the buildings and the machines, and partly of less durable things, such as the inventories, materials and supplies, etc.[29]

2. *The capitalized value of capital goods: capital in the sense of the value of the claims against assets; the concept capitalization as applied to a corporation; the concept capital as meaning the value of the proprietors' claims.* All real capital, however, can be conceived of in value terms rather than in physical terms. That is, instead of focusing our attention upon a capital good as the source of a service flow we can regard the stream of valuable services as having a present worth, which is no more than the summation of the present worth of all the valuable services that compose the stream. When we consider the streams of valuable services in this way, i.e., as being assigned a present worth, we usually refer to the procedure as the "capitalization" process. Each source of a valuable service flow acquires a "capitalized value." And if we use some common denominator like money we can now add together diverse things such as buildings, plant, materials, supplies, etc. In this manner we can speak of the total capital at the disposal of the business enterprise in value terms. This has the further advantage, moreover, that we can now include familiar assets like accounts and notes receivable because their worth in value terms can be recorded and added in with the "capitalized" value of real capital goods.[30] In this value sense, then, the capital of a business enterprise is no more than the sum total value of all its assets. This leads on to another usage of the word capital as applied to a business enterprise by a simple process of derivation.

We have shown how the total capital of the business enterprise can be reduced to value terms by means of the capitalization

[29] Observe that assets such as accounts and notes receivable and cash form no part of the concept of real capital at all; they would be simply claims against some of the valuable services yielded by real capital held by others.

[30] The significant thing on the value level of analysis is whether or not an item has value and if so how much: whether it is itself a capital good or not is not so important.

process. Now if the total value of all the assets is the total capital of the enterprise, it must also be true that the total value of all the claims against those assets is of an identically equal amount. In other words, instead of speaking of the value of the assets, we can, if we will, speak of the value of the claims against those assets. The value of the claims cannot be less or more than the value of the assets. Consequently people often speak of the total capital employed in a business enterprise as measured by the total money value of the claims against its assets. That is to say, people speak of the money value of the claims instead of the money value of the assets.

The claims against the assets are of two broad types: creditors' claims and owners' claims; the two kinds are exhaustive. In a corporation the owners' claims are represented by the shares of capital stock outstanding. The creditors' claims on the other hand are only partly evidenced by outstanding creditor securities in the form of bonds and (relatively) long-term notes: [31] accounts payable and promissory notes have also to be included among the creditors' claims. Nevertheless it is common to refer to the total face value of a corporation's outstanding securities as its "capitalization." So that when we say that the Acme Corporation is capitalized at $10,000,000, we mean that the face value of the creditor securities plus the par or stated value of the shares total this amount.[32] It is important to remember in this connection, however, that a corporation's capitalization will *not* be the same as the total value of all the claims against the assets and hence of the total value of all the assets; the capitalization does not measure the value of the total capital employed.

Perhaps unfortunately it is not uncommon for persons to refer to the "capital" of a business enterprise where reference is had only to the value of the owners' or proprietors' claims. This is true, for example, in the familiar formulation of the balance sheet equation in accounting as *Assets minus Liabilities equals Capital*. So, for example, people often speak of the proprietors' capital

[31] The distinction between long-term and short-term notes is of course partly arbitrary, five years being perhaps common.

[32] As Dewing well points out it is not always a simple matter to determine the capitalization of a large and complicated corporation. See Dewing, A. S., *The Financial Policy of Corporations*, New York (Ronald), 1934, pp. 13-14.

when they mean the value (computed in various ways) of the owners' claims in the corporation. This is apt to be confusing but possibly in most instances the context leaves little room for misunderstanding.

Thus it is that starting from the notion of capital goods yielding flows of services we pass easily to the capitalized value of these capital goods, to the value of the claims against such capitalized values, to the distinction between creditors' claims and owners' claims, to the emphasis that some of the claims are (in the corporation) represented by outstanding securities, and finally, to the accent upon the importance of the proprietors' claims. Logically the progression from one concept to the other is easy enough; but one has to be careful not to assign to all of them attributes that are only strictly true of some or one of them.[33]

There is yet another and quite important usage of the term capital to be considered, however, before we can leave the subject.

3. *Capital in the sense of free or disposable capital.* We often speak of a business enterprise as "procuring more capital" or of its "raising capital" for this purpose or that. If we stop and ask ourselves just what is being "procured" or "raised" here in the first instance the answer is clearly money. The money funds so obtained, of course, may be used to purchase capital goods in the narrow sense so that indirectly the enterprise is actually adding to its equipment. But it need not necessarily be so: the enterprise may want nothing more than to hold larger cash balances as a precautionary measure. This use of the word capital to mean literally money is very common, and, it may be observed, a fruitful source of confusion. When we talk of capital "available for investment" or refer to the "capital market" we very definitely do not mean

[33] Thus, for example, from the point of view of the individual security-holder *his* investment in a particular enterprise can be withdrawn by simply selling his shares to someone else, or as we often hear it said, the investment has the desirable quality of being "liquid." But it must never be forgotten that this is only true for the individual on the assumption that someone else is willing to take the shares off his hands at a price. The machines or building that are the "real" capital of the business enterprise cannot be disinvested in the same manner at all. What is true of the capital goods is not true of claims against these capital goods (the securities), and vice versa. One must be continually careful not to reason towards fallacious conclusions through assigning common properties and characteristics to all the various concepts of capital.

capital in the sense of capital goods.[34] What we have in mind here is liquid resources, i.e., money which is available for whatever use the borrower and the lender can agree upon. As has been pointed out many times, the essence of the idea of capital available for investment, or for transfer between industries, regions, countries, etc., is money, that is, the power to command the factors of production, including the stocks of capital goods already in existence. Capital in this sense is best prefixed by the adjective liquid or loan fund capital, or in the German terminology *Kapitaldisposition*. Possibly it is still better to say what we really mean, namely, money. This concept of capital meaning literally money is very commonly used and one needs to be careful not to confuse it with the other senses of the word already discussed.[35]

IV. SUMMARY

In a capitalistic economy the principal guide to and control of production is the institution of the price system. Within the price system, however, production is in fact organized on the basis of individual business enterprises.

The reasons for the existence of business enterprises as units of productive organization are the economies of organizing certain activities apart from the market mechanism; the advantages of so doing are accentuated in an economy that uses an intricate technology and which is characterized by progressive change and development requiring continual adjustments. The individual business enterprise as a unit for the computation of costs and incomes has important repercussions upon the volume and composition of the flow of goods and services in the economy. For some purposes it is useful to differentiate business enterprises on the basis of the kind of market situation in which they sell the commodities they

[34] The capital market sometimes means the market for new issues of securities and sometimes in addition the market for both new and old issues. It is apt to be a vague notion.

[35] The recent literature on monetary and business cycle theory has used the term capital in this sense of money a great deal so that it is now much more commonly met with than even a few years ago.

produce and/or in which they buy the productive agents and services they require for such production.

As applied to the business enterprise, it is important to distinguish between capital in the sense of the source of a valuable service flow, the capitalized value of this source as a derivative from the amount and time distribution of the items constituting the valuable service flow, the value of the claims against such capitalized values, and the several subdivisions of the total claims against capitalized values. Finally, the word capital in the sense of money or a generalized command over goods and services including factors or agents of production must be sharply differentiated from the many other usages of the term.

REFERENCES: CHAPTER II

(The references at the end of each chapter are divided into two groups. In general the first group contain items which are more easily accessible and of a more elementary character than the second. Although the second group contains typically more advanced works they should be comprehensible to any careful reader of the text.)

DEWING, A. S.—*Corporation Securities*, New York: Ronald, 1934, Ch. 2.

DEWING, A. S.—*Financial Policy of Corporations*, New York: Ronald, 1934, Book I, Ch. 1.

COASE, R. H.—"The Nature of the Firm," *Economica*, August, 1937.

DENNISON, H. S., and GALBRAITH, J. K.—*Modern Competition and Business Policy*, New York, 1938, Chs. 1-2.

HART, A. G.—"Anticipations, Planning and the Business Cycle," *Quarterly Journal of Economics*, Vol. 51.

IVERSEN, C.—*Aspects of the Theory of International Capital Movements*, Copenhagen, 1936; Introduction & Ch. 1.

KALDOR, N.—"The Equilibrium of the Firm," *Economic Journal*, Vol. 44.

ROBINSON, E. A. G.—*The Structure of Competitive Industry*, New York, 1932.

Chapter III

THE NATURE OF THE CORPORATION AND THE PROCESS OF INCORPORATION

I. The Nature of the Corporation. II. General Incorporation Laws and the Process of Incorporation. III. Foreign Incorporation and Corporations. IV. Summary.

～～～～～～

From almost the earliest times men have doubtless associated together for the pursuit of common ends. Indeed the existence of associations of individuals within the broader confines of the community as a whole seems to be an almost universal characteristic of human society even in its very lowest stages of development. Yet one cannot infer from the recorded or observed existence of such associations that analogues to our present-day corporate bodies have been familiar to all civilizations. One must distinguish between the plain historical fact that men have associated together for the better attainment of mutually common objectives and, what is quite another thing, the conceptualization of these associations as something distinct and apart from the particular individuals comprising them. One cannot deduce from the mere existence of associative activities in a particular society that the concept of the corporation is necessarily recognized and understood. Historically viewed, the corporate concept has only very gradually worked its way into men's modes of thinking. We have become so accustomed to the idea of "corporations" owning this and that, to their being in some sense legal persons with rights and duties, to their having perpetual existence, and to their drafting regulations for the flesh and blood persons of whom they are composed, that we are apt to forget that thoughtful and learned men of some earlier periods would have found such notions quite strange. The corporate concept has not always been a familiar component of

36

the apparatus of human thought. Yet to describe the origin and development of the corporate idea would require a book in itself and nothing of the kind will be attempted in the present volume.[1] Our immediate task in the present chapter is to indicate briefly what the corporate concept means [2] and implies in modern contexts, to describe how corporate bodies are brought into existence, and to consider certain other closely related problems.

I. THE NATURE OF THE CORPORATION

1. The sovereignty theory of the corporation: its association with the idea of a corporation as an "artificial" legal personality; the concessional aspects of the theory. 2. The criticisms of the foregoing view: emphasis on the reality of corporate personality; the idea of the corporation as a contract. 3. The partial sterility of the controversy: the purpose of law to subserve human personalities and relationships. Notion of corporate personality a convenient short-hand expression. Certain attributes of associations called corporations.

1. The sovereignty theory of the corporation: its association with the idea of a corporation as an "artificial" legal personality; the concessional aspects of the theory. At least in terms of mere numbers of adherents the most accepted view of the corporation in the United States is that corporate personality and privileges are to be had only through a grant of power from a sovereign authority. And under the constitutional arrangements prevailing in the United States, sovereign authority, of course, rests with the individual states, as Ohio, New York, California, etc. Probably the most hallowed and widely quoted expression of this sovereignty doctrine in American legal history is Chief Justice Marshall's opinion in the Dartmouth College case in 1819.[3] The Chief

[1] A brief word or two on a particular phase of the subject will be found in a note appended to this chapter. A short and very useful, but unfortunately undocumented, discussion of the matter is Abbott, C. C., *The Rise of the Business Corporation*, Ann Arbor, Mich. (Edwards Bros.), 1936.

[2] A good and easily accessible discussion of this problem will be found in Stevens, Robert S., *Handbook on the Law of Private Corporations*, St. Paul, Minn. (West), 1936, Chs. I, II.

[3] "A corporation is an artificial being, invisible, intangible, and existing only in contemplation of law. Being the mere creature of law, it possesses only those

Justice in this opinion, however, was reiterating an idea that was given forceful expression by Sir Edward Coke (1553-1633) in his *Commentaries on Littleton* published in 1598. The essence of this view of the nature of the corporation is that corporations come into existence only upon a grant of power from the sovereign authority, the State. Yet closely associated with the notion of a concession from the sovereign state is the further idea that the State thereby creates an "artificial," a "fictitious" person separate and distinct at law from the "natural" persons whose interests it embraces. The aggregate of the foregoing ideas, usually more elaborately and elegantly expressed, has come to be known as the "sovereignty" theory or the "fiction-concession" theory of the corporation. In its fictional aspects this theory of the corporation is wont to emphasize that for legal purposes the corporation is to be treated *as if* it were a person: a corporation owns property in the name that the sovereign has conferred upon it; it has the right to prosecute and defend by legal action in its own name; it is a person, in this legal sense, apart and distinct from the shareholders; the debts or assets of the corporation are not the debts or assets of the shareholders; at law, the corporation may contract with a shareholder just as if the two were in no way connected; so also, being a legal person created by a sovereign authority, a corporation may survive the death of all its shareholders and may only be brought to an end in the manner provided by the statute to which it owes its existence. Hence it is that a corporation is said to be a "fictitious" person, but a person at law none the less, a person capable of holding rights and bearing duties. Yet to say that a

properties which the character of its creation confers upon it, either expressly or as incidental to its very existence. These are such as are supposed best calculated to effect the object for which it was created. Among the more important are immortality, and, if the expression may be allowed, individuality; properties by which a perpetual succession of many persons are considered as the same, and may act as a single individual. They enable a corporation to manage its own affairs, and to hold property without the perplexing intricacies, the hazardous and endless necessity, of perpetual conveyances for the purpose of transmitting it from hand to hand. It is chiefly for the purpose of clothing bodies of men, in succession, with these qualities and capacities that corporations were invented, and are in use. By these means a perpetual succession of individuals are capable of acting for the promotion of the particular object, like one immortal being." *Trustees of Dartmouth College v. Woodward*, 4 Wheaton 518 (U.S.), 1819.

corporation is a legal person, an "artificial" person, need not imply that it is capable of all those legal relationships open to "natural" persons; while a corporation may not marry or make a will, it is yet true that for a vast number of legal situations it makes no difference whether the relationship involves two corporations, a corporation and a man, or merely two men: the legal principle is the same. For all relationships of this latter sort, of which there are a great many, the corporation is a fictitious legal person, or as F. W. Maitland has expressed it, "a right- and duty-bearing unit." [4]

If we turn now from the "fictional" aspects of the fiction-concession theory to the concession part of the doctrine we see that they are closely integrated. For, if a corporation is to be regarded as a "fictional" or an "artificial" person for legal purposes, it seems reasonable to insist that such personality could only be secured expressly from, or at least with the permission of, the sovereign. But the concession idea goes farther. In its more extreme formulations the sovereignty doctrine insists that the corporation is only called into being when the State grants it a charter; in other writers, however, the emphasis is on the charter grant as the act necessary to create legal personality. From the point of view of legal neatness and simplicity in application it must be admitted that the sovereignty concession view of the corporation has much to commend it. [5] And it may very well be true that its usefulness under present-day conditions is in no way impaired by the fact that historical research into the antecedents of the corporation lends it little support. Be that as it may, there is no question that the theory is rather widely held in the United States even though various writers are forever pointing out one or another of its weaknesses and deficiencies. An important practical manifestation of the sovereignty doctrine in the United States is the states' reservations of power to alter, amend or repeal corporate charters. While the extent to which such power extends is not entirely

[4] See his lecture "Moral Personality and Legal Personality" in Maitland, *Selected Essays* (ed. by H. D. Hazeltine, G. Lapsley, and P. H. Winfield), Cambridge, Eng. (Cambridge University), 1936.

[5] An excellent discussion and criticism of the fiction-concession theory of corporation will be found in Hallis, Frederick, *Corporate Personality*, Oxford (Oxford Press), 1930, Part I. Ch. I.

clear, it would appear that the State's (sovereign's) power to alter
or amend the charter relates particularly to the special privileges
granted to the corporate entity as such, rather than to the contractual relations between the shareholders and the corporation,
or the corporation and outside parties.[6] Yet this common statutory
provision is evidence that people still continue to think of the
corporation as a legal personality that exists by reason of a special
grant of privilege, a concession, from the sovereign; and what the
sovereign has granted it may also abrogate or take away.

2. *The criticisms of the foregoing view: emphasis on the reality
of corporate personality; the idea of the corporation as a contract.*
Different writers have at various times attacked the fiction-concession theory of the corporation. And, as might be expected, the
attack has focused now on the "fiction" doctrine and now on the
"concession" assumption of the theory.

Those who argue against the idea that corporations are fictitious
or artificial persons are likely to insist that corporations possess
personalities no less real than those habitually attributed to flesh
and blood persons. At law, so it is argued, personality is not something with which nature endows man but is merely a convenient
way of referring to the bundle of rights and duties which locate
him in the social scheme.[7] Especially among German scholars,

---

[6] See Ballantine, H. W., *Private Corporations*, Chicago (Callaghan), 1927, pp.
808-817, 823-832. The corporation need not continue in business under the state-
imposed amendments unless it accepts them.

[7] A recent writer has neatly expressed the view referred to in the following
language. "A 'person' or a 'personality,' it is declared, is not a human being nor
anything given in nature, but a group of rights and capacities, or at any rate a
group of legal relations, and this group owes its existence entirely to the recognition of it by the legal and institutional organization of the community. The
'personality' of an ordinary man would, in this view, be exhaustively described
in the list of rights and capacities which come into practical being only, we may
remember, when the individual performs certain specified acts in a certain specified way. In the same way, a different group of rights and capacities exists when
one or more of a number of specified individuals act in a determined way, and
to this grouping or complex of relations, the name of 'corporate personality' is
attached. One kind of personality is exactly of the same sort as the other. Neither
is in the least 'natural' and both are decidedly 'artificial' in the sense that they
are the result of a humanly planned scheme and both 'fictitious' in the sense that
the unit is imaginary, fanciful, the product of make-believe." Radin, Max, "The
Endless Problem of Corporate Personality," *Columbia Law Review*, Vol. 32
(1932), pp. 643-667, at p. 645. Professor Radin does not himself subscribe to this
view.

notably Gierke,[8] this insistence upon the reality of corporate personality proceeds to very considerable lengths. It is contended that corporations are not merely legally competent persons created by the State; that, on the contrary, they are persons every bit as "real" as natural persons and likewise capable of willing and acting on their own behalf. Indeed, it is argued, the very act of association together creates a unity, a living organism, possessing a common will which the law must recognize in the very nature of the case. The reality of "group persons" in the social order is strongly emphasized in contrast to the alternative view of corporations as "fictitious" persons.[9] Although the State does not concede corporateness or jural personality, according to Gierke's conception of the corporation, the State has, none the less, the important function of restricting and limiting its spheres of action. The corporate body must be confined in its actions by the State to those common interests and purposes which gave rise to the common will and hence to the association, the corporation. Thus, even according to Gierke's view, the State exercises a restraining influence over corporate activities even though the State in no sense can be said to bring the corporation into existence by concession. The State's function is to prevent corporate bodies from passing beyond their proper sphere of influence by confining their activities to the common purposes for which they spring into existence.

A less philosophical expression of certain ideas akin to, if not the same as, those of Gierke regarding the relation between the State and the corporation has come to be known as the "contract" theory. According to this theory the simplest view of the corporation is to regard it as a contractual arrangement between certain persons for the pursuit of common ends. The ends to be sought and the intentions of the parties are set forth by the terms of the contract. As a matter of public convenience the State may insist that such contracts be filed and open to inspection at a designated place; moreover, the State in its wisdom may deny that cer-

[8] Otto von Gierke was a German scholar whose principal work, *Das Deutsche Genossenschaftsrecht*, 4 volumes, Berlin, 1868, 1873, 1881, 1913, has been partially translated into English and edited with an introduction by F. W. Maitland as *Political Theories of the Middle Ages*, Cambridge, Eng. (Cambridge University), 1900.

[9] See Hallis, *op. cit.*, Part III, Ch. I, but especially pp. 146-149.

tain contracts are in harmony with public policy and refuse to recognize them—as for instance, when the State refuses to permit the invocation of the law to collect a gambling debt—but according to the contract theory, the State does not "create" the corporation in any sense, it merely recognizes it, or alternatively, refuses to recognize it. If one considers the ease and simplicity with which business corporations are brought into existence in the United States at present one must admit that the contract theory comes reasonably close to describing the prevailing practice.

3. *The partial sterility of the controversy: the purpose of law to subserve human personalities and relationships. Notion of corporate personality a convenient short-hand expression. Certain attributes of associations called corporations.* Such controversy over the most suitable conceptualization of the corporation bids fair to become perennial and it is doubtful if we serve any useful purpose here in carrying it further. Let us therefore point out one or two rather obvious considerations in conclusion and let the matter rest.

It is scarcely open to argument that the purpose of the law and legal institutions is to permit human beings the better to live together in organized communities. Legal relationships have no meaning for Robinson Crusoe before the advent of Friday. The consequence is that regardless of whatever concepts and constructions the law may find it convenient to employ, it must never lose sight of the fact that its ultimate concern is with flesh and blood human beings and their relationships with one another in society.[10] If this be granted, one may perhaps urge the view that corporations are merely one form that group activity of human beings in society may assume; not the *only* form of group activity to be sure, but a most important one. And if the corporation has any reason for existing as a mode of group activity it must be because

[10] Observe the following: "The only conduct of which the state can take notice by its laws *must* spring from natural persons—it cannot be derived from any abstraction called the 'corporate entity.' To be sure, the conduct of those individuals will be different when they are co-operating in their collective or corporate projects than when they are acting independently of one another—in a word, the 'psychical realities' will be different; but ultimately the responsibility for all conduct and likewise the enjoyment of all benefits must be traced to those who are capable of it, that is, to *real* or *natural* persons." (notes omitted) Hohfeld, W. H., *Fundamental Legal Conceptions*, New Haven (Yale Press), 1923, pp. 198-199.

it serves ends and purposes that natural persons in society are capable of holding. So also, the corporation is an acceptable form of group activity only to the degree that its use does not override or prevent the attainment of other ends which organized society regards as superior. The lower good must subserve the higher in any scale of values should conflicts develop. Consequently, occasions may arise when it is wholly reasonable to "tear aside the corporate veil" or "disregard the corporate fiction" in order that justice may be served or equity achieved. In view of the foregoing may we not argue that, in the first place, to call a corporation a "person" is only a convenient way of designating certain natural persons organized in a particular way and that we might, if we wished, express the same ideas in terms of the natural persons involved instead of in terms of the "corporation"? It would certainly be more cumbersome to do so, but it could be done. As a recent writer has said, "The need for such short-hand expressions is not only a primary requirement of all discourse; it is quite indispensable in law as in almost all social activities. It is simply impossible to say 'A. B. C. . . . . . . N stockholders, acting through R.S.T., their duly authorized agents,' have concluded a certain contract when it is possible to say that the Acme Co. has concluded it." [11] Such a convenient form of expression becomes the more useful in discourse as the number of natural persons composing the group increases. Hence, with the modern business corporation, the need for a "short-hand" expression is almost imperative. So many persons stand together in the corporation that the roundabout, yet alternative, mode of expression would hopelessly bog down even the simplest statement about them. Consequently we sensibly elect to refer to the complicated interrelations between real persons as an "it," the corporation, and endow "it" with legal personality. And for a whole host of problems that may arise and demand solution it is completely satisfactory to refer to the corporation as the possessor of legal rights and duties and to speak in terms that, taken literally, imply that the corporation is something entirely separate and distinct from its shareholders. Yet the entity

[11] Radin, op. cit., p. 652. The indebtedness of the present section to this article is gratefully acknowledged. See also Latty, Elvin R., Subsidiaries and Affiliated Corporations, Chicago (Foundation Press), 1936, Ch. II.

concept, the legal personality concept, is not capable of dealing with and resolving all questions of whatever kind; while doubtless useful and relevant for many purposes, none the less, fact situations may arise in which the entity concept is quite beside the point at issue. In cases of this sort our ordinarily convenient mode of reference must be dropped. To sum up: the law is ultimately concerned with natural persons; a corporation is an association of natural persons possessing powers and privileges accorded them at law as members of the corporation; for many legal purposes the corporation may be treated just as if it were a natural person, and we may call it an entity if we will; but for other legal purposes the entity concept is neither useful nor relevant because it does not bring out the points at issue between the natural persons for whom, in the final analysis, the law exists.[12]

When, therefore, we refer to the corporation as a person we merely designate certain characteristics of the association in a brief word. From the point of view of commerce and finance we specify that the members of the corporation are limited in their personal liability. All and sundry are served notice that they are to look to a specific fund of assets for the payment of their claims and not to the whole wealth of the associates. At least this is the general rule. Furthermore, by calling certain groups corporations, "persons" if we will, we indicate that the means of legal action against them is against them as groups and not their components as persons. So, for instance, one sues the corporation, the legal person; the corporation buys and the corporation sells; the corporation gives a mortgage; and the corporation is liable for torts. Yet another important connotation of calling the corporation a person is to emphasize that it is a financial and accounting unit: that is to say, it is a unit for the purpose of computing cost and measuring income. Indeed, in terms of the social consequences, the significance

[12] Note the following from Professor Radin's article (*op. cit.*, p. 665): "There is always a danger of indirection and confusion when, for any purpose and even for a moment, lawyers or publicists lose sight of the fact that their fundamental units are human beings, nearly all human beings, but nothing but human beings. These are persons in the proper sense of the term. Law exists for them to express their relations and subserve their needs. One of these needs is to speak of collectivities as though they too were persons. But an equal need is not to forget that they are not."

of the corporation as a unit for computing costs and income doubtless exceeds the limited liability feature. These are perhaps the
most important matters implied by easy reference to some groups
as corporations, although voluntary membership and transferabil-
ity of interest are significant if we have in mind chiefly business
corporations. Whether the State is itself a corporation is a question
we fortunately need not examine.

Yet if only some associations of individuals are to be known as
corporations, and if corporateness is to imply certain characteristics and privileges, it is only reasonable that "corporate personality" should be obtainable through complying with certain stipulations. To these requirements we now turn.

II. GENERAL INCORPORATION LAWS AND THE PROCESS OF INCORPORATION

*1. Corporations now brought into existence under general incor-
poration laws: the contents of the certificate of incorporation; the corporate charter. 2. The professionalization of the incorporation process.*

*1. Corporations now brought into existence under general in-
corporation laws: the contents of the certificate of incorporation;
the corporate charter.* Business corporations in the United States
are at present brought into existence under the terms laid down by
statute in the individual states. It is apparently well established
that incorporation is a power that inheres in legislatures, although
some few states have imposed constitutional limitations on the
legislative power to enact general laws on the subject. General
incorporation laws, of course, are simply statutes that specify just
how natural persons may bring a corporation into existence and
they take the place of the earlier method of incorporation by special legislative act.[18] Whereas the former incorporations by indi-

---

[18] General incorporation laws for religious, charitable and educational pur-
poses were passed by the individual states long before state legislatures enacted
general laws for business corporations. See Davis, Joseph S., *Essays in the Earlier
History of American Corporations*, 2 volumes, Cambridge, Mass. (Harvard), 1917,
Vol. II, pp. 16-17. Davis cites as a first instance of freedom of incorporation a
Massachusetts provision of 1799 permitting persons "by writing, associate and

vidual legislative act were often shrouded in mystery and ushered
in by intrigue, incorporation under general statutes has been made
simple and open to all without favor or privilege.[14] Under the general laws of the present day any group of individuals may bring
about the creation of a corporation by following the procedure
established by statute,[15] such as executing the necessary papers in
the proper form and paying the necessary fee.

In general, and apart from special corporations such as banks,
insurance companies, monied corporations, etc., the procedure of
incorporation follows approximately the following pattern in most
states. On proper forms there is prepared a certificate of incorporation (memorandum, articles of association) which contains,
in part, the following statements and information: A *name* by
which the corporation will be known. Since at law the corporation
is to be known as an entity distinct from its stockholders it must
have a name in which it may own property, defend or prosecute
legal actions and do various things. The corporate name, moreover,
must not be identical with, or presumably even directly suggestive

become Proprietors of any Aqueduct, or of any funds raised for making and
constructing the same. . . ." *Ibid.*, p. 17. It has been stated that the first really
modern general incorporation law for business purposes was that of Connecticut
in 1837. See Berle, A. A., and Means, G. C., *The Modern Corporation and Private
Property*, New York (Macmillan), 1932, p. 136. Other states subsequently followed until now all states and the District of Columbia have enacted general
incorporation laws.

[14] The development of business corporations, as distinct from the development
of the *idea of corporateness* which is briefly dealt with in a note appended to the
present chapter, has been a subject of research investigation by several scholars
in recent years. Among others the following may be mentioned as particularly
useful to readers who wish to pursue the subject. Du Bois, A. B., *The English
Business Company After the Bubble Act, 1720-1800*, New York (Commonwealth),
1938; Hunt, Bishop C., *The Development of the Business Corporation in England,
1800-1867*, Cambridge, Mass. (Harvard), 1936; Evans, G. H., Jr., *British Corporation Finance, 1775-1850: a study of preference shares*, Baltimore (Johns Hopkins),
1936; Todd, Geoffrey, "Some Aspects of Joint Stock Companies, 1844-1900,"
Economic History Review, Vol. IV (1932), pp. 46-71; Davis, Joseph F., *Essays in
the Earlier History of American Corporations*, 2 volumes, Cambridge, Mass.
(Harvard), 1917; Blandi, Joseph G., *Maryland Business Corporation, 1783-1852*,
Baltimore (Johns Hopkins), 1934.

[15] The statutes usually require at least three "corporators" although unless there
be an express or implied statement in the statute to this effect there is nothing to
prevent a state from creating a corporation where only one person is involved.
See Ballantine, *op. cit.*, p. 58. Infants and corporations as legal persons may not
become incorporators as a matter of public policy. A common requirement is
that at least one corporator be a resident of the state. See Stevens, Robert S.,
op. cit., pp. 108-113.

of, another corporation already chartered by and doing business in the same state. Some states require that the name include the word "corporation," "incorporated," or abbreviations thereof to warn the public that the association is a corporation. Just how closely the name chosen may approximate that of another corporation and not constitute an infringement is impossible to state in general terms.[16] The state, however, with the consent of the corporation, may change the latter's name or authorize it to do so by appropriate amendment. Besides a name, a corporation must also indicate in the certificate the location of its *principal office*, in order that persons seeking legal redress against it may know where to serve legal papers. Not infrequently nowadays the so-called principal office is not the place where the corporation will carry on any substantial fraction of its business, but merely an office maintained by the corporation to comply with the letter of the law. Until recently the statement of the *purposes and objects* of the corporation, the nature of its business, was among the most important parts of the certificate. Such a statement was regarded as important for two reasons. Firstly, since the corporation is a creature of the state (sovereign) authority it is important that the precise purposes for which special privileges have been granted should be clearly indicated. Secondly, from the point of view of the shareholders who venture their capital it is important that they know the kinds of business in which the enterprise may engage in order that they may be able to calculate the kinds of risks to which their capitals will be exposed. A person who was perfectly willing to commit his capital to the business of manufacturing gas from coal might well object to having his funds devoted to the search for natural gas pools of uncertain existence. The two undertakings are subject to quite different risks. In recent years, however, there has been a pronounced tendency for incorporators

---

[16] In some states the statutes expressly provide for the protection of the corporate name, but in any case the right to such protection exists at common law. A suit is proper by the corporation affected, either to prevent incorporation, or, if this has already occurred, to prevent the use of the infringing corporate name as granted by the state. The essential idea is to prevent one corporation from gaining advantage from the reputation and good-will created by another through deceiving the public by the similarity of names. In order to be protected in its name a corporation must use it, which seems to be reasonable. See Stevens, Robert S., *op. cit.*, pp. 114-120.

to seek and obtain the power to engage in many and varied lines of activity. The statement of the purposes, objectives, and powers of the corporation as commonly drafted nowadays is likely to be unrestrictive. This fact, coupled with the common provision permitting corporations to own shares of other corporations, has considerably lessened the danger of lawsuits alleging *ultra vires* acts.[17] It should be emphasized, moreover, that corporations have certain implied powers and others that are incidental to its main powers. For instance, to take and hold real property would be a power incident to other corporate powers unless expressly denied. It is worth noting also that where no public welfare question is at stake, corporate acts are presumed to be within corporate authority.

Other matters included in the certificate of incorporation are the amount of the authorized capital stock, the number of shares, the amount subscribed and by whom, including, of course, any classification of shares on the basis of preferences, priorities, etc. As a general rule the original incorporators must each subscribe to at least one share of stock and upon incorporation they automatically become stockholders. If there is the intention to limit the amount of indebtedness that the corporation may incur, this will also be stated in the certificate of incorporation.[18] Finally, there will be a statement giving the number of directors, the names and addresses of the incorporators, its proposed life-span (limited or perpetual) and any other special stipulations not contrary to the statute under which the corporation is being organized.[19]

According to the procedure in vogue in most states the above information properly prepared and assembled in triplicate and signed and sworn to by the incorporators is presented to the Secre-

[17] An act is said to be *ultra vires* when according to its charter the corporation is not permitted to carry on such an activity. The doctrine, however, has been used not only for the protection of stockholders, but also as an attempted means by which a corporation might escape performance of onerous contracts, etc. See Ballantine, *op. cit.*, Chapter VII, and Stevens, Robert S., *op. cit.*, Chs. VII, VIII.

[18] In some few states the statute itself may limit the total corporate indebtedness even though nothing is said about it in the certificate of incorporation. For example, in Arizona the amount of the indebtedness may not be greater than two-thirds of the amount of the capital stock even though there be no self-imposed limitation.

[19] In some states, e.g., Delaware, it is possible to include here a denial of the shareholders' pre-emptive right to subscribe to additional issues of stock of the corporation of any or all classes. See next chapter.

tary of State in the proposed state of incorporation. This official is usually charged with the duty of ascertaining that the provisions of the general incorporation statute have been properly satisfied; that is, he has no discretion in the matter and upon compliance with the statute must issue a charter to the corporation.[20] If all provisions of the statutory law have been properly met, one copy of the certificate of incorporation is filed at the Secretary of State's office, where it is open to inspection by any interested party.[21] The organizers of the corporation, upon payment of the proper fees and proof that they have subscribed to the required number of shares or that the necessary minimum amount of capital, if any, has been paid in, then receive from the Secretary of State their "charter," which is no more than one copy of the certificate of incorporation (duly signed and approved), taken together with the general incorporation laws of the state. This last, that the general incorporation law of the state is part of the charter, is important [22] because it gives the corporation certain of its powers and is the basis upon which the state imposes general rules on the corporation and its activities, e.g., the powers and liabilities of directors, the rules governing dividends, the procedure for dis-

[20] In a few jurisdictions, however, the Secretary of State is required to make sure that the objects of the corporation are not contrary to public policy. See Ballantine, *op. cit.*, p. 60.

[21] There is apparently a distinction between what Stevens has called "mandatory" and "directory" provisions of the general incorporation law. The idea is that certain portions of the statute are of greater importance than others because they are designed for the protection of the public; these are mandatory in the sense that if they are not complied with the corporateness of the association may be attacked either directly by the state or collaterally in private litigation and the courts will deny that a corporation has been formed. The directory provisions are those which are of little or no significance from the public point of view, and here if there has been an honest attempt at compliance the courts will hold that there has been "substantial" compliance and that therefore a corporation exists. See Stevens, Robert S., *op. cit.*, pp. 100-105 and the cases there discussed.

[22] The following from the New Jersey statute is more or less typical: "This act may be amended or repealed, at the pleasure of the legislature, and every corporation created under this act shall be bound by such amendment; but such amendment or repeal shall not take away or impair any remedy against any such corporation or its officers for any liability which shall have been previously incurred; this act and all amendments thereof shall be a part of the charter of every corporation heretofore or hereafter formed hereunder; except so far as the same are inapplicable and inappropriate to the objects of such corporation." *New Jersey General Incorporation Act* as amended at the end of the legislative session of 1931, sec. 5 (L. 1896, Ch. 185, sec. 5).

solution, etc. The third copy of the certificate of incorporation is filed in the county clerk's office of the county where the corporation has elected to maintain its principal office. When the requirements just described have been satisfied, the corporation has in most instances commenced its legal existence.[23]

2. *The professionalization of the incorporation process.* In earlier times all the above was usually performed by the parties directly interested in having the corporation brought into existence. And for small corporations, or corporations where there is no intention to offer securities for public sale, this method of direct participation in the incorporation process is often followed. On the other hand it is becoming increasingly common for corporations to be formed by specialists who engage largely or wholly in this kind of work. There are several organizations with country-wide connections which, for a fee, will procure a corporate charter in any state desired. The really interested parties need only to indicate in general terms the kind of corporate powers wanted, the amount and types of stock to be issued, the name, etc., and all the bothersome detail involved in the preparation of the certificate of incorporation, the original subscriptions, the holding of the first corporate meeting, the preparation of the minute book, and other details will be handled with marvelous efficiency and dispatch by unimportant clerks. Indeed, one concern engaged in this work boasts that it will procure any ordinary charter in less than twenty-four hours.[24] And now that the process of incorporation

[23] As might be expected, the exact time at which a corporation comes into legal existence is important for some purposes since until then it cannot act as a corporation. Ballantine states (*op. cit.*, pp. 61-62) that a corporation ordinarily comes into legal existence as soon as it has "accepted" its charter, which implies that it has complied with all the provisions of the general act. The California law provides that, "The corporate existence shall begin upon the filing of the articles and shall continue perpetually, unless otherwise expressly provided by law." California Civil Code (Hillyer's Cons. Supp. 1932), sec. 292. Yet notwithstanding a somewhat similar statutory provision in Ohio it has been there held that until capital has been paid in, directors elected, and by-laws adopted the incorporators are personally liable in a tort action. *Beck v. Stimmel*, 39 Ohio App. 510, 177 N.E. 920 as cited by Stevens, Robert S., *op. cit.*, p. 105.

[24] It is consequently not surprising that the number of new incorporations now far surpasses anything thought possible only a few decades ago. There seem to be no figures of the annual output of new corporations in the United States as a whole, but New York, whose laws are not the loosest among the several states, created no less than 290,494 corporations between 1920 and 1932. Cited in Senate

has been so simplified and standardized there is probably no harm in allowing persons to do through others what they could clearly do themselves.

There is another aspect of this tendency for incorporation papers to be prepared by persons skilled in the task that is especially important in the case of large enterprises which expect to raise their capital by means of a public sale of securities. Holding companies, investment trusts, and family concerns whose ownership is to be transferred to the general investing public, fall particularly within this group. In recent years investment bankers and their associates have been the ones to visualize the profit possibilities of such enterprises and to take the first active steps towards bringing them into existence.[25] This means that the provisions of the corporate charter are drafted by the investment banker with the assistance of his skilled attorneys. The persons who will be chiefly bound and limited by the document, however, are the shareholders and possibly bondholders who will ultimately provide the free capital for the enterprise. But at the time of drafting the contract which limits and defines their rights, their interests are neither represented, nor adequately considered, except insofar as the investment banker is aware that the security contracts must be salable, i.e., carry some appeal to those who are expected to buy them. The net consequences of this arrangement are not always entirely happy. The document as drawn by the banker and his attorneys will probably give the maximum in freedom and protection to the management and directors while shareholders' interests will be given secondary consideration at best. This is not surprising in cases where the investment banker intends to maintain "control" over the enterprise even after the financing has been completed. In particular, the powers and protections afforded management are likely to be strengthened by clauses in the charter allowing the directors to sell additional shares to whom and on

Doc. 92, 70th Congress, 1st Sess., *Utility Corporations*, Part 73-A, p. 83, note. Ripley, W. Z., *Main Street and Wall Street*, Boston (Little, Brown), 1927, pp. 16-18, cites figures for some few states that indicate that for these states the number of new incorporations per annum increased more than fivefold between 1900 and 1925. These states were among the more liberal in their laws, however.

[25] The present writer has dealt with this topic in part in an article, "The Origin and Development of the Public Utility Holding Company," *Journal of Political Economy*, Vol. 44 (1936), pp. 31-53.

whatever terms they desire, i.e., the pre-emptive right of share-holders is specifically denied; the voting rights of shares publicly owned are severely limited or denied entirely; and because of the very loose statutory provisions governing charter amendments even their few rights and priorities may be changed to their harm with comparative ease.[26] Not infrequently it is only after he has committed his capital, if ever, that the shareholder discovers the true nature of the security contract for which he has parted with his funds. But his rights, with few exceptions, will be those specified by the document which has been drawn by skilled legal talent at the behest of an investment banker.

III. FOREIGN INCORPORATION AND CORPORATIONS

1. Why persons seeking a corporate charter often select a state other than that where they propose to carry on most of the corporation's business. 2. Differences in powers and immunities: issuance of shares, rules governing dividends, shares issued for property, rules applicable to directors. 3. Differences in incorporation costs and annual fees. 4. Position of foreign corporations: sovereignty of individual states; federal constitutional limitations; comity; disability of a foreign corporation which has not complied.

1. Why persons seeking a corporate charter often select a state other than that where they propose to carry on most of the corporation's business. It might be supposed that a group of corporators would more or less naturally seek a corporate charter from the state in which they expected the corporation subsequently to carry on the major portion of its business. And for small corporations and those not contemplating engagements in interstate commerce it is doubtless typical for them to be incorporated at home. But in the case of larger enterprises and those expecting to do business on a nation-wide basis there are often cogent reasons why

---

[26] The amendment of the corporate charter is governed by the provisions of the statutory general incorporation law, but it is not necessary to select a state where the provisions are onerous. Something further is said about charter amendments in the next chapter, sec. I.

one state is preferable to others as a place of incorporation. Since in the United States each individual state is a sovereign authority and therefore has the power to engender corporations it is not surprising that the applicable laws are not identical nor equally attractive to prospective incorporators in all jurisdictions. From this point of view the relevant differences between the individual states are mainly of two types: (a) differences in the powers, privileges, immunities, etc., available under the respective general incorporation laws, and (b) differences in the costs of incorporation and in the amount and kind of taxes imposed upon corporations by the various states. Let us look into this.

2. *Differences in powers and immunities: issuance of shares, rules governing dividends, shares issued for property, rules applicable to directors.* The individual states have not followed identical policies in providing for the organization, conduct, and dissolution of business corporations. In most states the constitution merely states that the legislature shall provide by general laws, and not otherwise, for the organization of corporations.[27] Some few states (e.g., Louisiana and Virginia), on the other hand, have apparently thought such matters of constitutional import and their constitutions provide for the creation of corporations in rather detailed fashion. Constitutional stipulations are notably more difficult and cumbersome to amend than general laws and for that reason perhaps less satisfactory than general laws. This difficulty of amendment may in part explain why some states have lagged behind in what has been called the "race of laxity" towards more liberal provisions governing corporations.[28]

[27] For example, Maine: "Corporations shall be formed under general laws, and shall not be created by special acts of the legislature, except for municipal purposes, and in cases where the objects of corporation cannot otherwise be obtained; and, however formed, they shall forever be subject to the general laws of the State." *Constitution*, Art. IV, pt. 3, sec. 14. Similar provisions are to be found in many states.

A compact but useful digest of the state corporation laws and the more pertinent decisions thereunder is to be found in Sen. Doc. 92, 70th Congress, 1st Sess., *Utility Corporations*, Part 69-A, pp. 149-368. This compilation covers the modifications in the law up to July 1, 1934, and considerable use has been made of it in the present section. See also, Hills, George S., "Model Corporation Act," *Harvard Law Review*, Vol. 48 (1935), pp. 1334-1380, which describes critically important differences between the states.

[28] Some states are apparently very keen to liberalize their laws as a means of increasing their revenues. The Secretary of State's report for Delaware, for in-

A most important difference between the states of interest to incorporators is the statutory provisions governing the issuance of securities, especially shares of stock. In the case of shares of stock having a par value most states insist that the capital of the corporation shall be not less than the total par value of shares issued having a par value, and usually also that such par value shares may not

stance, reads very much like a report to stockholders by a competitive enterprise and opens with these words: "Delaware continues to be favored over other States by new enterprises seeking corporate charters; about one-third of all the corporations listed in Moody's Manual are domiciled here." A few sentences later the Secretary reports, "Certified copy fees of 1936, $79,767.65, were the highest of any year since 1930 when the revenue from this source was $88,784.45." State of Delaware, *Report of the Department of State for the Year 1936*, p. 4. It is interesting to note that the number of charters granted by Delaware from 1899, when the General Incorporation Law was enacted, to the end of 1936 was 43,187, of which 25,580 were in existence on December 31, 1936. *Ibid*.

The revenues derived are not negligible by any means. In 1935 Delaware collected fees in the corporation department of the Secretary of State's office of $233,885. *Ibid*. For the state of New York the similar revenues for 1935 were $1,633,164, State of New York, *Annual Report of the Secretary of State*, Legislative Doc. (1936), No. 44, p. 6.

The following figures show the growth in the number of new charters granted in a few states as reported by the respective Secretaries of State. The falling off since 1929 is very marked. Notice also that Delaware granted fewer charters annually in the years 1932-1938 than in any of the years 1918-1929. This is probably to be accounted for by the decline in the relative degree of superiority (from the point of view of incorporators, of course) of the Delaware statute over others in the later years.

	Delaware	New York	New Jersey
Av. 1909-1914 (incl.)	1,442	8,627	1,754
Av. 1915-1919 (incl.)	2,992	11,333	1,657
1920	5,747	15,103	2,588
1921	4,568	16,097	2,849
1922	5,095	18,160	3,500
1923	5,072	19,531	3,718
1924	4,379	19,549	4,257
1925	5,053	24,703	5,646
1926	4,778	25,388	6,109
1927	5,424	25,670	6,108
1928	6,250	26,817	6,558
1929	7,537	25,755	6,587
1930	5,611	23,867	5,289
1931	4,237	24,828	5,457
1932	3,564	24,901	5,627
1933	3,094	22,659	5,065
1934	2,476	18,537	4,191
1935	2,398	18,625	4,243
1936	2,598	18,805	4,499
1937	2,296	17,455	5,457
1938	1,659	15,649	

be issued as fully paid for a consideration less than their par value.[29] Shares of stock without par value have been growing in importance and popularity and incorporators are likely to have greater interest in the statutory provisions relating to them. Here the differences between the states are significant. According to Hills,[30] whose investigations are apparently exhaustive, the states fall into three classes in their treatment of stated capital in connection with the issuance of no par value shares. At the one extreme are those states that insist that the full amount received from the sale of no par value shares must be credited to the stated capital account and that there must be a minimum stated value (perhaps of $1 or even $5) for each no par value share issued. Indiana and Florida may be mentioned in this group. At the other extreme are states such as Delaware, Idaho, Maine and some others that allow directors to designate any portion of the amount received in exchange for the issuance of no par value shares as paid-in surplus rather than capital stock. Indeed, in Delaware, the directors are allowed sixty days from the date of issue in which to decide what portion of the proceeds from sale shall be designated paid-in surplus rather than stated capital.[31] The third group of states is willing to recognize some virtues in paid-in surplus in connection with no par value shares, but insists on a distinction between shares with preferences and shares without: shares with a preference in liquidation, but not others, must have an amount equal to the full consideration received credited to stated capital. California, Minnesota, Colorado, and Pennsylvania are examples. In Michigan 50 per cent of the consideration received from the sale of no par shares must be credited to stated capital regardless. By no means will persons proposing to incorporate find all the above-mentioned provisions relating to stock issuance equally attractive and hence they may select a state other than their own domicile.

[29] In California, however, "If par value shares have been issued as fully paid up for a consideration less than par, only the amount of the agreed consideration for such shares specified in dollars shall be credited to stated capital. . . ." *California Civ. Code*, sec. 300B as amended. According to Hills, *op. cit.*, p. 1361, Rhode Island has a similar provision. In Ohio, par value shares may be issued for less than par but an amount equal to the par value has to be included in stated capital. *Ibid.*

[30] *Ibid.*

[31] *General Incorporation Law*, sec. 14.

Closely associated with the question of the determination of stated capital is that of the statutory rules governing the payment of dividends. In some states dividends may be paid even though capital is impaired, while in others this is definitely illegal. In Delaware, for instance, a corporation may pay dividends, "(a) out of its net assets in excess of its capital . . . or (b), in case there shall be no excess, out of its net profits for the fiscal year then current and/or the preceding fiscal year"; [32] and similar provisions are to be found in Nevada, Maine, Indiana, New Jersey.[33] Certain states limit dividends from paid-in surplus to shares with preferences, and others add to this a provision that even then the preferred shareholders must be so informed. Such differences between the states in the applicable laws governing dividend payments are very considerable and may either attract or repel prospective incorporators.[34]

An important matter to incorporators and promoters is the attitude of the state towards shares issued for property and services. Some states follow the so-called "good faith" rule, which is to say that the judgment of directors as to the value of property and services accepted in payment for shares is conclusive in the absence of fraud. Others, notably New Jersey, Illinois, and Missouri, incline more to the "true value" rule. While Professor Dodd has emphasized that the actual differences between the state courts in this respect are far less than commonly supposed, nevertheless incorporators may yet prefer to "play safe" by avoiding those states which are reputed to be the more strict.[35] In Massachusetts a detailed description of the property and services accepted in payment for shares must be filed with the commissioner of corporations in order that its fair value may be better inferred.

[32] *General Incorporation Law*, sec. 34. The sentence goes on to limit such declarations where capital represented by shares with preferences is impaired.

[33] Hills, *op. cit.*, p. 1365.

[34] See, *ibid.*, pp. 1365-1370, for an illuminating discussion of the many provisions relating to dividends. Concerning the Delaware law on dividends one writer concludes, "There is such a thing as an illegal dividend in that State, rendering directors liable in that amount, but directors are so hedged in with safeguards as to render problematical the value of such a cause of action against them." Sen. Doc. 92, 70th Congress, 1st Sess., *Utility Corporations*, Part 69-A, p. 284.

[35] Dodd, David L., *Stock Watering*, New York (Columbia), 1930, especially Ch. III and the cases there cited and quoted.

The liabilities, powers, and qualifications of corporate directors are not identical in all jurisdictions. In some states directors must be stockholders, in others not. In Delaware, if the articles of asso- ciation so provide, a director may deal with the corporation in transactions in which he has a personal interest without disclosing that interest.[36] But the relations between the directors and the cor- poration and the directors and the stockholders are only defined in a minor way by the general incorporation law and probably statutory differences here are not an important reason governing the choice of a state of incorporation.

In the foregoing we have attempted merely to point out a few of the statutory variations between the states that may induce incorporators to select one state rather than another. There are of course many others, and in particular instances these may be of controlling importance, but they are too detailed to be described here.[37]

3. *Differences in incorporation costs and annual fees.* Apart from statutory laws of varying degrees of attractiveness to pro- spective incorporators in the different states there is the simple and obvious matter of the direct out-of-pocket cost of incorporation as between one state and another.[38] In Iowa, for instance, the au- thorized no par value shares are valued at $100 for purposes of determining the organization fee, which would mean for a cor-

[36] Professor Berle has caustically remarked on this point, "In a recent chapter it was written that directors might trade with their own corporation to the disad- vantage of the latter, even though they concealed their interest in the transaction. From the point of view of royal or government created corporation the clause must be considered wholly valid. If the government chooses to erect a concern of this sort, and has sole power of creation, it may, if it choose, grant thieves' licenses to directors." *Op. cit.,* pp. 24-25. On the powers and liabilities of directors in general see Ballantine, *op. cit.,* Chs. IX and X.

[37] One prime advantage of foreign incorporation regardless of what foreign state is chosen is the privilege obtained to bring suit in the federal as opposed to the state courts on the grounds of diversity of citizenship. This, of course, is a highly technical legal question whose ramifications cannot even be charted, much less explored, here. In particular many highly skilled corporation lawyers are of the opinion that the federal courts are apt to be more favorable than state courts to their clients in labor cases and cases involving enfringement upon the good- will of an established corporation, e.g., use of a similar name by another corpora- tion.

[38] The indebtedness of what immediately follows to the comprehensive compila- tion of Forest E. Keller and Fred Clarenbach in *Tax System of the World,* 7th ed., Chicago (Commerce Clearing House), 1938, pp. 176-180, is gratefully ac- knowledged.

poration (having more than 100 shares) a cost of 10 cents a share. Minnesota, Kentucky, and Utah also value no par value shares for fee purposes at $100. Other states, however, as Pennsylvania and South Dakota, tax no par value shares on the basis of value received; while Delaware, by contrast, charges a fee of one-half a cent a share for no par value shares up to 20,000 shares and thereafter the rate declines. On the other hand, Florida, up to 1,250 shares, assesses a tax of 20 cents a share. The differences in respect to par value shares are almost equally great but there is no need to labor the main point. Also relevant is the fact that while most states (e.g., Iowa, Colorado, Connecticut) levy the incorporation tax upon the *authorized* number of shares, a few (e.g., Illinois) use as a basis the number of shares actually issued.[39]

The relative costs of incorporation as between the respective states are not entirely determined by the costs of initial incorporation. All but a few states impose annual taxes on corporations based (usually) upon the amount of capital stock either outstanding or authorized. Here again the tax rates are by no means uniform. In Florida the annual tax is graduated from $10 for corporations with outstanding capital stock of $10,000 or less, to $1,000 for corporations with an amount above $2,000,000. By contrast California, Montana, New York, Indiana, Iowa, and Illinois levy

[39] An interesting sidelight on the relative costs of incorporation in the several states is the example cited by Dr. R. C. Larcom of Standard Brands, Inc., which was formed under the laws of Delaware on August 14, 1929. The capital stock authorized by the certificate of incorporation amounted to 21,000,000 no par value shares, divided into 1,000,000 no par value preferred shares and 20,000,000 no par value common shares. The following table shows what the organization fee would have been had the company elected to incorporate under the laws of the following respective states.

State of Incorporation	Organization Fee
Arizona	$ 85
Virginia	600
Nevada	2,100
West Virginia	2,500
Maryland	42,700
Delaware	43,050
Maine	43,050
Ohio	55,100
New Jersey	210,000
New York	1,050,000

As reported by Larcom, R. C., *The Delaware Corporation*, Baltimore (Johns Hopkins), 1937, pp. 22-23.

no similar tax at all. North Carolina imposes an annual tax of $1.75 per $1,000 of the sum total of capital stock, surplus, and undivided profits.[40]

While for small enterprises with comparatively few outstanding shares these differences in the incorporation costs and annual taxes would probably not outweigh the disadvantages of being a foreign corporation, the same cannot be said for large concerns with many outstanding shares. For the latter the added cost of being incorporated in one state rather than another may amount to a convincing figure. Consequently the incorporators may shop around instead of incorporating in the state where they expect to carry on the bulk of their business.[41]

4. *Position of foreign corporations: sovereignty of individual states; federal constitutional limitations; comity; disability of a foreign corporation which has not complied.* The foregoing discus-

[40] Dr. Larcom also prepared figures to show the annual franchise tax for Standard Brands, Inc., had it been incorporated under the laws of the following states. The capitalization used is that described in the previous note.

State of Incorporation	Annual Franchise Tax
Nevada	$ 5
Arizona	20
West Virginia	2,500
Delaware	25,000 (maximum)
Maryland	25,832
New Jersey	32,614
Virginia	33,100
Maine	52,525

Larcom, *op. cit.*, p. 24. As pointed out in the text some states do not impose any annual franchise tax so that not all states included in the note about incorporation fees appear here.

[41] Notwithstanding the tendency of incorporators to search out the most desirable state in which to seek a charter, almost two-thirds of the industrial companies listed on the New York Stock Exchange and the New York Curb Exchange in 1932 had obtained their charters from the four states of Delaware, New York, New Jersey, and Ohio. Of the companies then listed, Delaware had chartered 34 per cent of those listed on the New York Stock Exchange and 38 per cent of those on the Curb Exchange. For New York the corresponding figures were 16 per cent and 15 per cent; for New Jersey, 14 per cent and 7 per cent; for Ohio, 5 per cent and 5 per cent. In other words, although there are forty-eight states one small state, Delaware, had chartered more than one-third of the industrial corporations listed on the country's two largest exchanges. See *ibid.*, pp. 175-176.

These percentages are probably not indicative of present day trends, however, because the relative advantages of Delaware charters over others are now diminished; not that Delaware has become more restrictive: the others have simply become more liberal.

sion has carried within it the implication that a corporation chartered by one state will be able to carry on business beyond the
boundaries of that one state. And with some few minor qualifications this is indeed the fact situation. Yet it must be obvious that
there are certain problems to be overcome. In the first place, although a particular state may authorize a corporation to do business beyond its state borders it is equally clear that the authority
of the state loses all its force beyond its territorial limits. Hence,
if corporate personality is to be recognized beyond the boundaries
of the engendering state it must be because of some action or
acknowledgment on the part of other states and not because of
the extraterritorial force of the laws of the first. The grounds on
which the several states recognize each other's corporations as
corporations within their own jurisdictions are principally two:
first, the federal constitution does not permit the states to impose
burdens on interstate and foreign commerce; second, the doctrine
or principle of "comity" between the states.[42] Yet the doctrine of
comity does not prevent a state from attaching conditions and
requirements which must be met before it will recognize "foreign
corporations" as corporations within its boundaries.[43] If a sovereign authority deems it wise to insist upon compliance with certain
statutory provisions before corporateness will be conferred upon
its own citizens, it would certainly be reasonable for it to demand
that foreign corporations offer the citizens an equal protection.
And this right is well established. Overhanging the power of the
individual states in this connection, however, is the constitutional
power of the federal government over interstate and foreign commerce, and the right to insist upon the recognition of constitution-
ally guaranteed privileges.[44] Hence while a state has the power to

[42] Comity between the states means simply something more in the nature of
courtesy and accommodation rather than something existing as an enforceable
right. All states of the union, for instance, allow automobiles licensed in other
states to use their roads and highways provided certain simple requirements are
complied with. So also the states in general recognize the divorces granted to persons by the laws of other states.

[43] In the United States with respect to any given state a corporation is "foreign"
if it has been formed under the laws of another state or a foreign country, and
"domestic" if it has been formed under the laws of the instant state.

[44] As one might expect, the constitutional questions involved are complicated
and admit of no easy answer applicable to all situations. But see Stevens, Robert
S., *op. cit.*, pp. 827-836 and the cases there discussed.

control the activities of foreign corporations within its borders this power does not extend the whole way: interstate and foreign commerce may not be impeded, nor may the state discriminate unreasonably between citizens and non-citizens so that the latter are in effect denied equal protection and privileges at law.

In order to qualify and do business as a foreign corporation within another state, a corporation must ordinarily fulfill requirements somewhat analogous to those demanded of domestic corporations. In the main these include the following: to register as a foreign corporation by filing a copy of its articles of association, including a statement of its authorized capital stock and the amount issued; to designate an office within the state and an agent upon whom legal papers may be served; to pay the necessary fees and take out a license granting it permission to do business within the state as a foreign corporation.[45] The entry fee for foreign corporations is far from uniform in the various states. For example in Delaware and Maine there is a flat fee of $10; but in California the flat fee is $105, and in Tennessee $200. In New York the cost of registration for foreign corporations is 0.125 per cent for par value shares (or 6 cents a share for no par value shares), on that proportion of the corporation's capital employed in New York state, with a minimum fee of $10, plus a fee of the Department of State for filing and issuing a certificate of authority of $100. For a corporation with millions of no par value shares doing a substantial portion of its business in New York but incorporated elsewhere the total cost of registration would obviously amount

[45] The following from the New Jersey law is more or less typical. "Every foreign corporation . . . before transacting any business in this state shall file in the office of the secretary of state a copy of its charter or certificate of incorporation, attested by its president and secretary, under its corporate seal, and a statement attested in like manner of the amount of its capital stock authorized and the amount actually issued, the character of the business which it is to transact in this state, and designating its principal office in this state and an agent who shall be a domestic corporation or a natural person of full age actually resident in this state, together with his place of abode, upon which agent process against such corporation may be served . . . ; upon filing of such copy and statement the secretary shall issue to such corporation a certificate that it is authorized to transact business in this state, and that the business is such as may be lawfully transacted by corporations of this state, and he shall keep a record of all such certificates issued." New Jersey *General Corporation Act*, sec. 97.

to a considerable sum. New Jersey levies the same charge and taxes on foreign corporations for a certificate to do business in New Jersey as other states impose upon New Jersey corporations within their own jurisdictions.

Unless and until a corporation chartered by another state has complied with these requirements its corporate character has not been recognized by the foreign state, and important consequences in some circumstances may follow. In some states (e.g., Florida and Colorado) the officers and stockholders may be held personally liable for the corporate debts; again, the corporation may not maintain an action in the courts of the state until it has removed this disability by compliance with the statute including the payment of the stipulated fine.[46] But the exact statutory provisions are here controlling, and there are considerable differences between the several states.[47] All such legislative enactments are ostensibly intended for the protection of the citizens of the state, and therefore even though the corporation has not complied with the statute, legally competent residents may none the less maintain legal actions against it. In other words, an unqualified foreign corporation is liable but frequently may not prosecute.

In view of the penalties and disabilities attached to doing business within a state without having first qualified under the statute it is obvious that the exact meaning of "doing business" is of crucial importance. No sufficient discussion of the complicated legal questions involved can be undertaken here because the answer in any case depends partly upon the applicable state statute and partly upon the meaning of the phrase "interstate commerce."

[46] Stevens, Robert S., *op. cit.*, pp. 845-846, cites cases from Washington, Rhode Island, West Virginia, Alabama, and Pennsylvania to this effect.

The fines imposed are by no means negligible. In Delaware, for instance, transacting business without complying with the statute is a misdemeanor "and upon conviction thereof shall be fined not less than two hundred dollars nor more than five hundred dollars for each offense." *General Corporation Law*, sec. 193. In New Jersey the fine is $200.

[47] The following from the New York law renders contracts of unauthorized foreign corporations unenforceable. "A foreign corporation, other than a moneyed corporation, doing business in this state shall not maintain any action in this state upon any contract made by it in this state, unless before the making of such contract it shall have obtained a certificate of authority." *General Corporation Law*, sec. 218. A provision of this kind is very common.

Even though the legislature may enact laws that purport to define intrastate commerce such statutes are always subject to judicial review by the federal courts; in other words, the definition of interstate, and hence intrastate, commerce is not within the power of state legislatures. Where the question at issue is not one turning upon the definition of interstate commerce the disputes frequently hinge about such questions as to whether or not a single isolated transaction by a foreign corporation is "doing business"; is taking property in partial satisfaction of debt due doing business; or, is owning property *per se* doing business? While the several states are perfectly free to define what is *not* doing business, as Delaware, for example, has done, nevertheless the other question of what *does* constitute doing business is still largely dependent upon the full facts in each and every case.[48] Thus although there are real advantages in incorporating a new enterprise or reincorporating an existing enterprise in a foreign state, these gains are not in all cases entirely clear-cut and unalloyed. There are offsetting disadvantages to be reckoned in also.

IV. SUMMARY

The controversy over the precise legal character of corporations has not yet been terminated. On the one hand are those who urge the virtues of the sovereignty-concession theory: the view that corporations may only come into existence by a special grant of privilege from the sovereign which, by incorporation, creates an artificial person possessing some of the rights of natural persons.

[48] In recent years there has been evidence that at least some states have sought to exploit the tax revenue possibilities of foreign corporations doing business without first having qualified under the statute. State governments of late have been hard pressed to find additional revenues and perhaps for this reason they have sought to make the definition of doing business as all-embracing as the courts will allow. While one may only speculate on such matters, it seems reasonable to infer that the taxation of foreign corporations is regarded by many as a particularly desirable form of state revenue since the burden is believed to fall almost wholly on the foreigner. Yet it must be obvious that a like policy pursued by all the states will only raise the costs of doing business the country over to the detriment of all.

Others have insisted, on the other hand, that the State merely recognizes a personality that already has existence and reality; and that human "personality" is as much a creation of the mind as is corporate personality: neither is natural in any meaningful sense. An eclectic and matter-of-fact view of the corporation would emphasize that it is no more than a convenient legal device by which persons may associate together for the pursuit of acceptable ends; and that in the last analysis the ultimate entities with which the law must deal are real persons in society. By designating certain types of associations corporations we indicate that they have been formed in a particular way, that the associates have acquired the right to act as a unit for legal and commercial purposes, that the associates are not pledging their whole wealth to the venture, that membership is transferable, etc. But although the entity concept is notably useful as a short-hand expression there are certain problems for which it is irrelevant.

In the United States each individual state as a sovereign power has the right to recognize or to create corporations. Special act incorporation has given way to incorporation under general statutes. The corporation's charter, the legal evidence of its corporate character is no more than a properly prepared and accepted statement of its name, principal office, purposes and objects, capital, etc., taken together with the statutory law relating to corporations in that jurisdiction. The ease with which corporations are now formed and the tendency towards professionalization of the task are not without significance.

Those seeking to bring a corporate entity into existence have the choice of forty-eight jurisdictions in which to tender their application. The relevant differences between the states from the point of view of the incorporators are of two types: those relating to the kind of charter obtainable and those relating to the direct money costs of achieving and maintaining the corporate existence. A corporation chartered by one state and doing business in another operates in the latter as a foreign corporation and must comply with the stipulated requirements before its corporateness will be recognized for all purposes. The penalties for non-compliance are drastic in some jurisdictions.

A SUPPLEMENTARY NOTE ON THE HIS-TORICAL DEVELOPMENT OF THE COR-PORATE CONCEPT

A truly enormous literature relating directly or indirectly to the historical antecedents of the modern corporate idea exists and the present writer makes no pretense of having covered more than a very small fraction of it. The contributors to this literature, moreover, seem not to agree entirely on even all the ostensibly important points. Nevertheless a tentative word or two, especially on the church and the English borough in connection with the development of the idea of corporateness, may not be entirely out of place.[49] For it seems that it was out of the problems that the church and borough presented to medieval thinkers that the corporate concept found its way into English, and hence American, legal doctrine.

Although most scholars seem to agree that the corporate idea was familiar to Roman jurists [50] they also insist, usually, that there was no unbroken line of descent of the corporate concept from Roman times down through to Medieval England. On the contrary, the corporate idea seems to have arisen there independently in connection with religious and municipal life, and it was only when the concept of corporateness had attained some definiteness that Roman thinking on the subject was rediscovered and partially taken over to strengthen and cement the idea.

[49] Dewing, A. S., *Corporation Securities,* New York (Ronald), 1934, Ch. I, and especially pp. 19-40, contains a useful and well-documented discussion of some of the possible earlier prototypes of the corporation.

[50] Apparently Roman law clearly recognized the right of persons to form corporations for non-criminal purposes and when formed such corporations were treated by the law as legal entities. Some of the more important of these corporations performed quasi-public functions, or at least functions that we now commonly attribute to municipalities or states, for example, the cleaning of sewers, fire protection, and the like. Perhaps in recognition of their semi-public character, corporations of this kind were accorded special privileges, and were distinguished thereby from the *collegium illicitum,* which was just as much a corporate entity at law but had not been recognized as performing services of a public character. These corporate bodies, however, were not organized for profit, that is, they were not business corporations in the modern sense.

The associative pursuit of gain typically took the form of the *societas* which seems to have been more akin to our idea of the partnership. These took several forms, from a simple contract for joint administration of a single thing, for instance, a piece of land, to the *societas publicanorum,* which was a business partnership for farming out the collection of taxes, or the operation of a mine or

According to the eminent authorities Pollock and Maitland, English lawyers had begun to recognize at least the bare outlines of the corporate idea by the reign of Edward IV (1461-1483).[51] At any rate they had commenced to distinguish between mere conglomerations of men in townships, parishes, and gilds and "incorporated" bodies such as the Abbot and Convent of St. Albans, the Dean and Chapter of Lincoln, or the Mayor, Sheriffs, and Commonalty of Norwich. Yet even by the late fifteenth century, they had not come all the way. A really nettling problem was to distinguish between a man as a man and the same person as the head of a corporation. All corporations had a "head" who was a mortal man, and to distinguish between him as a flesh and blood person and as the present incumbent of whatever office was recognized as constituting the "head" of the corporation was not a separation that came easily to their minds. So, for instance, it was held in Edward IV's reign that the Mayor and Commonalty of Newcastle could not enter a bond to the individual who happened to be mayor; his private capacity was not recognized; a man, it was said, could not be bound to himself.[52] Yet, in more ways than one, the need for distinguishing between the particular incumbent of an office and the office itself as the medium through which the corporation took action, was of more than theoretical importance. However, if the late fifteenth century conception of the corporation was imperfect, legal thinking on the same problems a few centuries earlier was definitely crude. Let us first consider the church.

Even before 1066 there seem to have been "church" lands, in some sense, in England, although there is more than a suggestion that at an earlier time the church was thought of as belonging to the person

quarry. See, Radin, Max, *Handbook of Roman Law*, St. Paul, Minn. (West Publishing Co.), 1927, Ch. 12.

A different type of corporation, the *universitas*, was recognized by Roman law and was apparently the term applied to municipalities, townships, colonies, and the like. Although according to the legal doctrines of the time, the State alone could create such bodies this must have been no more than a rationalization since most of them undoubtedly antedated by a long period the full development of the Roman State. See Buckland, W. W., *Elementary Principles of the Roman Private Law*, Cambridge, Eng. (Cambridge University), 1912, pp. 56-57.

In the later Roman Empire the system of licensing and controlling these associations became more common. Radin (*op. cit.*, p. 270) declares that after the second century of the Empire corporations were rather infrequently organized. The earlier freedom with which corporations were formed seems to have disappeared.

[51] Pollock, Sir Frederick, and Maitland, F. W., *The History of English Law*, 2nd ed., 2 volumes, Cambridge, Eng. (Cambridge University), 1898, Vol. I, pp. 489-490. As will be presently observed the indebtedness of this note to this work is very large.

[52] *Ibid.*, p. 492.

upon whose land it stood. But apparently from the twelfth century onwards this ownership changes into a matter of patronage only.[53] Although in the Domesday Book local churches are both owners and owned objects, there are other difficulties: saints, in the technical sense, appear to be owners of property.[54] And in an age when religion loomed large on the social scene it is perhaps not surprising that persons should desire to bequeath a portion of their estate to one of the saints or even to the archangel. Yet the practical difficulties of bringing legal action against a heavenly saint must have been obvious enough from the first. Though the saint "owned" the land, it was quite clear that flesh and blood people occupied it, and undoubtedly disputes arose over what land belonged to the saint and what not. It would indeed be surprising if some practicable means had not been evolved for settling them. Accordingly we find the idea coming more and more into vogue that although the saint owns the land, the church holds it; or again, the Bishop of the diocese, or the Abbot, is conceived of as holding the land. There seems to have been no uniform pattern at first. Yet gradually the church becomes a "person." When this idea first begins to permeate sometimes the church as a whole (*ecclesia universalis*) and sometimes a portion thereof (*ecclesia particularis*) is thought to possess personality. The somewhat confused and not always consistent ideas then held about the church, however, were clarified by the study of the Roman Codes and Digests in England about the middle of the twelfth century; [55] for here scholars found the *universitas* of Roman Law. If the Roman ideas were not completely understood in England at first, they were no doubt clarified and consolidated by Innocent IV who, as pope (1243-1254), took over the Roman concept of the *universitas* and applied it effectively to the church. According to Innocent IV the church was an *universitas* but it was also a person, a *persona ficta;* the members of the church were not the church, they merely represented it, a *persona ficta* that could neither receive baptism nor be excommunicated.[56] Despite Innocent IV the full application of the corporate doctrine to all the complicated ques-

[53] *Ibid.,* pp. 497-498.

[54] Even in Roman times, after the Empire became Christian, rules had to be established for dealing with testaments by which persons left property to one of the saints but neglected to name a church or monastery.

[55] It is said that Vacarius, a learned scholar of the Roman Law, came to England about 1150 and began to teach at Oxford and Canterbury and that Roman Law was more or less continuously taught in England from that time onwards. Potter, Harold, *An Historical Introduction to English Law*, London (Sweet and Maxwell), 1932, p. 572.

[56] Pollock and Maitland, *op. cit.*, Vol. I, p. 502, point out that Innocent IV's conception of the church as a corporation included the deduction that the church could neither commit crimes nor do wrongs, but that this idea was not even then generally accepted. It is of course contrary to modern views.

tions of church property in England was only gradually accomplished in succeeding generations.[57] Nevertheless it seems to be generally agreed that by the fifteenth century the corporate concept had taken a firm hold in ecclesiastical thought in England.

The concept of corporateness, however, was not first developed in connection with church affairs and then by analogy applied to other bodies. While the concept was gradually being recognized in ecclesiastical matters somewhat similar problems in municipal affairs were there forcing its application too. A brief word on this (temporally) parallel development may not be out of place.

The English borough was a source of legal difficulties, even at the time of the Norman Conquest, because it did not quite fit into the feudal scheme of land tenure.[58] True, the borough land was said to be the king's land (*terra regis*), but only in the sense, apparently, that all the land of England was the king's.[59] In other words, the boroughs were not thought of as royal estates in the more restricted meaning. Although the number of boroughs in England decreased [60] in the two centuries following 1066, those that remained sought to procure, often by purchase, charters from the king that would set forth in written form the liberties they were accustomed to enjoy. The special privileges of the boroughs as listed in their charters are too numerous to be described at any length here but they did include the right to hold court; certain privileges of land tenure, as the right of the burgesses as a group to farm the borough land and to collect the revenues—tolls, court profits, mill profits, and perhaps house rents—formerly exacted by the sheriff for the king; [61] some few privileges of self-government, as the election of a mayor and bailiffs; [62] and finally, the charters

[57] In particular the transition from the church as a whole as a person, to the conception of smaller ecclesiastical groups—parish churches, abbeys, dioceses—as corporations, was one that came gradually and not altogether smoothly. But although this development cannot be treated here, see *ibid.*, pp. 503-511.

[58] A most interesting account of the historical development of the Borough of Cambridge is Maitland, F. W., *Township and Borough*, Cambridge, Eng. (Cambridge University), 1898.

[59] Pollock and Maitland, Vol. I, p. 638.

[60] This seems to have been especially true of the smaller boroughs where the expense of sending representatives to Parliament appeared proportionately great. In other cases the king or his lords felt it unwise to encourage "burgesses" to seek privileges. See *ibid.*, pp. 638.

[61] *Ibid.*, p. 651. Even the thirteenth century charters state that the king, not the burgesses, owns the land: "The burgesses of Cambridge hold the vill of Cambridge with all its appurtenances in fee farm of the king in chief, as in meadows, pastures, mills, waters and mill-pools with all franchises and free customs belonging to the said vill."

[62] As the towns grew in size and commercial importance they came to make by-laws and ordinances even though the charters did grant the privilege specifically.

granted to the burgesses of the borough the right to be free from the payment of market tolls within the borough and sometimes throughout the whole of England as well. The burgesses' freedom from market tolls and the accompanying trading privileges were highly prized, and in the words of Pollock and Maitland "it is chiefly in this character that it [the borough] becomes a person in the eyes of the law." [63] These charter rights to mercantile privileges apparently also carried with them the right of the burgesses to form an organization for the protection of these privileges; this was the gild merchant or market gild. In the main the gild merchant seems to have sought to enforce the recognition of the mercantile privileges in boroughs near and far; hence, the burgess venturing abroad as a trader got the backing of the association in obtaining proper treatment, that is, full recognition of his privileges as a burgess of the borough. Within the borough, on the other hand, the merchant gild holds court (the gild court) for the settling of disputes among the members. It must be recognized, however, that since not all burgesses were merchants, not all burgesses were members of the merchant gild.[64]

These then were the main privileges granted to the boroughs by the earlier charters. The charters were not irrevocable at first and the privileges granted thereunder were sometimes withdrawn by the king for non-use or abuse, although, at least in some instances, the payment of a fine was sufficient to restore them. Yet this very thought, that the *borough* itself could be fined or could have *its* privileges withdrawn, serves to emphasize the idea of corporateness. More and more the corporate concept comes to recognition: the burgesses are not properly conceived as proportional holders of the rights and privileges of the borough, but as temporal members of something more enduring; the king is sometimes found to owe a debt to the "community"; and the borough privileges do not pass away with the deaths of the existing burgesses. Pollock and Maitland neatly summarize the degree of corporateness of the boroughs as follows: "The best answer that we can suggest for this difficult question is that the lawyers are trying to retain old forms of speech and thought and to regard the burgesses as a set of co-proprietors, while at the same time they are beginning to know that the borough community differs in kind from all other 'land communities' and that Bracton had got hold of the right idea when he calls it an *universitas*." [65]

While scholars seem to agree that it is impossible to say just when the English boroughs became corporate, in the sense that they were

[63] *Ibid.*, p. 650.
[64] *Ibid.*, pp. 664-668.
[65] *Op. cit.*, Vol. I, p. 676.

thought of as corporations, it is perhaps reasonable to suggest that by the fourteenth century the boroughs were no longer conceived as simply a group of burgesses. The common seal, the enduring privileges, the property in tolls, the use of by-laws, all served to emphasize the at least quasi-corporate character of the borough. In the very nature of the facts the conceptual similarity, even identity, between the borough and the church could not long go unrecognized.[66]

One additional word in conclusion. Although the language used in these earlier times often seems to suggest that corporate bodies are created in some sense by sovereign authority we ought to recognize that this is more a manner of speaking than an accurate description of the course of historical development. In no very meaningful sense is it true that the English Crown created the boroughs as corporate entities; at the most, perhaps, it found it convenient to recognize by the written charter certain liberties or franchises which had long existed. To be sure, at a later time the king and his advisers found it both useful and profitable to insist that corporations could only come into existence by a special grant from the sovereign. While this idea was bolstered up by a not altogether unconvincing logic it did, none the less, and in spite of Sir Edward Coke (1552-1633), do violence to the historical facts. Historically the sovereign did not create the earliest corporate bodies.[67] They were corporations by prescription, that is something which had existed for so long a period that it became the basis of a legally recognizable right.[68]

[66] Pollock and Maitland, *op. cit.*, pp. 490-491, neatly describe the stage of development of the corporate idea by the fifteenth century in the following words. "They [the lawyers] demand that incorporatedness shall have some definite and authoritative commencement; the corporation does not grow by nature; it must be made, by the act of parliament, or of the king, or of the pope, though prescription may be equivalent to royal charter. The rule that the corporation can do no act save by a writing under its common seal they enforce with severity; it is an anomaly, a concession to practical necessities, that the commands of the corporation about petty affairs can come to its servants through less formal channels. The corporation is invisible, incorporeal, immortal; it cannot be assaulted, or beaten or imprisoned; it cannot commit treason; a doubt has occurred as to whether it can commit a trespass; but this doubt (though it will give trouble so late as the year 1842) has been rejected by practice, if not removed by any consistent theory. We even find it said that the corporation is but a name. On the other hand, it is a person. It is at once a person and yet but a name; in short, it is *persona ficta*." (notes omitted)

[67] See also Berle, A. A., *Studies in the Law of Corporation Finance*, Chicago (Callaghan), 1928, pp. 6-11.

[68] See the interesting note on custom and prescription in Salmond, Sir John, *Jurisprudence*, 8th ed. by C. A. W. Manning, London (Sweet and Maxwell), 1930, pp. 221-224.

REFERENCES: CHAPTER III

BURTCHETT, F. F.—*Corporation Finance*, New York: Harpers, 1934. Ch. 1.

DEWING, A. S.—*Corporation Securities*, Ch. 1.

GERSTENBERG, C. W.—*Financial Organization and Management*, New York: Prentice-Hall, 1934. Chs. 6, 7.

ARNOLD, T.—*The Folklore of Capitalism*, New Haven. 1937. Ch. 8.

FULLER, W.—"The Incorporated Individual, A Study of the One-Man Company." *Harvard Law Review*, Vol. 51.

HALLIS, F.—*Corporate Personality*, London, 1930, Introduction and Part I, Ch. 1.

LARCOM, R. C.—*The Delaware Corporation*, Baltimore, 1937.

RADIN, M.—"The Endless Problem of Corporate Personality," *Columbia Law Review*, Vol. 32.

TODD, GEOFFREY—"Some Aspects of Joint Stock Companies, 1844-1900," *Economic History Review*, Vol. 4.

WORMSER, I. M.—*Disregard of the Corporate Fiction and Allied Corporation Problems*, New York, 1927, Chs. 1-2.

WORMSER, I. M.—*Frankenstein, Incorporated*, New York, 1931. Chs. 1-4.

Chapter IV

THE RIGHTS AND OBLIGATIONS OF CORPORATE SHAREHOLDERS

I. The Rights of Shareholders. II. The Obligations and Liabilities of Stockholders. III. The Question of Par Value. IV. Summary.

~~~~~~~~~~~~~~~~~~~~~~~~~~~~

Although for legal and commercial purposes a business enterprise in the corporate form is an entity consisting of an aggregation of assets devoted to the acquisition of profits, it is also an entity in which certain persons have definable rights, and towards which some of these persons have ascertainable obligations. Those holding rights or claims against the corporate entity fall into the two broad classes of shareholders and creditors, in each of which there are several major and almost innumerable minor subdivisions. Since the relation of shareholders to the corporation and to one another is not wholly self-evident at the mere mention of the word "shareholder," the present chapter endeavors to explore and clarify its implications. Chapter V will consist of a similar discussion with respect to creditors. We shall then be in a better position to undertake an analysis of the corporate enterprise in its economic manifestations.

I. THE RIGHTS OF SHAREHOLDERS

1. Shareholders the owners of the corporation: ownership as a "bundle of rights." 2. The inherent and contractual rights of shareholders: voting rights, the pre-emptive right, right to prevent ultra vires *acts, the right to knowledge of the corporation's affairs, right to transfer ownership, right to participate in profits, right to net assets in dissolution. Summary. 3. The amendment of the corporate charter and shareholders' rights.*

1. *Shareholders the owners of the corporation: ownership as a "bundle of rights."* It is trite but true that the shareholders of a

72

corporation as a group are the owners, the proprietors, the residual claimants to whatever assets the corporation owns or possesses valuable rights in. And this statement holds regardless of the size or complexity of the corporate entity. To be sure, the position of all shareholders with respect to the corporation need not be identical; but we are now speaking of all shareholders considered as a group, not of the different classes, into which they are often broken up. Shareholders or stockholders are therefore owners above all else: they are the owners of the corporation.

We commonly hear it said—and the notion is useful—that the ownership of property consists of a "bundle of rights" in that property. Consequently, the essence of the shareholders' position as the owners of the corporation lies in the nature and character of their rights in and against the corporation. Now although in the case of any particular corporation one can define rather precisely the rights its stockholders possess, it is also true that most generalizations as to the rights of stockholders cannot be applied to a given instance of share ownership without qualification and amendment. The reasons for this annoying truth are to be found in the sources from which stockholders' rights are derived. On the one hand there are the so-called "inherent" rights of stock ownership, by which one means that certain rights attach to stock ownership in the very nature of the case unless they have been expressly altered by contractual agreement. So, for instance, if there were no written statement as to how profits were to be shared, all would (or should) understand that each share participated equally with all the others. Similarly, all shares would vote, and vote with equal weight, on all questions unless there were some written agreement to the contrary. Such inherent rights of shareholders are essentially common law rights, that is, rights established through the centuries by means of judicial decisions of the courts as cases came before them and were decided.[1] On the other hand,

[1] "The common law is the entire body of English law—the total *corpus juris Angliae*—with three exceptions, namely: (1) statute law, (2) equity, (3) special law in its various forms." Salmond, Sir John, *Jurisprudence*, 8th ed. by C. A. W. Manning, London (Sweet and Maxwell), 1930, p. 105. Again, "It is a form of case law having its source in the judicial decisions of the old courts of King's Bench, Common Pleas and Exchequer, and of the modern courts by which the system so established is now administered and developed." *Ibid.*

the rights of shareholders are derived from their contracts with the corporation by which their common law rights are either extended or modified. Unless the sovereign authority chooses to regard the contracting away of certain rights as contrary to public policy, there is nothing to prevent a person from modifying one or several of his common law rights as a shareholder. Thus, some shareholders may agree by contract to limit their participation in profits to seven dollars per annum and no more, or not to vote in the election of directors. The rights of shareholders, therefore, derive from two sources: first, the common law which attributes certain rights to shareholders *per se;* second, the contractual provisions to which they have agreed in the particular case and which, in some manner or other, abrogate their common law rights that would otherwise be controlling. What, then, are these inherent rights of shareholders which serve as the foundation for the more elaborate superstructures erected by contract?

2. *The inherent and contractual rights of shareholders.* The common law rights that ordinarily accrue to stockholders unless subject to contractual modification include the following:[2] (1) the right to vote their shares on all matters requiring a vote of the shareholders; (2) the pre-emptive right to subscribe to additional issues in proportion to their existing holdings; (3) the right to prevent the corporation from engaging in *ultra vires* activities; (4) the right to a knowledge of the corporation's affairs; (5) the right to transfer the ownership interest that the shares of stock represent to others; (6) the right to participate in any distribution of profits in proportion to their share interest; (7) the right to a proportionate share in the net assets available for distribution in voluntary and involuntary dissolution. These are the rights that attach to stock ownership unless the contract between the shareholder and the corporation has established a different arrangement.

There is one further point here, however. It will be recalled that in the previous chapter we emphasized that the general incorporation law under which a corporation has been brought into existence automatically forms a part of its charter. In other words,

---

[2] This list does not include absolutely all the rights that the common law has recognized as inherent in stock ownership but only the more important.

the corporation has agreed to the general incorporation law as a formulation of the general rules under which it will operate and function as a corporation. Many states have now codified certain common-law rules pertaining to the rights of shareholders in the general corporation law, so that, regardless of the common law doctrine, the statutory provision is controlling. Thus, for instance, the code will specify the procedure for amending the certificate of incorporation (articles of association), and if this provision is mandatory it overrides any agreement between the shareholders and the corporation on the question.

Let us now examine the inherent rights of shareholders and how they are often modified by contract.

a. *The right to vote.* As Professor W. H. S. Stevens has well said, ". . . stockholders vote not merely upon one but upon many matters so that the right to vote is to all intents and purposes 'a bundle of rights' to vote." [3] Although one ordinarily thinks of a shareholder's right to vote as relating primarily to the election of directors, this is by no means the only matter of interest or necessarily the most important. There are also such questions as charter amendments, the proposed issuance of additional stock having a claim to earnings prior to that of any shares now outstanding, a redefinition of stated capital for legal and balance sheet purposes, consolidations and mergers, the mortgaging of the corporation's assets in whole or in part, and perhaps others. But, unless there are contractual arrangements to the contrary, the right of each and every shareholder to vote on any and all of these matters (insofar as the general corporation law of the state requires a vote thereon), is beyond question; and the rule is one vote for each share held.

If the voting rights of all the shareholders in any given corporation are not identical, they may differ in a variety of ways by contractual agreement. From the simple common law rule of one share one vote on all matters the number of conceivable deviations is theoretically infinite. In the first place, each share might have

---

[3] Stevens, W. H. S., "Voting Rights of Capital Stock and Shareholders," *Journal of Business of the University of Chicago*, Vol. 11 (1938), pp. 311-348, at p. 312. This is an excellent study that warrants careful reading.

some multiple or some fraction of one vote.[4] The Great Western Sugar Refining Company, for example, allowed the preferred shareholders one vote for each share; but the common stockholders were only allowed one-twelfth of one vote for each share held.[5] Yet while such fractional or multiple arrangements between different classes of shares are interesting they are comparatively unimportant. In his study of 276 issues of preferred shares, whose listing applications were filed with the New York Stock Exchange between 1885 and 1934, Stevens found only 14 that con-tained multiple or fractional voting arrangements on a share-for-share basis.[6]

Since various questions may arise that require a vote of the shareholders it is quite possible for some groups of stockholders to have the vote on certain matters but not on all. One group of shareholders distinguished from the others by reason of a prior claim to dividends might, for example, have no voting rights in the election of directors, but be allowed to vote when the question at issue was the mortgaging of corporate assets. Moreover, the right of certain classes of shareholders to vote need not be constant under all circumstances and conditions: if preferred dividends have not been paid for some stipulated period, the preferred shareholders may then acquire, according to the terms of the contract of course, partial, equal, or even exclusive voting rights in the election of directors.[7]

Although the usual procedure in arriving at a decision on any question is simply to count the number of votes cast for and

[4] Here, of course, the fractions or multiples would have to be different for different classes of shareholders since otherwise the net result would be the same as giving each share one vote.

[5] As reported in *ibid.*, p. 314.

[6] *Ibid.*, p. 325.

[7] See the interesting instances of the F. W. Woolworth Co., California Petroleum Co., Simmons Co. and the Sherwin Williams Co. cited by Stevens in this connection. *Ibid.*, p. 334. Of 405 cases of preferred stocks listed on the New York Stock Exchange (1885-1934) having such contingent voting rights Stevens found that, "In nearly half of the cases the subsequent controls (47 per cent) are comparatively strong ones, exclusive (10.1 per cent), exclusive for directors (14.1 per cent), or a majority or even higher control of the directorate (22.8 per cent). Weaker equal and multiple share-for-share controls account for another 41.9 per cent." *Ibid.*, p. 336.

against it, it must be recorded that in some cases the reckoning is made instead on the basis of classes of shares. That is, granted that the shares are differentiated into classes on some other basis than voting rights, it is not infrequently true that no action can be taken on a particular proposal unless two-thirds, three-quarters, or some other percentage of the shareholders in a particular class vote affirmatively on it. So, for instance, before bonds could be issued, which would rank ahead of first preferred shares, 80 per cent of the latter might have to approve the proposal regardless of what percentage of the common stockholders had voted in favor of it.

It should be obvious that the number of possible permutations and combinations that may exist by contract with respect to shareholders' voting rights is well-nigh infinite. Voting may be by shares or by classes. Some classes may have the vote for some purposes but not for others. The votes per share may be fractional or multiple. And the right to vote in all these respects may vary from time to time with the financial condition, earning power, and the dividend distributions of the company. No useful purpose is perhaps served by endeavoring to describe all the conceivable variations that might be worked out by contractual agreement. So far as the basic principle is concerned, there is nothing to prevent a contract which allowed a particular class of shareholders to vote in leap years only; but of course most contracts are more purposive.

Since shareholders most frequently exercise their voting rights for the election of directors, a word or two on the relation between the directors and the shareholders may not be out of place. The theory has often been advanced that corporations as artificial beings must necessarily act through human persons, and therefore a corporation must have a board of directors. Yet the more obvious reason surely is that the affairs of a business corporation could not possibly be carried on effectively by all the shareholders together: centralization of control is indispensable to efficient operation.[8] Directors have been sometimes regarded as agents of the share-

[8] See Stevens, Robert S., *Handbook on the Law of Private Corporations*, St. Paul, Minn. (West), 1936, pp. 546-547.

holders [9] and at others as trustees for the shareholders. But neither term seems to describe their status accurately. It would appear to be well established that directors are expected to exercise their own judgment and not act as employees of the stockholders. As a New York court said: [10]

While the ordinary rules of law relating to an agent are applicable in considering the acts of a board of directors in behalf of a corporation when dealing with third persons, the individual directors making up the board are not mere employees, but part of an elected body of officers constituting the executive agents of the corporation. They hold such office charged with the duty to act for the corporation according to their best judgment, and in so doing they cannot be controlled in the reasonable exercise and performance of such duty. As a general rule, the stockholders cannot act in relation to the ordinary business of the corporation, nor can they control the directors in the exercise of the judgment vested in them by virtue of their office. The relation of the directors to the stockholders is essentially that of trustee and cestui que trust.

And perhaps this summarizes the relation between directors and shareholders about as effectively as a few words can.

b. *The pre-emptive right.* The right of shareholders to subscribe for additional issues of stock in proportion to their existing holdings was first laid down by a Massachusetts court in 1807 where it was said: [11]

Viewing a corporation of this kind as a copartnership, a power of increasing their stock, reserved in their original agreement, is a beneficial interest vested in each partner, to which no stranger can be made a party, but by the consent of each subsisting partner; and it is a power which the subsisting partners must exercise proportionably, and according to their interest in the original stock.

[9] Note the following: "In the strict relation of principal and agent, all the authority of the latter is derived by delegation from the former, and if the power of substitution is not conferred in the appointment, it cannot exist at all. But in corporate bodies the powers of the board of directors are, in a very important sense, original and undelegated. The stockholders do not confer, nor can they revoke these powers. They are derivative only in the sense of being received from the state in the act of incorporation." *Hoyt* v. *Thompson's Executor*, 19 N.Y. 207, 216. As quoted in *ibid.*, p. 547.

[10] *Manson* v. *Curtis*, 223 N.Y. 313, 119 N.E. 559 (1918).

[11] *Gray* v. *President, Directors & Company of Portland Bank*, 3 Mass. 363. Note that the shareholders are referred to as partners.

If this right did not exist there would be an opportunity for new shareholders to "appropriate" a portion of the undistributed profits earned before their funds had been invested. For example, suppose that earnings in the amount of ten dollars per share had not been distributed as dividends, and that further, the proposal was to sell an equal number of additional shares to outsiders at par value and no more. In that instance the new shareholders would appropriate one half of the total earned but undistributed profits previously attaching to the original shares, or five dollars per share. Furthermore, in the absence of the pre-emptive right the voting control of the corporation might well be re-allocated contrary to the interests of the existing stockholders. It is also true that where profits are divided between shareholders on the basis of classes rather than shares, an increase in the number of outstanding shares, to which existing shareholders were not permitted to subscribe, might alter the proportional division of net income inequitably. Hence from several points of view the pre-emptive right seems eminently necessary as the general rule.

The application of the pre-emptive right in practice is often difficult and confusing, and its interpretation has not been uniform in all jurisdictions. One question which has arisen is whether the right applies to already authorized but unissued shares, or only to increases in the amount authorized. Ballantine states that the weight of authority supports the view that the right applies to both. But he points out that some courts have restricted the right to the latter.[12] Where there are stock issues of different kinds, as is not uncommon in large corporations, the pre-emptive right is difficult to apply. For instance, if there are preferred shares outstanding, and it is proposed to increase the outstanding common shares, have the preferred shareholders the right to subscribe for them, and if so, what is the proper proportion of the new common shares which they must be offered?[13] Perhaps anticipating such

[12] *Private Corporations*, p. 421. According to both Ballantine and Berle the New York courts have restricted the right to increases in the amount of authorized stock. This seems unfortunate and contrary to the intended purpose of the right.

[13] In this case if the preferred shares were non-voting and limited in their claim on assets in dissolution, it seems clear that they are in no way affected by the increase in the outstanding common shares: the distribution of control and their share in assets will in no wise be altered adversely.

difficulties, the new Ohio corporation law specifically restricts the pre-emptive right to further issues of shares in the same class, although according to one authority this is contrary to the majority of the court decisions on the point.[14] Again, what of shares issued for property? Perhaps the general position of the courts on such questions, in the absence of explicit statutory provisions and where nothing is provided in the articles of association, is that the right should be upheld whenever the voting control or the rights in assets or earnings of existing shareholders would be adversely affected.[15]

In view of the difficulties already mentioned and certain others that might arise in corporations with complicated capital structures, and possibly also, because at times the pre-emptive right might limit the powers of the management control group, it is not surprising that many modern corporations deny the shareholders all pre-emptive rights in the articles of association. Indeed, the Delaware statute seems to go out of its way to encourage incorporators to do so. It is not so clear, however, that all things considered this denial is in the best interests of stockholders.[16]

c. *The right to prevent* ultra vires *acts.* A corporation is said to commit an *ultra vires* act when such act is not within the powers granted to it by the state and hence not contemplated by the shareholders because not included in the statement of powers and

---

[14] Frey, A. H., "Shareholders' Pre-emptive Rights," *Yale Law Journal*, Vol. 38, pp. 563-583 at p. 577.

[15] *Ibid.*, p. 583. Hills, in his "model Act" article, allows the insertion of pre-emptive right clauses in the articles of association, but they must be specifically written in, they are not granted by statute. He writes, "The 'right' of pre-emption was never intended to be a positive legal right, but rather an equitable remedy against the appropriation by a few persons or shareholders of voting powers and equities which properly belong to all the shareholders of one or more classes. Being an equitable remedy, its application has resulted in a confusion of successes and failures and in the creation of many exceptions with respect to preferred shares, treasury shares, shares originally authorized, shares issued for property, and the like. It is better not to attempt a codification of equities." Hills, *op. cit.*, p. 1357.

[16] It is said, however, that the right is practically never asserted by an ordinary shareholder but only by so-called financial "pirates" anxious to cause costly embarrassment to the corporation. See Drinker, H. S., "The Pre-Emptive Right of Shareholders to Subscribe to New Shares," *Harvard Law Review*, Vol. 43 (1930), pp. 586-616, at p. 615. I am indebted to Professor Henry W. Ballantine for pointing this out to me.

purposes to which they agreed.[17] Consequently, the doctrine has two aspects: first, that involving the state and the corporations; second, that involving the shareholders and the corporation.

The state's interest in corporate actions which are *ultra vires* is quite in harmony with the sovereignty-concession theory of the corporation. For, if the state "creates" the corporation, clearly the latter can have no powers that the state has not granted to it; consequently, corporate acts exceeding the powers granted are a nullity, as the phrase has it. Yet the rigid application of such a rule could be the source of injury to outside parties. Suppose that the corporation has received the full benefit of a contract, e.g., as a lessee, but then refuses to pay the rental on the grounds that the contract was *ultra vires*. Surely to allow such a defense would be unfair to the lessor. Hence while as a matter of public policy corporations should be restricted to the powers granted to them, a host of instances could arise where the mere fact of corporate incapacity is socially unimportant in comparison to the wisdom of holding persons to the agreements they have accepted.[18]

Our main interest in the concept of *ultra vires*, however, is in its relation to the rights of shareholders. Here the "contract" theory of the corporation provides a convenient basis for the doctrine: for in agreeing to the articles of association the shareholders have consented to have their capital investment exposed to the risks that the specified activities carry with them; they did not contemplate assuming the risks of ventures not named. Consequently, *ultra vires* activities are a breach of the agreement between the corporation and the stockholders. Therefore, a shareholder may properly bring legal action to prevent the corporation

[17] An *ultra vires* act is not an illegal act in the ordinary sense. It simply means that the corporation had no power to do the particular thing it has done or proposes to do. See Stevens, *Handbook on Private Corporations*, pp. 279-282.

[18] It is sometimes said that third parties are on "constructive notice" of the contents of the corporate charter and therefore the excuse of *ultra vires* is valid against them. But as a New York court once said, "A traveler from New York to the Mississippi can hardly be required to furnish himself with the charters of all the railroads on his route, or to study a treatise on the law of corporations." *Bissell* v. *Michigan Southern & N.I.R. Co.*, 22 N.Y. 258, 281. Quoted in Stevens, Robert S., *op. cit.*, p. 294. This seems more than a sufficient answer to the constructive notice doctrine so applied.

from engaging in them.[19] Notwithstanding this legal right, its present-day significance for shareholders is rather slight for two reasons: first, the statement of corporate powers in modern charters is likely to be broad and inclusive so that the danger of *ultra vires* acts is reduced; second, the amendment of the corporate charter in this respect is much easier than formerly, hence, bothersome limitations can be removed with comparative ease: in many jurisdictions a two-thirds vote of the shareholders is sufficient.

Because of the confusion in the courts over the doctrine of *ultra vires* some states—Vermont, Ohio, Louisiana, California, Michigan, Illinois, Minnesota, Pennsylvania, and Washington—have endeavored to cover the problem by statutory enactment.[20] This has been a recent development as the first state to do so was Vermont in 1915.

d. *The right to a knowledge of the corporation's affairs and condition.* While stockholders possess this right, it is not easy to say just how far it generally extends, because most states have reduced the ordinary common law right to statutory enactment and there are important differences between them. For example, in Arizona, "All books, papers, and records of the corporation shall at all times, during reasonable office hours, be subject to the inspection of any stockholder." [21] In Illinois, on the other hand, the right is restricted to shareholders of at least six months' standing, or to holders of at least 5 per cent of all the outstanding shares.[22] Such a time or percentage limit of the shareholder's right by statute is not uncommon. It is apparently firmly established that a shareholder has the right to inspect the list of stockholders and make a transcript thereof; but how much beyond this he may proceed will depend upon the statute and the presence of a proper motive. The right to examine books and records, of course, does not allow a shareholder to obtain information for improper mo-

[19] It is probably true that many corporations have engaged in *ultra vires* activities from time to time but that no shareholder has bothered to bring an action to prevent them either because he did not know they were *ultra vires*, or because he felt that the action taken was for, rather than against, his interests.

[20] See Stevens, *Handbook on Private Corporations*, Appendix, where the statutes in these states are described.

[21] Arizona, *Code*, 1928, sec. 584.

[22] Illinois, *Revised Statutes*, ch. 32, sec. 45.

tives unrelated to his position as a shareholder. Otherwise the right might seriously interfere with the corporation's regular business or allow competitors, who were also shareholders, to secure competitively useful information at a moderate cost.

For the purpose of better informing the shareholders some states now require that a statement of profit and loss and a balance sheet be sent to all shareholders at least annually, unless this requirement is specifically dispensed with in the by-laws.[23] In New York 3 per cent, and in California 10 per cent, of the stockholders have the right to demand from the officers of the company under oath a written statement of assets and liabilities.

e. *The right to transfer the ownership of shares to others.* The owner of a share of stock ordinarily has the power to sell it to whomever he may wish as he sees fit. This is, of course, one of the more important economic advantages of the corporate form of enterprise from the point of view of investors. Nevertheless, the right to transfer shares may be abridged by agreement between the shareholders and the corporation. The by-laws of the corporation usually indicate the manner in which shares may be transferred in order to protect the shareholders against fraudulent transfers. By-laws further restricting the right of transfer, such, for example, as a requirement that the shares to be sold must first be offered to the other shareholders or to the corporation, have sometimes been upheld and sometimes rejected.[24] Cases are certainly conceivable where such a provision might be necessary for competitive or other reasons and yet no harm to the general welfare result.

[23] For example, California: "The board of directors of every stock corporation shall cause to be sent to the shareholders not later than one hundred twenty days after the close of the fiscal or calendar year an annual report unless such report be expressly dispensed with in the by-laws.

"Such annual report shall include a balance sheet as of such closing date and a statement of income or profit and loss for the year ended on such closing date. . . .

"Such balance sheet itself or comments accompanying it shall set forth (1) the bases employed in stating the valuation of the assets and any changes in such bases during the preceding year; (2) the amount of the surplus, the sources thereof and any changes therein during the past year; . . . (4) the amounts, if any, of loans or advances to or from officers, shareholders and employees." *Civil Code*, sec. 358.

[24] See Ballantine, *Private Corporations*, pp. 447-448.

f. *The right to participate in profits in proportion to share interest.* No shareholder, as a shareholder, has any inherent right to insist upon the declaration of dividends.[25] The declaration of dividends is discretionary with the directors who are expected to exercise their best judgment in view of all the relevant facts affecting the enterprise as a whole.[26] And this seems a reasonable view since if a majority of the shareholders is convinced of the poor judgment of the existing directors in this respect they have an appropriate remedy in the election of a new board.

As already observed, each shareholder has the right to participate in profit distributions in proportion to his shareholdings unless some different arrangement has been established by contract.[27] It so happens, however, that it is on the basis of their rights to dividends that we most commonly differentiate shares into classes; for instance, when we speak of "common" shares and "preferred" shares.[28]

The number of deviations from absolute equality in rights to receive dividends is conceivably just as great as the variations in voting rights from the simple rule of one share, one vote. Indeed they both spring from the same source: namely, the right of free

[25] A dividend declared by proper action of the board of directors creates an account payable in favor of each shareholder affected, and such claim is a creditor's claim enforceable against the corporation as all other creditor's claims. It is not affected by subsequent insolvency provided the dividend was legal and proper at the time declared. Thus, for legal purposes, it is the declaration of the dividend rather than its actual payment which is the important step.

[26] As legal writers have frequently pointed out, the stockholders have only a right to "the exercise of honest discretion" on the part of directors. This general rule stands even though there may be large net earnings. For the most part the courts are unwilling to interfere with the discretion of directors unless there be a showing of bad faith or an arbitrary withholding of dividends. For instance, a court might intervene where an enterprise organized for profit is being operated with the avowed purpose of reducing profits. See *Dodge* v. *Ford Motor Co.,* 204 Mich. 459, 170 N.W., 668. Again, a court might intervene at the request of minority interests where it was demonstrated that the majority was endeavoring to force them into selling their shares by refusing to declare dividends.

[27] Not unlike the arrangement in a partnership where if no written agreement exists all the partners are assumed to be equal.

[28] According to the researches of Professor G. H. Evans, preferred stock first appeared in the United States in 1836 in connection with subscriptions by the state of Maryland to the stocks of two railroad and three canal companies. It was not until 1843 that preferred shares were sold to private persons. See Evans, G. H., Jr., "The Early History of Preferred Stock in the United States," *American Economic Review*, Vol. 19 (1929), pp. 43-58.

contract. In fact, however, and apart from a few isolated examples, the number of deviations from the typical pattern is much fewer. Of a total of 1094 listing applications for the New York Stock Exchange, examined by Professor W. H. S. Stevens, 961, or about 88 per cent, of them had a simple prior claim to dividends in a fixed amount and no more.[29] That is, of the issues studied, by far the greatest percentage were simple, ordinary preferred shares entitled to a fixed dividend rate and nothing additional. The alternative to a fixed initial preference is a preferred stock contract where the preferred shares are entitled to participate further in dividends according to the scheme provided in the agreement.[30] Such shares are called participating preferred.

The contract granting a preference in dividend distributions to a particular class of shares may provide for either a cumulative preference—that is, one which carries over from one year to another and which thus prevents dividend payments to more junior claimants until the fixed preference rate for each and every year has been met—or, a non-cumulative preference, in which case the net income of each year is subject to a definite preferred allocation, but the unsatisfied preferred claims of one year exert no influence on the manner of distributing dividends in subsequent years. The first is called cumulative preferred stock; the second, non-cumulative preferred stock.[31]

[29] Stevens, W. H. S., "Stockholders' Participations in Profits," *Journal of Business of the University of Chicago*, Vol. 9, pp. 114-132; 210-230, at p. 210.

[30] Of the remaining 133 issues (out of the 1094 studied by Stevens in the article referred to in the previous note) where the preferred was entitled to something more than a fixed initial dividend, "Eighty-three, or about 62 per cent . . . divide the profits after the payment of fixed initial dividends on both common and preferred equally share for share or on some other agreed basis." *Ibid.*, p. 226. The basis of participation in further profits may be on the basis of shares or classes. The latter, however, is comparatively rare, although Stevens mentions the Insuranshares Corporation of Delaware as a case in point. *Ibid.*, p. 124. In instances of this kind, clearly the number of shares in each class is important.

[31] The exact wording of the contract with respect to non-cumulative preferred shares is quite important. In some instances the dividends must be declared if earned, in others it is discretionary with the directors. Professor Berle started a lively discussion on this subject with an article in the *Columbia Law Review* in 1923 in which he urged that, on equitable grounds, non-cumulative preferred stock was entitled to cumulations in the same manner as cumulative preferred stock to the extent that its dividends had been wholly or partly earned; or, at any rate, that the earned but unpaid dividends could never be paid out to the

g. *The right to a proportionate share in the net assets in dissolution.* No shareholder or group of shareholders has a claim to specific assets but only a claim against the net asset values. And, unless a different arrangement has been agreed upon by contract, all shareholders are entitled to share in proportion to their holdings in the fund of net asset values after creditors have been paid their claims in full. As in voting and in participations in profits, the common law rule is that all shares stand on an equal footing in their rights in net assets in dissolution.

Not uncommonly, however, one or several classes of shares in a given corporation are granted by contract a prior claim against the net assets in dissolution. As with dividends, this prior claim may constitute the only claim on assets of the particular class of shares or it may be only the initial claim of the class. That is, they may be entitled to further participations on dissolution beyond their superior claims. Moreover, their rights may be different according as the dissolution of the corporation is voluntary or involuntary. Usually where shares are preferred as to dividends they are also entitled to any accumulated but unpaid dividends. And, finally, on top of all this the shares preferred as to dividends may be allowed a premium over and above their superior claim on assets in dissolution. Professor Stevens has tabulated the different provisions as to rights in assets in dissolution as on the opposite page.

The sometimes elaborate provisions relating to the partition of asset values in dissolution are probably not of great significance in the great majority of issues. For, if the corporation is successful, there will be no inducement to liquidate it and the profit possibilities of the opportunity will be exploited as long as possible. On the other hand, if the corporation is unsuccessful to the degree

common shareholders. The question was debated in the law journals for a number of years thereafter with the final conclusion, it would appear, that there were many different kinds of non-cumulative preferred shares and that while Berle's argument was applicable to some it was by no means generally true. See Berle, A. A., *Studies in the Law of Corporation Finance*, Chicago (Callaghan), 1928, Ch. V; Stevens, W. H. S., "Rights of Non-cumulative Preferred Shareholders," *Columbia Law Review*, Vol. 34 (1934), pp. 1439-1461; "Discretion of Directors in the Distribution of Non-cumulative Preferred Dividends," *Georgetown Law Review*, Vol. 24 (1936), pp. 371-396.

that failure occurs, the net assets available for distribution to shareholders in involuntary liquidation will be negligible. As is well known, creditors rarely receive the full value of their claims so that the likelihood of stockholders getting little or anything is very slight.[32] Nevertheless, there is certainly no harm in allowing the insertion of such provisions on the odd chance that they might prove valuable.

INITIAL PREFERENCE IN ASSETS IN DISSOLUTION OF CUMULATIVE AND NON-CUMULATIVE PREFERRED STOCKS RECORDED IN NEW YORK STOCK EXCHANGE LISTING APPLICATIONS, 1885-1934 *

Type of Participation in Assets	Cumulative	Non-cumulative	Total
Par or fixed sum	39	81	120
Par and fixed premium	1	3	4
Par and fixed sum in involuntary and par and premium or higher fixed sum in involuntary dissolution		1	1
Par and fixed premium and accrued or accumulated dividends	144	1	145
Par or fixed sum and accrued or accumulated dividends	449	5	454
Par or fixed sum and accrued dividends in involuntary and par and premium or higher fixed sum and accumulated dividends in involuntary dissolution	175		175
TOTAL	808	91	899

* From Stevens, W. H. S., "Stockholders' Participation in Assets in Dissolution," *Journal of Business of the University of Chicago*, Vol. 10 (1937), pp. 46-73, at p. 52. The "fixed sum" used in the table above applies, of course, in the case of shares without par value.

[32] An exception is to be noted where a corporation is forced to dissolve under court order, for example, as a consequence of a conviction for having violated the anti-trust laws.

It is clear also that cases might arise where merger or consolidation of a corporation with another could be construed as dissolution. According to Stevens, the cases are not in agreement on this point. In a Pennsylvania case, *Petry* v. *Harwood Electric Co.*, 280 Pa. 142, 124 Atl. 302, it was held that a merger was dissolution for the purpose of applying the clauses of the preferred stock contract. But in a New Jersey case, *Windhurst* v. *Central Leather Co.*, 107 N.J. Eq. 528, 153 Atl. 402, it was ruled that a merger did not amount to dissolution. See Stevens, Robert S., *Handbook on the Law of Private Corporations*, pp. 491-492.

In summary, we may re-emphasize the point stressed at the beginning of the present section: That there are certain inherent rights and privileges that attach to stock ownership *per se* in the sense that, if nothing is said about them to the contrary, they are assumed to accrue to the share owner and the courts will enforce them on a proper suit. On the other hand, these common law rights may be narrowed or extended by contract in any manner desired by the parties concerned so long as the modifications do not run counter to legal expressions of public policy. Furthermore, shareholders' rights can be combined within one contract in such a multitude of different ways that a complete catalogue of all the conceivable variations is quite impossible. Finally, in addition to the contractual modifications of shareholders' inherent rights there may be special rights added in particular cases, for instance, the right to convert shares of one class into those of another, or the right of the corporation to redeem the shares on proper notice at a specified price. But the main point to keep in mind is that in any given instance shareholders' rights are derived from the common law, the general incorporation statute under which the corporation has been formed, and the terms of the specific share contract between the shareholders and the corporation. Needless to remark, perhaps, short-hand names and descriptions of share contracts are likely to be decidedly misleading.

3. *The amendment of the corporate charter and shareholders' rights.* To all the foregoing there is one important qualification that must be touched upon before passing on to other matters: that is, the rights of shareholders may be modified after the contract has been drawn by an amendment to the corporate charter. This is indeed a highly complicated and (apparently) partially unsettled branch of corporation law. But the potential importance to stockholders of the power to amend the charter is so great that we cannot neglect it entirely. The few remarks here ventured, however, must be regarded as at best tentative.[33]

[33] The present section is based mainly on the excellent study of the problem made by the Securities and Exchange Commission. See Securities and Exchange Commission, *Report on the Study and Investigation of the Work, Activities, Personnel and Functions of Protective and Reorganization Committees*, Part VII, *Management Plans without Aid of Committees*, Washington, 1938, pp. 464-525.

The amendment of the corporate charter may be of greater or lesser importance to the shareholders. An amendment to change the corporate name is of quite a different order from an amendment that alters shareholders' voting rights and/or preferences, or constitutes a redefinition of stated capital. And, indeed, the law seems to distinguish between amendments which are "fundamental" and those which are "auxiliary." "Auxiliary" amendments have been defined as those "which do not change the nature, purpose, or character of a corporation or its enterprise, but which are designed to enable the corporation to conduct its authorized business with greater facility, more beneficially, or more wisely." [34] But such a definition does not enable us to differentiate between major and minor alterations.

With the exception of Iowa and Nebraska all states permit charter amendments on a vote of less than all the shareholders. Under most statutes amendments may be originated by the board of directors but must be approved by the stockholders (usually two-thirds) and properly recorded by the Secretary of State before becoming valid. Moreover, the statutes typically provide that even shareholders that do not usually vote must approve the amendment. Approval of the amendment, however, is sometimes (e.g., Delaware) by classes and sometimes without regard to classes (e.g., Arizona, Kansas, Kentucky, North Dakota, Oregon). Where the approval of amendments is on a share-for-share basis of voting it is clear that if the number of shares in the different classes was radically unequal it would be comparatively easy for, say, the common shareholders to outvote the preferred and by an amendment scale down the latter's rights.[35]

These broad statutory powers, however, have not been given an all-inclusive interpretation by the courts. On the other hand, the Securities and Exchange Commission has written: [36]

Actually, it seems impossible to deduce from existing decisions any rule to ascertain with certainty the validity of an amendment adopted

[34] *Mower* v. *Staples*, 32 Minn. 284, 286, 20 N.W., 225, 226 (1884), as quoted in *ibid.*, pp. 465-466.
[35] Where the simple two-thirds rule is provided in the statute without regard to classes the rule means two-thirds of the shares issued and outstanding, not two-thirds of those present at the meeting in person or by proxy. See *ibid.*, p. 475.
[36] *Ibid.*, p. 477.

by a majority of the stockholders pursuant to a clause which merely in general terms confers the power to amend upon a majority of the stockholders. The courts seem to have been guided by their notions of fairness in permitting or refusing to permit a majority of the stockholders to adopt various amendments under such a clause.

At least Delaware and California allow charter amendments to alter voting rights.[37] Ordinarily this would permit the common shareholders to modify the voting privileges of the preferred if they can vote sufficient shares. On the other hand, the courts on occasion have refused to sanction a reduction in stated capital in such a manner as to work real injustice on preferred shareholders.[38] Again, there is the problem of modifying contractual provisions relating to call features, redemption rights, etc. From the point of view of common shareholders there may be an advantage in altering clauses of this character after the contract has been drawn. The general rule appears to be, however, that the statutory law at the time the shares were issued is controlling.[39] Apparently the same rule governs the elimination of dividend preferences by charter amendment, and some of the newer statutes (e.g., Delaware) seem to contemplate such action. Yet amendments of this character may not be employed in Delaware as a means of eliminating accrued but unpaid dividends; that is, the amendment may not be retroactive.[40] Of course the shareholders of the class whose interests are being affected may wish to authorize the elimination of arrearages by a vote of their own number. But for preferred shareholders to relinquish their claims to accumulated and unpaid dividends is quite a different story from permitting the common

[37] ". . . the right to vote is not such a change in property rights as to be exempt from the tampering effect of amendment where general power to amend is reserved. It is but an alteration which concerns the internal management of the corporation and being such is not beyond the reach of an authorized general power to amend." *Morris* v. *American Public Utilities Co.*, 122 Atl. 696 at 705 (1923) as quoted in S.E.C., *op. cit.*, p. 481.

[38] *Kennedy* v. *Carolina Public Service Co.*, 262 Fed. 803 (N.D. Ga. 1920).

[39] S.E.C., *op. cit.*, pp. 493-496. It must be recalled, as we emphasized earlier, that the incorporation statute is part of the charter of the corporation and therefore binds the shareholders. That is, if the statute allowed amendments then security buyers are "on notice" and must accept them if carried through in the manner provided.

[40] *Ibid.*, pp. 506-510. A leading case is *Consolidated Film Industries, Inc.* v. *Johnson*, 197 Atl. 489 (Del. 1937).

shareholders to decide the issue solely by their greater voting power.

Overhanging all the foregoing there are usually said to be the protective limitations of equity. How far these extend is not altogether certain. Perhaps Professor Berle has stressed these equitable restrictions more than most writers; [41] but other legal scholars are less convinced of the practicality and effectiveness of these equitable remedies for the protection of minority groups.[42]

II. THE OBLIGATIONS AND LIABILITIES OF STOCKHOLDERS

1. Liability to the corporation. 2. Liability to creditors for unpaid subscriptions and fictitiously paid-up stock. 3. Theories of shareholders' liability to creditors: the trust fund doctrine; the fraud or holding-out theory; the statutory obligation theory.

1. *Liability to the corporation.* The obligations of shareholders extend in two directions, to the corporation on the one hand and to creditors on the other. Their liability to the former consists in their obligation to pay into the corporation on a proper call by the directors the amounts they have agreed to pay according to their subscription contracts to purchase stock. Although shares are not usually issued until they have been fully paid, sometimes less than the full purchase price is paid in at the time of subscription and even issuance. If the subscription contract should provide for specific payments on particular dates then the subscriber is liable for payment on those dates. Not infrequently, however, the date of call is not predetermined and then the directors may maintain a valid call against the shareholder for the unpaid balance. If, however, the shareholder has once paid into the corporation the full par value of his shares, and has in all respects fulfilled the obligations of his subscription contract, his liability to the corporation ceases under ordinary circumstances. Unless the arti-

---

[41] Cf. Berle and Means, *op. cit.*, Book II, *passim.*
[42] See S.E.C., *op. cit.*, pp. 519-524.

cles of association to which he has agreed provide for special levies or assessments the corporation has no further claim upon him. Nor may the state order a levy upon the shareholders for the benefit of creditors or others unless it has reserved to itself the right to amend the corporate charter, or unless the statutory law (which is part of the charter) expressly provides for an assessment. Furthermore, even if a majority of the stockholders should by means of a by-law order an assessment upon the shareholders, the corporation has no power to enforce payment from a shareholder who is unwilling to contribute.

2. *Liability to creditors for unpaid subscriptions and fictitiously paid-up stock.* The liability of shareholders to creditors lies in two directions: liability on account of unpaid stock subscriptions, and liability on account of watered or fictitiously paid-up stock.[43] The former has been indicated above as an obligation of shareholders to the corporation. The point to be added here is that creditors of a corporation have no direct claim against the shareholders on account of unpaid subscriptions, but only through the medium of the corporation. But any unpaid balance on stock subscriptions is an asset of the corporation and if creditors have not been satisfied they may take the necessary steps to enforce the

[43] This is the general rule although in some jurisdictions the constitution or statute provides for additional personal liability of stockholders. Generally this remedy of creditors against stockholders is secondary; that is, it may be brought into use only after creditors have exhausted all other means for the collection of their debts. As Ballantine has said, "It is well settled that stockholders are not personally liable for debts of the corporation either at law or in equity, unless such liability is expressly imposed by the charter, or by some statutory or constitutional provision." *Private Corporations*, p. 697. These constitutional or statutory provisions sometimes make the stockholders individually liable for debts of certain kinds only, such, for example, as the wages of employees, apprentices, etc. In other cases, where merely the word debt or indebtedness has been used, much litigation has ensued over what kinds of claims fall within the meaning of the word. The various decisions do not seem to agree very closely. For this and other obvious reasons it is not unusual for the corporation to insist on a "no recourse" clause in creditors' contracts, which clause limits the creditor to the assets of the corporation and he agrees to waive any claim he might have against the stockholders as individuals for non-payment.

It is important to keep in mind that where such individual liability is imposed upon shareholders by the statute the provision is entirely for the protection of creditors and for no others. That is, the corporation can in no sense regard such possible claims as being in the same category as unpaid stock subscriptions. The liability is to creditors and not to the corporation. See *ibid.*, pp. 696-717.

collection of these unpaid subscriptions.[44] The stockholders, however, are only liable to the amount of unpaid creditors' claims, and
not necessarily to the full amount of their unpaid subscriptions,
although as a practical matter the full amount is likely to be
necessary. Under such circumstances the defenses open to shareholders are apparently misrepresentation or fraud.

Shareholders' liability to creditors on account of watered stock
is more difficult to define. In essence the idea of watered stock is
that stock has been issued as fully paid and non-assessable when
in fact the shareholder has not paid into the corporation a consideration in value equivalent to the par value of the shares issued.
The legal principles and difficulties involved are not easily or
briefly described: there is first the question of what provides acceptable evidence that the stock has been watered, and secondly,
what liability attaches to shareholders who own such shares. It
is obvious that the courts should not penalize honest mistakes of
judgment as to the values assigned to property received by the
corporation in exchange for shares: hindsight cannot be substituted for foresight. Possibly for this reason courts have been rather
loath to interfere with the expressed judgment of the directors in
the absence of special showing. On the other hand, it would be
generally agreed that a mere resolution of directors as to the value
of assets should not be a useful device for defrauding creditors.
The whole question is a difficult one and space does not permit
any full treatment of it here.[45]

3. *Theories of shareholders' liability to creditors: the trust fund
doctrine; the fraud or holding-out theory; the statutory obligation
theory.* The liabilities of stockholders to creditors of the corporation have given rise to certain legal theories of capital stock which
attempt to provide a logical basis for shareholders' obligations.
These may be briefly mentioned.

[44] It must be emphasized that the interest of creditors, as such, is in the payment of their claims and in order for equitable remedies to operate on behalf of
creditors they must have exhausted their legal remedies without obtaining full
payment. In other words, so far as shareholders' contributions are concerned,
creditors have no interest therein unless their claims are unpaid or are in danger
of being unpaid. See next chapter.

[45] But see, Dodd, David L., *Stock Watering*, New York (Columbia), 1930. A
useful summary of this volume is to be found in Bonbright, J. C., *The Valuation
of Property*, Vol. II, New York and London (McGraw-Hill), 1937, ch. 23.

The so-called "trust fund theory" of capital stock seeks to emphasize the idea that the capital of a corporation is always subject to the prior claims of creditors as opposed to the rights of stockholders. As Professor Ballantine has said, "The principal office of the trust fund doctrine is to preserve the assets of a corporation as a fund for the payment of its debts against withdrawal by stockholders." [46] Thus the common legal provision that corporations may not pay dividends out of "capital" arises from the idea that the impairment of capital necessarily involves a reduction of a certain value sum set aside for the protection of creditors. In a sense what the trust fund theory seeks to avoid in a rather roundabout way is any impairment of the ability of the corporation to pay its creditors in full. Hence in corporate reorganization, according to the doctrine in the Boyd case, unsecured creditors who did not share in the plan of reorganization, although stockholders received something of value in the new corporation in exchange for their shares, have a valid claim against the new corporation.[47] The trust fund theory is perhaps of greatest meaning when applied to the capital of a corporation already in existence, and as such, it provides a reasonable explanation of certain legal principles governing the distribution of assets to stockholders, etc. At the same time, however, it contributes little to the formulation of proper principles in the case of watered stock.

The inadequacy of the trust fund theory for the problem of watered stock has been partly responsible for the formulation of the "fraud or holding-out theory." The nature of the fraud consists in the representation to creditors that capital in the amount of the par value of the outstanding shares has been invested in the enterprise when, in fact, some of the shares have been issued for an inadequate consideration (less than their par value) or none at all. Logically under this theory stockholders' liability would extend only to such creditors as were without knowledge of the

[46] *Op. cit.*, p. 672. Ballantine also quotes from *Scovill* v. *Thayer*, 105 U.S. 143, as follows, "The reason is, that the stock subscribed is considered in equity as a trust fund for the payment of creditors. . . . It is so held out to the public, who have no means of knowing the private contracts made between the corporation and its stockholders. The creditor has, therefore, the right to presume that the stock subscribed has been or will be paid up, and if it is not, a court of equity will at his instance require it to be paid." *Ibid.*, p. 672, n.

[47] *Northern Pacific Railway Co.* v. *Boyd*, 228 U.S. 482. See *infra*, Ch. XIV.

true circumstances surrounding the issuance of the capital stock. Creditors who were "on notice" could not subsequently claim they relied on the stated capital for the payment of their debts.[48] Such distinctions between earlier and later creditors, besides leading to confusion, are not an entirely adequate solution for the problem of watered stock.

Possibly the simplest and most straightforward theory to account for the obligation of stockholders to contribute full value for their shares is what Professor Ballantine has chosen to call the "statutory obligation" theory, a theory which regards this requirement as one imposed by the state as a matter of public policy. It is undeniable that one major advantage of the corporate form of enterprise is the state-recognized privilege of limited liability to the shareholders. Hence it is only reasonable that the sovereign authority should demand that if there is to be limited liability to the corporate associates, the privilege is only to be had provided the shareholders have complied with the statutory requirements governing the issuance of shares. Therefore the state may insist that stockholders' liability will be limited to the par value of their shares only on the assumption that the shareholders have actually contributed to the corporation property values in this amount for them. Such a theory of shareholders' obligations does away with any need for drawing a distinction between creditors who knew shares had been watered and those who did not. The principle is simply that if any meaning is attachable to limited liability, and if it is to be a device of real usefulness, then in the interests of the public welfare the state must prescribe how the privilege is attainable. The statutory obligation theory of capital stock would appear eminently reasonable and practical. While it is very doubtful if creditors do actually rely upon the stated capital of the corporation for the payment of their claims, nevertheless the state may well insist upon a certain minimum investment from all members of a corporation as an indispensable condition for the otherwise unlimited personal liability of the shareholders. It can be argued also that the state should insist that whenever shares are

---

[48] But in some jurisdictions the courts have held that this matter of being "on notice" makes no difference, although it is stated that this interpretation is based in part on the wording of the statutes. See Ballantine, *op. cit.*, p. 674

issued they should represent an equal value contribution from all those then acquiring them in order to protect the shareholders in their relations with one another. Indeed from a historical and practical point of view the really important aspects of stock watering are *not* the possible harm to creditors, which the courts have been inclined to stress almost exclusively. In the writer's opinion, the practice by which certain persons receive shares representing a proportionate claim on assets and earnings by delivering little or nothing to the corporation while at the same time others surrender cash in good faith for the same proportionate interest is the most grossly inequitable feature of the whole problem of stock watering. In short, the *de facto* fraud on cash purchasers is the real crux of the problem. So far as possible the state should insist that at any time when identical shares are issued they should represent an equivalent capital investment per share.

III. THE QUESTION OF PAR VALUE

1. The argument against par value shares. 2. Shareholders' obligation to the corporation in no par shares. 3. Shareholders' liabilities to creditors in no par shares. 4. No par shares and stockholders' relations to one another.

The various theories of capital stock discussed in the last section are chiefly applicable to par value shares. The question naturally arises as to what obligations and liabilities attach to stock ownership in the case of shares without a par value. May the same reasoning be applied, and if so how; and if not, what relationship does hold between shareholders and creditors under no par value shares? [49]

1. The argument against par value shares. The arguments which have been offered against par value and in favor of no par value shares have altered but little through the years. The requirement that the value contributed to the corporation must be at least equal to the par value of the shares issued has no doubt been

---

[49] North Dakota, Nebraska, Oklahoma, and the District of Columbia make no provision for no par shares.

bothersome at times and led to many questionable subterfuges. The most common adaptation to such laws has been to overvalue property (other than cash) and services received in payment for shares and then to have the shareholders so admitted to the corporation turn around and donate back to the corporation a portion of their holdings. The corporation could then sell these "donated" shares for cash at the best price obtainable and the then purchasers thereof would hold fully paid and non-assessable shares even though they had paid less than par for them. It is usually argued that some such arrangement is frequently necessary if the enterprise is to come into existence. The possibility of selling the shares for cash at their par value is held to be out of the question in many cases.[50] Hence it has often been argued that no par value shares permit directors to be more honest in their property valuations; although just how this result is the more likely to be achieved is not very clear. It has been argued also that many purchasers of par value shares were misled by the figures on the certificate into thinking that the shares were actually worth this amount. Hence, so it was urged, with the par value figure erased the purchaser could no longer be so deluded, but would seek to determine by his own investigation the true worth of the shares.[51] A more convincing argument against par value and in favor of no par value shares is that when a company wishes to raise more capital by

[50] Most such arguments usually carry within them the implicit assumption that the shares must have a $100 par value. But there is no reason why the par value might not be made smaller and the shares sold for more than par, or just at their par value. If shares will be purchased for cash at all there is no reason for going through the motions of overvaluing property and donating stock in order to permit such shares to be sold to the public at an appealing price. What a purchaser of shares is primarily interested in is whether the stock is full-paid and non-assessable, the fact that it is sold at more or less than its par value matters not at all if the first requirement is fulfilled. The real reason for the hocus-pocus with regard to par value shares issued for property is probably that it permits those who contribute property to secure their shares on more favorable terms than those who contribute cash.

[51] The kind of investor who would be misled by the printed figures indicating par value would certainly not be very well qualified to conduct any investigation of his own into their true worth. Furthermore, a prospective buyer usually never sees the certificate until after the purchase has been completed, and even then, under modern practices, the certificates are frequently left with a broker so that the purchaser never sees them in any case. If the purchaser were misled, in most cases it would be because the seller had led him to believe that they were somehow worth their par value.

the sale of shares it will be impossible to sell the additional shares at par if those already outstanding are selling below their par value in the market. If they are sold for less, then the discount will subsequently have to be amortized.[52] This may invoke a hardship on some corporations which, for one reason or other, do not wish to reduce their capital by formal action or to issue shares of another class. As was remarked in an important case, "To say that a corporation may not, under the circumstances above indicated, put its stock upon the market, and sell it to the highest bidder, is practically to declare that a corporation can never increase its capital by a sale of shares, if the original stock has fallen below par." [53] Perhaps the most convincing argument leading to the adoption of no par value shares, however, was that such shares frankly recognized that stock ownership meant a proportionate interest in the net worth of the enterprise with all the rights and privileges attaching thereto. Its original value was not necessarily its present value, and in the nature of the case any suggestion to the contrary was misleading.[54]

2. *Shareholders' obligation to the corporation in no par shares.* As Berle has pointed out, not all no par value statutes are identical, and hence no par value shares as permitted in one jurisdiction may be different in certain important respects from those issued in another.[55] Some no par value laws insist that a certain minimum capital contribution shall be paid into the corporation for each such share issued.[56] Berle would call this type "stated value" nonpar stock. The more common type of no par statute, however, simply requires a statement of the number of no par shares to

[52] Some few states now permit the sale of par value shares at less than their par value without rendering the purchasers thereof liable for further calls or assessment; in other words, these shares are full-paid even though sold for less than their par value. See West Virginia, *Code*, ch. 31, art. I, sec. 29; such authority must be conferred on the directors by the stockholders by special vote.

[53] *Handley* v. *Stutz*, 139 U.S. 417 (1891). This decision permitted the corporation to issue its shares for less than par value yet as fully paid. The facts of the case, however, seem to have been a little unusual.

[54] As we shall have occasion to observe below, however, the same argument could be applied with equal force to many asset figures, especially durable assets.

[55] Berle, A. A., *Studies in the Law of Corporation Finance*, Ch. IV.

[56] For instance in South Dakota the law apparently requires that no shares be issued for less than a minimum of $5. *Laws*, 1929, ch. 92, sec. I. There is also a provision that a corporation shall not begin business with a stated capital of less than $500.

be issued. States having the latter type of law then further provide that the capital of the corporation shall be either the full amount received in consideration for the no par value shares or that proportion thereof which the directors elect to designate as stated capital.[57] It is apparent that full-paid and non-assessable stock is not identical under these two kinds of no par value statutes. Where some minimum amount is required by the state it would seem that if this amount has not been paid in the shares are not fully paid and non-assessable.[58] In the other case, however, shareholders own fully paid shares when they have paid into the corporation such consideration as has been fixed by the directors or stockholders from time to time.[59] The price at which no par shares are to be sold may be fixed in the articles of association or, according to the agreement, the price may be left to be fixed by the directors or stockholders in general meeting on the basis of all the facts and circumstances at the time of sale.

3. *Shareholders' liabilities to creditors in no par shares.* What of the liabilities of shareholders to creditors under no par value shares? No par value shares were supported in many quarters on the grounds that the removal of par value would do away with the abuses and misrepresentations involved in "watered stock." One might suppose, therefore, that the protection of creditors would be greater under no par than under par shares. If anyone seriously believed this result would follow, the years since 1912 must have shattered any such hope. Much the most common type of no par statute allows stock to be fully paid and non-assessable provided only that the subscriber has delivered to the corporation all that he has agreed to pay. In Delaware there need be no alle-

[57] New York is an example of the first, and Delaware of the second.

[58] As Berle expresses it, "A fixed amount has been agreed upon in respect of each share; and this amount, multiplied by the total number of issued shares, is the capital attributable to such shares. The statute requires it; the incorporators have agreed to it; the subscribers of the stock are at least on notice of it; and the records in the office of the Secretary of State set forth the situation to all who inquire." *Op. cit.*, pp. 68-69.

[59] "Any and all shares without par value so issued, for which the consideration so fixed has been paid or delivered in good faith, shall be deemed full-paid stock and shall not be liable to any further call or assessments thereon, and the holders of such shares shall not be liable for any further payments in respect thereto." Michigan, *Laws*, 1931, no. 372, sec. 19. There are many statements of this kind in the statutes.

gation as to the value of the property contributed, it may merely be described, and the directors are allowed 60 days within which to affix a value upon the property tendered in payment for the no par shares issued.[60] The fact that directors are granted a two months' period in which to determine the value of the consideration received, however, in no way avoids any of the problems formerly associated with the valuation of property and services under par value laws. The corporation must keep books, and must therefore attach some money value to the property or services delivered to it in exchange for shares issued. The opportunity for over-valuations is as great under no par shares as under par value shares. The abolition of par value in itself is a negative idea only; it cannot simplify or remove the problem of arriving at a proper figure for property or services. So far as creditors are concerned, the net result, under the typical statute, is to protect promoters at the same time that creditors are denied their former remedies. This seems a strange consequence of a device which was to do away with the evils of watered stock. If under such statutes the ordinary rights of creditors against stockholders tend to disappear, then some provision should be established requiring a certain minimum capital with which the corporation will begin business, and which may not be reduced by dividends. Otherwise there is a

[60] As Professor Bonbright has observed, "Under the Delaware law providing for no-par stock, there seems to be no liability on the part of the promoter shareholder, provided he delivers to the corporation the precise pieces of property he contracts to deliver. As to the value of this property he need say nothing. He may even receive 10,000 shares of stock for a yellow dog and a dead cat without being subject to a further assessment; for he has made no claim as to the value of these two animals. It is, therefore, difficult to escape the conclusion that the Delaware law, in effect though not in form, has cut off the creditors' remedy of shareholders' liability when stock is issued for property or for services." Bonbright, J. C., "Dangers of Shares without Par Value," *Columbia Law Review*, Vol. 24, p. 460.

Consider also the following: "We are cited no authority, nor have we found any, supporting the right to recovery asserted by the trustee in bankruptcy. On the contrary, the generally, if not universally, accepted theory of the purpose of such statutes is that they are intended to do away with both the 'trust fund' and 'holding out' doctrines. . . .

"Granting that the courts should compel the payment of the consideration for which the no par value stock was issued by the corporation, it would seem, not only that the consideration contemplated by the corporation and its promoters has been paid, but also that the no par value stock had no tangible value." *Johnson* v. *Louisville Trust Co.*, 293 Fed. 857 (C.C.A. 6th, 1923).

See also *Allenhurst Park Estates* v. *Smith*, 101 N.J. Eq. 581 (1927).

serious danger that no par value shares may be employed by conscienceless persons in a manner to deprive creditors of even those few protections which they have traditionally possessed.

4. *No par shares and stockholders' relations to one another.* No par value shares are not without certain dangers to stockholders in their relations to one another. Under the typical par value statutes shares may not be issued for less than their par value. Hence every shareholder has the partial protection that no one else may receive a newly issued share in the enterprise for an amount less than he has originally contributed.[61] In the case of no par shares, however, it is common to provide that additional shares may be disposed of for such consideration as the board of directors may determine. The danger of such arrangements is that additional shares may be sold for an amount less than the true worth of the already outstanding shares; and insofar as this occurs the earlier shareholders will be harmed because a portion of their valuable interest will have been appropriated by the new shareholders. This could occur, however, only where the pre-emptive right has been contracted away. Whether shareholders have any remedy in equity in such situations seems to depend upon all the relevant facts of the case.[62] Seemingly no general rule can be laid down.

Another aspect of no par value shares of special interest to shareholders is the now rather common practice of crediting a portion of the proceeds from the sale of no par value shares to capital surplus rather than to capital stock. Capital surplus so created is in many jurisdictions surplus available for dividends. Under par value statutes the payment of dividends from "capital" has been typically illegal. The purpose of such provisions of course was to prevent unscrupulous directors from paying back to stockholders a portion of their original capital contributions in the guise of dividends.[63] Some no par value statutes, however, openly en-

[61] The protection is partial only, since if the pre-emptive right has been denied by the charter, then if new shares are sold for par when the book value or the capitalized earning power indicates a value greater than par, the new shares will appropriate some of the value attaching to the older shares. After the new shares have been issued, the new and the old will possess identical rights. See *supra* in the present chapter, I (2) (b).

[62] But see Berle, A. A., *Studies in the Law of Corporation Finance*, Ch. IV, and the cases there discussed.

[63] As already observed it was also intended as a protection to creditors.

courage the payment of dividends from capital surplus so created. It seems reasonable to argue that a sharp differentiation should be maintained between earnings and the source of earnings, otherwise much confusion and misrepresentation are likely to result. It is doubtful, however, if most shareholders realize the full implications of the apparently harmless provision that not all the proceeds received from the sale of no par shares must be credited to capital and hence made unavailable for dividends. Viewed historically and logically, the prohibition against the payment of dividends from capital, in the sense of the amount originally contributed to the corporation in return for shares issued, seems eminently proper and reasonable. In the case of par value shares each share issued required a payment to the corporation equal to its par value, and the capital stock account was simply the number of shares outstanding multiplied by their par value. Hence capital meant the amount originally paid in, plus any additions thereto from earned surplus; therefore a prohibition against dividend payments from capital need only insist that dividends not be paid which would reduce the capital stock account. Unfortunately in the case of no par shares this equivalence between the amount paid for the shares and the capital stock account is not necessarily maintained. Thus, while the statutes may still provide that dividends may not be paid from capital, capital, under many no par value laws, is interpreted to mean the amount appearing in the capital stock account, which may be considerably less than the amount paid by stockholders for their shares. In other words, while on the surface the same restrictions apply in no par as in par value shares, the protection to investors is reduced because they may receive back in driblets labeled dividends a sizable fraction of the amount they originally paid in; under the former this was typically impossible.[64]

Thus, despite the optimistic fanfare that accompanied the introduction of no par value shares of stock it is highly doubtful if

[64] Professor Berle has argued that in the absence of some explicit statement to the contrary the intention of purchasers of shares is that the whole amount paid in for no par value shares is intended as capital, and presumably would be subject to the same restrictions as in par value shares. In view of the wording of the statutes and decisions of the courts, however, this view seems more idealistic than the facts warrant. As to its desirability, however, there can be no doubt.

they have achieved anything beneficial from the broad public point of view. That they have protected promoters and corporate management in the pursuit of ends in conflict with those of shareholders in their capacity of investors can scarcely be denied; but the social wisdom of such protection is not easily demonstrated. Indeed, one wonders when all is said and done if no par value shares have not produced more harm than good. At any rate the alleged "advantages" which accrue from their general use by corporate enterprises have been grossly exaggerated.

IV. SUMMARY

The rights of shareholders define the relation that exists between them and the corporation of which they are the owners. These rights arise from three sources: the common law rights that have come to be regarded as attaching to stock ownership in the very nature of the case; the modifications or redefinition of these common law rights by statutory enactment; and the special terms provided in the written contract between the corporation and its shareholders. The number of ways in which these various rights can be combined and adjusted to suit the wishes of the contracting parties is very large indeed although some types of share contracts are more frequently employed than others. Even after the stockholders have had their rights defined by the share contract they may be subsequently altered by amendments to the corporate charter in the manner provided for when the contracts were drawn.

The obligations of stockholders extend both to the corporation and to its creditors. To the former they are bound to pay in full value for their shares as agreed upon a proper call by the directors. If creditors' claims are unsatisfied, shareholders are liable insofar as stock subscriptions have not been paid in full and to the degree that the shares are outstanding for which the corporation received an inadequate consideration in value terms. Shareholders' obligations to creditors have given rise to certain theories of corporate capital stock: the trust fund theory, the fraud or holding-out theory, and the statutory obligation theory. The last seems to provide the simplest logic on which to base shareholders' obligations to pay full value for their shares. It emphasizes that the special privilege of limited personal liability is only to be had on terms stipulated by the state in the interests of all parties concerned.

The usual theories of capital stock were developed with reference to par value shares. Partly because of the lip service paid to such doctrines in practice many persons felt that the abolition of par values entirely would promote honesty and fair dealing and at the same time encourage enterprise. Although not all no par value statutes are identical it would appear that shareholders' obligations to creditors have largely been swept away by the more common types. The net result has been to favor shareholders while stripping creditors of their former remedies, slight as these were. No par shares are not without their dangers to shareholders in their dealings with one another. The net gain from no par shares is problematical.

REFERENCES: CHAPTER IV

Burtchett, F. F.—*Corporation Finance*. Chs. 4-6.
Dewing, A. S.—*Corporation Securities*. Chs. 3-5.
Dewing, A. S.—*Financial Policy*. Book I, Chs. 2, 3.
Field, K.—*Corporation Finance*. New York: Ronald. 1938. Ch. 5.
Gerstenberg, C. W.—*Financial Organization and Management*. Ch. 8.
Hoagland, H. E.—*Corporation Finance*. New York and London: McGraw-Hill, 1938. Chs. 4-7, 14.

Austin, J. A.—"Stock Without Par Value" in *Sen. Doc. 92*, 70th Congress, 1st Session, Party 73-A, pp. 83-108.
Berle, A. A.—*Cases and Materials in the Law of Corporation Finance*, Minneapolis, 1930.
Berle, A. A.—*Studies in the Law of Corporation Finance*, Chicago, 1928. Chs. 3-6.
Colson, C. L.—"The Doctrine of Ultra Vires in United States Supreme Court Decisions," *West Virginia Law Quarterly*, Vol. 42.
Dodd, D. L.—*Stock Watering: the judicial valuation of property for stock-issue purposes*, New York, 1930.
Evans, G. H., Jr.—*British Corporation Finance, 1775-1850; a study of preference shares*, Baltimore. 1936.

EVANS, G. H., JR.—"The Early History of Preferred Stock in the United States," *American Economic Review*, Vol. 19 (1929), pp. 43-58.

EVANS, G. H., JR.—"Preferred Stock in the United States, 1850-1878," *American Economic Review*, Vol. 21 (1931), pp. 56-62.

FREY, A. H.—"Shareholders' Pre-Emptive Rights," *Yale Law Journal*, Vol. 38.

LIVERMORE, S.—"Unlimited Liability in Early American Corporations," *Journal of Political Economy*, Vol. 43.

WOOD, F. S.—"The Status of Management Stockholders," *Yale Law Journal*, Vol. 38.

Chapter V

THE RIGHTS AND REMEDIES OF CREDITORS OF THE CORPORATION

I. The Inherent Rights of Corporate Creditors. II. Extensions and Limitations of Creditors' Rights by Contract. III. The Anomalous Position of Bondholders. IV. Summary.

While both shareholders and creditors provide capital for corporate enterprises the relation of creditors to the corporation and its assets is different in many important respects from that of shareholders. In the previous chapter we indicated the general rights of shareholders and how these may be extended or restricted by contract. Similarly, creditors possess certain general rights and remedies which may be invoked in pursuit of their claims. And likewise these too may be refined and extended by contract. There is one notable difference, however: creditor-debtor relations between persons in the absence of special contract are, in general, not unique simply because one (or both) of the "persons" happens to be a corporation. That is to say, creditor-debtor relations in no sense spring from the existence of the corporate form; they would exist, at least in their simpler forms, had the corporation as we know it never developed. The concept and implications of stock ownership, on the other hand, are, in a very real sense, directly associated with and dependent upon the presence of the corporate form. If only the ordinary rights of creditors were involved there would be no reason to include here a special chapter dealing with creditors' rights. It so happens, however, that the application of the time-honored principles of creditor-debtor relations to corporations has brought about important extensions of the basic ideas and practices commensurate with the marked complexity of the modern business corporation. While the underlying philosophy has persisted, its application to involved situations has

106

led to forms and procedures that are unique in important respects: the idea of receivership, for instance, is simple enough; but an understanding of the basic idea itself gives but a faint suggestion of what receivership may mean for a large corporation. Again, since corporations, unlike real persons, may attain perennial existence, there are not the same obstacles to very long-time creditor-debtor relations. It would be unusual for real persons to draft a contract calling for the repayment of a large principal sum a century hence, yet such distant due dates are a commonplace among corporate debtors. Furthermore, legal ingenuity has developed a means whereby a corporation through a bond indenture may deal with a number of identically situated creditors as if they were one. Indeed, the relative permanency of corporate existence and its associative character have permitted an enormous ramification and elaboration of the simpler creditor-debtor relations between real persons. And it is mainly these which give corporate creditor relations the status of a special study within the broader field.

It is helpful, notwithstanding, first to take cognizance of the underlying position of creditors respecting debtors' property in the absence of special contract. The modifications and elaborations of creditors' remedies by contract will be postponed until section II of this chapter.

I. THE INHERENT RIGHTS OF CORPORATE CREDITORS

1. Creditors' procedure in law and equity to obtain payment. 2. Creditors' right to insist upon full value contribution by shareholders. 3. Fraudulent conveyances and corporations. 4. The granting of preferences. 5. The purpose in appointing a receiver for a corporate debtor's property. 6. The position of the receiver. 7. Summary.

1. *Creditors' procedure in law and equity to obtain payment.* A creditor, *qua creditor*, is entitled merely to collect from the debtor the sum of money owed to him.[1] In the broad and general

---

[1] The obligation of the present section to Glenn, G., *The Rights and Remedies of Creditors Respecting their Debtors' Property*, Boston (Little, Brown), 1915, is gratefully acknowledged.

sense his status as a creditor in nowise confers upon him any right to the specific property of the debtor. He is entitled to the payment of the sum of money owed him, to be sure; but in the absence of default the mode by which the debtor comes into funds with which to pay the claim is not his concern. Thus, the simple existence of a debt does not in and of itself set in motion any legal machinery. Although there is the familiar distinction between secured and unsecured creditors, it must be emphasized that the security is in reality "but an incident to the debt it secures, and a mortgagee is nothing more than a creditor secured by a mortgage." [2] In other words, secured creditors are not a class entirely apart, but simply creditors who have definable rights against some of the debtor's assets over and above those possessed by simple creditors.

In the ordinary run of events, of course, debts are paid when due and the inherent rights of creditors have no occasion for exercise. In the case of non-payment, however, by what procedure does the creditor seek the enforcement of his claim? [3]

If a debt is due and unpaid then the creditor may sue at common law for its payment. If the case be clear, i.e., there is no question of the money being owed, then the suit at law will result in a judgment. Now the importance of the judgment is notable. As Glenn emphasizes, in the first place the judgment gives the creditor a "claim upon the debtor" which, in the legal sense, he did not possess previously, i.e., the debt is determined at law to be owing and unpaid. That is, for legal purposes, there is no longer any question of the validity of the debt, of the fact that its due date has arrived, and that it has not been paid. In the second place, the judgment sets in motion certain machinery which will presumably lead to the payment of the creditor's claim. For a creditor who has had his claim reduced to a judgment, a "judgment creditor," is entitled, by means of a "writ of execution" which accompanies the judgment, to secure payment of his claim from the sale

---

[2] *Myer* v. *Car Co.*, 102 U.S. 1, as quoted by Glenn, *op. cit.*, p. 3.

[3] This brief excursion into such matters may seem an unwarranted digression. But it has been the author's experience that an elementary understanding of how creditors in general may proceed enormously facilitates comprehension of the more complex cases of the enforcement of creditors' rights, such as bankruptcy and corporate reorganization.

proceeds of whatever property of the debtor the sheriff finds it necessary to sell in order to meet the claim. The creditor's claim at law upon the debtor's property grows out of the judgment in an important sense: the judgment gives the creditor the right of realization upon his debt.[4] Armed with his judgment and the writ of execution the creditor's position is greatly strengthened.

The judgment and the ensuing writ of execution, however, only extend to those assets of the debtor which a common law court may recognize as property It must be emphasized, though, that not everything of value which a person would regard as an asset falls within the category of property at common law. For instance, a person's interest in a trust estate or an equity of redemption in a mortgage would not be property at common law. The usual practice among legal writers is to refer to such assets as "equitable assets," meaning thereby that jurisdiction over them resides in courts of equity as opposed to courts of law. Sometimes equitable assets are also called "choses in action." A recent writer describes these as follows: [5]

> This is the nondescript remainder—the choses in action. They consist of all less than present possessory rights which are nevertheless recognized at law. They are rights (and therefore "things") of a most highly incorporeal nature because no present possession is conceived to adhere to them. Thus in actual fact they represent little more than a right to bring an action. On the other hand the very reason for the right of action is itself the basis of their status as "things"—incorporeal "things"—for, as a class, they are all conceived to represent the right of the dispossessed to be repossessed—his persisting property in an object, possession of which he has temporarily surrendered or failed to gain. The recovery is of this object or its equivalent. Choses in action are thought of along somewhat the same lines as the future estates in land, which are at first included with them. They are slices of a right of possession which has been "protected upon the plane of time."

---

[4] Under certain circumstances, if the debtor freely admits his obligation to the creditor the formality of judicial determination of the debt is not essential. Moreover it is probably true that in a great many instances there is little difficulty in establishing the debtor's obligation because there is written evidence, e.g., a promissory note, of his acknowledgment of the debt.

[5] Noyes, C. R., *The Institution of Property*, New York (Longmans), 1936, pp. 278-279. If this somewhat long quotation does not clarify the concept entirely, which is quite probable, it is perhaps because no simple definition can be drafted in non-technical terms.

In order for the sheriff to assume control over property by writ of execution that property would have to be "the subject matter of a common law possessory action." [6] Fortunately for our purposes it is not necessary to indicate all the various kinds of property which fall within the definition of equitable assets. It suffices to recognize that certain of the debtor's assets in the ordinary meaning of that term cannot be reached by a writ of execution at common law.

But if the creditor's claim remains unpaid despite the writ of execution and the debtor has other assets, his equitable assets, which the writ cannot reach, what further remedy is available to the creditor in order to obtain payment?

Until comparatively recently the creditor's further prosecution of his claim was *via* a creditor's bill in equity. That is, a judgment creditor whose judgment was returned unsatisfied, or, as frequently expressed, a "creditor who had exhausted his remedy at law," could invoke the assistance of a court of equity by means of a judgment creditor's bill which, in effect, asked that the court compel the debtor to turn over to a receiver (a court appointee) those assets, unreachable at common law proceedings, which would yet permit the payment of the creditor's claim.[7] This somewhat circuitous procedure, however, has been shortened in recent times by statutory enactment so that the creditor may now achieve the same net result of filing a creditor's bill in equity by merely initiating so-called "supplementary proceedings" to his legal action.[8] In other words, the two proceedings are joined in a manner to expedite the relief available to the creditor. In this way, then, cred-

---

[6] Glenn, *op. cit.,* p. 7.

[7] A point of some importance, apparently, is that the equity proceedings were regarded as ancillary to the common law proceedings and that therefore the creditor had no claim to the assistance of equity until he had "exhausted his remedy at law." That is to say, until his judgment had been returned unsatisfied a creditor had no standing in an equity court. The creditor might, however, file a creditor's bill in equity either on behalf of himself alone, or on behalf of himself and others similarly situated. Unsecured creditors who did not have unsatisfied judgments, however, could not be parties to the bill.

[8] An interesting note describing briefly the similarities and points of difference between the older procedure and the new in the state of New York will be found in Hanna, J., *Cases and Materials on Creditors' Rights,* Chicago (Foundation), 1935, pp. 66-71. This note emphasizes that "supplementary proceedings" are statutory in origin and have largely superseded the older procedure.

itors are placed in a position to enforce their claims upon debtors by being able to reach out after both their common law and their equitable assets.[9]

Still leaving special contractual relations for subsequent consideration, is there anything peculiar in the situation when the debtor is a corporation? Do creditors of a corporation hold any special rights which do not obtain against real persons?

2. *Creditors' right to insist upon full value contribution by shareholders.* In the previous chapter we have already alluded to the doctrine that shareholders are obligated on various theories to contribute full value to the corporation for shares received. Both the trust fund theory and the holding-out theory seek to emphasize shareholders' responsibilities to creditors. While jurists have more or less abandoned the trust fund doctrine as untenable it may be emphasized none the less that even that doctrine gave creditors no right to insist upon full payment for shares unless they had "exhausted their remedies at law."[10] Nevertheless, as already pointed out in Chapter IV, the creditors, if their claims are unpaid, might well insist that shareholders contribute full value for their shares on the grounds that the incorporation statute has been violated: i.e., on the grounds of the statutory-obligation theory. All this, of course, is on the assumption that the corporation is solvent. An insolvent corporation is in a different position; and here, perhaps, the trust fund doctrine has greater cogency. As the United States Supreme Court once said:[11]

Solvent, it [the corporation] holds its property as an individual holds his, free from the touch of a creditor who has acquired no lien; free also from the touch of a stockholder who, though equitably interested in, has no legal right to, the property. Becoming insolvent, the equitable interest of the stockholders in the property, together with their conditional liability to the creditors, places the property in a condition of trust, first, for the creditors, and then for the stockhold-

[9] Needless to say this very brief sketch has ridden almost roughshod over certain important difficulties. In particular, our account has not even indicated the very knotty problems that may arise when assets of the debtor are located beyond the jurisdiction of the court. But see Glenn, *op. cit., passim.*

[10] See Stevens, Robert S., *Handbook on the Law of Private Corporations*, St. Paul, Minn. (West), 1936, p. 746.

[11] *Hollins* v. *Brierfield Coal and Iron Co.*, 150 U.S. 371, 383, as quoted by Stevens, Robert S., *op. cit.*, p. 747.

ers. Whatever of trust there is arises from the peculiar and diverse equitable rights of the stockholders as against the corporation in its property and their conditional liability to its creditors. It is rather a trust in the administration of assets after possession by a court of equity than a trust attaching to the property, as such, for the direct benefit of either creditor or stockholder.

3. *Fraudulent conveyances and corporations.* The prohibition against fraudulent conveyances in general operates with respect to corporations in the same manner as against real persons. A fraudulent conveyance may be said to consist in the transfer of assets by the corporation with "the intent or with the effect of hindering, delaying, or defrauding creditors." [12] An instance of fraudulent conveyance peculiar to corporations is the payment of a dividend which renders it insolvent.[13] Dividends, however, are probably a relatively unimportant instance of fraudulent conveyances. The recent Uniform Fraudulent Conveyance Act has simplified and expedited the remedies of creditors where fraudulent conveyances are demonstrated and proven, and the Act, of course, applies to corporate debtors as well as others. This statute which has been enacted by many states apparently permits the creditor to levy directly upon assets fraudulently conveyed—without the former necessity of first having them returned to the debtor—and then to follow the regular procedure in law and equity for the collection of claims already described.[14]

4. *The granting of preferences.* Where a debtor has more than one creditor an important matter is his right to grant preferences between them. The common law procedure and the ancillary relief afforded by courts of equity for the collection of debts do not pretend to restrain debtors from preferring one creditor to another. And subject to whatever modifications the individual states may have introduced by statute, a corporate debtor as any other may allow one or more creditors a preferred position over others.

[12] Stevens, Robert S., *op. cit.,* p. 751.

[13] The question of illegal dividends is, of course, not restricted to those inducing insolvency. And as a matter of fact dividends illegal for this reason constitute but a small fraction of the illegal dividend cases. Other restrictions on dividends usually impinge upon the corporation sooner. See *infra,* Ch. IX.

[14] An important point, seemingly, is that creditors' claims need not have matured in order to seek relief under the Act. See Stevens, Robert S., *op. cit.,* pp. 751-753.

Hence, so far as the law and equity courts are concerned, the general rule is "first come, first served" and creditors are entitled to payment according to their finishing positions in what has been called the "race of diligence." As has been recently said in an important case: [15]

To leave them [debtors] to the rude methods of common law debt collections would mean financial death to them and, because of the frightful waste which accompanies these methods, loss to creditors as well. More than this, creditors were forced by self-interest into a race to be first in at the death. Many a debtor was thus pushed into insolvency which might have been averted.

In other words, the ordinary procedures for the collection of debts do not prevent corporate debtors from preferring creditors one to another. And it has been stated that corporate assets do not form a "trust fund" for the benefit of creditors to be equitably divided among them unless proceedings for the "winding up" of the corporation have been undertaken.

5. *The purpose in appointing a receiver for a corporate debtor's property.* As just observed, the common law and equity procedures do not provide for any *pro rata* distribution of a debtor's assets among his creditors. The equity courts enter the picture merely as an aid to the achievement of justice at law, and since the law allows creditors to obtain preferences, the equity courts could scarcely alter the arrangement except on special showing. There is yet a further remedy, however, that is often invoked as an aid to the realization of creditors' rights and claims, namely, the appointment of a receiver. What is the purpose of receivership and under what circumstances may the court appoint a receiver for the assets of a debtor?

Particularly in the case of large corporate enterprises with durable and specialized assets, the pressure of creditors to secure payment of their claims may result in such a hurried dismemberment of the corporate assets that a substantial fraction of their value is destroyed. Under the circumstances, asset values tend to decline

---

[15] In *re. Philadelphia Rapid Transit Co.*, 8 F. Supp. 51, 53 (E.D. Pa. 1934) affirmed *sub. nom. Wilson* v. *Philadelphia Rapid Transit Co.*, 73 Fed. (2d) 1022 (C.C.A. 3d, 1934), as quoted by Gerdes, John, *Corporate Reorganization under Section 77B of the Bankruptcy Act*, Chicago (Callaghan), 1936, Vol. I, p. 5, note.

or disappear as a direct consequence of the procedure provided at law and equity for the payment of creditors. That is to say, the individualized actions of creditors defeat the common aims of creditors as individuals. In view of the purposes which equity courts are designed to serve—namely, to promote justice in situations where the law leaves something to be desired—it would be surprising if an equitable remedy had not been developed to obviate the bad result of creditors defeating their own ends. That remedy is the appointment of a receiver for the debtor's assets.

It must be emphasized that the appointment of a receiver for the debtor's assets is definitely regarded as a form of relief in aid of, and subsidiary to, the remedies of creditors already described. At least this is the general theory underlying the appointment of receivers. As a consequence the appointment of a receiver is discretionary with the court;[16] and furthermore, a creditor requesting receivership must give evidence that he has exhausted his legal remedies.[17] Although receivership is usually associated with insolvency a corporation need not be insolvent, in the sense of having an excess of liabilities over assets, before the court will appoint a receiver. It is sufficient if the debtor be unable to meet his obligations as they fall due.[18] Many states, however, have endeavored by statute to codify the conditions warranting the appointment of receivers; for the federal courts, however, there is no ruling statute

[16] Stevens, Robert S., *op. cit.*, pp. 758-771.

[17] The same qualification holds here as we have already noted in connection with equitable relief in general: that is, if the debtor in no way disputes either the validity or the amount of the creditor's claim, i.e., equitable relief would be granted as a matter of course, then the return of a judgment against the debtor unsatisfied is an unnecessary technicality. Some states have statutes which short-circuit the procedure in this way.

[18] There was always the latent danger that "unfriendly" creditors might upset the equity receivership by having the embarrassed corporation adjudicated bankrupt within the bankruptcy statute, i.e., an excess of liabilities over assets. To circumvent this risk it has apparently been a common practice to have friendly creditors also file involuntary bankruptcy proceedings against the debtor corporation. The following quotation is from a letter by an attorney active in such proceedings in a particular case:

"We have also filed today a petition in bankruptcy on behalf of the same creditors in the District Court. . . .

"Our practice in dealing with petitions of this kind is to apply for the appointment of a receiver in the bankruptcy proceeding after serving notice on counsel appearing for the various parties in the general equity receivership. Upon the service of such a notice the attorneys in the general equity receivership appear

and the historic principles governing the appointment of receiver hold.

From the point of view of creditors, the main consequence of placing the affairs of a debtor corporation in the hands of a receiver is that they are prevented from pursuing their ordinary remedies against it during the duration of the receivership. For the time being creditors may not dismember the property. And it is worth emphasizing that historically and in strict theory the appointment of a receiver was regarded as an action taken in the interests of creditors. Receivership does not destroy any priorities or liens that may have been secured by particular creditors prior to receivership; it does, however, prevent the granting of additional preferences and restrain the exercise of priorities already ceded.

Since the appointment of a receiver for the assets of a debtor corporation is a creditors' remedy, not a mode of relief for hard-pressed debtors, a petition for receivership must emanate from a creditor, at least formally. And furthermore a petition for the appointment of a receiver in the creditors' interests was always addressed to the discretion and wisdom of the court. This restriction led to the somewhat anomalous procedure called "friendly" or "consent" receiverships.[19] Although now comparatively rare among ailing corporations because of the superiorities of reorganization in bankruptcy under the revised Bankruptcy Act, the consent receivership is yet worth describing briefly.

in the bankruptcy court, deny the insolvency, in the bankruptcy sense, of the corporation, call the court's attention to the existence of the general equity receivership, and urge that the motion for a bankruptcy receiver be continued generally.

"The attorney representing the petitioning creditors in bankruptcy consents to the general continuance of this motion and the bankruptcy proceedings rest there indefinitely and until after the reorganization plan through the general equity receivership has been perfected and put into operation.

"Proof is then offered in the bankruptcy proceedings that the company is not insolvent and the petition is dismissed."

Securities and Exchange Commission, *Report of the Study and Investigation of the Work, Activities, Personnel and Functions of Protective and Reorganization Committees*, Washington (Government Printing Office), 1937, Part I, p. 246. Cf. *ibid.*, pp. 247-265.

[19] Dewing states that this method came into general use following the failure of the Wabash Railway in 1884. Dewing, A. S., *Financial Policy of Corporations*, New York (Ronald), 1934, p. 1118.

In its fullest stage of development the consent receivership came to be more a form of relief for debtors than an ancillary remedy of creditors. The procedure adopted was somewhat as follows. Let us assume that a corporation saw approaching difficulty in meeting creditors' obligations and feared the consequences of creditors' attachments. In the circumstances, the corporation would seek out a "friendly" creditor whose obligation was unpaid and have him request a court of equity to appoint a receiver for the corporation's assets. The creditor's "prayer" to the court would contend that the said corporation was unable to pay the debt and request that the court (in its discretion of course) appoint a receiver for the benefit of all interested parties. At the same time the corporation would file an answer to the creditor's contentions, admitting without argument his allegations, and urging likewise the necessity for the appointment of a receiver for its affairs.[20] The court would then consider the creditor's petition and the corporation's answer, and unless it appeared that receivership would clearly not conserve the assets, or that the action was not *bona fide*,[21] it would appoint a receiver.[22] Thus, while the formalities of procedure still retained the fiction that receivership is wholly a form of creditors' relief,

[20] Because a judgment *would* issue in favor of the creditor and be returned unsatisfied the creditor need not run through this formality. See Stevens, *op. cit.*, p. 767. That is where the debtor corporation admits the claim and its inability to pay a judgment is largely superfluous.

[21] Note the following in *re Metropolitan Railway Receivership*, 208 U.S. 90 at 110-111: "In this case we can find no evidence of collusion, and the Circuit Court found there was none. It does appear that the parties to the suit desired that the administration of the railway's affairs should be taken in hand by the Circuit Court of the United States, and to that end, when the suit was brought, the defendant admitted the averments in the bill and united in the request for the appointment of receivers. This fact is stated by the Circuit Judge; but there is no claim made that the averments in the bill were untrue, or that the debts, named in the bill as owing to the complainants, did not in fact exist; nor is there any question made as to the citizenship of the complainants, and there is not the slightest evidence of any fraud practiced for the purpose of thereby creating a case to give jurisdiction to the Federal court. . . . So long as no improper act was done by which the jurisdiction of the Federal court attached, the motive for bringing the suit there is unimportant."

[22] The action for the appointment of a receiver might be brought in either a state court or a federal court. In the case of large corporations with property located in several states there is usually an advantage to be had in having a federal court assume jurisdiction. In this instance the creditor filing the request must reside in another state from that in which the corporation is domiciled. Mere federal jurisdiction, however, does not avoid the necessity of ancillary receiverships.

it cannot be denied that, in fact, a receivership came to operate as much in the interests of debtors as of creditors. To what degree this end result was achieved as a consequence of the almost inevitable necessity of receivership for embarrassed quasi-public corporations is hard to say. But it must have been realized at an early date that the ordinary creditors' remedies were both inadequate and unsuitable for dealing with railroads or public utilities, for instance, in which the public welfare is superior to mere creditor-debtor interests. To break up such corporations would be an empty remedy for creditors. At the same time cessation of operations and dismemberment of the property would be clearly intolerable from the point of view of the general welfare. When the basic philosophy of receivership had been developed with respect to corporations "vested with a public interest," its extension to other corporations of large size was probably an easy step; for their very size and ramifications implied semi-public considerations.

6. *The position of the receiver.* Pending final disposition of the debtor's estate the receiver assumes full jurisdiction over it. The receiver derives his power from the court and his function is to conserve the assets and protect them in the interests of all parties involved. He is in no sense a representative of the interests of creditors even though they have brought about his appointment by their actions.[23] Since the public welfare may be involved directly or indirectly the receiver is often charged with operating the corporation, e.g., a railway company. And incident to the power granted by the court to operate the company, the receiver

[23] Note the following: "A chancery receiver is a ministerial officer, with the function of custodian, appointed by the court to hold property in litigation pending suit. He derives his authority from the appointing court, and not from the parties at whose instance he is appointed, and acts in behalf of no particular interest but guards the rights of all. It follows that a receivership cannot *per se* be the subject of a suit in equity, for the power of the court to appoint a receiver is based on the fact of real litigation between the parties, in which it becomes necessary to take possession of the property to which the controversy relates, in order to preserve and administer it. If the parties have no such controversy, and, desiring no lawful relief, institute a suit and have a receiver appointed, the appointment is void." Hughes, W. J., *Federal Practice*, St. Paul, Minn. (West), 1931, Vol. II, p. 328, as quoted by Gerdes, *op. cit.*, Vol. I, p. 29, note.

was sometimes given the power to borrow money through the sale of securities known as receiver's certificates.[24] During his incumbency the receiver is charged with operating the property efficiently and collecting the revenues therefrom in the interests of all parties concerned.[25]

Since, theoretically at least, the purpose of the receiver is to protect creditors' rights and not nullify them permanently, he must ultimately dispose of the property by sale for the benefit of creditors. And here an important point emerges. It will be recalled that one of the prime reasons for appointing a receiver initially was to prevent the dissipation of asset values through dismemberment and piecemeal sale. Now if the same end result of dismemberment is not to follow, the receiver must dispose of the corporate assets as a unit. But if the corporation be large, the number of possible purchasers at the receiver's sale will be rather narrowly restricted; for few individuals, obviously, will be able to tender a very large sum in payment for the assets as a unit. As the practice has developed it has been only the parties already in interest in the embarrassed corporation that offer a bid.[26] During the interim of the receivership the various parties in interest usually would have worked out a scheme of compromise between them, the so-called plan of reorganization, and the receiver's sale was a mere step in carrying this plan into effect. Just what the reorganization plan would be was determined in each case by a multitude of considerations: ordinarily, however, the strict letter of the applicable creditors' claims was modified. Before the receiver's sale actually took place the court fixed a minimum price, called the "upset" price, below which it would refuse to confirm the sale of the assets. From the point of view of the reorganization committee this was an advantage since it indicated roughly how much cash would have to be provided for those claim-holders against

----

[24] The issuance of receiver's certificates for corporations not affected with a public interest was quite rare.

[25] It may be noted in passing that the receiver appointed was often the president, the general-manager, or some other executive officer of the embarrassed corporation.

[26] On occasion another corporation has bid in the properties at a receiver's sale; but this is comparatively rare.

the corporation who did not assent to the reorganization plan. The payment of the upset price (or occasionally something more) was not made by the reorganization committee mainly in cash, but in the form of the claims the committee already held against the corporation. Cash was only provided in the amount necessary to pay off the non-assenters their proportionate amount of the sale price of the assets of the corporation. Thus, finally, through the receiver's sale, the creditors were able to levy their claims against the corporate assets that had been temporarily restrained from enforcement by the appointment of the receiver.[27]

7. *Summary.* To summarize the argument thus far: In general, creditors' rights against corporate debtors are no different from their rights against real persons. They have the right to sue upon the debt, to secure a judgment, and to levy upon the assets through a writ of execution. The aforesaid writ, however, can only reach assets that are property at common law. To levy upon "equitable" assets a creditor has the further remedy of a creditor's bill in equity or "supplementary proceedings." To the degree that their claims are unpaid creditors have the right to insist that shareholders contribute to the corporation full value for their shares. Fraudulent conveyances apply to corporations in essentially the same way as to real persons. To allow a hurried and piecemeal liquidation of the corporation's assets to satisfy creditors may yield less towards their claims than the sale of the corporate debtor's assets as a unit. Consequently equity courts often appoint receivers to hold the property intact with a view to its sale as a unit for the benefit of all concerned. Receivership is theoretically an ancillary remedy of creditors rather than a mode of relief for embarrassed corporate debtors. Until comparatively recent times, however, it was the normal vehicle for the reorganization of failed corporations at the instigation of "friendly" creditors, because in no other way could

---

[27] Something further is said on the procedure for the reorganization of corporations through the intervention of receivership in equity in Ch. XIV.

If no plan of reorganization could be worked out among the parties in interest whereby the assets could be sold as a unit, then the only remaining alternative was the piecemeal liquidation of the assets and the payment of creditors to the degree possible. In that instance the distribution among creditors was on a *pro rata* basis with due regard, of course, to any liens or attachments that particular creditors might have obtained before the receiver was appointed.

the assets be held together from the onslaught of creditors seeking payment. The ultimate sale of the assets as a unit by the receiver was usually to the reorganization committee.

II. EXTENSIONS AND LIMITATIONS OF CREDITORS' RIGHTS BY CONTRACT

1. The nature of bonds. 2. The indenture trustee. 3. The provisions of the indenture: a. pledges of assets, b. open and closed issues, c. sinking funds and redemption of bonds. d. maturity and acceleration thereof, e. miscellaneous provisions.

1. *The nature of bonds.* As an incident to the purposes for which they have been chartered, corporations acquire the power to borrow money. And almost all corporations do borrow money from time to time. More formal borrowings, however, such as bond issues which usually involve a formal statement of the corporation's covenants are customarily specifically "authorized" by the board of directors, even though the corporation has the general power to borrow money.[28] Bonds, which are formal agreements between certain creditors and the corporation, both modify and extend the ordinary rights of creditors.

The sale of bonds to a number of different persons could easily create certain bothersome problems for a corporation were special steps not taken to obviate them.[29] The most obvious complication

[28] The corporation's power to borrow money is almost uniformly granted by the incorporation statute. It is nevertheless customary to repeat the statement of authority in the articles of association. The articles may also, however, require that the creation of bonded indebtedness be first approved by the shareholders in formal meeting. Not infrequently preferred stock contracts require that no bonds or other security issue having a claim to assets or earnings ahead of such preferred stock may be issued without first securing the approval of the preferred shareholders.

[29] In common language the term bond designates a long-term debt instrument of a government, some subdivision thereof, or a corporation. Similar obligations of less than five years' duration are customarily called short-term notes.

In the more formal legal parlance, however, the word bond apparently refers to a sealed instrument; and on this basis some short-term notes are "bonds" too. We shall here adopt the looser usage and employ the term bond to refer to relatively long-term creditor obligations of corporations which have their foundation in a written document, the indenture. See Lyon, H., *Corporations and their Financing*, New York (Heath), 1938, p. 226.

for the corporation is that each bondholder, although possessing exactly the same written agreement, might place a different interpretation on his rights and the corporation's obligations. Hence a bond issue held by a number of different persons might automatically expose the corporation to the risk of innumerable actions at law originating in alternative interpretations of the bond contract. Confusion and costly litigation would be the almost certain result. In view of these contingencies almost all present-day corporate bond issues consist of two parts. The first consists of "the bond" which individual investors purchase and hold. This instrument is evidence that the owner thereof possesses certain rights and claims against the corporation because his "bond" is part of an elaborate agreement between the corporation and all other persons holding like "bonds" of the corporation. The full rights of the bondholders and the covenant of the corporation are contained in an instrument called the bond indenture. The indenture is the second, and in some respects the more important, part of the bond issue.[30] Partly because of the contingent difficulties already mentioned, and partly for other reasons, the indenture provides that the bondholders' approach to the corporation is not direct and individual but rather as a group *via* a third party, the so-called trustee under the indenture. In other words, by the use of a trustee the corporation is enabled to deal with a whole group of persons as if they were one. The obligations of the corporation are technically to the trustee; and obversely the bondholders' claims and remedies against the corporation are not those of ordinary creditors, but rather by way of inducing the trustee to act on their behalf.

Before examining some of the more important parts of the indenture as a document let us first consider the position of the trustee and his relationship to the bondholders and the corporation.

---

[30] Some few corporate bond issues, usually only where the agreement is short and simple, have no indenture; the full contract being contained in each "bond." The growth of large corporations with far-flung properties and interests, and hence large bond issues, has made an indenture almost indispensable. The contract is often so lengthy that its full text could not possibly be set forth in a document of convenient proportions. Nowadays each bond contains only a brief summary of the contents of the indenture. If perchance the full agreement and the digest on the bond do not agree then it is not settled which is controlling. See Dewing, A. S., *Corporation Securities*, New York (Ronald), 1934, p. 205.

2. *The indenture trustee.* As we shall observe in more detail shortly, the modern indenture specifying the rights of the bondholders and the obligation of the corporation has tended to become a very formidable document. And, *a priori*, it would seem reasonable to suppose that someone would be responsible for ascertaining with due regularity and diligence that the terms of the contract were not being violated. A single creditor with a claim against another is assumed to be guided sufficiently by his self-interest to search out lapses in the debtor's fulfillment of his obligations. Where the debtor is a corporation, and perhaps 10,000 persons scattered far and near compose the bondholders, it is manifestly impossible for each and all to search out the debtor's deviations from the letter of the obligation. Consequently the bondholders need an intermediary or representative to watch for violations of the terms of the agreement. Likewise, as already noted, it is convenient for the corporation to deal with the bondholders as a unit through a single person.

In theory, the trustee under the bond indenture is the individual charged with representing the bondholders in dealings with the corporate debtor. While originally a natural person, the trustee nowadays is almost invariably a corporation such as a bank or trust company, since the finite life of any human may prove a disadvantage. If anyone ostensibly represents the bondholders by observing the corporation's fulfillment of its covenants and reporting violations thereof, that person is the trustee. Certainly his title of trustee suggests care and diligence, caution, wisdom, and conservation. In the absence of concrete information to the contrary one would expect the trustee to notify the bondholders of any lapses by the debtor, such as failure to maintain the property as provided, failure to pay taxes due, failure to remit interest or to maintain a sinking fund, failure to use the proceeds of the loan as promised, failure to maintain a certain required ratio of current assets to liabilities, etc., etc., according to the particular contract. And as a matter of fact a trustee under a bond indenture is usually *given the right* to do all these things and more besides if he so desires. But having full authority to do certain things and actually performing them are two different things. One does not necessarily imply the other.

As the trustee's functions and responsibilities have come to be defined and interpreted in latter-day times they afford bondholders precious little protection. Indeed one sometimes wonders whether it is more accurate to describe the modern trustee as the representative of the bondholders or as a protector and shield for the corporation against the bondholders. One would suppose, for instance, that, at the very least, a trustee would report to the bondholders such an important matter as a default or impending default on the interest due.[31] Yet apparently many trustees felt they had no obligation in that direction unless requested by a specified percentage of the bondholders.[32] While this state of indolence and non-responsibility on the part of trustees is partly the result of their having divided affiliations, as the Securities and Exchange Commission has clearly shown, it is also traceable to certain broad exculpatory clauses within the indenture itself. As the judge opined in an important case: [33]

> The facts in this case show, perhaps as clearly as can be imagined, how utterly unjust to the investing public is the modern trust indenture.
> The cruel fact is that not only is the trustee not required to exercise that greater skill and watchfulness and prudence and skill which it has, but it is even absolved from exercising merely the ordinary care which a single individual should exercise as to his own affairs. . . .
> The trustee under a corporate indenture, on the other hand, has his rights and duties defined, not by the fiduciary relationship, but exclusively by the terms of the agreement. His status is more that of a stakeholder than one of a trustee.

As the Securities and Exchange Commission has demonstrated, the trustee under the bond indenture cannot be regarded as the protector and representative of the bondholders in any significant sense. He is little more than an appointed and nominal representative of the bondholders through whom they may take action if they organize and are willing to indemnify him for any trouble

[31] See Securities and Exchange Commission, *Report on the Study and Investigation of the Work, Activities, Personnel and Functions of Protective and Reorganization Committees*, Part VI, *Trustees under Indentures*, Washington, 1936, esp. pp. 37-55.

[32] *Ibid.*

[33] Judge Rosenman in *Hazzard* v. *Chase National Bank of City of New York*, as quoted in S.E.C., *op. cit.*, p. 22.

or expense incurred. Otherwise, apparently, he is content with an easy conscience, come what may.[34] Perhaps the trustee's very limited responsibilities to the bondholders are less an occasion for astonishment when one considers that almost invariably the borrowing corporation and the investment banker undertaking the sale of the securities select him and define his obligations. Under the circumstances the indenture is more likely to favor the corporation than the bondholders.

While the trustee under the modern indenture need not do much for the bondholders on his own behalf, the bondholders individually and collectively can do little or naught themselves without acting through him. As already emphasized, the bondholders' approach to the corporate debtor is through the trustee. And commonly the trustee need not act even when requested unless a certain fraction (25 per cent and sometimes more) of the bondholders ask him to do so and undertake to indemnify him accordingly. In practice, of course, the net result is apt to be that the trustee will do nothing until a bondholders' protective committee has formed and urged him to take such action as he might have taken earlier. Meanwhile much valuable time will have elapsed. It is also

[34] Note the following by a trust company officer before the Securities and Exchange Commission:

"Q. You think the corporate trustee is merely a mechanical agency?

"A. Yes.

"Q. That is, it is a sort of finer bookkeeping agency, and also an instrument, vehicle, as you put it, which can be put in motion by the bondholders?

"A. By the bondholders.

"Q. Would you say that that defines all the duties of a corporate trustee?

"A. I would." (S.E.C., *op. cit.*, p. 4.)

That some trust officers have been conscience-stricken by such an attitude is indicated by the following:

"If an event of default happen, the responsibilities and difficulties accumulate around the trustee's devoted head. Suppose one occurs and the required number of bondholders do not get together and form a protective committee, and there is no one to make request of the trustee to proceed under the foreclosure clauses of the indenture: What shall the trustee do? He can sit back with folded hands and say that the proper number of bondholders have not called his attention to the default and he has not been indemnified under the terms of the agreement, therefore he will do nothing. This may be strictly within the letter of the indenture, but, as Scripture has it, 'The letter killeth, the spirit maketh alive.' Is it not a reproach against any issue of bonds that the trustee has so wrapped himself up in non-responsibility clauses that his signature on the back of a bond is mere waste of ink?" W. G. Littleton, vice-president, Fidelity-Philadelphia Trust Co., as reported in *ibid.*, p. 45.

well established that any legal action taken by a single bondholder, or a group thereof, must be for the benefit of all the bondholders who are parties to the indenture.[35]

By and large the duties of the trustee have become largely mechanical such as receiving and paying interest, certifying that a particular bond is part of the issue named in the indenture, and a few minor details of a clerical nature. The amount of protection he affords the bondholders by a diligent exercise of care for their interests is likely to be very small; or, perhaps more accurately, what he is *required to do* under the terms of the indenture is very small.[36]

3. *The provisions of the indenture.* Although the bondholders' action against the corporation is by way of the trustee, the indenture contains an elaborate recital of the bondholders' rights over and above the rights of ordinary creditors and how they may be exercised. We cannot describe here, of course, the full text of any bond indenture; but since the forms have tended to become standardized we may indicate briefly some of the more frequently recurring provisions.

a. *Pledges of assets.* A corporation often seeks to reassure its bondholders by pledging specific assets as security for the loan. That is, the corporation reinforces its promise to pay by granting the bondholders a definite, but contingent, claim against specified

[35] "Assuming for the purposes of this case that, under the peculiar terms of this mortgage, these bondholders had the right to file this bill without calling upon the trustee to act—a point upon which we express no opinion—they had no right to a decree for their exclusive benefit. If a single bondholder has any right at all to institute proceedings, he is bound to act for all standing in a similar position, and not only to permit other bondholders to intervene, but to see that their rights are protected in the final decree." *New Orleans Pac. Ry. Co.* v. *Parker,* 143 U.S. 42, as quoted by Berle, A. A., *Cases and Materials in the Law of Corporation Finance,* Minneapolis, (West) 1930, pp. 562-563. See also Stevens, Robert S., *op. cit.,* pp. 761-762.

[36] The trustee's point of view regarding any action he might take on behalf of the bondholders is partially understandable. There is the danger to him that his action might cause loss to the bondholders and that he would be liable for such losses to the bondholders. Consequently the trustee is almost certain to demand an indemnity bond before proceeding to do anything that might so expose him. On the other hand, the trustee is typically surrounded with exculpatory clauses which attempt to protect him so long as he acts within the limits of his trust. There is perhaps some tendency, however, for the courts to interpret such clauses in favor of bondholders when disputes arise. See Stevens, Robert S., *op. cit.,* pp. 759-764.

assets. Where real property is involved this pledge takes the form of a mortgage, and the mortgage may be a first, a second, or some subsequent lien with respect to the assets involved.[37] And in truth in corporate bond issues the mortgage is often a first mortgage on some property but junior to some antecedent mortgage on the remainder. Since a mortgage relates to specific assets, the indenture will contain a recital of the property subject to the lien. With respect to such property the corporation agrees to pay the taxes, to keep it insured where insurable, to maintain it in good repair, etc., etc. In brief, the company agrees, in effect, to keep the pledged property in such a condition as will provide continuous and equal protection to the bondholders.

Since the corporation may wish to sell certain of the pledged assets because they are worn out, obsolete, etc., and to replace them with others, the indenture usually provides that the company may do so and that the substitute assets shall come under the lien. Where the pledged assets are documents in evidence of property rights, e.g., bonds and shares, etc., the conditions governing the withdrawal of the collateral are important. Some collateral trust bonds, for instance, have been rendered well-nigh worthless to investors because of the great freedom allowed the corporation in withdrawing and substituting collateral pledged as security.

If no prohibition were imposed, the corporation might subsequently grant to other creditors a lien superior to that now afforded the instant bondholders. Consequently, the covenant usually provides that during the period the bonds are outstanding the corporation will not grant any lien superior to that now accorded to the present bondholders.

If there is the intention to pledge as security to present bondholders any additional property subsequently acquired by the corporation, then the indenture will contain the "after-acquired property" clause. This clause, if rigidly formulated, brings under the mortgage whatever assets the corporation may come to own after the bonds have been issued. Although nominally an added protec-

[37] For our purposes the distinction between the title and lien theories of mortgages is not important. But see Walsh, W. F., "The Development of the Title and Lien Theories of Mortgages," *New York Law Quarterly Review*, Vol. 9 (1932), pp. 280-309.

tion to the bondholders, the corporation can ordinarily avoid it by means of a subsidiary or a leasing arrangement should it prove too restrictive.

b. *Open and closed issues.* The indenture will specify the aggregate principal amount of the bonds that may be issued by the corporation under this document. Often the corporation will not wish to issue at once bonds to the full amount allowed under the indenture. The issue is then said to be an "open" issue, which means nothing more than that the corporation may execute further bonds under the same indenture.[38] And, conversely, bonds are said to be parts of a "closed" issue when no more can be issued under the same indenture. So-called "open-end" issues are common in large corporations which anticipate more or less continuous growth and therefore a continuous need for capital. In open-end bond issues the indenture usually sets forth certain terms and conditions under which additional bonds may be issued: e.g., that more bonds may be issued in exchange for property at not exceeding, say, 80 per cent of its appraised value; or provided that earnings are more than twice annual interest charges on the bonds already outstanding and those about to be issued. In this manner the bondholders are ostensibly protected against over-borrowing by the corporations.[39]

c. *Sinking funds and redemption of bonds.* Partly for its own assistance in repaying the debt and partly as an attraction to investors, the corporation often agrees to pay to the trustee a certain annual sum to be applied towards the reduction of the net bonded

[38] On the basis of unpublished studies by W. L. Dayton, J. D. Richer, and P. Donham, Dewing reports that of a random selection of 960 mortgage bond issues brought out between 1920 and 1929 inclusive 48 per cent were open issues and 52 per cent were closed. For the period 1925-1929 the percentage of open issues was higher than for the period 1920-1924; and for the period 1930-1932 inclusive a study of 120 issues brought out during that interval showed a still higher ratio of open to closed issues than for the period 1925-1929. In short, open issues seem to be increasing in importance. Indeed, Dewing states that open issues were rare before 1901. Among railroads and public utilities open-end bond issues seem to be predominant by a wide margin. Some railroad and public utility bond indentures specified no maximum upper limit at all. See Dewing, A. S., *Corporation Securities*, New York (Ronald), 1934, pp. 218-220.

[39] As can well be imagined, there are ways and means by which the corporation can comply with the letter if not the spirit of such clauses; e.g., by friendly appraisals, adjustment of net earnings, figures, etc.

indebtedness. According to the terms of the indenture the trustee is required to apply the monies so delivered to the purchase of the bonds of this issue (often at a price not exceeding a specified figure), or to call by lot for redemption a certain fraction of the bonds outstanding, or to invest the funds at interest. In the case of railroads, what are sometimes called sinking fund clauses provide that the funds shall be used for improvements to the railroad property rather than for reducing the net indebtedness, on the theory, doubtless, that the security behind the bond issue is similarly improved thereby.[40]

The payments into the sinking fund may be regular and absolute or irregular and conditional. Both types are common, although among the Class I railroads the latter is much more frequently the arrangement.[41] Where the payments are conditional they may be contingent upon gross or net earnings, dividends, the ratio of current assets to liabilities, the total indebtedness, or such other measures of the earning power or financial position of the corporation as may appear reasonable to the persons drafting the indenture, i.e., the corporation's officers and its bankers. The essential logic of the sinking fund is, of course, that with a gradual reduction of the

[40] A very recent study reports: "In general, the so-called "sinking fund" provisions in the indentures of the fifty-one large Class I railroads are of four major types. One group of indentures requires the payments to be used for the extinction of the funded debt. This is subject to qualification in those cases where sinking fund debt is not initially available at or below a specified price. . . . A second group divides the fund set aside into two parts, one to be used for the redemption of debt and the other to be devoted to improvement of the mortgaged property. A third group of indentures sets up funds which can be used for (1) the extinction of funded debt, (2) improvements to the mortgaged property, or (3) both, at the option of the mortgagor.

"Besides these three types, there is a fourth group of funds. This consists of a few indentures containing covenants requiring the corporation to set aside funds to be invested solely in additions, betterments, or improvements to the mortgaged property." Stevens, W. H. S., *Railroad Sinking Funds and Funded Debt*, Washington (Interstate Commerce Commission, Bureau of Statistics), 1939, p. 10; this is perhaps the most completely up to date study of the subject available.

[41] For Class I railroads "Nearly 30 per cent of the sinking fund indentures require unconditional payments to the fund but this type of contract accounts for less than 8 per cent of the total sinking fund debt, conditional or voluntary payments applying to the remainder, or over 92 per cent of the total debt. Again, nearly 76 per cent of the indentures require the sinking fund payments to be devoted exclusively to debt redemption (pure sinking funds) though with qualifications if sinking fund debt is not initially available. . . . But these covenants apply to less than 46 per cent of the sinking fund debt." *Ibid.*, pp. 20-21.

debt and no adverse change in the earning power of the company the security of the bonds will increase.

Since the corporation may wish to undertake additional financing at some time, or to remove its bonded indebtedness entirely, or to take advantage of a fall in the rate of interest at which it can float securities, the bond indenture will commonly contain a clause permitting the corporation to "call" the bonds for redemption on any interest date by giving due notice. The price at which the bonds are callable may be at an unvarying price throughout their existence or at a fluctuating price, usually a declining price as they approach maturity. Ordinarily, too, the indenture provides that if the bonds are called before their due date, a premium above par will be paid to the holders thereof.[42]

d. *Maturity and acceleration thereof.* Bonds, being creditor obligations, specify a date at which the principal comes due. Nonpayment of the principal constitutes default as a matter of course. Also, the corporation agrees to pay interest in the interim between issuance and maturity according to the arrangement specified in the indenture. Generally speaking, interest must be paid semiannually and irrespective of the earnings or cash position of the corporation; but in "income" bonds or "adjustment" bonds, which usually are issued in the course of corporate reorganization, the interest payment is made conditional upon earnings, current asset or cash position. Unless the bonds be of this sort, the failure to pay interest on the appointed date constitutes a default by the corporation under the indenture, and the due date of the principal is accelerated.

While a default in interest payments is perhaps the most serious violation of the covenant by the corporation, it is not the only lapse which may bring about an acceleration of the due date of the principal. Two recent authors have written the following in this connection: [43]

[42] Dewing reports that certain studies made under his direction showed that, of 410 bond issues brought out between 1925 and 1929, 116 were callable at 102 per cent of par and 143 at 105 per cent of par. In other words, more than 63 per cent were callable at these two figures. See Dewing, A. S., *Corporation Securities*, pp. 232-234.

[43] McClelland, R. A., and Fisher, F. S., *The Law of Corporate Mortgage Bond Issues*, Chicago (Callaghan), 1937, p. 575.

Typical events of default are nonpayment of interest, nonpayment of principal, failure to keep specific covenants of the indenture (insurance coverage on property, etc.) filing of voluntary or involuntary petitions in bankruptcy, the commencement and continuation of proceedings for reorganization or otherwise under section 77B of the Bankruptcy Law, and any other special agreements that the parties may desire, as, for example, default under a prior mortgage or failure to manufacture or mine property of specified gross value or quantity during a given period—in short, the happening of such events as the creditors (and possibly the trustee) deem to be adverse to, or to lessen the probability of, repayment of the loans.

Since, however, the trustee is not required to do very much by way of seeking out violations of the indenture by the corporation, the bondholders are likely to be aware of default thereunder only when there is non-payment of interest, or of interest and principal.[44] And in fact the indenture often provides that the trustee shall take no cognizance of default by the corporation unless it be brought to his attention by a specified percentage of the bondholders.[45]

e. *Miscellaneous provisions.* Apart from the foregoing, particular bond indentures may contain additional covenants too numerous and diverse to be described here. Indeed, as we have already noted with respect to capital stock, the limit on variations between contracts is set only by the ingenuity of the human mind. Some bonds are serial, for instance: a certain proportion of them mature at regular intervals. Others are convertible into common

[44] In strict accuracy the acceleration of maturity is not brought about in most cases by actual default on bond interest. Rather, the corporation, foreseeing it will be forced to default at the next interest period, will initiate proceedings for the appointment of a trustee in bankruptcy, or, prior to the recent amendments to the Bankruptcy Act, for the appointment of a receiver in equity. Under the usual indenture the appointment of a trustee or receiver constitutes default and accelerates the maturity of the principal.

[45] Note the following from an indenture: "Unless and until the Trustee shall have received written notice to the contrary from the holders of not less than ten per cent in amount of the Bonds outstanding, the Trustee may assume that for the purposes of this Indenture no default has been made by the Company in the payment of any of the Bonds or of the interest thereon or in the observance or performance of any of the covenants contained in the Bonds or in this Indenture and that none of the events of default has happened." Indenture of the Indiana Flooring Company as reproduced in Berle, A. A., *Cases and Materials in the Law of Corporation Finance*, Minneapolis, Minn. (West), 1930, pp. 527-528.

or preferred shares of the capital stock of the company. Still others are guaranteed with respect to principal and interest by another corporation. So, for example, one often speaks of convertible bonds, of serial bonds, of guaranteed bonds, etc., or by some other name which draws attention to this or that provision of the indenture which is thought to be of especial importance for the purpose at hand. But the significant point is that a bond indenture is a complicated contract extending from the bondholders to the indenture trustee and from the trustee to the debtor corporation, and the various provisions of the contract do not lend themselves to an easy designation by a word or phrase which can be very descriptive. In the last analysis a bondholder's rights are the ordinary rights of creditors plus those provided by his contract and it is to his contract that he must look for any accurate description of them.

Although the diversity between bond indentures is probably greater than that between capital stock contracts, nevertheless the great bulk of the issues fall into rather standard patterns. In the United States the railroads and public utilities have probably introduced a greater variety of types of bond issues than all other industries together. Yet for the 51 Class I railroads having total funded debt on December 31, 1935, of $9,233,012,424, 75.20 per cent of this funded debt was mortgage bond debt; collateral trust bonds were 8.41 per cent, income bonds, 2.84 per cent, equipment issues, 5.34 per cent, and all others 8.21 per cent.[46] No similar figures appear to be available for public utilities bonds; but here too certain common types seem to predominate, such, for instance, as mortgage bonds among operating companies, and collateral trust bonds and debentures among holding companies. Consequently, although unusual issues exist and are interesting in themselves, they are relatively unimportant among the great mass of bonds outstanding which more or less follow traditional patterns with minor variations in this provision or that to suit the peculiarities of a particular situation.

As we emphasized above, the important thing to remember is that by virtue of their position creditors have certain rights at law and equity by which they may endeavor to bring about the pay-

[46] Stevens, *Railroad Sinking Funds and Funded Debt*, p. 18.

ment of their claims. Over and above these general rights certain others may be added by contract, e.g., the pledge of specific assets, the right to exchange their creditor obligations for shares of stock, etc. And likewise their ordinary rights may be restricted by the contract: as, for example, bondholders being forced to act through the trustee in pursuing their remedies rather than by proceeding directly against the debtor in the ordinary way. But in the last analysis the rights of creditors are those at statute law, common law, and equity, plus or minus any extensions or restrictions by contract.

III. THE ANOMALOUS POSITION OF BONDHOLDERS

Although with the passage of the years corporate bond indentures have become increasingly complex and, if possible, even more solemn and pious, one wonders nevertheless if in the last analysis the realistic view is not to treat the whole formal recital as so much "mumbo-jumbo." This may seem heresy at first blush; but the conviction is buttressed by facts of common knowledge none the less.

If a business enterprise with bonds outstanding is successful it will pay the interest thereon and the principal at maturity. The self-interest of the shareholders acting through the directors is to do so, and the bondholders may rejoice in their foresight or good fortune. The ultimate concern of the bondholders is that they be paid their principal and interest as agreed; the elaborate covenants of the indenture relating to depreciation policies, sinking funds, current assets, etc., are not important in and of themselves to bondholders, but only to the degree that the corporation's behavior in these respects may endanger the payment of bond interest and/or principal.[47] Presumably the corporation might mismanage its affairs

[47] Whether a corporation makes sufficient or insufficient depreciation charges to care for the decline in the value of its depreciable assets is really not of any special interest to bondholders so long as the corporation is able to pay interest and principal as the indenture provides. The provisions about depreciation are of course indirectly relevant: for the computation of profits available for dividends

in any way imaginable; and yet so long as it continued to pay the bondholders the monies stipulated by contract, the latter might remain completely unconcerned. And the only sources from which bond payments can be made are the operations of the business or the liquidation of its assets.

On the other hand, if the corporation is not successful to a degree, regardless of its good intentions, it cannot pay the bond interest. In that event the bondholders ostensibly may take such steps for the payment of their claims as the indenture provides.[48] But it is common knowledge that ordinarily the bondholders are prevented from pursuing their contractual remedies at once and in full. Rather, the corporation will have induced action in equity or bankruptcy to forestall the exercise of creditors' remedies: a receiver will have been appointed in equity or a trustee in bankruptcy and during his incumbency the bondholders are effectively estopped from pursuing their stipulated rights. Moreover, the net result, if not the underlying theory, of so restraining creditors is to allow time in which to prepare a "readjustment" or "reorganization" plan. Now the very essence of any such plan is to settle creditors' claims in a way different from that required by the indenture. To be sure, the bondholders usually dictate the reorganization plan in part; and they may be able to insist upon smaller rather than larger sacrifices; but regardless, the bondholders typically emerge from the shuffle with something less than full payment or less than their full rights and remedies under the bond indenture. In other words, what they finally receive is likely to

without deduction for depreciation and the paying of dividends on this basis may produce the result that the corporation will be unable to refund the bond issue at maturity and hence be unable to pay off the existing bondholders. And this doubtless is the reason why bond indentures contain provisions about depreciation, dividends, etc. It is perhaps unnecessary to remark, however, that the faithful charging of depreciation by no means assures that the bondholders will be paid off in full at maturity. Although the regular accounting charges for depreciation have been made the property may still have little value on an earning power basis. The point to be stressed is that all such indenture provisions are supplementary to bondholders' primary concern with interest and principal payments.

[48] It must be remembered that all the bondholders under any one indenture stand in an identical position and must share equally one with another. The principle of first come first served does not apply to bondholders of the same class. See *supra*, note 35.

be something less than their contract stipulated. It is of course easy to see why that is often unavoidable; but that does not alter the fact situation.

Let us consider the problem from another point of view. Suppose that the bondholders were not prevented by receivership, etc., from pursuing their remedies under the contract. Suppose that, step by step, they relentlessly pursued their rights under the indenture and at law in general. What would be the result in most cases? The corporation's officers have been unable to make the enterprise earn enough to pay the bond interest, consequently it defaults, and the bondholders take the property through foreclosure of their mortgage. If the property has any value that value derives from its ability to earn a net income in its present use or some alternative employment; and its value will be proportionate to its earning power. Assuming honest endeavor by the management, the very fact of default is itself evidence that the property cannot earn an income as great or as regular as that anticipated when the bonds were sold. It follows, therefore, that the mortgaged property is worth something less than the face value of the bonds here and now. The bondholders have two alternatives: they may try to sell the pledged assets as a whole or piecemeal, or may attempt to operate the assets in such a way as to yield the maximum income. In either case, however, if we assume good management prior to default, the bondholders have suffered a loss in value. Very frequently the mortgaged assets are so highly specialized that they are useful, and therefore valuable, only for the particular purpose for which they were constructed, e.g., a railway terminal, an apartment house, an automobile plant, etc. In other words, where a loan is secured by specialized equipment the mortgage lien may add little or nothing to the chance of payment if default occurs. The very fact of default is evidence that the assets are not worth what they cost, and presumably too, not worth the face value of the bonds secured by them. The value of the assets is a derivative from what they can be made to earn and default is *prima facie* evidence that they cannot be made to earn enough to pay the bond interest. Hence, regardless of the estoppel of creditors' remedies by receivership or bankruptcy, the elaborate covenants under bond indentures can by no means assure the bondholders full payment of their obligations. Thus, while it might be fairer if bondholders were allowed to proceed as their contract allows, this would not guarantee them final satisfaction of their claims against the corporation.

Where does all this leave us? The indenture is of little interest to the bondholders if the interest is paid regularly and the principal repaid at maturity. On the other hand, if default occurs, the course of events is typically not according to the solemnities of the indenture; usually the corporation is reorganized which means that the bondholders' claims are often abrogated and scaled down, or the bondholders seize the property only to discover to their sorrow that the property is worth no more than what it can be made to earn, and that on this showing their total claims will have to be scaled down likewise. In short, the indenture is of little moment if there is no default, and it does not determine the course of events or ensure full payment of bondholders' claims if default does occur. At the most, perhaps, it determines the order of priority among creditors; if there are several mortgages on the same assets, those holding a first mortgage will doubtless be in a stronger position than those holding junior mortgages. Thus, perhaps in the final analysis one ought not to regard the added rights of bondholders under an indenture as of any vital significance; they are of no importance prior to default, and after default they do little more than determine relative priorities. On the only occasion on which it might be of some relevance, the strict language of the bond indenture is but rarely honored in full.

IV. SUMMARY

A bondholder is in the first instance a creditor of the corporation and as such he has the ordinary legal and equitable remedies available to creditors to attempt to secure payment of his obligation. His further rights as a bondholder are essentially superadded to those of ordinary creditors and are defined and limited by the agreement between himself, the indenture trustee, and the corporation.

The indenture trustee stands between the corporation and the bondholders in the sense that the obligations of the corporation run to the trustee and the rights of the bondholders against the corporate debtor extend through the trustee. By means of the indenture trustee the corporation is able to deal with all the bondholders under the same indenture as if they were one person. Although the trustee has broad permissive powers his required functions have tended to become mechanical in character so that in effect the net protection afforded bondholders by the trustee is not as great as might be supposed. Bond indentures which define the rights of bondholders are formidable documents by which the debtor often pledges property as security for debt, agrees to establish a sinking fund, agrees to issue further bonds under the indenture only under certain conditions, defines what will constitute default for purposes of accelerating the maturity date of the debt, etc. The designation of bonds of different kinds is often by means of a reference in the title to a particular clause in the indenture which is deemed to be especially important.

Despite the elaborate covenant between the corporation and the bondholders it is none the less true that in case of default the order of events is not according to the procedure defined in the indenture except in a general way. Corporations are frequently reorganized rather than liquidated and in reorganization literal compliance with the terms of the indenture is rare. On the other hand the terms of the indenture are not likely to be of great interest so long as there is no default. The position of bondholders is therefore somewhat anomalous.

REFERENCES: CHAPTER V

BURTCHETT, F. F.—*Corporation Finance*, Chs. 7-12.
DEWING, A. S.—*Corporation Securities*, Chs. 6-8, 10.
DEWING, A. S.—*Financial Policy*, Chs. 4, 5.
FIELD, K.—*Corporation Finance*, Chs. 6-9.
GERSTENBERG, C. W.—*Financial Organization and Management*, Chs. 10-13, 17.

GRAHAM, B., and DODD, D. L.—*Security Analysis*, New York and London: McGraw-Hill, 1934, Chs. 18, 19.
HOAGLAND, H. E.—*Corporation Finance*, Chs. 8-13.

———

FINNEY, D.—*Finding Capital for Business*, London, 1931.
JAMISON, C. L.—"Trading on the Equity by Industrial Companies," *Michigan Business Studies*, Vol. 6.
POSNER, L. S.—"Liability of the Trustee under the Corporate Indenture," *Harvard Law Review*, Vol. 42.
SHAFFNER, F. I.—*The Problem of Investment*, New York, 1936, Book III.
WALSH, W. F.—"Development of the Title and Lien Theories of Mortgages," *New York University Law Quarterly*, Vol. 9.

Part Two

ECONOMIC ASPECTS OF CORPORATE ENTERPRISE

Chapter VI

NOTES ON THE ECONOMIC THEORY
OF PROMOTION

*I. Equilibrium Analysis and the Promotion of New Enterprises.
II. The Proposed Enterprise and the Probable Yield on Investment.
III. Aggregate Investment and Working Capital Needs. IV. The
Acquisition of Capital and the Financial Plan. V. Summary.*

The promotion of new business enterprises into existence is an everyday occurrence which has often been described from various points of view. The order of treatment adopted here, however, will deviate from the familiar types of discussion in certain respects. In the main we shall endeavor to present a treatment of the problem of promotion that is essentially general in its application to business enterprises of all kinds. Although each instance of the promotion of a new enterprise raises certain special difficulties peculiar to itself, the degree of similarity between the problems presented from one case to another is sufficiently great to warrant certain generalizations concerning them.

Our first task will be to describe, if we can, the kind of economic situation that gives rise to the inception of new enterprises. In its broader economic aspects the promotion of a new enterprise is essentially a problem in capital investment and the redistribution of economic resources, e.g., land and persons, between employments. Consequently we need to examine briefly the kind of occasion that gives rise to an opportunity for a new enterprise to come into existence. We pass then to a discussion of the essential problems raised in the investigation of the probable net returns to be had from the investment of capital in the opportunity that the new enterprise proposes to exploit. This will carry us into an analysis of cost factors and those having to do with the probable receipts from sales of the product. Granted that the investment opportunity proves on investigation to be promising, there remain the problems of determining what the aggregate investment ought to be, including an allowance for working capital needs. Finally, the needed liquid funds will have to be raised by offering security contracts for sale in the capital market; and here again decisions of some importance will have to be made.

I. EQUILIBRIUM ANALYSIS AND THE PROMOTION OF NEW ENTERPRISES

General works on economic theory usually have little to say on the matter of the promotion of new enterprises. The general treatises at the formal level of analysis have concentrated their attention upon movements toward equilibrium and the nature of different kinds of equilibria when attained. An equilibrium adjustment to any given set of economic facts, which are taken as "data," consists in such a combination of prices, rates of output, rates of purchase, earnings of the factors of production, distribution of the agents of production between employments, etc., that no further adjustments therein are profitable so long as the underlying data remain unchanged. The aim, more or less, has been to indicate how far and in what directions changes in the prices of products and factors and their utilization will have to occur before they will come to an end in the sense that mutually consistent adjustments have been achieved. Thus, with respect to a particular industry, we commonly say that an equilibrium adjustment exists when the earnings of the factors of production are at such a level that there is no inducement for factors to shift out of, or into, the industry from other employments. Traditionally the discussion of equilibrium has distinguished between short-run adjustments and long-run adjustments.[1] Although the differentiation between short-run and long-run equilibrium is shadowy when stated in general terms, it assumes more definiteness when applied to a specific problem. So, for example, we often say that an industry is in

[1] See, for instance, Marshall, Alfred, *Principles of Economics*, 8th ed., London (Macmillan), 1920, Book V, chs. iii-v.

short-run equilibrium where the enterprises already established within it, and therefore committed to a given *scale* of production, have no incentive either to contract or expand their rates of utilization of fixed plant.[2] On the other hand, it is quite clear that such a state of affairs might exist and yet the industry not be in long-run equilibrium: despite the existence of a short-run equilibrium adjustment already established, enterprises might have an incentive to increase their scale of operations and there might be an inducement for new firms to enter that industry.

The significance of the foregoing for the problem of the promotion of new enterprises is simply that the bringing into existence of new enterprises betokens the existence of a disequilibrium situation which the influx of new firms will tend to remove.[3] The disequilibrium may be no more than that the earnings of established enterprises in a particular industry are known (or believed) to be higher than in alternative employments for capital of equivalent risks. The larger earnings may be the resultant of any number of causes: an alteration in consumers' tastes, a technological improvement, the discovery of a new source of raw material supply, an increase in population or a shift in its distribution, etc. In any case, already existing firms are securing returns such as to invite the establishment of new enterprises.[4]

---

[2] The distinction between *scale* of production and the *rate of utilization* from any given scale is dealt with in sec. II of the present chapter.

[3] There is an alternative possibility on theoretical grounds. Instead of the promotion of new enterprises being evidence of a disequilibrium situation calling for a redistribution of economic resources between alternative uses, it may be nothing more, under some circumstances, than evidence that certain persons hold demonstrably false expectations as to how large the returns from capital investment in the proposed venture are likely to prove. Especially in the retail trade, where the entry of new firms requires very little investment, it seems to be true that persons are very prone to hold absurdly optimistic views concerning the returns available to new enterprises. The perennial crop of "Dress Shoppes," "Book Nooks," etc., that "waste their sweetness on the desert air" for a few short months before passing out of existence seems to be explainable primarily on these grounds.

[4] It might be asked why the already existing enterprises do not merely expand their scale of operations and thus preclude the necessity of new firms. To some extent this occurs of course. But it is conceivable that each firm already in the industry would have no incentive to change either its volume or scale of production, thus leaving room for new enterprises to enter with profit. Such a state of affairs would exist if each enterprise were maximizing profits (i.e., marginal cost equaled marginal revenue), so that to increase the scale of production would mean a reduction and not an increase in the individual net profits of the established enterprises, i.e., the diseconomies of scale exceeded the economies. All this

A new firm may of course enter an industry even though established firms using generally known production methods are not making unusual profits. In this case the new firm proposes to employ new methods, a new combination of the agents of production, which others will not be able to adopt immediately; if the new combination is superior, the new enterprise will be able to secure very favorable returns. It was probably not true for example that the profits in retailing food products were unusually high at the time chain food stores of the self-service type were first introduced. Such a new technique of making the product or rendering the service may or may not be protected by a patent: yet even though unprotected by legally enforceable monopoly rights the new concern may none the less acquire an important quasi-monopoly position by being the first to employ the new methods. From one point of view, it might be argued that the very promotion of a new enterprise suggests that the proposed concern is believed to possess some element of monopoly unavailable to enterprises in general.[5] This may be no more than the possession of some special information, e.g., that the market undervalues the ability of the manager, or that the true relation between

might be true and yet the existing firms be securing larger net earnings per unit of capital investment than available elsewhere. Hence the appropriate adjustment is the entry of more enterprises. In the real world, perhaps, it is usually true that the response to superior earnings is both an expansion of existing firms and the entry of new concerns.

[5] A little reflection will indicate that the problem of promotion in a form at all analogous to that which it assumes in the real world cannot be formulated under the rigid and simplifying assumptions of pure competition and perfect knowledge. The abandonment of these assumptions is a prerequisite to any meaningful discussion of the promotion problem. For if pure competition and perfect knowledge prevailed then the productivity and earnings of all factors of production at the margin would be equal in all employments, while the rewards to entrepreneurship would be proportional to efficiency. Under the circumstances no capital investment could secure more than the current rate of interest, and no entrepreneur could expect a larger reward from self-employment than from working for someone else. Furthermore, under these twin assumptions (pure competition and perfect knowledge) there is no reason to suppose that enterprises would be necessary at all since all the organization of production could be carried out directly through the price system. (See Chapter II.)

Pure competition without perfect knowledge would however permit situations in which new enterprises could be brought into existence. But it is more useful to admit the possibility of monopolistic or imperfect competition as well. For many important types of promotions are dependent upon individual differences between enterprises of a quasi-monopolistic sort.

costs and receipts is not that generally supposed, but in any case some special conjuncture which gives promise of a rate of return to capital investment, in excess of, or certainly not less than, the going rate of interest. For if the new enterprise is to secure free capital in the competitive market it must promise a net return at least equal to the current rate of interest. Unless possessors of free funds believe the yield on capital to be at least this large they will be unwilling to purchase the security contracts or otherwise provide the capital which the enterprise will need to come into existence. In other words, it is not sufficient that the return to capital be positive; it must be at least equal to the rate of interest. Strictly speaking, however, this generalization applies only to those new enterprises which propose to appeal to the competitive market for free capital. For many small enterprises annually brought into existence this may not be true.[6]

II. THE PROPOSED ENTERPRISE AND THE PROBABLE YIELD ON INVESTMENT

1. The problem of costs in the proposed enterprise: a. cost variations related to volume of production with scale given. b. alternative combinations of the factors of production and the economies of scale. c. uncertainty factors and the choice of the scale of production. d. summary. 2. The problem of gross income: price and demand for the product: a. factors affecting probable demand. b. summary. 3. The promoter.

If any proposed new enterprise is to warrant actual promotion and realization it can only be because the prospective returns to

[6] Observation suggests that many small firms are organized even though the prospective return upon capital is less than the rate of interest. Not infrequently a man will form a "business of his own," using his own capital when the prospective return to capital exclusive of any imputed return for his own services is very small or negligible. This would seem to be true of the ebb and flow of small retail enterprises. The full explanation of this phenomenon is not easy, although it seems probable that blind optimism and a strong desire for independence play a large part. Seemingly many persons will pay a high price for the privilege of being "their own boss," while many others grossly overestimate their own ability to manage an enterprise skillfully and profitably. In any case any rational appraisal of the probable returns to capital would seem to suggest the manifest un-

capital are in excess of the going rate of interest. What returns to capital are likely to be had from a particular investment opportunity, however, will not be immediately obvious. The belief that there is room for a new enterprise which will yield a return to capital higher than the rate of interest is only the first step; before the enterprise comes into existence it is usually necessary to carry out a rather thorough "investigation" in order to determine more precisely what returns may be expected from the proposed venture. In the parlance of corporation finance an "investigation" must necessarily be undertaken.

An investigation of the probable returns to capital to be invested in a particular business enterprise is simply an attempt to determine the probable net income stream of the proposed concern. And it is also axiomatic that net income is a function of two factors: costs and gross receipts from the sale of the product or service. Thus the nature of any investigation of the feasibility of promoting any proposed enterprise resolves into an examination of the probable costs and the probable receipts.

1. *The problem of costs in the proposed enterprise.* Unless the circumstances are most unusual it is quite unlikely that the per unit costs of production of the proposed product or service will be constant and invariable regardless of the volume (or rate) of output or the scale of production. And this distinction between alternative scales of production and the volume of output from a *given* scale needs to be made precise. The term "scale of production" refers to the particular aggregate of fixed assets with which the enterprise operates and that is not subject to alteration in the short period. In essence scale of production has reference to that particular combination of certain of the factors of production, e.g., land, specialized capital goods, management, and a skeleton labor force, to which are applied varying amounts of labor, materials, etc., to produce varying quantities of the finished product as a rate of output. From another point of view, the scale of production is that combination of the factors which is unalterable over

wisdom of bringing into existence a large proportion of the many small concerns which are formed yearly. The practice will undoubtedly continue, however. See also note 3, *supra.*

a given time period and whose costs cannot be avoided or reduced.[7]
For example, a cotton textile manufacturing concern has a certain
complement of machinery and equipment housed within buildings
of a given size which it can use more or less intensively in the
production of cotton fabrics by varying the number of laborers
employed and the quantity of yarns and other materials used.
We say that it is a textile concern of a certain *scale*, and that other
textile concerns on either a larger or smaller scale are known to
exist. Or again, we say that this hospital is a 100-bed hospital and
that one a 300-bed hospital, meaning that this is the scale to which
it is now committed. The scale of production then is the combination of the factors of production to which the enterprise is
bound in the short period. We must say "in the short period"
because over a succession of short periods it is possible for the
scale to be changed. Our textile concern can build a new plant,
install much new machinery; our hospital can add a new wing or
another story to the building, so that it is no longer a 100-bed
hospital.[8]

By the phrase "rate of output" or "volume of production" where
the scale as above defined is assumed to be given, we mean quite

[7] It might be thought better to define "scale of production" in terms of the
capacity output of fixed factors. But a little reflection will suggest that "capacity"
is a highly flexible notion; does it mean the *maximum* output which the plant is
capable of producing under any circumstances, or does it mean that rate of output at which average total costs are minimized, or does it mean something between
these two possibilities, and if so where? For these reasons it seems better not to
define scale of production in terms of capacity. The notion "scale of production"
applied to the municipal subway system in New York City, for instance, certainly
has meaning even though we could not say what its capacity is in terms of the
fixed factors.

[8] Just what factors of production, and hence what cost items, fall within this
category is clearly determined by the length of the time period under consideration. If we take a *very* short period of time, say, an hour or a day, then the enterprise is "committed" in all sorts of directions from which it cannot retract.
On the other hand, if we think in terms of several months the number of commitments is fewer but most of the machinery, the buildings, office equipment,
plant layout, etc., are still unalterable. And for still longer time periods the degree
to which the enterprise is bound to a given scale becomes less and less.

In discussing problems of this kind it is usual to postulate some time period
during which it is impossible for the enterprise to alter the particular combination of certain of the factors of production. This then becomes the scale of production to which the enterprise is assumed to be committed. There is no intention to suggest that the scale of production is completely unalterable regardless
of how long a time period is allowed to elapse.

a different thing. Here we refer to the fact that it is possible to use the fixed factors of production to which the enterprise is committed with varying intensities. The cotton textile company may vary its output from, say, zero yards a day to 11,000 yards a day by hiring more people and using more materials, power, light, supplies, etc. The hospital may be a 100-bed hospital, but at one time it can be only half occupied and at another, because of an epidemic, it may be crowded beyond the point of optimum efficiency. By using the fixed factors with varying degrees of intensity the flow of product can be raised or lowered. This is what we mean by volume of production or rate of output.

a. *Cost variations related to volume of production with scale given.* With any *given* scale of production and with *given* prices of input factors the per unit cost of salable product will average more or less according as the enterprise in question is operated farther from or closer to capacity. The explanation of this phenomenon lies largely in two directions. In the first place, if all costs of production are included, there are certain items which are more or less invariable in their aggregate amount with different volumes of output. As a consequence, these items of cost will be smaller per unit the larger the output.[9] But the behavior of average total cost will depend upon the behavior of average variable costs over different volumes of output, since total average cost at any point is simply the sum of average fixed cost and average variable cost at that volume. In other words, it is a question of the rate of decline of average fixed costs per unit of output in comparison to the rate of decrease or increase in average variable costs. What assumptions are appropriate with reference to variations of average variable costs? Three possibilities are open: as an aggregate, variable costs may increase less than proportionately, proportionately, or more than proportionately to the increase in output. If the possible range in the variation of output is from zero to N units per time period (where N is the absolute maximum irrespective of how many units of the variable factors are applied), then it seems reasonable to suppose that average variable cost will at first decline and then subsequently increase. In other words, at

[9] A curve of average fixed cost at different volumes of output will be a rectangular hyperbola.

first the output will increase more than proportionately to the increase in aggregate variable costs, and later less than proportionately. This is no more than reasonable. Any enterprise is technically designed to be operated at maximum efficiency at some particular volume of output per time period. At any different rate of output below or above this the enterprise will operate at reduced efficiency. The ideal or optimum volume of output is that at which the output per unit of cost is a maximum, i.e., the point of least average (total) cost. Beyond this point average total cost is likely to increase (perhaps rapidly) because of overcrowding within the plant, increased spoilage of materials, overtime wage rates, inability of the management to be equally effective, etc.[10]

The significance of the above in the investigation of the feasibility of a new enterprise is simply that once any given scale of production has been adopted, average total costs of production will be a function of output. It is quite inappropriate to assume as is sometimes done that costs per unit will be independent of the amount produced, although the latter, of course, will have to be related to the amount sold.

b. *Alternative combinations of the factors of production and the economies of scale.* For an enterprise which is about to come into existence there is no reason to suppose that only one scale of production is possible. Except in a few very unusual cases it is possible to produce any desired salable commodity or service by more than one method. That is, both practically and theoretically the same end result can be achieved by adopting different combinations of the factors of production. For instance, one can keep automobile trucking equipment in good working order by

[10] Some recent statistical studies seem to indicate that the average variable cost curve is well-nigh horizontal over a considerable range of variation in the rate of output. This means, of course, that the marginal cost curve would be nearly horizontal too. If this statistical evidence is reliable and typical, as some are inclined to hold, it would be very significant both practically and theoretically. However, it is too early to generalize about such matters in the author's opinion even though some instances do seem to exist. It is worth pointing out, however, that on the theoretical side, a strictly horizontal average variable cost curve would mean, under conditions of pure competition, that the output of the individual firm is undefinable: one could not postulate how much a given wheat farmer would plan to produce even though the price of wheat and the prices of input factors were given. See J. T. Dunlop, "Price Flexibility and the Degree of Monopoly," *Quarterly Journal of Economics*, August, 1939, pp. 522-534.

having the repair work done in one's own shops or by hiring a non-affiliated garage to do the job. One can manufacture automobiles by doing certain necessary operations by hand methods or by machine methods. In short, one can use relatively few capital goods and relatively much labor as factors of production in the fabrication of a particular commodity, or alternatively, one can use relatively little labor and many more capital instruments; the possibilities of variation are often considerable.

This problem of the different possible combinations of the factors of production from which the proposed new enterprise must select may be conceived of in either of two ways: from the point of view of efficiency, a technological concept, or from the point of view of economy. Although both yield identical results when applied to any given problem it is useful to recognize that they are but two aspects of the same thing. From the standpoint of efficiency one asks: What combination of the factors of production of various kinds will give the maximum output of salable product per dollar of investment in the proposed enterprise; in other words, what scale of production is most efficient? From the point of view of economy, one asks: What scale of production, what combination of the agents of production, will give the minimum average total cost of production per unit of output? But the two answers must necessarily indicate the same scale of production as the optimum. For, if we say a particular combination will give the maximum output of salable product per unit of investment, a little reflection will reveal that that is the same thing as saying that each unit of product is being produced at a minimum cost. Sometimes one way of looking at the problem is more convenient than the other; but there is really only one problem, not two.

For many small enterprises about to be promoted into existence the amount of money capital available for investment reaches a definite upper limit at a relatively small figure. The maximum sum which it is possible to raise to inaugurate the enterprise is often small because there is no possibility of selling security contracts to investors through the organized capital market. Investment bankers will not undertake to underwrite the small corporation's offerings at any reasonable fee in relation to the amount of capital to be raised and as a consequence the funds must be raised from relatives, friends, business associates, supply houses, and the like. In cases of this sort the problem of selecting the scale of production resolves itself into one of determining what scale of production is most efficient within the limits of the amount of capital available.[11]

We have yet to inquire, however, how it is that average costs of production should be different for different scales of production when the different scales are compared at their optimum rates or volume of production. As we have already shown, the optimum rate of production for any given scale is that at which average total costs of production are a minimum.

If all the factors of production were divisible into infinitely small particles, like grains of sand for instance, and were also available in perfectly elastic supply, then there would be no reason for large enterprises to have lower average costs (when operating at their optimum volume) than small ones. But in fact the agents of production are not infinitely divisible; although this difficulty is more applicable to some than to others. Because of the practical indivisibility of hired human services below certain limits their costs do not increase proportionately with the increase in

[11] Where, however, there is an attempt to raise capital by the sale of security contracts the efforts are likely to be abortive. A recent writer, now Director of Research of the Securities and Exchange Commission but formerly economist with a large investment banking house, comments: "Apparently, it is difficult to raise funds for these companies, at least in part, because of the absence of banking assistance. Studies of the Commission have indicated the following facts with reference to these promotional ventures: (a) there is a general absence of any firm banking commitment, with only about one out of every twenty issues having firm underwriting; (b) there is apparent inability thoroughly to distribute these securities, since, of about 45% of the total amount and 40% of the total number of issues for which registration under the Securities Act was effective, not one share of stock nor one bond was sold within the year following the effective date of the registration statement, and, on the average for all issues, less than 20% of the amount effectively registered was actually sold within this period (about 85% of the total sales being made within the first six months, after the effective date); (c) the investor pays a disproportionate cost for this investment in such companies because of the watering of stock by issues to promoters, the latter receiving on the average, about ¾ of the equity securities for less than one-quarter of the total investment, or about ten times as much as the public for an equal dollar of investment; (d) the expenses of distribution are high, averaging about 10% to 15% of the amount contributed by all investors." Gourrich, Paul P., "Investment Banking Methods Prior to and Since the Securities Act of 1933," *Law and Contemporary Problems*, Vol. IV (1937), No. 1, pp. 53-54, note.

output possible with a larger scale. For example, to take an absurdly simple case, within certain limits a night watchman can inspect plants of different sizes with roughly the same effort, and certainly the cost of watchman's services do not increase proportionately with the size of plant. Similarly with certain administrative costs—buying, selling, supervising, etc.—the increase in cost is less than proportionate to the increase in output possible with a larger scale.[12] More important perhaps than this "lumpiness" of labor increments is the lack of complete divisibility of specific capital goods. In essence, however, this is not entirely, or perhaps even principally, a matter of physical impossibility. The difficulty is essentially that the cost of capital goods does not decrease proportionately to the reduction in their work capacity. It is possible to make many machines in progressively smaller and smaller sizes, but their purchase price does not decrease in proportion to their ability to render useful services. The cost of manufacturing electric generators in larger and larger sizes, for example, rises much less than the increase in their generating capacity. And there are numerous instances of the same phenomenon. If there are many capital goods used in a particular productive process of which this is true, an obvious advantage accrues from having the scale of operations large enough to make use of capital goods in the larger sizes.[13]

The other advantages of larger scale arise essentially from two sources: First, the possibility of a greater degree of specialization of both men and equipment within the larger scale. These are

[12] This is partly the reason why small issues of securities cannot be handled by investment banking houses. The costs which the investment banker must undergo —investigation, negotiation, etc.—do not decrease proportionately with reduction in the size of the issue. If a $10,000,000 issue can be handled profitably with a three point "spread" between buying price and selling price, a $100,000 issue may well require an eight point margin, even assuming the risks are identical in the two issues. See previous note.
[13] Professor Florence in an illuminating discussion of these matters argues that the economies of larger scale rest essentially on three principles of efficiency: (1) the principle of bulk transactions, which is really the idea that certain costs as an aggregate increase less than proportionately to the increase in output (see text above); (2) the principle of massed reserves: ". . . the greater the number of items involved the more likely are deviations in their amounts to cancel out and to leave the actual result nearer to the expected result." (Professor F. H. Knight also makes much of this point as an explanation of large scale enterprise even

familiar and have often been recounted from Adam Smith's day onwards. They need no further comment. Second, is the tendency of an enterprise as it operates on a larger scale of production *relative to other enterprises in the same industry* to attain a larger degree of monopoly power both with respect to things it buys and products it sells. In the degree that being relatively large permits the firm to exert a favorable influence upon the prices of products it buys from others or the prices at which its immediate competitors offer their wares for sale, there is an advantage in large scale operations.

One or two further observations concerning the advantages of larger scale may not be out of place. There seems no reason to suppose that the advantages and lower costs of larger scale proceed gradually and without interruption as the scale of the enterprise is increased.[14] That is, it seems more likely there is typically more than one optimum size of enterprise in most industries. Just how many optimum sizes there are likely to be will depend largely upon technological factors and the nature of competition in the particular industry. But it does seem probable that in many industries there are "in-between" sized firms neither small enough to achieve the greater flexibility of quite small firms nor large enough to achieve the full advantages of large scale operations.

It is perhaps unnecessary to add that the advantages of larger scale leading to lower average unit costs do not continue indefinitely as the scale of operations is increased. It has been often observed that after a point the increasing diseconomies of larger scale

where there are no economies of greater specialization. See his *Risk, Uncertainty and Profit*, pp. 254-5.) (3) the principle of multiples: which is simply the idea that a certain size is essential to make full use of several different kinds of specialization which are capable of being combined in one productive process. See Florence, P. S., *The Logic of Industrial Organization*, London (Kegan Paul), 1933, Ch. I, but especially, pp. 16-20.

[14] As Mr. E. A. G. Robinson has pointed out, the optimum scale of operations for the enterprise may not be identical with the optimum for each of its branches considered individually. The best size from the point of view of physical production may be other than the best size for maximum marketing efficiency. When therefore we speak of the optimum scale we must be understood to mean that scale which will give maximum net returns through time in the given situation when all factors are considered. This might mean a different scale, for instance, than if production costs were nil and marketing costs alone considered. See his *Structure of Competitive Industry*, New York (Harcourt, Brace), 1932.

more than offset the economies in other directions. In large measure these diseconomies appear in the increasing inability of the management to maintain an effective control over the various parts of the organization, with the result that there is a decline in efficiency and a rise in unit costs. Furthermore the scale of operations at which these diseconomies begin to assume significant proportions is perhaps somewhat smaller than is commonly supposed. If it were not for the quasi-monopolistic advantages which tend to accompany increasing size it seems likely that the technically optimum size of firm in most industries would be considerably smaller than it actually seems to be.

c. *Uncertainty factors and the choice of the scale of production.* In considering the effect of uncertainty upon the appropriate combination of the factors of production in the proposed enterprise, we may conveniently distinguish between two types of uncertainty: first, uncertainty with reference to the kind of product which the enterprise is likely to be producing in the future; and second, uncertainty with reference to the degree to which the demand for the given product of the firm will fluctuate through time, because of changes in consumers' preferences, variations in their incomes, etc.[15] The first influences the appropriate combination of the factors by enhancing the desirability of using relatively more agents of a non-specific sort. If the probability is that the enterprise will find it necessary to alter its product frequently then it will be clearly inadvisable to use highly specific capital goods of a durable nature. Rather, it will pay to employ a combination of the factors using mostly non-specific capital goods and considerable labor. And to this extent the optimum-sized scale of production is likely to be small. It is noteworthy, for example, that in industries like the women's garment trade, novelties of various kinds, and the like, where style changes and product differentiation are common and frequent, the combination of the factors is one involving relatively few fixed capital instruments, and those non-specific (e.g., sewing machines), and a great deal of labor.

---

[15] Cyclical changes could also affect the cost situation. To some extent the advantages of owning rather than renting certain agents of production on short term are simply that the firm knows what its costs for certain factors will be over relatively long periods.

The contrast with electric power companies or oil refining companies in this respect is very marked. In the latter style changes are negligible and hence large durable capital goods of a high degree of specificity are widely used. Furthermore, it may be true that the industry which the proposed enterprise intends to enter is one in which technological improvements are going ahead very rapidly so that presently available machinery is soon rendered obsolete. In that instance a new firm will be unwise to select a combination of the factors of production using much durable and costly capital equipment. Over the last decade this seems to have been true in certain industries, for example, aeroplane manufacturing.

The influence of the trade cycle upon the optimum size of firm is not altogether clear. Insofar as different scales of production mean different proportions of capital and labor employed in the process one observation seems relevant: once capital takes the form of fixed capital instruments, it is difficult to disinvest it, at least in the short period, should slack times or business depression ensue. And to that extent capital costs must be borne regardless of the volume of operations. Labor costs, wages, are not of this character, however. The enterprise hires, i.e., rents, labor under short-term contract, and when the demand for the product drops off the enterprise tends to avoid this cost by lowering wages or discharging the employees in whole or in part. While, to be sure, the firm will be forced to contribute something to the support of the unemployed, under the more usual arrangements, it will not contribute an amount equal to the reduction in its own wage bill. Thus, if there were no business cycles, no slack periods, the ideal (most economical) combination of the factors might be one involving a relatively large proportion of fixed capital equipment and relatively little labor. Yet where one must expect slumps, during which all firms in the industry will experience less than capacity operations, such a combination may be uneconomical. Over a period which includes both prosperity and depression the most suitable factorial combination may be one embracing relatively more labor and relatively fewer fixed capital instruments simply because the costs of labor need not be borne by the firm during the slump;

they can be in large part passed back to the community as a whole.[16]

d. *Summary*. We have been suggesting in the foregoing that before any new enterprise is brought into existence there should be a reasonable presumption that the rate of return to capital will exceed the rate of interest. While the rate of interest is known, an investigation is necessary to determine the probable yield to capital in the contemplated use. Since net income will be a function of gross income and costs, such an investigation necessarily means an investigation of probable costs and probable receipts from the sale of the product. With respect to costs we have sought to indicate that for any given scale of production per unit costs will vary with the degree of utilization, tending to decline to a minimum representing the most efficient volume of operations for the particular scale. Also, however, we have emphasized the economies and diseconomies of large scale production or that all scales of production when operated with maximum efficiency do not yield identical average costs per unit of output. Finally, in any estimate of the probable production costs it is essential to bear in mind that the enterprise will be operating in an uncertain world characterized by flux and change and that certain commitments in the form of fixed capital instruments are inherently inflexible in the face of changed conditions and their costs must be borne. Hence the optimum scale and form of production will tend to be partially determined by a consideration of such factors. It is matters of this kind, then, that must necessarily be reckoned with in determining what costs of production the firm is likely to incur in its proposed venture.

Yet costs are only one element in the determination of net income and therefore the net return to capital. The other determinant is gross income from the sale of the product and to this we must now turn.

[16] This might seem to contradict what was said earlier to the effect that the enterprise as such owns no labor but only capital. The contradiction, however, is only apparent. For what we mean here is that a relatively larger amount of the total capital will consist of circulating or working capital necessary to hire laborers, etc., and relatively less committed to capital goods with a high degree of specificity.

2. *The problem of gross income: price and demand for the product.* (a) *Factors affecting probable demand.* Under the assumption of atomistic perfect competition the demand curve for the product of the individual firm is assumed to be infinitely elastic; that is, at the ruling price determined by the whole demand and supply situation, the single firm can sell as many units as it can produce without affecting the price. We have already indicated that this is generally not the applicable assumption to make in investigating the feasibility of a new business enterprise.[17] Monopolistic competition is more in accord with the typical case. As a consequence, the investigation of the probable income from the sale of the product is in essence an attempt to determine, or estimate as closely as possible, the nature of the demand curve for the product of the proposed new firm. And, as for any demand curve, it is a question of the functional relationship between the price and the amount sold. Clearly there is no easy answer to this problem. In recent years "market surveys," sampling, and other ingenious devices have been tried with varying degrees of success in an attempt to determine as accurately as possible the probable demand for new products about to be introduced. These techniques are too intricate to be described here but a few general observations are in order.[18]

Many new enterprises are brought into existence each year which propose to do no more than produce commodities which are already being produced by existing firms. In this instance the new company proposes to encroach upon the business of existing firms by offering a slightly better product, providing better service, or utilizing useful business connections obtained in various

---

[17] Unless of course the proposed enterprise intends to produce one of the staple commodities. Here the problem becomes that of attempting to estimate the probable course of the market price of the product through future time. That is, the individual producer can afford to assume that he will be able to sell the whole of his output at the ruling price. But what that price will be is indeterminate, and the individual considering entering the field must necessarily entertain some expectations about its probable course.

[18] See, however, Smith, G. C., *An Outline for Market Surveys*, St. Louis, Mo. (The Industrial Club of St. Louis), 1930, for a detailed account of the nature of these investigations. It seems to be true that more and more of these investigations of the probable demand for new products are being undertaken by firms specializing in this kind of work.

ways.[19] Not infrequently the demand for the product which the new concern proposes to offer will be a derived demand, and therefore dependent upon the demand for some final product already upon the market. For example, the demand for a new machine for retreading used automobile tires will clearly be dependent upon the demand for retreaded tires. If, of course, the new machine will substantially reduce the cost of production of the final product and hence its price, it will be quite inappropriate to assume that the current demand for the final product will not increase. In other cases the price of the product will necessarily be dictated rather strictly by substitute products already on the market. In order to sell any retreaded automobile tires one would have to market them for a price less than that of new tires. Not uncommonly the price may be almost wholly prescribed by custom, as for instance, a new magazine or newspaper.[20] For many new enterprises that propose to offer a new type of capital good the demand curve is very likely to be discontinuous. Instead of small gradations in the number of units sold as the price is varied the movement in probable sales may be by fits and starts. Possibly between, say, a price of \$1,000 and a price of \$1,010 there may be no perceptible change in the quantity sold whatsoever. While if the new machine is markedly superior to existing machines doing the same operation, then it may be true that almost as many will be sold at \$1,400 as at \$1,000.

Whatever special characteristics of the demand for the product

[19] As, for example, when a person decides to branch out for himself, having first established connections and obtained a knowledge of the trade as an employee of some other firm.

[20] Recently in the United States there has been a veritable flood of new magazines. One of them is rather interesting as a study in promotion. Before it was decided to go ahead with the venture at all an attempt was made to assure a certain minimum circulation by the sale of pre-publication subscriptions at a favorable price, i.e., less than the post-publication price. Upon the basis of the investigation it seemed safe to assume a probable demand of 250,000 per week, and accordingly presses were leased, and the enterprise launched. It developed that the actual demand was much greater, and, according to the information available, the necessity of operating the presses, etc., at a much greater intensity than was originally contemplated, caused costs per unit to rise sharply. The result has been substantial losses even though the demand for the product far exceeded expectations. But to increase plant capacity requires time, in this case apparently some many months. The company reports that it soon hopes to increase the scale of operations sufficiently to reduce costs and ultimately make a profit.

of the proposed enterprise are discoverable by study and investigation, it must always be kept in mind that the purpose in studying it is to ascertain, so far as possible, what gross income the new enterprise can expect to obtain. The firm's gross income will be simply the arithmetical product of the number of units sold multiplied by the price received for them.

It is perhaps necessary to add a word on the problem of estimating the probable gross income for that ever-growing group of enterprises whose prices and products are subject to regulation by public authority. In the United States such enterprises are commonly referred to as public utilities. Economically speaking, the characteristically important thing about public utilities is their ability to charge discriminatory prices for their products.[21] In other words, an enterprise of this sort is in reality confronted with the problem of estimating the demand curve for its product in several different markets which it is itself in a position to create. In these several markets the prices which the enterprise will be allowed to charge are fixed within rather definite limits by public authority, at least in the United States. Furthermore, in part because of a local monopoly and an absence in most instances of suitable substitute products, it is apparently somewhat easier to determine in advance the probable unit sales in the respective markets. As a consequence gross income may be estimated more accurately than in non-public utility enterprises.

While one can estimate the probable production costs with some degree of accuracy it must be admitted that estimates of the probable demand curve for the product, and its variations through time, are subject to a wide margin of error. The reason is that the factors which can affect the demand curve for any particular product are more various and more unpredictable than the changes affecting costs. Theoretically, the demand for the product of a particular enterprise will be affected in a greater or lesser degree by a change anywhere in the economic system. Each firm is cer-

[21] See Batson, H. E., "The Economic Concept of a Public Utility," *Economica*, November, 1933. Mr. Batson discusses at some length the reasons why public utilities are more likely to wish, and to be able, to charge discriminatory prices. He would not allege that this desire to charge discriminatory prices is only to be found in public utilities, but that elsewhere it is usually overbalanced by other tendencies.

tain to be affected by product changes, price changes, changes in sales effort, etc., on the part of its immediate competitors. But broader changes affecting the whole industry may likewise occur; and the plight of the individual firm is not rendered more comfortable by the knowledge that its competitors are similarly chafed. Finally, changes in the volume of business activity as a whole through time, the cycle phenomenon, impinge upon different industries and different firms within each industry with unequal force.[22] The demand for the product of an individual firm, therefore, is subject to a variety of influences from many directions. Consequently, it is not surprising that efforts to predict its probable amount and duration for a new enterprise are enormously difficult at best. Finally, as contrasted with costs, the rapidity with which changes may occur is many times greater. In fact from one point of view, the very essence of the problem of business fluctuations as it impinges upon the individual firm is the unequal rates of change that occur between demand factors and supply factors, i.e., between receipts and costs. Whereas sales can drop off sharply almost overnight, costs cannot be similarly pared on short notice. Consequently losses are incurred.

b. *Summary.* The above discussion has endeavored to make the point that the investigation of the feasibility of a new enterprise is essentially an attempt to determine the probable gross income by means of a thorough study of probable costs of production and probable gross income from the sale of the product. In any real world instance of promotion the two parts of the investigation are of course intimately connected: any discussion of the probable costs with different scales of output must of necessity be related to the probable demand for the product at varying prices. There would be no sense or logic in having an enterprise large enough to take full advantage of the economies of large scale operations if the demand for the product is such that it would be impossible to sell anything approaching that number at a correspondingly low price. Even though large scale production methods are often capable of reducing costs substantially, it is also true that the

[22] See Mills, F. C., "Changes in Prices, Manufacturing Costs and Industrial Productivity, 1929-1934," *National Bureau of Economic Research,* Bulletin no. 53, December 22, 1934.

number of units sold at the reduced price may be much less than that necessary to permit the profitable adoption of those methods. Sales increase with a reduction in price, but not by a sufficient amount. Consequently the cost studies and the gross income studies must be closely integrated with one another.

In conclusion a word must be said in answer to an objection which has no doubt been present in the reader's mind through the last several pages: Do business men in fact proceed in this manner? To some extent it must be admitted that general observation rather prompts a negative answer. Nevertheless the logic of the method of investigation outlined above would perhaps be admitted. Certainly business men do consider proposed ventures on the basis of their prospective profit possibilities, and this necessarily means investigation of probable costs and probable receipts; and to neither of these is a clear-cut answer ready to hand. Hence more complete studies of the above type are imperative. But, it will be objected, the business man's calculations are of a far less formal sort; and this must be admitted for many investigations. But this is not in fact so irrational as might at first appear; for the nature of the investigations is such that rather soon one realizes that further study and inquiry yield relatively little increased precision in the estimates. In other words, the investigations themselves have a cost, and as in all economic calculations one must compare the results with the costs. Beyond a point it is futile to hope for greater accuracy in one's estimates, the problem being what it is. It is therefore unwise to incur additional costs in an effort to secure greater precision. But that by and large people do investigate seems beyond question. And if one "investigates" a proposed enterprise he studies its profit possibilities, which means forming estimates of probable costs and probable receipts: an examination of supply factors and demand factors.

3. *The promoter*. The foregoing analysis has been developed without any specific mention of a person or persons called a promoter. This term is essentially one borrowed by economics from the law and finance. And in these latter disciplines the noun is loosely used to designate those individuals who play an active part in bringing new enterprises into existence. The precise functions

which presumably define him are not entirely clear, especially at law, but in general his most important activities apparently are discovering unusual opportunities for profitable capital investment and bringing these to the attention of persons possessing investible funds or in a position to solicit them from others. In this respect, therefore, it is the "promoter" who carries out the initial investigation of the profit possibilities of the contemplated enterprise. In the usual case, others, such as investment bankers, will check and recheck his estimates before actually launching the venture. Yet very frequently the "promoter" is the one who first sees that an investment opportunity exists.

It is clear that for analytical purposes it matters little whether this function of seeing investment opportunities devolves upon a particular group of real persons specializing in such tasks or whether it is variously performed by numerous individuals. In a capitalistic society, or in any other, for that matter, in which cumulative growth and change are occurring, some persons must necessarily decide where economic resources may be applied most effectively. That some persons should specialize in this work is perhaps no more than to be expected; but this is not to say that in reality the same *kind* of thing is not undertaken by others who bear no distinctive label. The really important fact is that in a dynamic economy there is a need for such activities being continually undertaken. What specific real persons carry them through will tend to vary according to circumstances of time and place.[23]

[23] Unfortunately in the popular mind the term promoter has come to be associated with a particularly brash and unscrupulous type of person endeavoring to foist worthless corporate securities upon a gullible and defenseless public. While such individuals do exist we should not thereby forget there is an important promotion function to be performed; and that not all persons who render these services are *ipso facto* open to censure.

In highly developed capitalistic countries promotional activity in connection with large enterprises, mergers, consolidations, etc., has tended to gravitate into the hands of financial institutions. Investment bankers especially tend not only to underwrite the capital requirements of enterprises which others have fostered and created but also actively promote new opportunities on their own initiative. Their intimate contacts with many established enterprises and persons seeking outlets for idle funds tend to give them an advantage over individual promoters. It cannot be said, however, that the social consequences of investment banker promotions have been uniformly desirable. See in this connection Myron W. Watkins, "Promotion," *Encyclopaedia of the Social Sciences*, Vol. XII, pp. 518-21.

III. AGGREGATE INVESTMENT AND WORKING CAPITAL NEEDS

1. The limits to profitable investment in the proposed enterprise. 2. The essence of the working capital problem. 3. Uncertainties and working capital needs. 4. Special working capital needs of a new enterprise.

As we have insisted throughout the present chapter, an indispensable preliminary to bringing a new enterprise into actual existence is for someone to investigate the probable returns to capital if invested therein. Enterprises do not form themselves nor appear indiscriminately and at random; by and large each new venture has its antecedents in someone's conclusion that here is an opportunity for investing capital to secure a rate of return in excess of the rate of interest.[24]

1. The limits to profitable investment in the proposed enterprise. Now while the prospective return to capital in the proposed new enterprise must exceed the rate of interest if the venture is to warrant promotion, in each particular instance there is the additional problem of determining at what point the returns from further investment fall *below* the rate of interest. It may be obvious that *some* capital will yield a return greater than the going rate of interest; but it may be less apparent how rapidly the returns per unit of investment decline as the total investment increases. In other words, we must determine for each new enterprise how much capital does it need, or alternatively, how much capital can it profitably employ. Unless the circumstances are very unusual one ought not to assume that the rate of return per unit of investment will hold constant regardless of how much capital is invested in the particular concern. While the rate may at first increase as

[24] That enterprises are often promoted into existence on the basis of conclusions drawn from *insufficient* evidence goes without saying. Our contention is merely that people *do* investigate before proceeding; and that, rationally, going ahead with a venture is evidence of a belief that the net returns to capital investment here are greater than those available elsewhere. We use the phrase "rate of interest" to indicate the returns on capital invested in alternative uses, due allowance being made for risk elements.

the total investment is augmented, nevertheless, almost inevitably in any given opportunity it will subsequently decline. And if this be true, it means there is a definite limit to how much capital the proposed enterprise can profitably use. In answering "how much," the ruling principle is the same as that applicable in all problems involving the allocation of scarce resources: namely, that the total capital investment in the enterprise should be extended up to the point at which the (estimated) rate of return on a further increment is just equal to the rate of interest.[25] So far and no farther should the total investment be carried in the enterprise to be promoted. When we have determined at what total investment this point is reached we have ascertained how much capital the new concern can profitably employ.

A thoroughgoing investigation of probable receipts at different prices and probable costs with alternative scales of production, such as we have outlined in section II, ought to indicate approximately how much capital the proposed enterprise can profitably employ. There is another aspect to the problem of the quantity of capital to be invested, however, which persons dealing with a given project in the real world would consider separately. This is the matter of working capital needs and the allowances necessary because a new enterprise does not attain its full power and strength the instant its incorporation papers are filed. Let us look into this.

2. *The essence of the working capital problem.* In formal theoretical analysis the question of working capital and the delays incident to getting started may be disregarded or treated as mere fric-

[25] It is important to observe that the (prospective) returns on invested capital in the new corporation must be thought of in terms of successive increments of investment and the returns thereon. In other words, the average rate of return on the whole capital employed is of no special relevance in determining how much capital to commit. When we have determined at what total investment the marginal rate of return is equal to the rate of interest we are merely saying that to invest more (an additional unit of investment) would yield a smaller return than what the same capital would earn if invested elsewhere. Notice also that when the *marginal* rate of return to investment is equal to the rate of interest that the *average* rate on the whole investment will be greater. The only exception would be where the average rate was constant from the very first and equal to the rate of interest. If the average rate is constant and greater than the rate of interest then the proposed enterprise can utilize *any* amount of capital. But this case is absurd on the face of it.

tions. Yet in the uncertain world in which business enterprises carry on their operations they cannot be disposed of so easily.

By "working capital" business men and accountants usually mean such assets as cash, accounts and notes receivable, inventories of raw materials, goods in process of production, finished goods, marketable securities and perhaps others under some circumstances. The sum of these items is usually termed "gross" working capital while "net" working capital is this figure *minus* the firm's obligations to pay cash over the proximate future—usually over the next twelve months. Either gross or net, working capital is held to be distinguishable from "fixed" capital on the grounds that the components of the former are regularly, and more or less continuously, being converted into and out of cash while the transformation of the latter is more gradual. Some writers even prefer the term "circulating capital" to "working capital" as more descriptive. The distinction, although essentially one of degree, is none the less sufficiently marked probably to be useful for many problems.

In the discussion of working capital, however, it seems to the present writer that there are really two ideas which ought to be separated.

The first idea is to draw attention to the fact that certain assets can be converted into cash (or are already cash) on very short notice without any significant sacrifice of their book value while certain other assets can be liquidated on short notice only at a considerable sacrifice. Notice that the important point here is convertibility into cash without *sacrifice* of value on short notice. Any asset—with the possible exception of goodwill in the technical accounting sense of capitalized earning power in excess of some going rate—may be turned into cash on short notice *at a price;* but with land, buildings, machinery, etc., the prices at which they are convertible into cash on short notice are substantially below what might be received for them if time is allowed in which to find suitable buyers. If we must, we could probably sell the building for cash this afternoon if we put the price low enough, but we could get a better price if we had a month or two to find a purchaser. This emphasis on cash or near cash assets without value sacrifice is important to persons outside the firm because it is evidence of debt-paying ability *without* disrupting the enterprise or actually bringing its operations to an end (liquidation). From the point of view of the persons in charge of the concern the emphasis on cash or near cash assets is important because it is evidence of the firm's ability to finance operations, purchases, etc., and to pay debts without resort to additional financing. Notice that working capital in this sense would include cash, receivables, marketable securities and inventories if they are not too highly specialized; in some cases the only items would be cash and marketable securities. To repeat: used in this sense, working capital emphasizes that certain assets are convertible into cash on short notice without value sacrifices.

The other idea associated with working capital and of which the adjective circulating is more descriptive is quite different. Here there is an effort to point out that within a certain asset group the component parts change according to a more or less regular pattern. Cash, it is said, is exchanged for raw materials; raw materials become goods in process, then finished goods, then accounts receivable, and then cash again. Here it is this circular flow to which attention is drawn and not the matter of convertibility into cash at all. On this basis items like marketable securities would not be included because they are not part of this circular flow. This circular flow may be important for some purposes but in the writer's opinion its significance can easily be exaggerated, for a similar type of thing is true with respect to fixed or durable assets also. But regardless it is important to keep the circular flow idea distinct from the liquidity idea.

If we ask what determines the amount of working capital necessary for any particular enterprise now in existence or about to be established we at once raise the question why any working capital is needed at all. If a business enterprise were perfectly synchronized in all its parts and all its operations, then working capital problems would disappear. For perfect synchronization would mean in the sphere of production and sales, for example, that the finished salable product emerged from the fabrication process at exactly the same time rate of speed as it was sold to buyers. Likewise the enterprise would absorb raw materials and supplies at precisely the same rate. Viewed in terms of money receipts and money outlays per unit of time the volume of cash receipts would exceed (or fall short of) the volume of cash outlays by just that amount representing the net profit (or loss) on operations for the time interval. And if profits were distributed continuously the firm would neither possess a cash balance nor require one. All cash received from sales would immediately be paid out as expenses or dividends. To be sure, even under these assumptions, the firm would possess working capital assets at any instant of time consisting of goods in process of production and accounts receivable, unless the production of ultimately salable product were instantaneous and all sales for cash. But so long as the rate of absorption of the product by buyers remained constant and there were no price changes, the sum of goods-in-process and accounts receivable would remain at a fixed figure through historical time. There would be no problems at all associated with working capital; the enterprise could simply treat these assets as non-depreciating items of constant value. And given the fabrication period technologically imposed and the credit terms of sale one could state exactly their value sum.

So soon as we state the conditions under which working capital problems would disappear, however, we discover why business enterprises in the real world encounter working capital problems. It is simply not true for most enterprises that cash outlays synchronize perfectly with cash receipts, although leads and lags are less pronounced in some concerns than others. A water company in a region where rainfall is more or less evenly distributed throughout the year comes close to the ideal case: cash receipts over any interval closely parallel cash outlays; seasonal and cyclical variations are negligible. At the other extreme, for instance, would be an enterprise making nothing but fireworks whose only sale was on some annual national holiday. In other words, the need for working capital is, in part, occasioned by the imperfect synchronization of cash receipts and outlays imposed by the technical conditions of production, and the degree of seasonal and cyclical variation in output, prices and sales.[26]

[26] By cyclical variations we refer to those general changes in the level of economic activity termed alternations from "prosperity" to "depression." We are not suggesting that these follow a consistently uniform pattern that can be predicted in advance and precisely for the particular enterprise. But merely that those general changes in production, employment, prices, and real income in the whole

3. *Uncertainties and working capital needs.* The working capital requirements of the individual firm are not wholly prescribed, however, by these considerations. Business concerns carry on in a world where unpredictable developments and non-fulfillment of expectations are the rule rather than the exception. As a consequence any enterprise can look forward to an unending series of partially or wholly unexpected developments which may affect it in an untoward or favorable manner. Against such eventualities one of the most useful precautions for the individual firm is a substantial cash balance or the possession of other assets easily convertible into cash without loss on short notice. The contingencies against which business concerns will find liquid assets a convenient assurance, although varying between industries of course, will often be favorable as well as unfavorable. The following are perhaps typical: the default of an important trade creditor, a chance to buy materials or supplies at a large price concession, an unforeseen need to expand output greatly on short notice, sharp changes in the prices of products or inputs, being forced into a price war, or the development of a favorable juncture for starting one, etc.[27] A business enterprise's appraisal of its cash needs for these purposes probably does not remain constant from boom to depression but doubtless increases during a downswing and declines as prosperity proceeds. But the main point of our argument is clear: if a business firm expects unforeseen developments without knowing their precise and particular character perhaps the most effective preparation for them is to hold cash or near cash assets.

Thus we observe that the need of any particular enterprise for working capital arises partly from the imperfect synchronization of cash receipts and outlays, partly from the technical conditions

economy, loosely referred to as the "business cycle," will inevitably impinge upon the single enterprise for better or worse.

[27] Mr. J. M. Keynes calls this motive for holding cash the "precautionary-motive." What Mr. Keynes calls the speculative motive, i.e., changes in the willingness of individuals and business enterprises to hold cash consequent upon changes in the rate of interest, will not be dealt with here since it is not particularly germane to our immediate interest: the promotion of new enterprises. This must not be interpreted, however, as a denial of its validity for Mr. Keynes' problems. See, his *General Theory of Employment, Interest, and Money*, New York (Harcourt, Brace), 1936, Ch. 15.

of production and sale of its product, and partly from the inherent uncertainties of business as it is met with in real life.

Almost needless to say, there is no reason to suppose that the firm's needs for working capital assets arising from the reasons indicated will remain constant throughout different phases of the business cycle; indeed it is common knowledge that they fluctuate considerably. The varying needs for working capital raise the question of what proportion of the maximum requirements ought to be supplied by long-term contract and what by short-term. To provide the maximum anticipated working capital needs by permanent or very-long term financing methods creates the problem of investing idle resources during slack periods when the assets are not needed directly in the business. On the other hand, to provide only the bare minimum by permanent financing exposes the firm to the risk of being unable to borrow at reasonable short-term rates as its needs expand. No general answer to such questions is possible on *a priori* grounds; but in each new venture a solution can usually be formulated having acceptable accuracy.

4. *Special working capital needs of a new enterprise.* We observed earlier that a new enterprise will almost inevitably pass through a stage in its early history when its need for liquid resources will be especially great. The favorable relation between costs and income indicated by the investigation and which induced promotion is not usually attained within the first week or sometimes even the first few years. Rather, sales are small and only increase gradually as a competitive position within the industry is won. The especial importance of this common experience for the promotional problem and the determination of the necessary capital is simply that during the gestation period cash outlays will exceed cash receipts by a wide margin. Hence the firm will need an abnormally large beginning cash balance to finance itself until such time as cash receipts more nearly synchronize with cash disbursements. Thus the firm will need a large cash balance to tide it over that interval. Depending upon the product and the nature of the competition the firm will suffer losses on operations for a longer or shorter period.[28] For these reasons, due allowance for

[28] Such accounting losses are but one of the costs of getting going and are as

such losses must be made in determining how much capital the firm can profitably employ and ought to raise by the sale of security contracts. And in this connection an overdose of pessimism concerning the length of the gestation period is much better than a mild optimism; for the whole scheme may be brought to naught by the simple inability of the firm to finance itself over the initial slack period in which cash outlays far exceed cash receipts. As a practical matter it is almost impossible to overstress the importance of this point.

IV. THE ACQUISITION OF CAPITAL AND THE FINANCIAL PLAN

1. Alternative sources of capital for the promotion. 2. Considerations affecting the financial plan.

If the investigation as outlined in section II has been carefully undertaken the wisdom of proceeding further with the proposed venture or dropping it entirely should be apparent. Assuming that the results of the investigation are encouraging, i.e., that a rate of return to capital in excess of the rate of interest seems assured, the process of launching the new enterprise may be carried forward. The promoters now must consider alternative ways and means of raising the necessary capital.

1. *Alternative sources of capital for the promotion.* A new enterprise may or may not propose to appeal to the organized capital market for funds. As already observed many enterprises are not able to use the facilities of the organized capital market, either because of their small size or the character of the venture. By the phrase organized capital market in this connection we mean that grouping of investment bankers, brokers, commission houses, etc., which facilitates the raising of (relatively) long-term capital for industry and commerce through the sale of security contracts. While individual houses differ somewhat in their conception of "desirable" ventures or promotions, nevertheless most such con-

much a part of the permanent investment from the economic point of view as plant and equipment.

cerns are predisposed to avoid the securities of new enterprises which are quite small or in relatively unknown fields. Neither the automobile industry nor the electric power and light industry in the United States were able to secure free capital from the organized capital market during their early history. Both were apparently regarded as too speculative for conservative investment houses. To some extent the attitude of the investment bankers of course was inherently rational: both industries *were* highly speculative in their early days and the mortality of firms was quite high. It should be recognized furthermore that investment bankers are primarily, although not entirely, middlemen who must be guided in their purchases by what the ultimate purchasers consider desirable investments. And it is probable that around the turn of the present century both the aforementioned industries were regarded by many "sound" people as highly dubious. Somewhat the same difficulties beset new enterprises in relatively untried fields at all times. The banker may feel that the enterprise has remarkable prospects but if he is convinced his clients will *not* think so, he is perhaps forced to reject the promoters. Traditionally very speculative new enterprises, such as mining ventures, ordinarily may not appeal successfully to the better investment houses at all. The reason here is perhaps partly because such enterprises are associated in the public mind with semi-fraudulent schemes. Just how many concerns of this kind succeed in securing capital is something of a mystery. Apparently the methods are varied and essentially opportunistic: friends, relatives, and business associates of the conceivers of the new enterprise are apparently cajoled into putting up the needed capital. Often of course considerable difficulty is encountered in acquiring any capital beyond the amount those directly associated with the enterprise are themselves able to provide.[29]

In economic theory we speak of an enterprise securing liquid funds from the capital market. In the real world this means that

[29] Sometimes wealthy persons, perhaps investment bankers in their private capacity, are willing to risk sizeable sums in new ventures provided they are placed in a strategic position and the prospects of high returns seem favorable. Such persons often "take over" the enterprise from those who are soliciting capital. They are undoubtedly in a strategic position since the "idea" without capital to

corporations sell security contracts to persons with cash to invest. We have already indicated in a previous chapter however that there are many kinds of security contracts. Some decision has to be reached therefore as to the specific kinds of security contracts which the new enterprise may offer with greatest advantage. In financial literature the particular combination of security contracts by which a corporate enterprise raises its capital is termed its "financial plan." Let us look into this financial plan concept more closely.

2. *Considerations affecting the financial plan.* Fundamentally the very nature of the financial plan serves to accomplish three things: (1) secure the capital the enterprise needs to carry on its operations; (2) determine the distribution of control between the parties furnishing capital; (3) establish the rules, priorities, etc., governing the distribution of the corporate net income. In drafting the financial plan, therefore, it is important to select that combination of security contracts which, in view of all the relevant data, best fits the needs of the particular enterprise. Generally speaking the plan will be drawn primarily from the point of view of those upon whom its formulation devolves: the promoters with the assistance of investment bankers or whoever will assure the necessary capital. Alternatively, perhaps, we might argue that the financial plan will cater chiefly to the interests of those who will ultimately occupy a proprietary position in the corporation. In fact these two contentions come to much the same thing since those actively interested in bringing the enterprise into existence will typically come to own securities representing a residual proprietary interest, e.g., common stock.

The investigation will not only have indicated the advisability of organizing the new enterprise; it will also have shown how much capital in total and what kinds and types of assets are necessary. The aggregate amount of free capital will in itself partly determine the financial plan. A combination of bonds, preferred stocks and common stocks quite suitable for an enterprise of $10,-

give it realization is completely barren. It is probably true that many fortunes are the result of supplying capital to new enterprises in which the percentage returns per unit of investment in the early life of the company run into two and three figures. Many millions are lost annually however in new ventures which come to naught.

000,000 would not be equally satisfactory for a $1,000,000 corporation identical in all other respects. For small enterprises the higher costs more than outweigh the advantages of numerous kinds of securities in the financial plan.[30] Apart from the absolute amount of capital to be raised another important factor tending to determine the financial plan is the degree of regularity in the prospective income stream. If the nature of the enterprise is such that net income is likely to fluctuate greatly from one period to the next, perhaps rising markedly in boom periods and falling drastically during depression, then it will be unwise to enter contracts which require a fixed annual payment regardless of the fortunes of the corporation.[31] Even assuming such securities can be sold the corporation is probably wise to avoid their inclusion in the financial plan under the circumstances.[32] A similar objection pertains to leasing arrangements involving a fixed annual rental. Conversely, of course, if earnings are likely to be comparatively regular from period to period fixed return securities may be used in the financial plan with safety and profit.

If securities are to be exchanged directly for assets rather than being first sold for cash, as often happens in new enterprises, the sellers of the assets may dictate rather rigidly the kind of securities they will accept. This may well be the case, for instance, with assets contributed by the promoters or others directly associated with the formation of the enterprise. Even so, if time is an important element, somewhat onerous terms may be preferable to the costly delays incident to ordering anew the construction of capital instruments (e.g., buildings, machinery, etc.).

Whatever the financial plan selected it must make provision for the allocation of control of the enterprise between the different contributors of capital. Presumably the desire for a voice in con-

---

[30] The point is that with relatively small issues of securities the cost of negotiation, drafting mortgages, maintaining a trustee, etc., do not decline proportionately with the decrease in the size of the security issue. To some extent these costs tend to be a fixed aggregate, hence for small issues the cost is proportionately quite high.

[31] The degree of fluctuation in net income will tend to be greater the farther removed is the enterprise from consumers' goods markets.

[32] If the risks are large security buyers are unlikely to place much credence in solemn promises to pay a fixed annual return per unit of investment. In short the security would probably be unsalable.

trol is predicated on either or both of two beliefs: (1) that a voice in management will produce for those possessing it a more favorable income stream, either in amount or distribution in time, than if control rests with others; or, (2) that direct control reduces the possibility of the dissipation of the capital investment.[33] In other words, a desire to exercise control or have a voice in it betokens a strong belief in the superiority of one's own judgment and policies. If the group directly responsible for creating the new enterprise is convinced of the necessity of maintaining control, the financial plan will tend to include relatively more bonds and non-voting shares. Necessarily, perhaps, this will mean that the group desiring to control the corporation will have to offer other capital contributors more favorable contractual terms in other directions, e.g., greater assurances of regular returns, pledges of assets, a higher rate of return, etc. How great sacrifices it will pay to undergo in order to retain control of the enterprise will depend upon how highly the promoters value the control privilege. There is undoubtedly some elasticity of substitution among security buyers between the contractual provisions relating to amount and priority of income claims, security of principal, a voice in management, etc.; but it is not complete. The primary aim in drafting the financial plan is to discover that "ideal" combination of security contracts which will raise the capital on terms most favorable to the new enterprise, which, as we have already indicated, means most favorable to the common stockholders. But the latter are constantly restricted by the important limitation that the securities offered must raise the capital, i.e., they must be sold. This means that although the security contracts are drafted by the proprietary interests they must carry sufficient investor appeal to induce purchase.[34] In one sense the interests of common stock-

[33] From one point of view these are really two aspects of the same thing; since the danger of loss is one contingency in the future income stream. But perhaps persons tend to think of them in somewhat different terms. Any security holder who values the voting privilege in a corporation must do so because it permits *him*, and others like him, rather than someone else, to select the persons in whom he will place his trust. Psychologically of course control may be desired for its own sake.

[34] This may appear to endow investors with somewhat greater perspicacity than is usually credited to them. It is easy, however, to overemphasize the degree of innocence and stupidity among security buyers. In recent times the importance

holders and of those who are expected to contribute capital on different contractual terms are at opposite poles in this respect. From the standpoint of the investor the ideal contract would be one which requires the enterprise to provide a maximum of security of principal (first mortgage on all assets, guarantees of various kinds, etc.), a respectable annual income as a guaranteed minimum, and in case of unusual success a generous share in the large profits. Those forced to seek capital, however, will wish to promise little in security, guarantee no return on the investment whatsoever, and restrict the gains from unusual success entirely to themselves. Obviously neither group can be completely satisfied; concessions will be forthcoming on both sides.[35]

The financial plan, therefore, is essentially a compromise; and ideally it should raise the necessary capital and provide for the allocation of control and the distribution of net income on terms most beneficial to the enterprise in the given circumstances. What the optimum compromise actually is in any particular instance of course may be somewhat difficult to determine with absolute precision. But there seems no reason to deny that this is what is being sought subject to the frailties of human judgment.[36]

of institutional investors such as insurance companies, banks, investment trusts, etc., has grown enormously and these are perhaps equally sophisticated with the sellers.

[35] The language above rather suggests that there is some formal negotiation between the sellers of security contracts and the ultimate purchasers. This is of course contrary to the facts. In general the contract is drawn wholly without consultation with the ultimate purchasers. They either accept or reject it by purchasing it or not when presented to them. Yet in an indirect way there is considerable negotiation in the interest of the ultimate buyers on the part of investment bankers. They necessarily have an interest in the appeal the final contract will have to the ultimate purchasers; and for this reason the financial plan is very often different from what it would be if the promoters had their way entirely. If the investment banking house is to underwrite the financial plan, then it must be even more careful to insist upon security contracts which have an investor appeal.

[36] We emphasized above that in determining the probable optimum combination of the factors of production due allowance would have to be made for uncertainty and change. Similar considerations must be kept in mind in drafting the financial plan. What seems the most suitable financial plan here and now may not be the most desirable at some subsequent time in view of changed conditions. Consequently it is important for the enterprise to allow for as much flexibility as possible in its financial plan. With respect to bond contracts this means avoiding "closed" issues, issues containing the after-acquired-property clause, and noncallable issues. In preferred stock contracts non-callable features and clauses nar-

V. SUMMARY

Fundamentally the inception of a new enterprise is warranted on economic grounds provided there appears to be an opportunity for the investment of capital in the particular employment under consideration to yield a rate of return greater than that elsewhere available. Since the probable returns per unit of investment will not be immediately obvious, an investigation will be necessary to determine how large they promise to be. Because net returns are a function of costs and receipts this means that the investigation will primarily concern itself with a thorough study of these factors. Cost of production is not entirely self-evident in its meaning. With any given scale of production cost of production will tend to be a function of the rate of utilization of that scale. Yet for an enterprise about to be brought into existence the scale of production has yet to be determined; it is not given in advance. Consequently the investigation of probable costs consists first, of a study of costs with different scales of production, and second, of a study of varying costs of production with varying degrees of utilization of alternative scales. It will be found that there are often certain economies to be had from large scale production.

The estimation of the probable receipts from the sale of the product which the enterprise proposes to turn out is less susceptible of accurate prediction than probable costs. In the first place, the quantity sold will vary with the price at which it is offered. On the other hand, the quantity sold at any given price will not remain constant in the course of time but will rise and fall with changes in buyers' tastes, the prices and product variations of substitute commodities, and alternations in the general level of economic activity from prosperity to depression. Nevertheless, out of such highly complicated and often interrelated variables one must

rowly restricting the borrowing powers of the corporation should be avoided if possible. Similarly there is also something to be said in favor of serial maturities. In regard to these flexible features of the financial plan, as with others, however, the drafters will not have an altogether free hand, but will be forced to consider what investors wish to buy as well as what they would like to sell.

distill the estimates of the probable gross receipts from the sale of the product.

The estimates of gross receipts and costs together suggest whether or not the probable net returns per unit of capital investment promise to be larger or smaller than those available on alternative opportunities for investment, and indicate the amount of the difference.

While the investigation to determine probable net yield per unit of invested capital will have indicated how much capital investment is warranted, separate study is usually necessary to determine the likely working capital needs of the proposed enterprise. The crux of the working capital problem lies in the imperfect synchronization between the rate of flow of cash receipts and the rate of flow of cash outlays. The technological aspects of the productive process, seasonal and cyclical factors, and uncertainties tend to be the primary determinants of the amount of working capital required.

A corporate enterprise will raise the funds necessary to bring the proposed venture into existence by offering security contracts for sale to investors. The combination of security contracts which it will find advisable to offer will depend upon the regularity of probable net income, the attitude towards control, and the aggregate amount of capital to be raised.

REFERENCES: CHAPTER VI

BURTCHETT, F. F.—*Corporation Finance*, Chs. 19, 21, 22.
DEWING, A. S.—*Financial Policy*, Book III, Chs. 1-4.
GERSTENBERG, C. W.—*Financial Organization and Management*, Chs. 1-3.
HOAGLAND, H. E.—*Corporation Finance*, Chs. 15-18.

Chapter VII

THE MAXIMIZATION OF PROFITS: ECONOMIC ASPECTS OF ENTERPRISE OPERATIONS

I. The Maximization of Net Returns. II. Variations in Physical Output with Scale Given. III. Variations in Cost in Relation to Changes in the Rate of Output. IV. The Demand Curve and the Marginal Revenue Curve. V. The Optimum Rate of Output. VI. Changes Which Alter the Optimum Rate of Output. VII. Summary.

~~~~~~~~~~

Having already pointed out the economic character of the business enterprise (Chapter II) and the circumstances under which new firms come into existence (Chapter VI) we shall endeavor to clarify in the next few chapters some of the economic problems associated with already established concerns. The present chapter endeavors to explore the meaning and implications of the ever common phrase "maximization of net income" when applied to business enterprises.

Although it is generally agreed that the aim and purpose of business enterprises in a capitalistic economy are to maximize net returns (net income), a little reflection will indicate that the meaning of this statement is not nearly so self-evident as might appear at first glance. To be sure, economic theorists in recent years have considered the problem at length so that we now have a fairly complete body of propositions about it which are matters of common knowledge among persons schooled in that discipline. But the application of these economic principles of maximizing net returns to business enterprises as we find them in the real world has been something less than complete. There would seem to be no obvious reason, however, why the apparatus of economic theory should not be useful for the analysis of business operations. The problem of maximizing net income or of "obtaining the

178

largest profit," as the business man would be more likely to express it, is so fundamental in all business conduct that any clarification of its meaning that economics can provide is all to the good. Consequently, it is worth our while to explore the subject at some length. If occasionally the treatment seems a little abstract and "theoretical" it is perhaps worth recalling the words of an eminent scholar who once said, "There is nothing so 'practical' as sound theory."

I. THE MAXIMIZATION OF NET RETURNS

1. The meaning of maximizing net returns. 2. Uncertainties and the maximization of net returns.

1. *The meaning of maximizing net returns.* When we speak of maximizing net income we must necessarily mean maximizing returns to some person or group of persons. It makes no sense at all to talk of maximizing returns without indicating specifically or by implication to whom or to what returns are being maximized. Here, of course, by maximizing returns we mean maximizing returns to the enterprise. We conceive of the enterprise as consisting of an aggregate of assets the returns from which it endeavors to make as large as possible. It must not be assumed that the assets which the firm has under its control are fixed and invariable in their amount. By selling more shares of stock or by issuing bonds the enterprise can increase the total assets available for the obtaining of a net income. But as repeatedly emphasized in earlier chapters, increasing the total assets available necessarily means increasing the total value of the claims against the assets. Furthermore, the claims against the assets fall into the two broad classes of creditors' claims and owners' claims. Both in corporate enterprises and others, however, the utilization of the assets in a manner to yield the maximum net income has a clear reference to the partition of the net income between owners and creditors. The primary aim in the conduct of the enterprise is to maximize the net income to the owners. Creditors are regarded as a class

apart, and borrowing operations are only undertaken when they will add to the net income of the owners of the enterprise. Consequently, when we speak of maximizing returns to the enterprise we really mean maximizing returns to its owners. The phrase maximizing returns to the enterprise is only a short-hand expression for the more precise expression maximizing net income to the owners, the shareholders, of the enterprise.[1]

What then do we mean when we say that an enterprise is endeavoring to maximize returns? Clearly we do *not* mean the attempt to maximize immediate gross income. A corporation is not trying to secure the largest possible gross income from sales. Rather it is seeking to maximize its net income in some sense yet to be defined. It is not true, however, if for a moment we adopt the accounting notion of net income, that the corporation is trying to maximize this figure for the current period or even for the next succeeding period. We would recognize at once that a business enterprise rarely acts in such a way as to make as much as possible, say, "this month." Broadly and typically the business enterprise looks forward to a well-nigh perpetual existence composed of an endless series of "months" in each of which it hopes to obtain a net income. In other words, what the enterprise is concerned with is the *stream* of net income items running forward into the future perhaps indefinitely far. Essentially the objection to taking some action to increase the net income to be secured "this month" is simply that the repercussions of that action upon the net income items of subsequent months are on net balance unfavorable. To take a simple example: let us assume that the enterprise has some merchandise which it can dispose of this month for a known price payable in cash. What objection is there to doing so? Clearly, the

[1] The distinction between obtaining the maximum net income from the utilization of the assets under the control of the enterprise and maximizing the returns to the owners is more verbal than fundamental in the great majority of cases. For if the enterprise is so operated as to produce the maximum net income from its assets this will also mean that the returns to the owners have been maximized. Ordinarily creditors' claims are a fixed maximum rather than proportionate to aggregate net income. Consequently the maximum net income from the use of the assets in production will mean also that the residual available to the owners has been maximized. If a corporation, for example, has bonds outstanding and the shareholders endeavor to obtain the maximum residual after bond interest, this means the same thing as securing the maximum return before bond interest.

objection is that the same merchandise might be sold next month for a much higher price. And this brings us to the next point.

At any point in time the enterprise has at its disposal a certain fund of resources, assets, which can be applied towards the securing of a net income stream. Indeed the resources have a significance to the firm simply and solely because they are the means by which the enterprise is able to obtain a net income stream. These assets consist of land, buildings, machinery, materials, merchandise, evidences of property rights, cash, etc. And each asset item has alternative uses, although the number of alternative uses is greater for some than for others. In the case of cash the kinds and types of assets for which it might be exchanged are almost countless. Machinery, apart from the alternative of selling it for cash, can be used in production now, or it can be used later. By using it now we decrease the number of useful services which can be secured from it subsequently. Raw materials can be converted into finished goods of different kinds either now or later. For each asset, the following sets of alternatives are available: (a) use here and now in the present, or at some future time; and (b) use at any given time (now or later) in one of a variety of possible employments. Essentially the problem of operating the business enterprise to yield the maximum net income consists in making the best choices between the alternatives available with respect to each and every asset. That is, at any instant of time the enterprise has a certain stock of assets, each of which is capable of yielding a valuable service flow (either now or later) or of being exchanged for some other asset (again either now or later) which will yield a different service flow in value terms. One asset will be exchanged for another in the market or transformed into another (e.g., when raw materials are made up into finished goods) within the confines of the enterprise whenever the substitute asset obtained has a greater value. And, of course, the enterprise will endeavor to acquire by exchange those assets having the greatest value to the firm and to part with those which are least significant to the enterprise in terms of the valuable services they can render. So, for instance, a firm gives up cash to obtain raw materials because the latter will contribute more to net income than will the retention of cash. The essence of maximizing net returns to the enterprise is the selection of those asset exchanges and those asset transformations (without resort to the market) which render the net income stream available to the enterprise a maximum.

According as the assets are utilized or exchanged in different ways the income streams obtained will differ. And as we have just argued in the previous paragraph, the aim is to select the largest income stream from among all the choices available. Since the individual items in the different income streams will vary in their size and distribution over time, some way has to be found of reducing them to comparable terms. For example, one stream might consist of items as follows: $10 this "year," $100 next "year," $450 the third "year," and nothing thereafter, while another might have the form $2 this year, $15 next year, $600 the third year, $5 the fourth year and nothing thereafter. Which is the larger of the two income streams? Obviously that one which has the larger present worth when both are discounted at the *same* rate of interest.[2] Those ways of using the assets which give small returns in the near future must yield considerably larger returns in the more remote future in order to be superior to

---

[2] The simple arithmetical procedure for finding the present worth of a single future payment or a stream of payments running forward into the future is for some obscure reason difficult for the beginner to grasp. Consequently a word of explanation may not be out of place.

If the rate of interest (discount) is 4 per cent, the present value (worth) of $1.00 due to be received one year from today is $\frac{1.00}{1.04} = .96151+$ cents because .96151 cents placed at interest today at 4 per cent would amount to $1.00 a year hence. Similarly $1.00 due two years from today at a 4 per cent discount rate is $\frac{1.00}{(1.04)^2} = .92454+$ by a similar mode of reasoning. Consequently the present worth of $1.00 receivable a year from today *plus* $1.00 receivable two years from today is $\frac{1.00}{(1.04)^1} + \frac{1.00}{(1.04)^2} = .96151 + .92454 = 1.88605+$. Thus, to generalize, if we let i be the percentage rate of discount—4 per cent, 6 per cent or whatever—per period (commonly although not necessarily a year), then the present worth of $1.00 receivable any number (n) of periods hence is $\frac{1.00}{(1+i)^n}$, where n is any positive number. Similarly a stream of non-identical receipts $A + B + C + D \ldots N$ would have present worth indicated by the general formula

$$\frac{A}{(1+i)} + \frac{B}{(1+i)^2} + \frac{C}{(1+i)^3} \cdots \frac{N}{(1+i)^n}$$

In this form the expression is quite general: any figures desired can be filled in for the symbols.

alternative methods which yield immediate though smaller returns almost at once. The simple basic principle can be stated in quite general terms. If we represent any one of these income series extending through future time by the expression $D_1 + D_2 + D_3 + D_4 + D_5 + \ldots D_n$, where the D's simply represent the money payments to the owners at successive points in time, it is obvious that given some rate of discount this series has a present worth which we may designate W_1. If the assets are employed in a different manner, a different income stream will result, and using the same rate of discount, the second stream will have a different present worth which we may designate by W_2. Similarly, each alternative income stream will have a corresponding present worth which we may indicate by the symbols, W_1, W_2, W_3, W_4, W_5, $\ldots W_n$. Obviously that income stream will be the largest which has the greatest present worth. In other words, the enterprise would endeavor to select that income stream whose present worth (W) is the largest.

If we so desire we can express the same fundamental notion in another way. We have just said above that the enterprise will endeavor to select that income stream among all those available which has the greatest present worth. We also indicated that the enterprise would obtain this maximum income stream by (a) exchanging assets already held for assets of greater worth to the firm, and (b) by transforming assets it now has into assets of greater worth to the firm. In other words, starting at any point in time with a given combination of assets which is the result of decisions made in times past, the enterprise will endeavor to obtain that new combination of assets which will yield the maximum income stream. But this is exactly the same thing as saying that the enterprise at all times will seek to maximize the present worth of its assets, for the combination of assets which will yield the maximum income stream must be that combination of the assets which has the greatest present worth. The one is exactly the same as the other: in one instance we look at the flow of income and in the other we emphasize the source of this flow.

We have argued that the enterprise will endeavor to employ its assets so as to yield the maximum of all possible income streams available. And we have seen that this is the same as saying that the enterprise will at all times endeavor to maximize the present worth of its assets. However, let us look into the matter of the income stream and its components a little more closely. Let us assume that the optimum income stream is of the form $D_1 + D_2 + D_3 + \ldots D_n$ where D_n represents either the ultimate liquidation of the enterprise at some finite point in time now taken as given, or alternatively, that n is infinity in which instance the enterprise is assumed to continue indefinitely: no liquidation is contemplated. In defining the D's in the paragraph above we said that they represented the cash made available for distribution to the owners. In the corporation this would mean that the respective D's stood for the cash dividend distributions to the shareholders at successive points in time. Since we are considering all the shareholders as a group, the D's represent aggregate cash dividend payments at successive intervals and not dividends per share.[3] Let us assume that D_n represents an ultimate liquidating dividend to the shareholders. It is this stream of dividend payments that the enterprise is endeavoring to maximize, measured, of course, by its present worth. Now one caution must be entered to avoid a possible misinterpretation. We have *not* said that any individual D in the series is itself an item of net income in any sense. For if we consider any one term in the dividend series by itself and wish to compute what fraction of it is net we can only do so by computing what sacrifices were entailed in acquiring it then rather than later. That is, we cannot take the item, say, D_3 in the cash dividend series and regard it as net income for it is certainly not net income. Only that portion of it is net after we have deducted for the sacrifices inevitably entailed in acquiring it. What are these sacrifices? Clearly they are the effects produced upon the amount and time distribution of all the other D's in the series because D_3 is so placed in time as it is and is of the face amount that it is. Hence, if using the resources in a particular way will permit a cash dividend in the amount and at the time represented by D_3, the proportion of D_3 which is net can only be determined by computing what effect D_3 had upon the size and time distribution

[3] It is not necessary to assume that the D's are so spaced in time that they represent quarterly dividends paid to shareholders. They may be quite irregular in their location in time, including certain "special" dividends of various amounts.

of D_1, D_2, D_4, D_5 . . . D_n. It is the effect upon these earlier and subsequent D's that determines the "costs" involved in obtaining D_3, hence the proportion of D_3 which is net. For example, a corporation might offer for sale at a cheap price a product which was poorly made of shoddy materials but whose defects were not apparent to purchasers. By so doing the concern might make a large immediate gain which would permit large cash dividends in the very near future. But because the buyers would soon discover the defects of the product, sales and hence dividends would soon come to an end. The stream of D's would be short-lived. The enterprise would have been wiser to have adopted a policy which would have yielded smaller immediate dividends but a larger dividend stream in terms of present worth.[4] Or again, many concerns will often make small adjustments for a person at no charge at all even though the latter believes he should pay. By such a policy they hope to build up a favorable disposition on the part of prospective buyers which will result in a larger dividend stream.

2. *Uncertainties and the maximization of net returns.* It must be emphasized that business enterprises operate in a world which is characterized by uncertainties. New enterprises are always appearing on the competitive scene, new products are being offered to buyers, the techniques of production do not remain constant, and there is the ebb and flow between prosperity and depression which affects all business enterprises in a greater or lesser degree. This uncertainty element has two important repercussions upon the solution of the problem of maximizing net returns to the owners of the enterprise.

The first important effect is that items in the dividend stream which are far distant in time are accorded a very small present worth by those charged with the operation and management of the enterprise. The longer one is forced to wait before the results (in terms of distributable sums to the owners) of any given application of resources will be forthcoming, the less certainty is there that they will ever be received at all. One can feel reasonably

---

[4] It is a fact of common experience that the merchandise offered for sale by street barkers, concessionaires at circuses, etc., is often gaudy and of poor quality. The hope of repeat business here is no part of the seller's plans, hence he endeavors to extract the maximum return here and now.

confident perhaps that next week's sales will not deviate greatly from this week's; but the sales to be had during the corresponding week two years from now are something about which the average business man holds only vague surmises. Between now and then a war may intervene, a new product may appear, a new competitor may enter the industry, or a business depression may overtake the economy. Of course, the unforeseen developments may be favorable as well as depressing. But the important point is that the number of changes which can impinge upon the situation to alter the amount and time distribution of the terms in the D series is so great that those far distant can only be accorded a very small present worth. The degree to which uncertainties of this character are significant varies greatly from one industry to another. Hydroelectric power companies often construct dams which are expected to be useful for almost an indefinite number of years. Railroads, dock and wharfage companies, mining concerns, etc., similarly look forward to receiving valuable services from fixed investments over a long series of years. The contingencies which they visualize as reacting upon them unfavorably are comparatively fewer. Nevertheless, even here the present worth accorded to items in the D series that are long postponed is probably quite small.

The second consequence of uncertainties for the problem of maximizing returns to the owners is that those in charge of the enterprise are constantly revising their expectations and their plans of operations. At the present juncture it will appear that a particular course of action will yield the maximum income series. But before the enterprise has proceeded very far in the chosen direction new knowledge has become available that justifies a greater or lesser modification of the plan of operations originally contemplated. Starting from any point in time the enterprise will attempt to readjust its asset holdings and to undertake those asset transformations which will yield the maximum returns. Yet before three months have passed those in charge of the corporation will perhaps find that, on the basis of what they now know but did not know three months earlier, a slightly different readjustment of asset holdings and transformations will yield the maximum income stream. Such changes in plans may be necessary because of a change in the relative prices of the factors of production, the appearance of a new technique of production, a shift in consumers' tastes, or merely a revision of the expectations of the managers concerning any or all of these matters. Consequently, when we say that a business enterprise will endeavor to maximize net returns by planning asset exchanges and transformations we do not mean to imply that having once formed a self-consistent plan of operations in this respect it will hold to this plan come what may. On the contrary, the plans are always in the process of gradual modification as new knowledge becomes available. But the alterations in the plans are always in the direction of what now appears likely to yield the maximum income: the stream of *D*'s having the greatest present worth.

II. VARIATIONS IN PHYSICAL OUTPUT WITH SCALE GIVEN

An established enterprise will endeavor to maximize returns. And it does this by selling physical products or "services" to outsiders for a money price. The rendering of these services or the production of these products typically necessitates the use of factors of production which involve costs. As a consequence the behavior of costs per unit of physical product (or service) will be a function of the behavior of total output as the number of units of the factors applied in production is varied. It is apparent at once that the important cost determinants are whether output increases proportionately, or more or less than proportionately, to the increase in the factors applied in production: in other words physical input-output relationships and the cost of the input factors.

The physical relationships holding between units of input and units of output are essentially technological in character. The economist as such is interested in them only insofar as they partially determine, as indeed they must, the behavior of cost per unit of product. In general, economists carry their analysis forward on the assumption that these physical input-output relationships (the production functions as they are sometimes called) are given. Nevertheless it is helpful to examine briefly just what types of production functions are likely to rule in the individual enterprise.

We shall assume in the following discussion that the enterprise, a going concern, is committed to some given combination of the factors of production: a certain combination of buildings, machines, land, etc., to which may be applied laborers, materials, supplies, etc., in order to produce a certain output as a rate of flow per unit of time. In short, the enterprise is committed to a given "scale" in the sense defined in Chapter VI.

If we apply to this given combination of fixed factors varying amounts of one variable (e.g., a laborer provided with certain tools and materials which we call a "unit" of the variable) we should expect the physical output to be a function of the number of units of the variable factor applied. Mathematically speaking it is self-evident there are only three possibilities: that the total output will increase proportionately with the increase in the number of units of the variable factor applied, more than proportionately, or less than proportionately. What is the typical case to be expected in the absence of special conditions? Technologically the fixed factors probably were designed to be used with some particular combination of this and other variable factors. If so, then as more units of this variable factor are added the *total* product will at first increase more than, but subsequently less than, proportionately to the increase in the variable factor. And it is not at all inconceivable that ultimately the total might reach an absolute maximum and even subsequently decline if still more inputs were added. This familiar phenomenon of production arises from the fact that up to a point we have been improving the productive combination from the technical viewpoint; the fixed factors are combined with a more efficient number of units of the variable factor. It is also obvious that the degree to which output would at first increase more than proportionately to the input of the variable factor would depend upon how large were the fixed factors relative to the variable factor to begin with. If the fixed factors were quite small it is possible there might be no range at all over which total output would increase more than proportionately to the increase in the number of inputs of the variable.[5] Provided, however, we are dealing with homogeneous input factors, we could vary these one at a time and prepare a schedule showing the changes in physical output as more units of the variable were applied to the given fixed factor.

The primary objection to this procedure is simply that in most business enterprises of which we have knowledge the variable factors of production applied to increase output would not be homogeneous. They would consist for instance of laborers of different kinds, materials, kilowatt hours, etc., which have no common denominator.[6] Consequently it is impossible to add these together as physical items. For purposes of economic analysis, however, this non-homogeneity of the factors is less serious than at first appears. The business enterprise as such is concerned with money receipts and money cost outlays; the physical inputs and outputs are of interest only insofar as they determine money costs and money receipts. Henceforth we may take the physical input-output relationships as given and concentrate our attention on the behavior of money cost as output is altered. This will have a dual advantage: first, it will emphasize that money cost and not physical variations in output *per se* are important; and second, the problem of numerous types of variable factors having no common denominator vanishes, for now we can add them in terms of their money cost to the enterprise. Hence, in what follows when we say there is a given increase in the money cost outlay

[5] Although it is customary in describing the behavior of product output as the number of variable factors applied to some given fixed factor is gradually increased to take a case where the total output first increases more than proportionately to the increase in the number of variable factors applied but later less than proportionately, this need not necessarily be the relationship. The familiar examples, such as an acre of land to which are applied various "doses" of labor and capital to yield increments in total product which are first more than proportionate and then less than proportionate, are only conceivable because an acre was too much land with which to begin. If the assumption had been, say, a quarter of an acre of land instead of an acre, the optimum combination of the factors would have been achieved perhaps with the very first "dose" of labor and capital. Consequently over what range one obtains more than proportionate increases in the total product depends upon how large is the fixed factor relative to the variable factor units when the process is begun.

[6] This difficulty would not arise if each laborer required a given fixed complement of materials, power, hand tools, etc. For analytical purposes these could all be lumped together as a "unit" of the variable. Such cases, however, are probably few and far between.

on variable factors of production we shall always assume that this money sum is applied in the purchase of physical producing agents in such a way as to give the maximum possible increase in physical output and/or in net receipts. We need to say "and/or net receipts" because the enterprise might find it necessary or advisable to leave the product unaltered in physical terms but to spend money on advertising or sales efforts of other kinds. The selling costs such as advertising are just as much costs as money spent for materials and therefore must be included.

Let us now examine the relationships between variations in cost and variations in output.

III. VARIATIONS IN COST IN RELATION TO CHANGES IN THE RATE OF OUTPUT

1. The commitment to a scale of production and sunk costs. 2. The concepts of average and marginal cost. 3. The relation between average and marginal cost curves. 4. The average total cost curve.

1. *The commitment to a scale of production and sunk costs.* It has been observed above that an established enterprise is at any point in time committed to a particular combination of the factors of production, in the form of buildings, machines, land, etc., which it is not possible to change in the short-run.[7] These commitments are the result of past decisions of management policy; but for the present purposes the sunk costs which they represent are of his-

---

[7] The degree to which these factors are unalterable is of course a function of the length of the time period. For different enterprises in different industries the time required to alter the scale of operations will be vastly different. For any particular enterprise, however, it ought to be possible to specify rather accurately a time period during which no substantial alteration of the scale of output is possible. As a matter of fact, of course, in no one enterprise is there any rigid dividing line between a long period over which the scale of operations is alterable, and a short period during which no alteration of scale is possible. For purposes of analysis, however, it is convenient to employ the assumption. Cf. Viner, Jacob, "Cost Curves and Supply Curves," *Zeitschrift für Nationalökonomie*, Band III, Heft 1 (1932), pp. 23-46 at p. 26.

One further point in this connection may be mentioned. How long a time period is assumed necessary to change the scale of operations is dependent upon what cost outlays the firm is willing to undertake. That is, if we wish to change

torical interest only. These fixed factors, from another point of view, may be regarded as that scale of operations to which the enterprise is committed in the short period under consideration. If such sunk costs are really sunk, in the sense that their amount can in no way be altered during the short period, then they constitute a fixed aggregate sum whose amount is independent of the volume of output from the given scale. Being fixed in amount for all rates of output, they are therefore in no way important in determining how much to produce over the period of time for which they are fixed. Just what cost items will fall within this category will depend upon the enterprise in question and the time interval under consideration. Interest on bonds outstanding, insurance, property taxes, a skeleton labor force, the salaries of managers, some depreciation, obsolescence, etc., would perhaps be the most common items of this type.[8] If their amount is assumed to be a fixed aggregate sum for all rates of output between zero and maximum physical capacity, it follows obviously that their average amount per unit of output will be progressively less as the volume of production is increased. A curve depicting their average amount per unit of output at different rates of output will be a rectangular hyperbola.[9] The cost of the license plates per mile of travel by automobile becomes continuously less and less with each mile traveled.

2. *The concepts of average and marginal cost.* The significant cost elements in determining what is the appropriate output for the enterprise to produce under given conditions are those costs which are incurred as a result of producing rather than not pro-

the scale in a relatively short period of time it will no doubt be technologically possible to do so; but only at a tremendous cost in comparison to the cost of doing so more slowly. Thus, even in a brief space of time the scale of operations may be enlarged, and therefore output increased. Whether it will pay to do so will of course depend upon the relationship between costs and receipts. During a war-time boom it may pay to construct factories by floodlight, but not usually.

[8] It is important to note that not all depreciation should be included for the reason that at least in part depreciation is a function of the rate of production. In this connection see the discussion of Mr. J. M. Keynes on "User Cost" in his *General Theory of Employment, Interest and Money*, New York (Harcourt, Brace), 1936, Ch. 6.

[9] A rectangular hyperbola is simply a curve of such a character that the product of the ordinate and abscissa for all points on the curve is a constant. It is a curve whose equation is of the form $(xy) = K$.

ducing. By making cost outlays in certain directions and in various amounts the firm in the typical case can increase its output. Our interest here is with the behavior of these costs which arise as a result of producing more rather than less. We shall refer to them as variable costs, although there is no implication that with respect to each component item that it increases proportionately with the increase in physical output.

The most realistic assumption with reference to these variable costs is that their *aggregate* amount increases progressively with every increase in output: [10] the larger the volume of output the larger the total variable costs. From these data of aggregate variable costs at different outputs we can compute two important and useful cost figures per unit of output: average variable cost and marginal cost. For any rate of output for which we know total variable cost, average variable cost would simply be this figure divided by the output. If Xn is the total variable cost when n units are produced (n being any positive figure), average variable cost would simply be $\dfrac{Xn}{n}$; hence for all values of n we can compute average variable cost, $\dfrac{Xn}{n}$. If, therefore, we know the behavior of aggregate variable cost we can compute therefrom the average variable cost of production per unit at different volumes of output. Such values when plotted on a graph (whose horizontal axis measures units of output and vertical axis cost of production in money terms) and connected up to form a curve would indicate the average variable cost of production at different volumes of output.

Our other cost concept, marginal cost, is simply the increment in cost incurred as a consequence of increasing output by one

[10] The possibility that *aggregate* variable cost will decrease as output increases seems too inconceivable to be worth serious consideration. That total variable cost would remain constant over certain relevant ranges of output is a theoretical possibility which at times may be almost approached in practice. It essentially implies that the technological conditions of operation are such that it is impossible to have either more or less than a certain given complement of variable factors in order to operate at all. And further given this complement, the amount of product or service it is possible to render is a variable within certain limits. Some of the more recent regulations governing the operations of railroads and steamships, e.g., the requirement of a "full crew," create cost conditions of almost this sort. But cases of this kind are unusual in the writer's opinion.

unit from any given point. This is also derivable from the total
cost data. As we have said, the marginal cost at any point n is by
definition the cost incurred by adding one more unit to the output.
It is obvious, therefore, that its amount may be simply determined
from the total variable cost data by deducting from the total cost
of $(n + 1)$ units, the total cost at n units. Since total variable cost
increases as output is increased it follows that the difference between total cost at $(n + 1)$ and total cost at n must be positive.
By giving n different values it is a simple matter to compute marginal cost at any point and to plot the different values graphically.
Thus from the total variable cost data we can derive average
variable costs.

3. *The relation between average and marginal cost curves.* A
little reflection will indicate that two curves, one showing average
variable cost and the other marginal cost, must bear a definable
relation to one another. We suggested above that the fixed factors
of production to which the business enterprise is committed in
the short period have been designed in most cases to be used with
a certain complement of variable factors. As a consequence over
a certain range physical output will increase faster than the increase in variable factors applied. But if this be true then average
variable cost will be declining over this range. At some point (rate
of output), however, average cost must cease falling and commence to rise, for if it fell continuously it would ultimately strike
the horizontal axis which would mean that some very large output could be produced at zero average variable cost per unit.
Since this is absurd the average variable cost curve sooner or later
must cease falling and commence to rise. What of the marginal
cost curve? So long as the average cost curve is falling it must
mean that the amount added to cost by producing one more unit
is less than the previous average. For if the average cost when n
units are being produced is greater than when $n + 1$ are being
produced it must mean that the amount added to cost in raising
output to $n + 1$ was less than the average cost at n. Average cost
cannot continue to decline indefinitely however; sooner or later
it must cease falling and begin to rise. But it is impossible that the
average cost could rise unless the amount added (the marginal

cost) becomes greater than the previous average. Hence it must be true that the two curves intersect at the point of least average cost, i.e., when the average cost curve is neither falling nor rising. Beyond the point of intersection both curves must be rising, but

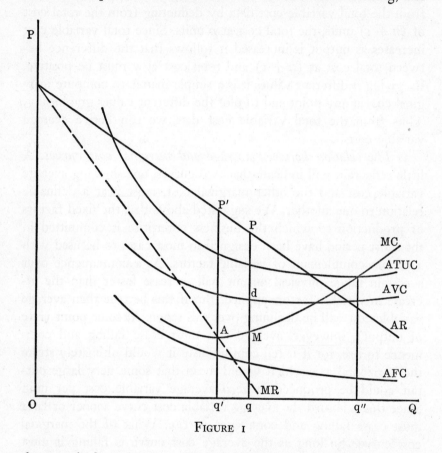

FIGURE I

the marginal cost curve will be rising the more rapidly. These relationships are shown diagrammatically in Fig. 1.

A further relationship between the average variable cost curve and the marginal cost curve may be indicated. Suppose we should wish to know the total variable cost of producing any given volume of output. Taking any point q on the horizontal axis (indicating rate of output) we may erect a perpendicular until it meets the marginal cost curve (MC) and the average variable cost curve (*AVC*) at points *M* and *d*, respectively. The total (variable) cost at *q* is of course the average variable cost at that point multiplied by the number of units produced, or, the rectangle having *Oq* as its base and the distance *dq* as its altitude. But also the total variable cost at *q* is the sum of all the increments in cost up to that point, that is the area subsumed under the marginal cost curve (*MC*) up to *M*. Thus the relationship between the average and marginal cost curves is such that the total variable cost at any point (any volume of output) is indicated geometrically by either: (a) the rectangle whose base is the output and whose altitude the average variable cost at that point; or (b) the area subsumed under the marginal cost curve up to that point. Obviously these two areas must be equal, and this must be true for any output. Thus between an average cost curve and a marginal cost curve this relationship must hold.

4. *The average total cost curve.* The foregoing discussion has been concerned only with variations of average and marginal cost where cost included only those items incurred in as a result of producing more or fewer units. In other words, the analysis was concerned entirely with the short period. But although the life of a business enterprise consists of a series of short periods these periods taken together produce a long period. While over a short period, as above defined, it is irrelevant to consider those sunk costs which can neither be avoided nor reduced, over a long period these costs are equally important with the variable costs. If an enterprise is to continue operations over an indefinite period it must cover *all* its costs. It is important therefore to have a curve of average costs which will include not only variable cost items but sunk cost items too.

As already noted a curve of average sunk costs would be a rectangular hyperbola for the short period. What, then, would a curve of average *total* cost per unit of output be like for the short period? This is easily answered. The average total cost at any point would be the sum of the average sunk cost (*AFC*) and the average variable cost (*AVC*); this would be true for any point. Therefore it follows that from a curve of average variable cost at different outputs and the rectangular hyperbola indicating average sunk cost at different outputs it is a simple matter to construct a curve showing average total cost at various points. Such a curve is indicated in Fig. 1. For certain purposes this curve will be very useful.

IV. THE DEMAND CURVE AND THE MARGINAL REVENUE CURVE

The cost data alone are insufficient to define the most profitable rate of output in the short period. Such data must be related to the behavior of gross receipts from the sale of the product; or stated otherwise, the supply conditions must be related to the demand conditions.

In economics the functional relation between price and the amount sold per period of time is usually indicated by means of a demand curve. Drawn in the familiar manner a demand curve shows how many units of the product buyers will purchase at different prices per unit of time (e.g., per day, week, etc.). We are interested primarily in the demand curve for the product of an individual firm and except in very unusual circumstances such a curve (*ATUC*) will have an elasticity greater than unity.[11]

Any demand curve may be interpreted as an average revenue curve; that is, it indicates the average gross revenue per unit of product sold when different amounts are sold. The total revenue (gross) received from the sale of any quantity is simply the number of units sold multiplied by the price. If at price P, the number of units sold is q, it is obvious that the total revenue is $P \times q$.

From a demand curve or average revenue curve it is possible to derive a marginal revenue curve in a manner symmetrical with our cost analysis. For instance, at price P, let total revenue be

[11] While it is possible that a demand curve for the product of all producers might have an elasticity less than unity this is unlikely over the relevant range for the single firm unless it has practically no direct competitors. But see Chamberlin's analysis of the case where all sellers are assumed to meet any price reduction by any one of them immediately. Chamberlin, E. H., *The Theory of Monopolistic Competition*, Cambridge, Mass. (Harvard), 2d ed., 1936, pp. 81-100.

$P \times q$. If now the number of units sold were to be increased by 1, i.e., $(q + 1)$, the total revenue will be the product of $(q + 1)$ and P''. P'' will be ever so slightly less than P: it is not shown in Fig. 1. If we now deduct from this second product the amount of the first (i.e., $P'' (q + 1) - P (q)$) the residual must necessarily be the amount added to revenue as a result of selling one more unit. This remainder is clearly the marginal revenue at that point, that is, the amount added to total gross revenue as a result of selling one more unit. By giving P (or q) different values we could compute the marginal revenue for each point on the average revenue curve. At least for the present we shall assume that the demand curve for the product of the enterprise has an elasticity greater than unity over a considerable range of prices. This must necessarily mean that marginal revenue is positive over the same range. Given the demand curve therefore it is possible to compute marginal revenue at any point; and if these values are plotted and connected into a curve we have what is called a marginal revenue curve.

If the demand curve for the enterprise has an elasticity greater than unity but less than infinity it means that the average revenue per unit decreases as the number of units sold increases.[12] But if the average revenue curve is falling, the marginal revenue curve must be falling even more rapidly or the average could not fall. Hence the marginal revenue curve will lie below the average revenue curve (the demand curve); and so long as the demand curve continues to have an elasticity greater than unity the marginal revenue curve will remain above the horizontal axis, i.e., have positive values. A demand curve (*AR*) with its corresponding marginal revenue curve (*MR*) is shown in Fig. 1. Because straight line demand curves are so much easier to draw they are here used. There is no implication, however, that most enterprises do in fact encounter straight line demand curves.

[12] If the demand curve is a horizontal straight line (infinitely elastic) the average revenue per unit of product sold is a constant. But if average revenue is constant, the marginal revenue is also constant and equal to it; therefore, the marginal revenue curve is the same as the average revenue curve, in this case both being a horizontal straight line extending to the right from the price (determined by the demand and supply forces in the market as a whole).

V. THE OPTIMUM RATE OF OUTPUT

Our analytical apparatus has now been elaborated to include two pairs of concepts which are useful in understanding the economics of enterprise operation. On the one hand we have an average cost curve and a marginal cost curve; on the other, an average revenue curve and a marginal revenue curve. Our problem is now to determine from these data what volume of output and sales will yield the enterprise its maximum return under the given conditions.[13] This should be comparatively simple: for we have one curve showing the increments in cost as more units are produced and another showing increments in revenue as the number of units sold is increased.

In the first place, unless the average revenue per unit sold is in excess of (or at least equal to) the average variable cost there will be no output whatsoever by the firm.[14] For to produce and sell under the conditions that the average receipt per unit of product sold is less than the average direct cost per unit of output produced is to involve the firm in an avoidable loss. Generally: at any and all times total receipts from the sale of the product must at least be equal to the total direct cost outlays which are incurred in production. There is clearly no necessity or incentive for the firm to incur an avoidable loss.

Assuming then that total revenue must always be at least equal to total direct cost outlays, what volume of output will maximize net returns for the enterprise?

[13] To simplify the analysis at this point it is assumed that output and sales proceed at the same rate; that is, sales per unit of time and output per unit of time are the same. This is of course equivalent to the assumption that the firm maintains its inventories at a constant figure through time.

[14] A possible exception to the above statement may be mentioned. If the firm is involved in a sales promotion campaign to build up the demand for the product it may pay to sell at less than the direct cost of production; it may even be worth while to give the product away. Cases of this sort turn upon considerations of future income as opposed to current income. The aim in selling at a very low price (or at zero price) is of course to influence the demand curve in a favorable direction. In other words, the aim is to secure more favorable returns in subsequent periods.

Here two curves are especially relevant: the marginal cost curve and the marginal revenue curve; the first shows the amount added to cost as a result of producing one more unit, the second, the amount added to receipts from selling one more unit. Now clearly so long as the marginal cost curve is below the marginal revenue curve it means that each additional unit produced and sold adds less to cost than it does to receipts; and it will pay to increase output and sales. But as output and sales are increased marginal cost rises, and since marginal revenue either remains constant or falls, there must be a point at which the marginal cost curve intersects the marginal revenue curve, i.e., where the two are equal.[15] But when marginal cost equals marginal revenue it means that the last unit produced adds to revenue exactly as much as its production adds to cost. For outputs and sales larger than this amount, more is added to cost than to receipts, and an avoidable loss is incurred on these units. Therefore, it follows that the output which will yield maximum returns is that output at which marginal cost equals marginal revenue. The point at which marginal revenue is equal to marginal cost is of course that rate of output and sales indicated by the point of intersection of the two curves. In Fig. 1 this is point A. Marginal cost is equal to marginal revenue in Fig. 1 at a rate of output Oq' which is sold at a price $P'q'$. By producing at this rate and selling at this price the enterprise is maximizing its returns under the conditions postulated.[16]

Before passing on to other matters of a related character it is worth noting several significant points on our curves so that we can refer to them conveniently by name without having to employ a diagram to illustrate the discussion.

As already indicated the optimum rate of output for the enterprise where the scale is given is that rate at which marginal cost is equal to marginal revenue. In Fig. 1 this is a rate of output Oq'

[15] Marginal revenue will only be constant for the case of pure competition where the marginal revenue curve is horizontal at the level of the ruling price.

[16] Under pure competition where the demand curve for the single firm is a horizontal straight line extending to the right opposite the ruling price, the marginal revenue curve traces out the same line, and the most profitable output is that at which marginal cost is equal to price.

which is sold at the price $P'q'$. It is found by erecting a perpendicular from the horizontal axis through A, the point of intersection of the marginal cost and marginal revenue curves. Hence
when in subsequent discussion we say that MC is equal to MR,
this is a brief way of indicating that the firm is maximizing returns under the given conditions.

For reasons already given both the $ATUC$ curve and the AVC
curve fall over a certain range as the rate of output is increased
and then they subsequently rise. And the marginal cost curve
(MC) intersects both $ATUC$ and AVC at their lowest points. But
the lowest point on $ATUC$ is that rate of output at which average
total unit cost is a minimum. In other words, when operating at
this rate of output, Oq'' in Fig. 1, the enterprise is producing at
maximum efficiency: per unit of resources applied the enterprise
is securing the maximum output of product.[17] This point is often
called the least cost point. It must be emphasized, however, that
because $ATUC$ is a minimum or even AVC is a minimum it does
not necessarily follow that the enterprise should produce at this
rate. The enterprise is endeavoring to maximize returns, not to
minimize costs. Consequently the behavior of costs has to be
related to the behavior of receipts.

One further observation may be made in closing. Unless a
segment of AR lies above AVC or, in the limiting case, is tangent
to it, the enterprise will not produce any output at all. For, if
everywhere throughout its range AR is below AVC, it means that
at all rates of output the enterprise is producing and selling at an
avoidable loss. Since the enterprise has no incentive to incur an
avoidable loss there will be no production and sales if these conditions hold. The same is *not* true, however, when AR lies below
$ATUC$ but above AVC. Here the firm is suffering a loss but a
smaller loss than it would incur should it not produce at all. Although the firm is producing and selling at a loss, it is none the
less minimizing those losses. It is maximizing its returns under the
conditions prevailing at the time.

[17] See *supra*, Ch. VI, sec. II, 1, (b).

VI. CHANGES WHICH ALTER THE OPTIMUM RATE OF OUTPUT

The previous section has endeavored to show that the enterprise will maximize its net receipts by producing at that volume of output at which marginal cost is equal to marginal revenue. At any juncture in time of course just what volume of output this will be may be quite different. What kinds of changes could alter it?

For purposes of analysis it is convenient to divide these changes into those affecting the cost side and those affecting the demand side.

Concerning the first it may be pointed out again that the fundamental relations determining the shape and slope of the average and marginal cost curves are (a) the physical relations existing between applications of variable factors of production and variations in output; (b) the per unit prices of the variable factors. It is apparent, therefore, that any change in the production functions, or any change in the per unit prices of the factors, will alter the curves and therefore the output which will yield the greatest returns. Technological changes of one sort or another could modify the most productive combination of the factors and hence the different amounts of each used. More common, however, is some change in the prices per unit of the particular factors of production which the firm hires or purchases. The effect of a higher per unit cost of any agent of production tends to be two-fold. In the first place, insofar as it is possible to substitute other agents of production for this (now) more costly agent there will be an incentive to do so. It may be, of course, that the character of the agent is such that the elasticity of substitution is zero; in that case no substitution is possible and the cost curves are altered accordingly. If the wage rates of railway locomotive engineers and firemen rise and there is no possibility of increasing the length of the trains operated for the present, then the railroad has no alternative but to pay the higher rates. Even though wage rates have risen, each train must have one engineer and one fire-man. Consequently there is no possibility of using less of these now more costly agents of production. In the second place, if some substitution is possible it will mean using more of the other agents than formerly and less of this particular one, and again the cost curves will be changed. Here the production functions are the same but because of altered prices of one (or several) of the agents it is more economical to combine them in a different pro-portion. Any change, therefore, which alters the cost schedules will alter the optimum volume of output quite apart from any change in the demand schedule.

The other type of change which will alter the output of the enterprise is that arising from the side of demand.[18] The kinds of fact situations which bring about a change in demand are too numerous to be described. The possible changes in demand *curves*, however, are rather simple to portray. These are essentially two: first, the curve might move to the right (an increase) or the left (a decrease) without changing its slope. Assuming that the firm had been maximizing returns previously by producing up to the point at which marginal cost was equal to marginal revenue, an increase in demand will mean a rise in price and an increase in output. Conversely, a decrease in demand would mean that re-turns will now be maximized with a smaller output sold at a lower price. If the demand curve changes at the previously estab-lished price, the enterprise will be aware of it through either an increase or decrease in the rate of absorption of the product by buyers. Inventories will be declining or increasing. Diagrammati-cally this case of a shift without change of slope is illustrated in Fig. 2. Here *AR* is the original demand curve and *P* the original price. An increase in demand causes price to rise to *P'* and a de-crease a fall to *P''*, the corresponding outputs being respectively *M'* and *M''*. *MC* is of course the marginal cost curve.[19]

It is possible however that the change might be of a different

---

[18] The case of perfect competition is not here considered. Under perfect com-petition, however, a firm would be immediately aware of any change in demand by the obvious fact of a price change.

[19] In this and the succeeding case it should be observed that the results are partially dependent upon the shape and position of the marginal cost curve. For instance in Fig. 2 if the marginal cost curve should only commence to rise *after*

sort; demand might become more or less elastic at higher or lower prices while remaining unchanged at the previously established price. This case is illustrated by Fig. 3. Here as before let AR be the original demand curve and P the price at which output

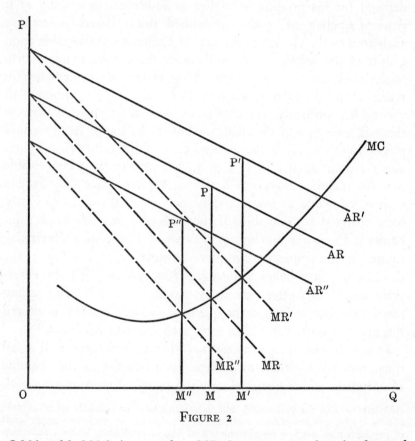

FIGURE 2

OM is sold, MC being equal to MR. Suppose now that the demand curve pivots around P to assume the new position AR'. The new marginal revenue curve is MR' which is equal to MC now when output is OM'. Returns will now be maximized by producing and

it has intersected the three marginal revenue curves it is not so certain that P would be greater than P'' but less than P'. It might be but it is not certain. It would depend not only on the fact that marginal cost is falling but on how rapidly it were falling. The reader can see the results for himself by drawing different marginal cost curves intersecting the three marginal revenue curves in various points. A similar qualification holds for the succeeding case.

selling OM' units at price P'. Similarly if the demand curve should rotate around P to the position AR'' price should be increased to P'' and output curtailed to OM''.[20] In cases of this sort the individual producer might not be aware at all of any change in the demand for his product at higher or lower prices so long as it remains unchanged at the established price. There is nothing analogous to the change in the rate of absorption consequent upon a shift of the *whole* curve. And under the circumstances a firm might continue for some time selling at the old price when in reality it would increase its returns by altering it. Although in general it is probably true that when there is a change in demand there is a change in the quantity buyers will take at all various prices. In other words, the demand curve shifts rather than rotates about a point such as P in Fig. 3. Nevertheless it is conceivable that the quantity buyers will take at a given price may remain unchanged while at lower and higher prices the quantities may have changed considerably. If, because of a rise of people's incomes in the lower brackets or because of a successful advertising campaign, the demand curve pivots around P (e.g., in Fig. 3, the demand at prices below P changes from AR to AR') the enterprise would be better served by reducing its price and selling more units. But so long as the quantity sold at P remains unaltered the firm would never realize such a change had occurred.[21]

In conclusion, then, we may say that an enterprise will at all times seek to maximize its returns by producing at that volume of output at which marginal cost and marginal revenue are equal.

[20] Any firm in the real world will necessarily have to consider what indirect effects, if any, will result from a change in price. A rise in price for certain kinds of products may cause a certain amount of consumer ill-will; while a reduction may cause purchasers to revise their notions of its worth. See Smith, Henry, "Discontinuous Demand Curves and Monopolistic Competition: A Special Case," *Quarterly Journal of Economics,* Vol. 49 (1935), pp. 542-550. This merely re-emphasizes our contention in section I of the present chapter that the firm must consider the consequences in terms of future receipts of any step taken to increase them in the current period.

[21] Parenthetically it may be remarked that one of the aims of advertising expenditure is to render the demand curve more elastic at prices below that now ruling and less elastic at prices above that now charged. In other words, one purpose of advertising is to attach buyers more firmly to the product. But this means that buyers would continue to prefer it at prices higher than those now ruling and that if the price were reduced only a little existing buyers would purchase

No enterprise, to be sure, is ever in a position to determine the demand curve for its product throughout its whole length. But in reality this is no objection to the foregoing analysis since it is quite unnecessary that the firm know this. Let us assume the firm

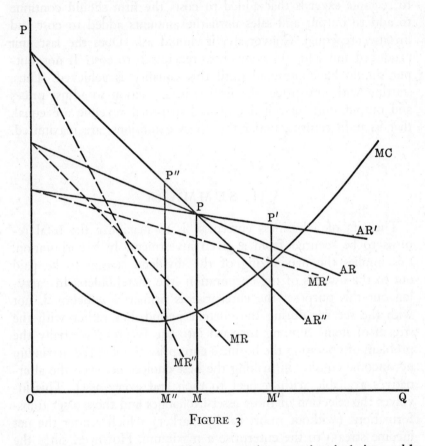

FIGURE 3

has fixed some price at which a certain quantity is being sold. Now what the firm must consider is, Will the production and sale of an additional unit add more to income than it will to cost? An

many more units and a whole flood of new buyers would be induced to purchase. In diagrammatical terms: in Fig. 3, if the original demand curve were *AR*, advertising would hope to convert it into the position of *AR'* below *P* and of *AR"* above *P*. However, advertising would be expected to move the curve to the right at *P* as well. But it may be of some importance to observe that advertising is not only aimed at shifting the demand curve to the right but at altering its elasticity as well.

"additional unit" is here used to mean the smallest variation in output it is practical to consider. In many cases the "unit" might be several hundreds or even thousands of the final product, e.g., boxes of matches or pairs of shoes. So long as the amount added to receipts exceeds that added to costs the firm should continue to add to output and sales until the amounts added to cost and income are equal. Conversely, it should ask, Does the last unit produced and sold add as much to receipts as to cost? If not, output should be contracted until this equality is achieved. Thus, starting with any price, the firm is in a position to adjust prices and output until marginal cost and marginal revenue are equal, that is, until returns, under the given conditions, are maximized.

VII. SUMMARY

The aim of a business enterprise is to maximize the total re-*c*urns to be secured from a given investment. In a corporation, this implies the maximizing of the dividend stream to be paid out to the owners of the corporation—the shareholders. In carrying out this purpose, the enterprise is primarily concerned, not with the returns during the current period, but rather with the stream of items running forward into the future. Essentially the problem of operating the business enterprise to yield the maximum net income consists in making the best choices between the alternatives available with respect to each and every asset. This involves the selection of those asset exchanges and those asset transformations (without resort to the market) which render the net income stream to the enterprise a maximum. However, since the value of a group of assets is determined by their ability (in combination) to yield net returns over a period of time extending into the future, the problem of maximizing net income becomes that of maintaining that asset combination having the greatest present worth. Yet the aim is always to secure that *stream* of returns having the greatest present worth so that often the enterprise will forego substantial but short-lived returns in favor of those smaller but more enduring, provided their present worth is greater. The element of uncertainty, which is characteristic of business as a whole, influences the solution of the problem of maximizing net returns in two important ways: (a) net receipts to be had in the far distant future are accorded a very small present worth and (b) constant revision of expectations and plans of operation is necessary as more accurate knowledge becomes available.

To obtain this income stream the enterprise sells physical products or services to others for a money price. Such activity necessitates the use of certain factors of production with their accompanying costs. The exact relationship between the input of factors of production and the output of goods and services, assuming a given scale of operation, depends upon technological considerations which largely determine the degree of efficiency at each rate of operation. To facilitate this study, we may discard the physical input-output relationship in favor of its monetary manifestations in terms of costs and returns.

For any given scale of production, there are certain fixed costs which are not affected by the rate of output and which may not be altered over the short period. Thus for a short period, these costs have no influence in determining the appropriate rate of output; this is found rather from an analysis of average variable cost and marginal cost. Nevertheless, in the long run average total costs must be covered if the enterprise is to survive.

These cost data alone, however, are insufficient to determine the optimum rate of output. The average revenue and marginal revenue data must be included in the analysis to determine the point of maximum returns to the enterprise. With these revenue factors known, the optimum rate of production may be demonstrated to be that rate which equates marginal cost and marginal revenue; that is, the rate at which the last unit produced and sold adds to revenue exactly as much as its production adds to cost.

The actual volume of output indicated by the foregoing analysis changes from time to time as a result of variations both in cost and in revenue factors. Cost factors fluctuate with two general types of changes: (a) changes in the prices of the factors of production and (b) technological changes modifying the optimum combination of factors of production which the firm employs. Demand may vary for innumerable reasons, although the two types of changes are variations in elasticity and slope, and shifts in the position of the whole curve.

REFERENCES: CHAPTER VII

CHAMBERLIN, E. H.—*The Theory of Monopolistic Competition*, Chs. 1, 2, 4, Cambridge, Mass.: Harvard, 1933.

ROBINSON, JOAN—*The Economics of Imperfect Competition*, Ch. 2, London: Macmillan, 1933.

BOULDING, K. E.—"The Theory of a Single Investment," *Quarterly Journal of Economics*, Vol. 49.

CARLSON, SUNE—*A Study on the Pure Theory of Production*, London, 1939.

CASSELS, J. M.—"On the Law of Variable Proportions," in *Explorations in Economics:* Essays in Honor of F. W. Taussig, 1936.

DENNISON, H. S., and GALBRAITH, J. K.—*Modern Competition and Business Policy*, Chs. 3-4.

MARSCHAK, J., and MAKOWER, H.—"Assets, Prices, and Monetary Theory," *Economica*, August, 1938.

ROBBINS, L.—"Certain Aspects of the Theory of Costs," *Economic Journal*, March, 1934, Vol. 44.

ROBINSON, E. A. G.—"The Problem of Management and the Size of the Firm," *Economic Journal*, June, 1934, Vol. 44.

WILLIAMS, J. B.—*The Theory of Investment Value*, Cambridge, Mass., 1938.

Chapter VIII

SOME PROBLEMS IN THE DETERMINATION OF INCOME FOR AN ELAPSED PERIOD

I. The Accounting Concept of Income. II. The Valuation Problem in the Computation of Accounting Income. III. Accounting Reports and the Business Enterprise in Relation to the Economy. IV. Summary.

Our contention throughout the previous chapter was that a business enterprise endeavors to maximize returns to the owners of the concern. And on analysis we saw that this reduces to the aim of obtaining that combination of the assets which will yield the stream of cash payments (dividends) to the owners (shareholders) having the greatest present worth. We also showed that an alternative form of expression for the same principle was to say that the enterprise seeks to maximize the present worth of its assets, for the significance of the assets to the firm is their ability to contribute to the realization of the desired stream of dividends. But since the present worth of the assets which the enterprise is endeavoring to maximize is necessarily equal to the present worth of the claims against those assets, and since the claims are creditors' claims and proprietors' claims, we can just as well say that the enterprise endeavors to maximize the present worth of the proprietorship claims. In other words, the effort to maximize returns to the owners of the enterprise consists in trying to maximize the present worth of the ownership claims against it. Although for business enterprises in the real world the application of the principles we sought to develop is probably somewhat less precise than our analysis might suggest, nevertheless it would probably be agreed that this is essentially what business corporations are endeavoring to do. In the nature of the case principles must be formally and precisely stated to be correct and to be useful. Vague generalizations are not helpful since their logic and meaning do not stand forth clearly. An accurately stated principle on the other hand is applicable to all sorts of fact situations differing from one another in irrelevant details because a principle emphasizes the essential similarity and logic common to them all. The only alternative to precise principles is simply to assume each case is unique and a law unto itself: no useful generalizations are possible or have yet been discovered. With respect to many kinds of phenomena experience and reflection demonstrate this is not true. Hence in our analysis of the meaning and implications of maximizing income we have sought to be precise, and to this extent formal, since we have tried to state the principles in terms applicable to all kinds of business enterprises organized for private gain. Nothing we have said so far, however, must be interpreted to mean that no problems arise in making the allowances necessary when these principles are applied. However, we shall postpone these difficulties from consideration until a later section of this chapter.

I. THE ACCOUNTING CONCEPT OF INCOME

1. Accounting and the balance sheet equation. 2. The treatment of durable assets in the computation of accounting income. 3. The sources of the accountant's difficulties.

Our discussion of maximizing returns to the owners of the enterprise in the preceding chapter was strictly forward-looking in character. We argued that the enterprise endeavors at all times so to apply its resources as to yield the dividend series having the greatest present worth. That is, all the terms in our D series were forward in time from the present moment. The thing to be maximized in the operations of the business was returns yet to be received.

Although primary interest attaches to the present worth of the proprietorship claims (necessarily a derivative of returns yet to be received), business enterprises are nevertheless accustomed to determine periodically their "income" for a period which has already elapsed. It is income in this sense of returns during some period *which has already passed* which is the primary concern of the accountant, and what we usually imply in everyday language when we say, for instance, that the Acme Corporation is very "profitable." We mean that computations of earned income by accounting methods have indicated favorable changes in the computed value of ownership claims over the past several periods. No accountant in 1939 would ever compute the change in the value of the proprietorship claims for the calendar year 1941, although he might prepare certain "budgets" for the two years 1940 and 1941. If accounting is concerned with the computation of income for some period that has already expired, what is the relationship between income in this backward-looking accounting sense and returns in the forward-looking sense by which the value of the assets and hence the value of the proprietorship claims are determined? This question will bear examination.

1. *Accounting and the balance sheet equation.* Accounting, as everyone knows, is built around the so-called proprietorship equation. This equation is simply that in value terms assets equal liabilities plus proprietorship. Necessarily these two must be equal since by definition the value of the claims of the owners is simply the total value of the resources of the enterprise minus any claims on those resources possessed by creditors, sometimes called "outsiders." As we have repeatedly emphasized, the resources have value to the enterprise solely because they may be employed to yield valuable services through future time. And the *amount* of value to be attached to the resources at any instant in time must necessarily be a derivative from the prospective stream of returns *as now computed* on the basis of information *now* available. Knowing the value of the resources and the amount of the liabilities at an instant of time we can deduce the value of the proprietorship claims. Now let some period pass, say, a year, during which the enterprise conducts its operations always with the aim of maximizing the present value of the proprietorship claims. At the end of the year let the value of the assets, creditors' claims, and hence proprietorship be again determined. And let us assume further that the proprietors neither withdraw nor add assets during the year. Almost inevitably the value of the proprietorship

will be different at the end of the year than it was at the beginning. For at the end of the year the value of the assets must be computed on the basis of the *then* prospective returns they are expected to yield. Similarly the claims of outsiders will probably have changed too. But if both assets and liabilities have changed it would be pure accident if the proprietorship did not also change. What is this difference in the value of proprietorship? It clearly must be the income of the proprietors for the period just ended. Since the change in proprietorship may be either an increase or a decrease, so also income may be positive or negative.

From one point of view accounting is no more than a rather highly developed technique for computing and recording such changes in the value of the proprietorship claims from period to period. And it does this of course by recording changes in the value of the particular asset and liability items as these occur and/or as they are recognized. The change in proprietorship is determined simply by subtracting the revised value of the liabilities from the revised value of the assets. It is worth repeating again that if it were not for uncertainties, i.e., that people's expectations are not exactly realized in practice, there would be no necessity for such computations from period to period. If anticipations were always perfect we could specify the value of the proprietorship claims at any and all points in the future here and now. Given the income stream and the rate of discount the determination of the value of the proprietorship claims at any juncture in the future would be a simple arithmetical problem. In fact, however, the size and time distribution of the income stream are tinged with uncertainty; and people are continually revising their previous estimates. In one important sense accounting is simply a means of recording the net changes in the estimated value of proprietorship from the beginning of a period to its end. If anticipations were always correct then the value of these claims at the end of the period could be determined and recorded at its beginning. But anticipations are not perfect; they are being continually revised. Suppose, for instance, that at the beginning of a period it is estimated that the value of the proprietorship claims *at the end of the period* will be V, and let us assume further that the rate of discount is i. However if the value of proprietorship claims at the end of the period is now reckoned to be V, and if the rate of discount is i per period, the *present value* of these proprietorship claims must clearly be $\frac{V}{1+i}$. Let us now assume that the period has just ended and that, on the basis of what is *then* known, the value of the proprietorship is again computed and found to be not V, as anticipated, but $(V \pm a)$, a being the divergence between the estimate at the beginning of the period and that at its end. If we like, a is the amount by which the expectations held at the beginning of the period are now thought to have been incorrect. It is clear at once, however, that the income for the period just ended is $(V \pm a) - \left(\frac{V}{1+i}\right)$, which may be positive or negative. This expression which we may designate by the symbol I (income), so that $I = (V \pm a) - \left(\frac{V}{1+i}\right)$, is essentially what the accounting technique is endeavoring to determine. Let us reiterate that I, as defined, is the expression for income in the accounting sense for a period that has already expired. In accounting practice, of course, numerous ancillary devices are typically employed in order to facilitate the calculation of I; the most important of these, perhaps, being the so-called subsidiary proprietorship accounts or the expense and income accounts. But these are no more than aids to the primary aim of accounting which is to provide a means of recording changes in the value of proprietorship claims through time. Theoretically the value of the proprietorship claims could be recomputed at stated intervals or in such a way that their value could be read off from the records at any instant. As we shall note presently the usual practice is a compromise.

2. *The treatment of durable assets in the computation of accounting income.* Our argument has been that income in the accounting sense, I, is determined by the formula $I = (V \pm a) - \left(\frac{V}{1+i}\right)$. While this is the theoretical procedure for determining income relating to a past period in accounting the actual practice contains certain aberrations from this formula or "ideal." [1] In some

[1] Note the following: "If absolutely accurate balance-sheets could be prepared at the beginning and at the end of a period, the difference between their surplus accounts (withdrawals, dividends, and allowances being considered) would rep-

measure these are forced on the accountant by the exigencies of practical affairs but also they partially result from the use of certain fictions as convenient assumptions. Let us examine these modifications of the strict logic.

Perhaps the most important modification of the formula in accounting practice is the use of a unique, and in a sense arbitrary, assumption in assigning revised values to certain types of resources from period to period. Our contention has been that the value of any asset to the enterprise is a derivative of the prospective benefits consequent upon its possession. Now the accountant recognizes that certain items of equipment possess an ability to render valuable services to the enterprise for more than one accounting period, an accounting period being simply that time interval for which income is regularly computed. It is in revising periodically the values of these durable items that the accountant employs a particular assumption which ought to be made more explicit.

An accountant assumes that at the time of purchase any item is worth its purchase price to the enterprise. In the case of machines, etc., having a usefulness of more than one accounting period, the purchase price to the enterprise is assumed to indicate their then present worth as determined by the valuable services they are expected to render. Logically of course a particular machine must be worth at least this much to the concern or its acquisition is irrational.[2] The value of the machine having been

resent the net income or deficit for the term; but the valuation and revaluation of capital assets involve too much speculation to permit the recognition of such a practice as satisfactory." Montgomery, R. H., *Auditing, Theory and Practice*, New York (Ronald), 1927, p. 360.

In our terminology we would simply say that *a* is zero. In this case of course the income of the enterprise would be exactly equal to the rate of interest multiplied by the value of the net worth at the beginning of the period.

[2] Economists will observe that what the accountant takes as the then value of the machine is only the limiting case. If the machine is worth this much and no more then the purchase is marginal, which is to say it is a matter of indifference whether the firm acquires it or not. In most instances its worth to the enterprise undoubtedly is estimated by those in control at something more. This is because there is a certain "lumpiness" in the things the enterprise purchases. If they were all divisible into very small units the firm would continue to purchase until the last unit was just worth its cost price to the enterprise.

Presumably what the accountant does here is accept the purchase price as an unbiased judgment of its worth. His experience no doubt has emphasized the proneness of owners to be overly optimistic concerning the present worth of the things they possess. Hence, unless he is ready to accept the purchaser's estimate

once determined in this manner it is thenceforth assumed in subsequent accounting periods that the original estimate was correct and that there is no necessity for changing it.[3] Consequently, given the number of periods over which the machine was originally expected to yield services, it is assumed to decline in value to the enterprise by a proportionate amount each accounting period. Thus, if at the time of purchase it is expected to yield valuable services to the enterprise for n periods it declines in value to the enterprise each period 1 nth of its purchase price. In other words, in accounting the implicit assumption regarding durable items of equipment is that absolutely correct estimates of their value to the enterprise can be made at the time of their purchase: the appropriate assumption is perfect expectations.

The consequence is that in determining the income for any expired period, i.e., the change in the value of proprietorship, it is thought to be unnecessary to revise the value estimates of durable items of equipment made at the beginning of the period. Given their estimated service life and their purchase price, their value at all points in future time is assumed to be determinable. Stated otherwise, we might say that the periodic revisions of the

or make one of his own, perhaps the most reasonable procedure is to accept the purchase price as the most reasonable measure of value to the enterprise.

From another point of view one might argue that the purchase price is the most reasonable because it is the market price representing the judgment of many individuals. Such an argument would be greatly strengthened if perfect competition could be assumed. For then the selling price of the machine would equal its cost of production which would in turn be determined by the value of the factors in alternative uses. Hence the selling price would represent the collective judgment of the individuals of the economy as to its worth. Except in a very rough way it is unlikely that any such thought sequence has entered into accountants' reasoning.

[3] Some thoughtful students of accounting incline towards the position that the purpose of accounting is to record historical "cost" to the enterprise and to undertake to allocate these costs between accounting periods. Consequently, they would urge that the accountant, *qua* accountant, is concerned to deal with values in no other sense. From this point of view accounting is a log of the day to day voyage of the business enterprise rather than a process of "shooting the sun" at periodic intervals. Observe the following: ". . . it seems desirable to emphasize the fact that accounting is not essentially a process of valuation, as some writers on accounting and some economists conceive it to be. . . . Primarily, accounting is historical in its approach, with valuation entering into it at times as a safeguard. The emphasis is on cost, though where an asset is intended for sale and its selling value is known to be less than cost, the lower figure may be substituted for cost." May, George O., *Twenty-five Years of Accounting Responsibility*, New York (American Institute Publishing Co.), 1936, Vol. II, p. 309.

value of the proprietorship claims are carried through on the special assumption that for an important group of assets the original estimates of their value were quite perfect. This assumption of perfect expectations may not strike the reader as an accurate description of what the accountant does with respect to "capital assets." But to the writer it seems logically unassailable. Anyone familiar with accounting would admit that the usual procedures with respect to depreciation are such that it is possible to say at the time of an asset's acquisition what "book value" it will have at any time in the future. This would certainly seem to mean that it is assumed that its value can be predicted with strict accuracy. In the accounting literature this idea is perhaps usually expressed in the *dictum* that the proper basis for depreciation charges is original cost.[4] On occasion, if the original estimates are seen to be seriously in error, the accountant will sanction their revision.[5] But the point to be stressed is that they are not *continually* revised from period to period as a consequence of all changes, internal and external to the enterprise, affecting their ability to yield valuable services.

[4] "The accounting function in relation to capital assets is to measure and record not the fluctuations in their value but the extent to which their usefulness is being exhausted through age or use, and to make proper charges against income in respect of such exhaustion, based on the cost of the property exhausted, with the intent that the property shall stand on the books at its salvage value when the term of its usefulness is ended." *Ibid.*, pp. 310-311. It may be observed, however, that "usefulness" to the business enterprise is largely meaningless unless it means productive of valuable services. The enterprise is not concerned with usefulness except from this point of view.

[5] There are essentially two ways by which such revised estimates of their discounted earning power are carried through. If the "book value" of the asset is believed to be wrong it must either overstate or understate the proper value as now computed. To correct it we may either change its present book value and alter the value of the proprietorship claims immediately, or, we may increase or decrease its book value in subsequent periods by revising our estimate of the number of accounting periods over which the asset will yield valuable services to the enterprise, i.e., change the depreciation rate. In the latter case although the book value of proprietorship is not now changed it will be subsequently affected by the revisions now undertaken. Neither alteration however is made to affect "income" as computed by the accountant for the current period. The charges or credits are made to "capital" in the accounting language.

The other occasion on which revised estimates of the value of the asset are placed on the books is when the asset is disposed of to persons outside the enterprise for either more or less than its book value. Here again the difference is charged or credited directly to the stated value of the proprietorship claims, it is not included in income. But by revising the stated net worth we are indicating that the past computations of income were incorrect.

Hence, although accountants and economists would probably agree that for any expired period income is properly defined as the change in the estimated value of proprietorship, one must not assume that when an accountant computes net income for an enterprise according to "standard practice" he purports to measure the *entire* change in net worth. To be sure he computes the change in the *book* value of net worth; but the change in book value will only reflect the complete change in proprietorship on the special assumption that the depreciable assets (and land) have been assigned originally and permanently correct valuations. The change in net worth as shown by the change in the proprietorship *accounts* has, therefore, a misleading appearance of identity with the *concept* of net income as the change in the estimated value of proprietorship.[6]

3. *The sources of the accountant's difficulties.* Before passing to a consideration of some of the specific problems encountered in determining the net income for a past period let us note the basic sources from which these difficulties spring.

We have already shown that if expectations were always perfect it would be a simple matter to write down the significant accounting figures for the enterprise for all future time. The essential difficulty of an uncertain future is that the net results in value terms of any given application of resources are imperfectly predictable. From one point of view this is the most serious limitation within which the accountant has to work. But there are others.

It is frequently suggested that the difficulties of the accountant

[6] As Professor Bonbright has said, "The exposition is all the more necessary because many writers, misled by the formal procedure by which the accountants determine income, have identified the accounting concept with the 'increased-net-worth' concept. That is, they have assumed that the income of a business during a given period is measured by the increase in the net worth of its assets during that same period. This misconception arises because, as a matter of convenient form, net income is derived by a comparison of the *book* values of the assets at the end of the year with their *book* values at the beginning. The difference in these book values may be treated as income. What is overlooked is the fact that the book values themselves are not ordinarily adjusted so as to reflect changes in actual values. Fixed assets, for example, are traditionally valued at cost minus conventional allowances for depreciation—which means they are not valued at all." Bonbright, J. C., *The Valuation of Property*, New York (McGraw-Hill), 1937, Vol. II, p. 905.

would disappear if individuals were satisfied to make no computations of the change in the value of the proprietorship claims until the final liquidation of the enterprise. This is really tantamount to our previous contention about uncertainties and their significance for the accountant. For if no computations are undertaken until the enterprise has ceased operations for all time, the enterprise no longer possesses a future about which doubts may exist. By definition its termination means the disappearance of its uncertain future. Since many concerns expect to maintain a perpetual life and since the life span of real persons is finite there are obvious reasons why the computation of changes in the value of proprietorship cannot be postponed until the dissolution of the enterprise. Business concerns are organized for profit purposes and they are typically perpetuated so long as the profit possibilities appear attractive, and often longer. As a rule they are only dissolved after the proprietors' investment has been at least partially dissipated. Consequently is it unsatisfactory to postpone all calculations until the termination of the venture: periodic determination of the probable value of the proprietorship claims is the well-nigh universal rule. And the necessity for periodic estimates magnifies the difficulties of the accountant. As is common knowledge the revisions in the value of the proprietorship are usually undertaken no more frequently than quarterly, although theoretically they might be undertaken daily if the information supplied was deemed to be worth its cost of preparation.

A third major difficulty for the accountant arises from the fact that his computations and estimates necessarily run in terms of value or worth to the enterprise which he is in no position to compute independently. That is, the magnitudes with which he works are value magnitudes and since he cannot compute these on the basis of his own knowledge and experience he must adopt certain "rules" or "principles" to assist him in inferring value changes. In certain circumstances there seems to be a tendency to forget that the ultimate purpose is to record value changes and not to seek to establish the universal applicability of the rules and principles which often give evidence of value changes and their degree. Nevertheless by almost any criterion the position of the accountant in this respect is not particularly happy. He must report value changes in the enterprise without being qualified to determine *de novo* how great these changes are.

II. THE VALUATION PROBLEM IN THE COMPUTATION OF ACCOUNTING INCOME

1. The direct valuation of assets. 2. The indirect valuation of certain types of assets. 3. Revaluation accounts and the valuation of proprietorship.

The general tenor of section I may seem to have been unduly critical of prevailing accounting practices. This, however, was quite unintentional. What we were essentially endeavoring to show was the relationship between the *concept* of income in economics as forward-looking and the *concept* of income in accounting as backward-looking. Now not infrequently it comes about that a *concept* is perfectly clear-cut and logically unassailable at the same time that very grave difficulties are encountered in applying the concept statistically to day to day affairs. The concept of depreciation, for example, can be formulated with reasonable precision; but to determine *how much* any particular machine has depreciated in a given period is less easy. So it is with income in the accounting sense: the concept is not especially difficult but its application to particular cases raises some knotty problems. The accountant as a practitioner can neither brush these difficulties aside nor refuse to deal with them. Furthermore, he does not possess unlimited time and money, the expenditure of which might increase considerably the precision of his statistical results. As a consequence he must make the best compromise he can in view of the difficulties of the problem and the limited resources of time and money at his disposal. Let us examine these compromises somewhat further than we have already.

We have argued that the accounting *concept* of income is simply the estimated change in the value of the proprietorship claims from the beginning of a period to its end. And according to the accounting (or balance sheet) equation, assets minus liabilities measure proprietorship. Now if statistical difficulties arise in determining the change in the (estimated) value of proprietorship between any two dates it must be because there are difficulties in computing the precise value of assets and/or the precise amount of outsiders' claims: for the value of proprietorship is by definition the difference. The difficulties or problems are therefore those of valuation.

1. *The direct valuation of assets.* The assets of a particular enterprise might be broken up into almost any number of groups although certain classifications are ordinarily employed. The usual designations such as land, buildings, machinery of various kinds, accounts receivable, inventories, cash, etc., are familiar to everyone. For purposes of the problem immediately at hand, the valuation problem, a more useful classification of assets is on the basis of the kind of valuation methods usually adopted. As Professor Canning has emphasized, the valuation of any asset may be determined directly or indirectly; [7] and for some assets presumably a choice is available.

For most components of that group of assets known as current the usual procedure is direct valuation. If an enterprise has $10,000 as a deposit in a solvent bank the present value of that item cannot be more or less than that sum since values are nowadays expressed always in money terms. So also with notes receivable with definite due dates little difficulty arises in determining their present worth, due allowance being made of course for the possibility that some are not fully collectible; similarly with accounts receivable. [8] These assets are comparatively easy to evaluate because the

---

[7] Canning, J. B., *The Economics of Accountancy*, New York (Ronald), 1929, especially Chapters X-XII. The present discussion has been considerably aided by this excellent volume. At p. 198 Professor Canning makes the following useful clarification: "A theory of value may be conceptual only—most theories of value are. But theories of valuation are statistical. They do not go beyond the bounds set by the data that are, or that may become, available. A theory of valuation treats of selecting a set of procedures appropriate for discriminating data in the form of money-valuations. It is but an elementary and specialized kind of statistical theory. Statistical theory is a theory of measurements that are subject to error."

[8] The interest accrued on notes receivable is usually separately recorded. With open book accounts it is not customary to include any deduction for the time

time interval forward over which they will yield returns to the enterprise is quite short. The value of marketable securities to the enterprise is likewise easily determinable by reference to the market quotations. The comparative simplicity of assigning reasonably accurate valuations to these items arises from the very short interval over which the valuable services they will yield to the enterprise has to be projected.

Inventory valuation for balance sheet purposes raises certain difficulties which cannot be dealt with at length. The bothersome snag here seems to be that the accountant has the choice of two techniques of valuation: one direct and the other indirect. In valuing current assets the rule is usually to employ a direct valuation method; in valuing current durable assets an indirect technique is employed. With respect to inventories the accountant has both valuations, he knows cost and he knows market price. Which should he use? More often than not the dilemma is avoided by urging the virtues of understatement and therefore adopting the rule of "the lower of cost or market." In a sense this combines the disadvantages of both with few of the advantages of either.[9]

The payments which the enterprise will have to make to nonproprietors for commitments already made, the liabilities, can typically be assigned reasonably accurate value amounts. The usual procedure, however, is to assign them a figure which indicates the amount of money the enterprise will have to pay at a point of time in the future rather than the (negative) present worth

interval between the date of the balance sheet and the due date of each account. Accounts receivable are usually listed in the balance sheet at their "face" value less some allowance for uncollectibles or "bad debts." Since accounts payable by the enterprise are similarly treated these minor discrepancies tend to offset one another. No doubt the accountant could make his valuations of these items more precise at a cost, but the increased accuracy in the results is probably not worth the candle.

[9] Cf. Canning, *op. cit.*, pp. 214-228. The writer has seen a compilation by a prominent firm of public accountants which seems to indicate that more than 50 per cent of the enterprises the firm examined used an out and out "cost or market whichever is lower" rule of inventory valuation. Also a considerable additional number used very slight modifications of it to give substantially the same results. The 50 per cent figure for the frequency of the cost or market rule is also confirmed by the study of Fjeld, E. I., *Balance Sheet Classification and Terminology*, New York (Columbia), 1936, pp. 62-63. See also Daniels, Mortimer B., *Corporation Financial Statements*, Ann Arbor, Mich. (University of Michigan), 1934, Ch. 8.

of such liabilities. Thus a bond issue is carried among the liabilities at its face value although it may not become due for another decade. The fact that the unpaid interest coupons on the bonds are not recorded, however, serves as an offset here. Such an overstatement of liabilities is less serious of course when the due date is near at hand; but it still exists. Here again, as with the current assets, greater precision could be obtained at a cost in time and money, but it is doubtful if, in view of the other limitations upon the accountants' results to be discussed presently, the more accurate figures would be worth their cost.

If the accountant had no asset valuation problems more serious than those occasioned by current assets and current liabilities his task would be vastly lighter than it now is. Unfortunately, as already observed, he is also faced with the difficulty of assigning revised values from period to period to assets whose ability to yield valuable services to the enterprise extends a considerable distance into the future.

2. *The indirect valuation of certain types of assets.* As repeatedly emphasized, the value of any asset to an enterprise is conceptually a derivative from the prospective valuable services its possession will add to the total. Now in arriving at a value for items expected to yield valuable services to the enterprise over several accounting periods there is a dual problem: first, the services to be received are basically physical services to which a money value has to be affixed; second, there is the question of what outlays will be entailed in order that the asset may render these valuable physical services through future time. The difficulty does not end here, however. For the services to be received from, say, the machine in question do not have a separate market in which they will be sold. The machine yields valuable services in furthering the production of some final product, its particular services are not themselves sold in the market for a money price.[10] If they

[10] As Professor Canning has written, "But the condition of independent, or primary, valuing of the service unit *in terms of money* can be fulfilled when, and only when, those services *are separately to be exchanged for money*. To the extent that a price per unit of service, whether for all or part of the service, can be rationally forecast we can value directly. But the items under consideration are those not to be sold or rented but to be used in conjunction with others for the making of a product that is to be sold." *Op. cit.*, p. 232. Italics in original.

were, their present worth might be more easily determinable. An alternative procedure might be to estimate how much the enterprise would have to pay for a similar instrument which would yield equally valuable services to the enterprise.[11] This might or might not mean purchasing an identical machine; the important thing is services of equal significance to the enterprise.[12] Obviously this is merely one particular kind of indirect valuation. Even here, however, no little trouble will be encountered in determining how much the enterprise would have to pay to secure alternative agents capable of yielding services of equivalent value to the enterprise. Conceptually the problem is not difficult, but statistically the task is troubling, time-consuming, and expensive. And to this is added the further objection that empirically equally skilled computators would attach varying margins of error to the results.

As a consequence of all the foregoing it is perhaps not surprising that accountants are usually unwilling on their own initiative to assign revised values to durable asset items at the end of each period. The accountant is doubtless aware that in most instances original cost less conventional depreciation does not accurately portray the present worth of the valuable services to be received from the asset; but he is also impressed with the inherent difficulties and costs of determining an appreciably more precise valuation. Consequently he is perhaps to be censured rather less than is customary for simply taking original cost less depreciation as a rough approximation of probable value.[13] And it should be noted further that when sufficient evidence becomes available the accountant is usually willing to record the revised valuations. The position of the accountant in the preparation of balance sheets is perhaps best summarized by saying he insists upon "acceptable" evidence before valuing fixed assets at other than cost less depreciation.

[11] Note we have said, "would have to pay," and not "could afford to pay." For, the latter, assuming the enterprise already has a certain aggregate of other assets, might be anything up to the full present worth of the total prospective net income. In most cases however some substitution is possible.

[12] See Canning, *op. cit.*, p. 243.

[13] Such approximations become decidedly less trustworthy, of course, in a period of rapid changes in the purchasing power of money. For a suggested method for handling such difficulties in the accounting procedure see Sweeney, H. W., *Stabilized Accounting*, New York and London (Harpers), 1936.

3. *Revaluation accounts and the valuation of proprietorship.* While the accountant ordinarily follows the general principles just described in valuing particular assets as separate items, he sometimes applies more or less blanket revisions of the asset total or of the statement of net worth. In general these take two forms according as they aim to revise the value of proprietorship claims upwards or downwards. Though the accountant is perhaps loath to raise the book value of particular assets above their purchase cost he nevertheless will often sanction the inclusion of an item such as "good-will" or "going concern value." What this means in effect is that all the assets taken together in the particular productive combination in which they exist have a present worth exceeding the sum of their individual valuations determined by accepted techniques. Not uncommonly the accountant will merely draw attention to the existence of such an excess by recording it at $1, but make no effort to state its amount. Presumably the only purpose served by so doing is to place each person on notice that such an excess probably exists. In other cases, however, it may be fixed by capitalizing the amount by which current earnings upon the book value of the proprietorship exceed the going rate of interest. While good-will as an asset is not regarded with complete favor by accountants there is no denying its existence in the sense used in some instances. And if attention is drawn to it in the balance sheet statement it may serve to emphasize that the sum total of the other assets as stated does not fully reflect their true present worth.[14]

On occasion the accountant offers a suggestion in the balance sheet that the asset or liability figures are liable to a possible downward revision. The usual method here is to include among the subsidiary proprietorship accounts certain special "reserves" which imply that the asset and/or liability accounts do not portray the full picture. Very frequently these so-called reserves show the presence of certain contingencies which may reduce the size of the net income stream in the future and hence the present worth

[14] Sometimes the practice is to call attention to probable understatements in the balance sheet by means of appended footnotes which point out that such and such an asset has a market value or has been professionally appraised at a figure exceeding its book value by a stated amount.

of proprietorship. Thus we may have reserves for non-productive expenditures as when a railroad is forced to remove a grade crossing; or reserves for certain special but uncertain losses, or undecided actions at law which might affect the enterprise adversely.[15] One probably need not add that such "reserves," which are subsidiary proprietorship accounts, have nothing whatever to do with the existence or non-existence of cash balances held by the enterprise.

Hence, in addition to the valuations assigned to particular assets and liabilities, more or less general revisional accounts are frequently included in order to indicate more accurately the probable present worth of the proprietorship claims. Even with their inclusion, however, any accountant would admit that the precise dollars and cents figures give a specious aura of certainty to the results which is inevitably belied by the very nature of the problem.

III. ACCOUNTING REPORTS AND THE BUSINESS ENTERPRISE IN RELATION TO THE ECONOMY

1. Inferences and deductions from accounting reports. 2. Accounting reports and the direction of new capital investment.

While most persons would doubtless agree that in a capitalistic economy the aim and objective of business enterprises are to secure the maximum possible net return, it is not so generally recognized and appreciated that about the only way of measuring the achievements of individual concerns in this mutual pursuit is by the use of accounting methods. Despite whatever comments we have offered concerning the aberrations of accounting practice from the strict realization of its objective of recording changes in the value of the proprietorship claims, the fact remains that accounting is almost the only technique that is widely used for this purpose. As a consequence it is most important that the ac-

[15] Dewing, A. S., *Financial Policy of Corporations*, New York (Ronald), 1934, Book IV, Ch. 5, treats of these various reserve accounts at considerable length.

counting statements as reported and studied should be computed with an accuracy commensurate with the nature of the problem and data available. We are not suggesting for a moment that the difficulties with which the accountant has to deal are trivial and easily solved. On the contrary a good many of the problems do not lend themselves to a demonstrably "correct" solution because they deal with futurities which are *ipso facto* uncertain to a degree. On the other hand, it is of the utmost importance that persons do not read conclusions and facts from the accounting statements which, in the very nature of the case, cannot be derived from them. Accounting statements should be prepared with the degree of accuracy and precision that the data allow; but equally there should be full recognition of the limitations of the data from which the statements are prepared. The necessity for both accurate statements and sophisticated readers lies in the fact that accounting reports are made the basis of important decisions by persons within the enterprise and those external to it. And these decisions have important consequences. Consequently the degree of misinformation and misinterpretation should be reduced to a minimum.

1. *Inferences and deductions from accounting reports.* We have argued that the essence of economical management is so to apply resources as to maximize net returns. But we have pointed out also that uncertainties and ignorance necessarily attend any attempt to achieve this end in practice. In considerable measure the procedure is one of trial and error. The results of various "trials," however, are set down in accounting terms. That is, those charged with policy formation in the individual enterprise will almost inevitably measure the success of alternative policies by their effect upon net income as shown by the accounting statements. Consequently it is most important that these statements reflect as nearly as possible what they purport to measure. Otherwise disastrous errors of policy may remain undisclosed for long intervals. Thus, because in the internal operations of the enterprise accounting records tend to become policy determining, their preparation and interpretation ought to be carried out with care and accuracy. Possibly one of the gravest consequences of the current interpretation of accounting records is the inference

drawn therefrom concerning price policy. Business concerns have an unholy fear of "selling below cost" which means average total cost as shown by the records, including some of the often doubtful refinements of "cost accounting." In Chapter VII it was shown, however, that average *total* cost is not particularly important in short-run analysis. The relevant consideration is always marginal cost and marginal revenue. Although accounting records are not designed to reveal this information there is no reason why one need infer that all costs are alike for purposes of determining the appropriate price and output at any given time. To know that average total cost is so much is interesting but does not suggest at all that the firm must not sell below this figure if it is to maximize profits. It may very well make more or lose less if it reduces price below total cost provided only that the increase in sales income more than offsets the increase in cost outlay. The costs which will be incurred regardless of the volume of production are mostly irrelevant in determining present price policy. So far as possible then, the accounting technique should be sufficiently refined to indicate the uses, within the enterprise, from which resources should be withdrawn and to which they should be applied. To achieve the maximum net income from its resources an enterprise needs some means of measuring the net income derived from alternative uses of its resources. Accounting is approximately the only available means of comparing past anticipations with actual results in the internal conduct of the enterprise.

The accounting statements of the individual corporation have also an important influence upon its external relations. Its reported net earnings will tend to affect its credit rating and its ability to raise more capital for expansion by appeal to the competitive market. In large measure it is on the basis of the reported net earnings that we label this corporation "successful" and that a failure, or on the other hand, cite this management as "progressive" and that ineffective.

To be sure there is some irrationality in the great significance often attached to reported net income for past periods. In the first place, the past records of the corporation are only indicative to the degree one may assume that the future conditions within which the firm will operate will be similar to those of the past. One might well argue too that the record of past earnings indicates the ability of the management to cope with the changing conditions of the past. And that while conditions will no doubt change in the future one may assume that the present management will be able to cope with them with equal facility. In an uncertain world this is perhaps a very reasonable position. Very frequently, but not always, these are tenable assumptions. Again, it is commonplace that the reported net income of a corporation is partially discretionary from period to period, albeit without the full approval of the professional accountant. Yet once published, the figures seem to acquire a halo of precision which is not easily dispelled. There is here almost a curious contradiction in the attitude taken towards the statement of profit and loss as contrasted with that taken towards the balance sheet. No one is surprised when a company's shares sell in the market at a figure considerably greater or less than their book value. This is accepted as a matter of course on the ground, no doubt, that the balance sheet is at best a rough approximation. Yet persons have a strong tendency to accept the earnings statements almost unreservedly as a basis for far-reaching deductions. Here it seems to be almost forgotten that the income statement could not be prepared without the balance sheet and that the reported net income for any period is conceptually identical with the change in net worth as shown by the balance sheet. In an important sense there is no reason to attach much greater validity and accuracy to the one than to the other. Yet in all probability stockholders and those with free capital available for investment will continue to attach greater significance to the statement of income and expense than to the balance sheet.

The computation of net earnings is therefore likely to be of great significance because of the inferences drawn therefrom by persons dealing with but unassociated with the actual conduct of the corporation. In the circumstances every effort should be made to portray the true state of affairs as clearly as possible.

2. *Accounting reports and the direction of new capital investment*. More important than the welfare of the individual enter-

prise is the significance of accurate calculations of income by all business enterprises for the economy as a whole.

It is generally agreed by economists that the allocation of free capital to its most productive uses is an indispensable condition for the maximization of the general welfare. Under modern conditions this process of capital allocation is achieved through two media: the market for new capital issues (as opposed to refunding issues) and the re-investment of earnings by already established concerns. Only the new issue market need concern us at this point. Apart from certain imperfections in the market (which affect small enterprises most seriously) the holders of liquid capital allocate their funds to those corporations which give promise of making it yield the highest returns. But for established concerns the criterion by which the allocation of investible funds is determined tends to be the past earnings records of the competing bidders. We have already commented on the necessarily tentative character of these records and the simultaneous tendency to accept the figures without much qualification. But there is a further point. It is often assumed that such statements offer a reliable indication of the productivity of *additional* capital in the respective corporations. Expressed as aggregates or average rates of return upon capital already committed, reported net earnings really throw no light on this question at all. The important question is the marginal productivity of capital as between competing concerns or alternative uses and not average rates of return derivable from earnings statements. As we shall see more in detail in the next chapter it is quite possible for average rates of return on past investment as shown by accounting records to be distressingly low at the same time that the *marginal* productivity of capital in the enterprise is quite high. Yet under the ideology of the capital market currently accepted it would be most unlikely that an enterprise so situated would be able to sell securities to finance new investment.

There is an additional point here. In a rapidly changing society it might be argued that the need is less for feeding additional resources into already established concerns than for supplying funds to new enterprises designed to exploit the investment opportunities created by progressive economic changes—such as the appearance of new products, improved techniques for the manufacture of existing products, shifts in population, alterations in consumers' tastes and the like. Yet as the investment market is now organized there is little question that those who are associated with the flotation of new security issues strongly favor business corporations with a satisfactory record of past earnings. It is not here suggested that this represents any conspiracy on their part or anything of the kind: no doubt investment banking houses are inclined to such preferences because they find it easier to dispose of such issues to those with funds to invest. But the fact remains that their disposition in this regard makes it very difficult for unproven concerns, i.e., corporations not possessing a long record of satisfactory earnings, to secure funds with which to carry out capital investments that would yield high returns. Promising investment opportunities may go begging because persons with investible capital have been led to believe that an acceptable earnings' record must be offered before any commitment is warranted. But by definition new enterprises to undertake new investment opportunities have no past history on which to base an appeal for funds. Furthermore, in the degree that the economy is increasingly characterized by change and development in all its aspects, the less reliable as a guide to the future are the reported earnings of established corporations for times past. The net result of the foregoing may well be misdirected capital investment within the economy on a considerable scale, and an increased hesitancy on the part of investors to make commitments of any kind. In short, aggregate investment within the economy may decline and refuse to rise again with any ease. For a capitalistic economy the maintenance of new investment at a high level seems to be a *sine qua non* to full employment and a high level of real income.

IV. SUMMARY

Whereas the notion of maximizing returns to the owners of the enterprise is essentially forward-looking, for numerous reasons corporations report periodically on the results, in terms of changes of net worth, of their operations for a period that has transpired. Income in the accounting sense is income in retrospect and conceptually it is the change in the value of the proprietorship claims from the beginning of a period to its end. The increase or decrease in the value of proprietorship which accountants compute statistically, however, is calculated on the special assumption that durable assets have been assigned permanently correct valuations at the time of their acquisition. Care is therefore necessary to avoid identifying the concept of income for an elapsed period with the statistical applications of this concept (with modifications) in the preparation of accounting reports. In revaluing assets to estimate the change in the value of net worth accountants use direct methods where the information is readily available but draw inferences from historical outlay cost where it is not. Overhanging the whole revaluation procedure is an observable bent on the part of accountants towards the virtues of understatement. The essential difficulty that the accountant faces is that he is forced to report his findings in money value terms without being in a position to undertake on his own initiative any complete and thorough study of the changes in these money values.

From the broad social point of view there is a great need that accounting statements be prepared with the maximum degree of accuracy and interpreted with an appropriate appreciation of their limitations. Especially the practice of reasoning from the past earnings records of business corporations to firm conclusions concerning their probable future earnings and their ability to employ additional capital that will yield high returns is at best very tenuous. The tendency also in the new issue market to favor already established concerns rather than new enterprises, which by definition have no past earnings records on which to base an appeal for funds, may make it more difficult for a highly developed capitalistic economy to maintain a high rate of real capital investment.

REFERENCES: CHAPTER VIII

DEWING, A. S.—*Financial Policy*, Book IV, Ch. 3.
GRAHAM, B., and DODD, D. L.—*Security Analysis*, Chs. 31-34, 37, 38, 42-45.

CANNING, J. B.—*The Economics of Accountancy*, New York, 1929.

DANIELS, M. B.—"Corporation Financial Statements," *Michigan Business Studies*, Vol. 6.

HOSMER, W. A.—"The Effect of Direct Charges to Surplus on the Measurement of Income" in *Business and Modern Society*, edited by E. P. McNair and H. T. Lewis, Cambridge, Mass., 1938.

LINDAHL, ERIK—"The Concept of Income" in *Economic Essays in Honour of Gustav Cassel*, London (Allen and Unwin), 1933.

LITTLETON, A. C.—"The Concept of Income Underlying Accounting," *Accounting Review*, March, 1937.

MARPLE, R. P.—*Capital Surplus and Corporate Net Worth*, New York, 1936.

PREINREICH, G. A. D.—"Annual Survey of Economic Theory: The Theory of Depreciation," *Econometrica*, Vol. 6.

WARSHOW, H. T.—"Inventory Valuation and the Business Cycle," *Harvard Business Review*, Vol. 3.

(unsigned)—"Market Capitalization Rates of Industrial Earnings," *Harvard Business Review*, October, 1927; Vol. 6.

Chapter IX

PAYMENTS TO PROPRIETORS IN THE FORM OF DIVIDENDS

I. The Marginal Principle in Dividend Distributions. II. Legal Rules Governing Dividend Distributions. III. The Dividend Policy of American Corporations. IV. Dividend Policy and the Business Cycle Problem. V. Summary.

One reason why business enterprises find it impracticable to postpone computing changes in the value of the proprietorship until the dissolution of the enterprise is that shareholders expect the corporation to make regular or occasional payments on account called dividends. Whereas the corporation as such may contemplate a well-nigh perpetual existence, its individual shareholders have a finite life, and in large measure it was the expectation of dividend payments during their own life span that prompted them to make their original investments in the corporation. As a consequence there is a need for an accounting and reporting of corporate income in retrospect at regular intervals. And, as we shall have occasion to note shortly, the law has found it necessary to establish certain legal rules governing the declaration of dividends to protect the parties in interest; in order to apply these rules some statistical determination of income such as the accounting technique provides is probably indispensable.

Before proceeding to an examination of the economic questions that dividend payments present there is a minor matter that must first be disposed of.

Recent years have seen a great proliferation of the different kinds of things that pass under the name of dividends. We have cash dividends, stock dividends, scrip dividends, "property" dividends, and perhaps others. But fundamentally there are really only two kinds of dividends: first, those which involve a transfer

233

of assets from the corporation to its shareholders, and second, those which do not. Only dividends of the first type where something of value is given over to the shareholders by the corporation involve any change of the economic position of the enterprise. All others which leave the sum total of resources at the disposal of the enterprise unchanged are not "dividends" in any significant sense at all. Indeed it would have been better had the term dividend never been applied to the latter, but the usage has now become so common that we must accept it. Where the corporation actually transfers assets from itself to the shareholders, i.e., reduces the total resources in its possession, the asset transferred is almost invariably cash. On strict theoretical grounds there is no reason why any kind of asset might not be paid over to the shareholders by the corporation as a dividend. If there are numerous stockholders, however, the choice is practically restricted to assets divisible into relatively small and homogeneous units. In what follows immediately below we shall mean by a dividend the transfer of cash to the shareholders. For the present we shall omit dividends of type two from the discussion.

I. THE MARGINAL PRINCIPLE IN DIVIDEND DISTRIBUTIONS

1. The marginal principle illustrated. 2. Qualifications to the principle in application.

In the corporation, a multiple proprietorship enterprise, the reinvestment of earnings is but one method of increasing its capital investment. And logically there seems no reason to suppose that the ordinary marginal principles of capital investment would not apply. If we may assume that directors are endeavoring to maximize the net returns to the shareholders, then clearly no portion of the earnings ought to be reinvested unless the return upon the increment of capital employed promises to be at least as large as could be earned upon the same capital employed elsewhere, i.e., outside the enterprise. So long as the prospective return from further capital investment in the enterprise is not less than the rate of interest on alternative investments of equivalent risk, the directors may properly increase the employed capital by reinvesting earnings.

1. *The marginal principle illustrated.* In order to bring into clear relief the basic considerations involved in dividend distribution let us take the following simplified case. Assume a corporation which, according to the best calculations it is practical and economical to undertake, shows an increase in the value of the shareholders' claims of $1,000,000 during the year just ended. Assume but one kind of shares to be outstanding. Assume further that the cash account shows a balance larger by $1,000,000 than the balance at the beginning of the period. Finally, assume that the directors wish to act in the best interests of the shareholders. Under the conditions here assumed, what considerations determine the wisdom of paying dividends to the stockholders, and in what amounts?

Where there has been an increase in the value of the proprietorship claims, such increase represents an increment in the total stockholders' investment in the enterprise. The question confronting the directors, therefore, is the wisdom of retaining this increased investment within the corporation as opposed to paying it out to the shareholders in dividends. Here, as elsewhere, the ordinary marginal principles governing the application of resources apply. Clearly no portion of the increased capital (now in the form of cash) ought to be retained within the enterprise unless the returns thereon promise to be at least as large as could be earned upon the same capital employed elsewhere, i.e., outside the corporation. So long as the prospective returns upon the capital if retained in the enterprise are not less than the returns available on other investments of equivalent risk the directors may very properly retain the whole amount within the corporation rather than pay any of it to the shareholders as dividends. The directors do not have a schedule showing the exact rates of return to capital in various parts of the economy, nor of course does anyone else. They must infer these returns from the rates of interest ruling in the market on free capital applied in opportunities of approximately equal risk. The market rates presumably indicate the judgment of holders and borrowers of free capital concerning the probable return to capital in various uses. Practically the directors must accept this composite judgment, and henceforth we shall use the term rate of interest to indicate the returns available on free capital in alternative uses.

The basic marginal principle applied to dividend distribution may be illustrated by a simple example. Assume our corporation in the period just ended shows a net profit of $1,000,000.[1] If now it be estimated that by retaining the whole $1,000,000 the net income in subsequent periods will increase to $1,060,000, the marginal returns on the additional capital are clearly at an average rate of 6 per cent on a rather large increment. If the returns elsewhere were no greater than 6 per cent it might be inferred that the stockholders would be best served by retaining the whole amount. But this is a very crude calculation since all we know is that the average return per dollar of increased capital investment is expected to be 6 per cent. In order to know more definitely we should have to determine the prospective increase in aggregate returns to be derived from retaining different proportions of the $1,000,000. In the following hypothetical schedule the $1,000,000 is broken up into units of $100,000 and the resulting increase in net income is shown both as a cumulative aggregate and by increments: [2]

---

[1] It might be supposed that a relevant question was, on how much "capital" are net earnings $1,000,000. This, however, is unimportant for the question. The book investment might be 5, 10, or 25 million and it would make no difference to the present question, i.e., how much of the present increase in net assets should be permanently retained within the enterprise. This question turns entirely on the relative returns to be had from capital investment within the enterprise as compared with investment elsewhere.

[2] The figures in the table may be interpreted to mean either a constant increment in net earnings per period through all future time over what they would be without any increased investment, or as a stream of additional income items whose individual terms are different, but which, when reduced to a present worth, have a value equivalent to a perpetual stream whose terms are constant. In symbolic terms: the present worth of $r_1 + r_2 + r_3 \ldots r_n \ldots \infty$ equals the present worth of $a + b + c + d \ldots n$ where the r's are identical but the terms a, b, c, etc., are not. In any actual corporation the returns would in fact fluctuate considerably from period to period and would be expected to do so. The increment in earnings from reinvestment is here assumed to be $r_1 + r_2 + r_3 \ldots \infty$.

It is not really necessary to formulate the proposition in terms of a perpetual income stream at all. The enterprise may be regarded as endeavoring to maximize its present worth, and therefore the retention of earnings is justified if it increases

SCHEDULE I

If investment be increased by:	Total increased earnings	Marginal increments in dollars	Average rate of return on total increased capital	Rate of return on the successive increments
$ 100,000	$10,000	$10,000	10.0%	10.0%
200,000	19,500	9,500	9.75	9.5
300,000	28,500	9,000	9.50	9.0
400,000	36,500	8,000	9.12	8.0
500,000	43,500	7,000	8.70	7.0
600,000	50,000	6,500	8.33	6.5
700,000	54,500	4,500	7.70	4.5
800,000	57,500	3,000	7.18	3.0
900,000	59,000	1,500	6.55	1.5
1,000,000	60,000	1,000	6.00	1.0

From an examination of the schedule it is clear that if the returns available on capital invested outside the enterprise are 6 per cent then not much more than 60 per cent of the earnings should be retained, for beyond $600,000 the capital yields less than it would elsewhere. Theoretically the directors should declare dividends of not much less than $400,000 if they are intent upon the best possible use of stockholders' capital.[3]

The marginal principle is not restricted in its application to cases where the aggregate net income will actually be increased. Additional capital investment may be necessary to prevent earnings from falling in subsequent periods. If we suppose as before a corporation with net income of $1,000,000 in the period just ended, and further that the whole of this amount must be retained if the subsequent net income is to remain at $1,000,000, the ques-

the present worth by more than the amount retained, i.e., within the enterprise the capital has a productivity greater than the rate of interest. This formulation would give identical results, of course, with that used in the previous paragraph. See also *supra*, Ch. VII, sec. I, 1.

[3] It may be objected to the foregoing that "outside" investment, i.e., investment in assets not directly employed in the productive process in which the enterprise is engaged, may be undertaken by the corporation as well as by the stockholders as individuals. Theoretically there is nothing to prevent the corporation from securing whatever returns the market affords, e.g., by purchasing securities in other corporations. In this case the corporation would take on the characteristics of an investment trust. Practically, in the writer's opinion, however, unless returns in wholly new fields appear unusually promising the directors are likely to direct the additional free capital available into familiar channels, such as expanding plant or into "hoards" of bank balances or government bonds. This problem cannot be fully discussed here, however.

tion then obviously becomes, how much will earnings fall if the additional capital is paid out to the shareholders in dividends. Let us suppose that with no additional investment earnings it will fall permanently to $950,000 and that the following schedule represents the increments in earnings above $950,000 resulting from retaining different fractions of the current year's earnings ($1,-000,000): [4]

SCHEDULE II

If investment be increased by:	Total earnings will be:	Marginal increment in earnings above $950,000	Average rate on total increased capital employed	Average rate on successive increments
$ 0	$ 950,000	$ 0	. . .	. .
100,000	958,500	8,500	8.50%	8.5%
200,000	966,500	8,000	8.25	8.0
300,000	973,500	7,000	7.83	7.0
400,000	979,500	6,000	7.37	6.0
500,000	985,000	5,500	7.00	5.5
600,000	990,000	5,000	6.66	5.0
700,000	994,000	4,000	6.28	4.0
800,000	997,500	3,500	5.93	3.5
900,000	999,000	1,500	5.44	1.5
1,000,000	1,000,000	1,000	5.00	1.0

If the rate of interest be 6 per cent as before, then not more than 40 per cent of the current period's net income should be reinvested by the corporation. For while the *aggregate* returns will be maintained by retaining the whole amount, beyond the fourth $100,000 each unit will yield less in the enterprise than it will outside. Hence, even though earnings will decline as an aggregate, the stockholders will be better served if dividends of $600,000 are paid than if the directors endeavor to maintain earnings at $1,000,-000 by reinvesting the whole amount. There ought to be nothing surprising of course in a decision to permit net income to decline when to maintain it constant involves a cost (sacrifice) in excess of the return.

Directors in endeavoring to maximize the returns to stockholders should therefore determine the amount of the dividend by comparing the returns from additional capital investment within the

[4] The expected decline in future net income may be the result of any number of factors. This schedule is to be interpreted as in the previous example, see *supra*, note 2.

enterprise with the rate of interest. If it be objected that this in-volves difficulties, since it is not easy to predict with accuracy what returns will result from a given capital investment, the point will be readily granted. But the mere fact that it is difficult in no way relieves the directors from the necessity of attempting to find out. The directors must have *some* reason for investing more rather than less, unless one is willing to argue that the determination of dividend payments should be handled without regard to the eco-nomic considerations involved. If the directors are to exercise reason in arriving at a decision, then the appropriate logic runs in terms of increments of returns from increments of investment, a marginal analysis.

2. *Qualifications to the principle in application.* Let us now relax somewhat the rigidly simplifying assumptions with which we began and see if the basic principle just enunciated still ap-plies.

The case of a small corporation in the process of expansion might appear to be an exception. Many such enterprises find the facilities of the organized capital market partly closed to them at the same time that direct security sales by the company itself are not feasible. If the existing shareholders have no further funds to venture, then almost the only available means of increasing the long-term investment is by not paying dividends. In itself this involves no violation of our principle. The advantages of increased size, however, may not be continuous from the small or medium-sized firm to the relatively large concern to which this enterprise aims to grow. Such situations are neither unknown nor difficult to understand. But if the corporation must pass through a stage of relatively low earnings before reaching the desired size, then for a few years the additional capital will yield returns less than the rate of interest, only rising above it when sufficient capital has been added to bring to the company that size at which the advan-tages of larger scale begin to appear with full force. If the subse-quent increased earnings are large enough the directors may very properly retain all earnings for a few years even though in the interval the increased returns received are very low or non-existent. A somewhat similar situation often prevails in new enter-prises. As a general proposition, the items in the prospective income stream may at first be very low or have any other time shape imaginable, although of course the longer the period of low returns the larger must they be ultimately in order to justify the investment. The question is always the comparative present worth of alternative income streams from investment within as opposed to investment outside the enterprise.

We assumed initially that the full amount of the earnings of the year were manifested by an increase in cash. This assumption will often be contrary to fact. Corporate executives often announce that despite large earnings they are unable to declare dividends because of the inability of the enterprise to spare cash from working capital. Here two situations need to be distinguished even assuming the price level is comparatively stable.[5] It is not unusual for a corporation to report large earnings which have not yet been realized in cash, being tied up in receivables. This is at worst a temporary situation, assuming the accounts or notes to be collectible (i.e., the earnings genuine), and within a relatively short period the funds should be available for dividends or other use. If, however, the earnings have already vested themselves in assets which will not, or cannot, be soon converted into cash, the decision to increase the capital investment has already been taken, and the dividend question confronts an already accomplished fact. The aggregate investment has already been increased and has taken a more or less permanent form.

There is yet one further possible disposition of the increase in net assets other than raising permanently the capital investment in the enterprise or paying dividends to the shareholders. Many enterprises often partially finance themselves by the sale of bonds or long-term notes. At a subsequent time, however, it may appear

[5] An especial difficulty may arise during a period of rapidly rising prices. During such periods an increased dollar amount of working capital will be necessary to carry on the same physical volume of business. At the same time the earnings as ordinarily computed will probably show a considerable increase. A large portion of such increase, however, will not be available for distribution to shareholders because additional cash will be required to finance the purchase of merchandise in the same physical volume as before. In no physical sense is the firm expanding its operations necessarily, yet it is unable to part with cash without serious harm despite the fact that earnings as reported have greatly increased. See Arthur, H. B., "Inventory Profits in the Business Cycle," *American Economic Review*, Vol. 28 (March, 1938), pp. 27-40, and the citations there given.

wise to substitute ownership claims for creditors' claims. Under the circumstances it is possible for the aggregate stockholders' investment in the corporation to increase even though the total capital employed may not change. As an alternative to the sale of additional shares at once, creditors' claims may be liquidated gradually by using the increased cash made available by retaining earnings. Such a change merely increases the relative shares of stockholders in total assets. Instead of paying dividends or increasing the aggregate capital invested certain prior claimants to both income and assets are removed.[6] The same reasoning of course would apply to preferred stock or other issues possessing claims prior to common shares.

II. LEGAL RULES GOVERNING DIVIDEND DISTRIBUTIONS

1. The parties in interest. 2. Statement and consideration of the rules.

It would be surprising indeed if the law had not endeavored to establish rules governing the declaration and payment of dividends. For here innumerable fact situations are possible out of which conflicts of interest and thus disputes may easily develop.

1. *The parties in interest.* It is helpful in a preliminary view of the legal rules to ask what parties conceivably could have any interest in the declaration and payment of dividends by private corporations.[7] Presumably these reduce to three: the sovereign authority, creditors, and finally stockholders. Either in the constitution

---

[6] Assume a corporation with the following balance sheet: *Assets:* Cash, $20,000; Other assets, $70,000; *Liabilities and Net Worth:* Bonds, $50,000; Capital Stock, $40,000. If we assume that during the next period the corporation earns $10,000, which is all realized in cash, then cash will be $10,000 greater and a Surplus item of $10,000 will appear. If now bonds are paid off to the full amount of the earnings, cash will again fall to $20,000, bonds will reduce to $40,000, while total stockholders' equity will remain at the increased amount of $50,000. Total investment in the corporation is unchanged although shareholders' proportionate interest has increased.

[7] We omit from consideration here those special problems which may arise in corporations "affected with a public interest."

or the general incorporation laws the state might wish to lay down certain rules governing dividends as a matter of public policy. Such constitutional or statutory provisions are in theory simply rules formulated for the common good. The interests of stockholders and creditors in dividend payments on the other hand are essentially private rather than public in character. First, what of creditors' interests?

The interest of creditors in dividends arises from their possession of claims against the corporation which are as yet unpaid. These claims may be for either principal or interest and may arise from any number of causes. Now except under very unusual conditions the means of satisfying (liquidating) these claims is cash. And since a dividend is a cash payment to shareholders, it is only reasonable that the creditors, whose rights are prior to those of the stockholders, should have an interest in such cash disbursements. Clearly their interests and rights spring from the possibility that cash dividend disbursements may endanger the corporation's ability to pay their claims. With other than this creditors are not really concerned.

The interest of stockholders in dividends arises partly from their relations *inter sese* and partly from their relations to the corporation. The charter usually defines the former and its provisions are not usually difficult to apply.[8] The latter, although similarly stipulated, is less easy to define and more difficult to circumscribe. Perhaps the most important legal rules governing the relations between the stockholders and the corporation are a recognition of the comparative ease with which directors might mislead the stockholders even though the former ostensibly represent the latter. More specifically, there has been no little concern over the possibility of the corporation returning to the shareholders as "dividends" a portion of their original capital contributions. The law

---

[8] The charter, it will be recalled, includes also the general incorporation law of the state. See *supra*, Ch. III. Some very special problems may arise, however, in connection with so-called non-cumulative preferred stock. Apparently no generalizations are possible however, the question rather turning upon the precise wording of the security contract. See Stevens, W. H. S., "Stockholders Participation in Profits," *Journal of Business of the University of Chicago*, Vol. 9 (1936), pp. 114-132; 210-230.

has apparently developed a logic of its own, drawing distinctions between capital as a source of income and the income itself, and not unnaturally this reasoning has been applied to dividend questions. As we shall note shortly, however, the "rules" established on this matter are neither simple nor clear.

The interests of these three, then—the sovereign, creditors, and stockholders—have led to the formulation of certain legal rules restricting the declaration of dividends. What are these rules?

2. *Statement and consideration of the rules.* According to most scholars there are essentially four rules governing the payment of dividends by a corporation. To use Bonbright's formulation, these are: [9]

1. No dividend may be paid when the company is insolvent or when the payment would result directly in insolvency.
2. No dividend may be paid unless the value of the assets, after the payment, exceeds a certain sum in excess of the corporate debts, this minimum sum constituting the "capital" of the corporation.
3. No dividend may be paid except from the balance of earned and hitherto undistributed profits.
4. No dividend may be paid except from the current profits of the year as of which the dividend is declared.

Professor Bonbright indicates almost immediately that rules 1 and 4 are of minor consequence. The insolvency rule is really a modern form of the Elizabethan statute prohibiting fraudulent transfers; if a corporation is insolvent a dividend by transferring assets to shareholders is fraudulent against creditors whose claims are superior and exhaustive.[10] Rule 4 is likewise of no special moment

---

[9] Bonbright, J. C., *The Valuation of Property*, New York (McGraw-Hill), 1937, Vol. II, pp. 915-916 and Ch. 27. This chapter was based mainly on certain articles by Joseph L. Weiner (one in collaboration with Bonbright) appearing in the *Columbia Law Review* in 1928 and 1929. Almost any text on corporation law will contain a similar if somewhat less complete account of the same principles.

[10] See Weiner, J. L., "Theory of Anglo-American Dividend Law: American Statutes and Cases," *Columbia Law Review*, Vol. 29 (April, 1929), pp. 461-482, at 463-467. Mr. Weiner writes (p. 465): "Few cases involving dividends can be found where the issue turns on solvency, and in only two of them did the court consider which of these two meanings should be given to 'insolvency' as used in a dividend statute. One construes insolvency as an ability to meet maturing debts; the other adopts the second meaning." (Notes omitted.) The reason the insolvency rule is not of much practical importance is that other rules would come into operation in most cases before insolvency is reached.

since apparently only a few statutes contain it. We may therefore simplify our discussion by confining it to rules 2 and 3.

Rule 2, sometimes called the "capital impairment" principle, is ostensibly aimed at the protection of both shareholders and creditors. Under either the "trust fund" or "holding-out" doctrines of capital stock a corporation is supposed to maintain a fund for the protection of creditors as a substitute for unlimited personal liability.[11] Stockholders are also to be protected against the return of their original contributions as dividends. The essence of the difficulty in applying the rule, however, is the meaning of the term capital. What creditors have a right to forestall is the dissipation of assets by dividends which destroy debt-paying ability. It is only capital in this sense which is important to them. As applied and interpreted on the other hand the rule relates mainly to the *account* called capital on the credit side of the balance sheet. So long as none but par value shares were in use the difficulty was not serious, for the total par value of the outstanding shares was the amount of "capital." And this figure, except under peculiar circumstances, was the amount the shareholders in the aggregate had paid in as a more or less permanent capital contribution. So long as this figure was not reduced there was some presumption that creditors and shareholders were being protected as the law intended. With the appearance of no par shares, however, the so-called "stated" capital is not necessarily indicative of the amount stockholders have permanently committed. What then is the proper interpretation of the capital impairment rule? Does capital mean the amount appearing in the *account* called capital stock or ought it to mean, as was undoubtedly intended originally, the total value sum enduringly ventured by the stockholders? Apart from these difficulties we may observe that under the capital impairment rule a corporation could not pay dividends while it had a deficit but it could presumably pay out as a dividend any amounts received above par value (or stated value) in the sale of shares. Furthermore, so far as the capital impairment rule goes the *kind* of assets which together give a value total in excess of the liabilities is

[11] See *supra,* Ch. IV, sec. II.

largely irrelevant. After the payment of the dividend perhaps liquid assets suitable for paying creditors might be almost entirely absent and yet capital be "unimpaired." [12]

Rule 3, frequently called the net profits rule, would seem to have been intended mainly as a protection to shareholders and only incidentally to creditors. Whereas the capital impairment rule creates serious difficulties concerning the proper interpretation of "capital," the net profits rule raises uncertainties of almost equal magnitude concerning the construction to be placed upon "profits." In the previous chapter we noted that the accounting computations of income or profit for a past period are based on certain special assumptions concerning the valuation of durable assets. The concept of net income is not strictly applied in computing profit for a particular period. What the statutes and the courts seem to have in mind by profits is something analogous to the accountants' *computations* of net income.[13] That is, there seems to be a tendency to regard the accountants' methods as indicative of the only logically defensible manner of determining profits. Hence courts are frequently unwilling to sanction dividends "out of" unrealized appreciation of durable assets. What the profits rule would presumably allow is any "profit" which standard accounting practice would report as a profit. Under this interpretation, be it noted, a premium on the sale of shares would not be "profit" and therefore not a proper basis for the declaration of dividends. On the other hand, a profit for any period might be reported and

[12] A special modification of the capital impairment rule is usually made for corporations organized to exploit exhaustible resources. Here the so-called wasting asset theory is applied. The doctrine is that such enterprises have as their sole purpose the exhaustion of limited natural resources and to require them to maintain capital intact would mean converting them into investment companies which the shareholders would not desire. There are certain logical and other difficulties with the doctrine which need not detain us here; but in general the courts recognize it. See Weiner, *op. cit.*, pp. 477-482.

[13] "Computations" is italicized in the above for the reason that the concept of income for a past period in accounting is simply the net change in the value of proprietorship during the period. The reported net income on the other hand does not undertake to revalue all the individual assets at the end of the period. We have already indicated that the reasons for this procedure are not logical but rather practical. The law, on the other hand, would seem to have assumed that the only logical way to compute profits is as the accountants in practice find it necessary to report changes in proprietorship, i.e., by making certain simplifying assumptions concerning the value of durable assets.

presumably a dividend paid, even though the corporation had a net deficit, i.e., "capital" as previously described was impaired.

Logically, then, there would seem to be two rules restricting dividends, even though neither one considered independently is rationally unassailable.

If all shares of stock had a par value, and if credits to surplus only arose when the full earnings of any period were not distributed as dividends, then the capital impairment rule and the net profits rule would be merely alternative formulations of the same thing. For an enterprise could not pay dividends in excess of past or present earnings without impairing its capital, nor on the other hand could there be an excess above capital without the presence of undistributed profits. If, however, "surplus" may arise from other than undistributed earnings, and the term "profits" has meaning even on the assumption of a partial deficiency in the original capital contribution, there are *two* restrictions on dividends and not one only. What seems to have happened in the interpretation of these two rules is that the courts have assumed that the really special case just noted is the general one, and that therefore a corporation is entitled to pay dividends if it qualifies under *either* of the two rules. Thus at law there seems to be a general presumption that the presence of surplus on the balance sheet is evidence of past earnings undistributed. In the case of no par value shares this may be quite contrary to fact if "earnings" is interpreted in the sense of the accepted accounting procedure for reporting earnings. "Capital surplus" and "surplus" arising in other ways are not the same as earned surplus. Similarly, even though a corporation has a deficit, implying thereby that the original or stated capital is impaired, the courts seem willing none the less to attach meaning to the statement that there has been a "profit" for the period just ended, and hence, under the profit rule, dividends are not contrary to law. Hence what are really two rules have come to be interpreted by the courts as merely alternative expressions for one idea, and therefore if a corporation is qualified to pay dividends under one rule it is *ipso facto* qualified under the other.[14] The very special conditions under which this would be true and the many possibilities under which it very definitely would not be true have

[14] See Bonbright, *op. cit.*, Vol. II, pp. 918-920.

apparently gone undifferentiated by the courts in their interpretations of the statutes.[15]

The importance of the legal rules governing dividends just discussed has been greatly reduced by the ever more common practice among corporations of redefining their capital as the occasion demands. If a company is intent upon paying dividends and the law seems to prohibit, the usual procedure is to redefine the capital for legal purposes so that a surplus item is made to appear on the balance sheet. By this adjustment par value shares of the older type are able to secure those advantages to the corporation which have made no par shares so very popular. Probably most corporations can avoid the restricting influence of the legal rules governing dividends by such a change.

If the legal rules governing dividends have been designed to protect creditors in the collection of their claims and to assure stockholders against the impairment of their investment it cannot be said that they go very far towards accomplishing either. Debt-paying ability is largely a matter of the composition of the corporate assets as between liquid and non-liquid items. It really has very little to do with the question of whether shareholders' capital is impaired or intact. A corporation could have a large surplus in the accounting sense because assets were valued on an historical-cost-less-depreciation and yet be unable to raise cash to pay creditors. Conversely, capital could be impaired and yet cash be more than sufficient for all creditor obligations. Consequently, if the legal rules governing dividends related to some index of debt-paying ability rather than to shareholders' capital they would

[15] Cf. the following: "The lack of distinction between the two rules arises from the fact that most judges and legislatures are likely to and often do identify 'surplus,' which is the only source of dividends under the usual interpretation of the capital impairment test, with accumulated 'profits.' They have not often distinguished between a *capital* surplus, as being available for dividends under the capital impairment test, and an *earnest* surplus, as being alone available under a profits test. The only situation where a court would be likely to draw a distinction is the case where a company has issued stock below par and where it has not yet made good the capital deficit by the reinvestment of earnings. In that case, while most courts would probably hold, contrary to the New Jersey holding on this point, that no dividend may be paid under a capital impairment statute, they would also probably hold that this deficit need not be made good before a company is deemed to have profits available for dividends under a profit limitation." Weiner, J. L., and Bonbright, J. C., "Anglo-American Dividend Law: Surplus and Profits," *Columbia Law Review*, Vol. 30 (March, 1930), p. 332.

afford creditors more protection. Unfortunately it is not an easy matter to formulate any such rule that would be generally applicable to all corporations.

In setting up rules governing the payment of dividends for the protection of shareholders in their relation to the corporation, there would seem to be no sound economic reason for insisting that capital investment should remain undiminished. It might often be eminently wise for the corporation gradually to disinvest and return to the shareholders the funds they committed instead of continuing on in an unprofitable venture. Provided creditors were assured of payment and that shareholders were informed what was taking place, i.e., that some of their original investment was being returned to them, there would be no harm in permitting dividends of this character. If, however, as many are inclined to argue, shareholders' capital ought to be kept intact so that it will yield an undiminished income stream, then it ought to be recognized that the maintenance of capital for legal purposes, i.e., "stated" capital, by no means assures this objective. To maintain legal capital intact guarantees nothing concerning earnings because earnings have no necessary relation to what the assets cost originally.

III. THE DIVIDEND POLICY OF AMERICAN CORPORATIONS

1. The statistical evidence. 2. Usual explanations of this policy. 3. Stock dividends in relation to the foregoing. 4. Concluding observations.

In Section I we sought to formulate certain general economic principles drawn from the theory of capital investment which would seem to apply to the problem of dividends and the reinvestment of earnings in private business corporations. In Section II we have seen that dividend payments are hedged about with certain legal rules which are partly restrictive and partly enabling. It is within the confines of these rules that any particular corporation must determine its dividend policy. That is, the principles of capital investment, in so far as dividends are concerned, necessarily operate within this legal framework. With these reservations in mind, what can we say concerning the "principles of dividend distribution" as that term is ordinarily used in financial literature?

1. *The statistical evidence.* In some measure one may infer the policies of dividend distribution followed by American corporations by noting what they have done in the past. It is well established statistically that American corporations have usually paid out during periods of prosperity an amount considerably less than their full earnings as dividends. Conversely during depression periods total dividend distributions have exceeded earnings by a substantial margin. The following table compiled from recognized sources illustrates this very clearly:

TABLE I

(All figures in millions of dollars)

FABRICANT *

Year	Aggregate net income before payment of dividends but after income profits taxes	Net cash dividends	Per cent of net income	Corporate savings (undistributed net income)	Corporate savings as reported in Statistical Abstract †
1919	6,910	2,600	37.6	4,310	
1920	4,280	2,900	67.5	1,380	
1921	—70	2,600		—2,670	
1922	4,300	2,640	61.3	1,660	1,747
1923	5,720	3,310	57.9	2,410	2,528
1924	4,870	3,430	70.4	1,440	1,575
1925	6,830	4,020	58.8	2,810	2,957
1926	6,630	4,450	67.1	2,180	2,337
1927	5,730	4,780	83.4	950	1,115
1928	7,500	5,170	68.9	2,330	2,479
1929	7,950	5,780	72.7	2,170	2,320
1930	1,260	5,660	449.2	—4,400	—4,255
1931	—3,240	4,200		—7,440	—7,327
1932	—5,470	2,640		—8,110	—8,001
1933	—2,520	1,950		—4,470	—4,481
1919-1933	50,680	56,130	110.7		

* See National Bureau of Economic Research *Bulletin* no. 50 (April 18, 1934), p. 10, for years 1919-1930 and *Bulletin* no. 55 (April 11, 1935), p. 7, for years 1931-1933. These figures exclude tax-exempt corporations and life insurance companies.

† *Statistical Abstract of the United States,* 1936, p. 252.

So far as the statistics are indicative American corporations have apparently considered the non-payment of the full earnings of prosperity as a cardinal principle of dividend policy. These figures are of course aggregates and do not therefore indicate the many differences between individual corporations. Nevertheless it is hardly open to dispute that the practice of "plowing back" a relatively large proportion of the earnings of prosperity has been very common. So far as the statistical evidence is suggestive this appears to be the one outstanding result of whatever dividend policies have been followed. What explanations or reasons may be adduced for this "policy"?

2. *Usual explanations of this policy.* Doubtless the most obvious reason why corporations do not pay dividends to the amount of their full net earnings is simply that the cash position of the enterprise will not permit it. But unless the decision to apply the increased net assets in augmenting plant and equipment or other not easily liquidated items has already been made, there should be only a temporary lag between the determination of the earnings and the payment of dividends in cash to shareholders. Insufficient cash may explain a particular year; but it does not explain why dividends paid should be consistently less than earnings.

Sometimes it is argued that corporations are "conservative" in their dividend distributions because the directors are inclined to distrust the earnings statements as reported, and fear the consequences of a dividend which might be ruled illegal. This would apply mainly to corporations which had no surplus in the accounting sense. After a reasonable accumulation of surplus has been attained the legal dangers tend to become almost non-existent. The fear of the illegality of dividends might explain why some few corporations seek to accumulate surplus; but it will not suffice as a generalization applicable to most corporations.

More reasonable and convincing is the argument that corporations wish to accumulate a surplus credit against which undetermined losses of subsequent periods may be debited without impairing the original paid-in capital. But there are two aspects to this achievement. On the one hand, is the desire to accumulate a surplus credit against which losses may be charged; on the other is the fact that surplus accumulation in this manner automatically means increasing the capital investment in the enterprise. Surplus against which to charge losses that may develop is necessary largely to satisfy the legal requirement as to impaired capital. If this is the only end to be attained it seems unreasonable to proceed to it by increasing the investment. The redefinition of capital for legal purposes is comparatively easy under modern corporation laws, and should a particular corporation find its stated legal capital impaired, then it could take the steps necessary to redefine its capital. To achieve a surplus credit by means of increasing the capital investment seems unwise unless the additional capital can be made to earn as much within the corporation as elsewhere.[16] Nevertheless some such reasoning as this no doubt has been partly responsible for corporations not paying out their full earnings. Here again, however, unless surplus is actually reduced by losses and needs to be built up again, surplus accumulation need not go on indefinitely.

We come now to the argument that corporations reinvest a relatively large fraction of their net incomes during good years in order to stabilize their dividend rates through prosperity and depression. In order to achieve this end, which is generally regarded as desirable, it is important to realize that the reinvested earnings must be kept in a relatively liquid form. It is no argument to urge reinvested earnings in order to stabilize the dividend rate, and then use the funds for plant expansion which automatically precludes easy disinvestment during depression. Furthermore, if the funds are reinvested in securities they must be issues which will not suffer a decline in price during depression when they are to be sold to maintain dividends. This almost restricts the choice to gilt-edged, low-return issues which stockholders could purchase for themselves with equal facility.[17] It requires no special managerial ability to buy government bonds and subsequently to sell them. But doubtless by so reinvesting the earnings a small but steady dividend rate could be maintained.

It is not entirely clear just what advantages to the shareholders are believed to accrue from a regular and steady dividend rate.

[16] As already observed, of course, if creditors' claims are reduced surplus might increase yet total capital investment remain unchanged.

[17] There may be a problem here for small shareholders whose total dividends would be too small to buy a bond. In that case they could buy them indirectly through deposits in savings banks.

Usually it is alleged that a stable dividend long maintained increases the credit standing of the corporation, facilitates the raising of additional capital, and builds a loyal group of stockholders who hold the shares for "investment" as opposed to speculation.[18] But as to the first, the credit standing of the corporation, this is a matter of the ability of the corporation to pay its debts and to continue to do so; it depends upon cash resources which are not necessarily connected with earnings.[19] By refusing to pay dividends and building up large cash balances an enterprise could no doubt raise its credit rating to almost any desired level; but it is doubtful if beyond rather narrow limits it is in the shareholders' interest to do so. That corporations which have maintained a steady dividend rate probably find it easier to sell securities than those with an irregular record is no doubt true. But this is scarcely to say that the first has "caused" the second. More reasonable is the explanation that a steady dividend rate is indicative of persistently good earnings; and if it be assumed that the future is likely to be similar to the past there is an increased likelihood that the proffered securities will earn the promised return. In other words, the ability to raise more capital from security sales is largely dependent upon the prospective income which investors believe will accrue to their owners. The past dividend record is relevant only in so far as it throws light upon the future earning power. A loyal group of shareholders is presumably one whose members hold their shares continuously through good times and bad, although it is not clear why this is advantageous to the "corporation" which in this connection must mean the management. Theoretically a corporation exists for the benefit of its owners, the stockholders; it is difficult to attach meaning to the suggestion that it is better for shareholders

[18] See for example, Dewing, A. S., *Financial Policy of Corporations*, New York (Ronald), 1934, pp. 623-626. But also compare *ibid.*, pp. 616-620, and Wilbur, D. E., "A Study of the Policy of Dividend Stabilization," *Harvard Business Review*, Vol. 10 (April, 1932), pp. 373-381.

[19] It may be argued that a corporation which pays regular dividends must so manage its working capital as to be able to part with cash at quarterly intervals. Therefore there is less likelihood of creditors being unpaid since if cash is regularly made available for dividends, it could, if necessary, be used to pay creditors. Hence a steady dividend rate is evidence of the management of working capital in a manner which protects creditors. Thus a steady dividend rate may indirectly call forth a better credit rating. If this be the argument it is essentially sound.

if shareholders do not change through time, unless it is meant it is better for *some* shareholders if the others are not a frequently changing group.

3. *Stock dividends in relation to the foregoing.* The net result of the foregoing reasoning on "plowing back" earnings is to reduce cash dividend distributions during boom periods to an amount substantially less than earnings. This urge to expand through retaining a large fraction of the increased net assets indicative of net income has no doubt been largely responsible for the popularity of the stock dividend. So far as the shareholders are concerned, either individually or collectively, a stock dividend adds nothing to the total value of their claims regardless of its amount. For par value shares, a stock dividend is simply a formal recognition by the corporation that some proportion of the undistributed earnings of the past are to be retained in the business more or less permanently. This permanency is given formal expression by a transfer from one proprietorship account to another; a transfer from surplus to capital stock.[20] Logically a stock dividend adds no more to the value of an individual's holdings than if the corporation having had two accounts called respectively Chairs, Type A, and Chairs, Type B, and for no special reason decided that one account, Chairs, was sufficient. Calling a portion of total proprietorship by one name rather than another can add nothing to its total value. And this is exactly what stock dividends achieve. The corporation parts with nothing of value nor do shareholders receive anything of value. Immediately after the declaration of a stock dividend assets are precisely what they were before. Stock dividends in no way inhibit any expansion plans the management of the enterprise may have in mind. The same holds for scrip dividends and others which do not require the corporation to part with assets.

Despite the foregoing, stock dividends seem to have a certain popularity among shareholders. While they would prefer a cash dividend, probably a stock dividend is thought to be better than nothing. In part this attitude is no doubt based upon a misconcep-

[20] For no par value shares it may be unnecessary even to transfer an amount from surplus to capital stock. Under some statutes a corporation could keep on declaring stock dividends for almost an indefinite period despite zero earnings.

.tion of what a stock dividend entails. More rational is the often not-unfounded belief that the old cash dividend rate will be maintained on the now larger number of shares outstanding. In this instance the total cash dividend received by the stockholder will be larger than before and to this extent his position is improved. Also it may be true that a stock dividend by reducing the market price of the shares will make them attractive to a larger number of persons and thus enhance their aggregate market valuation over what it would have been otherwise. A policy of regular and continuous stock dividends may lead to somewhat strange and not altogether happy results.[21]

4. *Concluding observations.* It would of course be absurd to argue that corporations should never reinvest earnings. Yet it seems equally absurd to believe that most corporations are usually justified in not distributing more than, say, 50 per cent of their net income, e.g., the often quoted "dollar for dividends dollar for surplus" maxim. Whether it is rational or irrational will depend upon the marginal returns from increments of investment. Economically speaking, it might be the essence of wisdom for many corporations to terminate their existence by a gradual process of disinvestment, thereby retrieving as much as possible of the shareholders' original investment. Some difficulties of a legal and accounting sort may arise in carrying this process to final completion. Yet logically there is no reason to suppose that the "opportunity" which justified the inception of the corporation warrants its perpetual maintenance in the face of changed conditions. In some ways there is much to be said economically for treating all enterprises as if they were mining properties where no one regards "maintaining capital intact" as of any importance. Nor should the attempt to maintain an indefinite existence by further investment be made unless the returns equal the opportunity cost. Yet ob-

[21] A curious mode of reasoning may set in operation a kind of self-levitation in the market value of the shares. The shares are given a certain value because of the regular stock dividends which are expected to continue. There is some tendency to value the dividends at the current market price of the shares before their number has been increased. But if the stock dividend is so valued the already outstanding shares warrant a still higher value. The thing may become circuitously cumulative. See Graham, B., and Dodd, D. L., *Security Analysis*, New York (McGraw-Hill), 1934, Ch. 30, but especially pp. 344-349.

servation and reflection suggest that once a business has been organized, frequently almost every conceivable means will be employed to "keep it going," practically regardless of the irrationality and costs involved. What small earnings are made are retained year after year and the directors and executives defend their policy, if at all, in generalities and a fervent prayer for a better future.

Section I of this chapter attempted to apply the accepted economic principles of capital investment to the problem of dividend distribution. *If* the declaration of cash dividends in prosperity has been determined by directors on this basis then (inferentially) they have generally estimated the returns upon *some* additional capital in their respective corporations to be at least equal to the rate of interest, and presumably somewhat greater, for the empirical data show that during prosperity dividends are less than earnings by a large margin. By and large corporate directorates must believe that within their own enterprises the productivity of capital at the margin (prior to any increased investment) exceeds the rate of interest. On *a priori* grounds the presumption of this being true for almost all enterprises is open to suspicion. Unless one is willing to argue that competition succeeds in establishing equal returns to capital at the margin in all employments some boards of directors must be mistaken, some misdirection of capital investment must result. In the very nature of the case, however, one cannot compute statistically just where and how much malinvestment of capital has occurred.[22]

A more accurate description of the reasoning of corporate directors is perhaps that they have not considered the dividend question in marginal terms at all. On the contrary, habit and custom have played a large part and have led directors to be at once optimistic and "conservative"; rules and principles, certainly relevant and useful in many cases, have been applied generally to almost all corporations without much thought as to their applicability in each instance. An understanding of marginal analysis would have been better for all concerned.

[22] This point is dealt with at some length in a note appended to the present chapter.

IV. DIVIDEND POLICY AND THE
BUSINESS CYCLE PROBLEM

The traditional dividend policy of American corporations has been both defended and criticized in terms of its broader economic consequences. It has been argued that where corporations typically pay dividends considerably less than their full net incomes during prosperous years there is a tendency towards misdirected capital investment, overinvestment, or hoarding. On the other hand it has been urged that the policy of reinvesting a large fraction of the earnings of boom periods allows dividends to be distributed during depression and therefore assists in the maintenance of aggregate consumers' outlay. Let us examine these arguments very briefly.

Insofar as corporations do not distribute dividends equal to their net incomes they may apply these funds in the purchase of capital goods (including here materials, inventories, etc.), in the acquisition of easily salable securities, or merely in augmenting their bank balances. If the corporations use the undistributed net income in the purchase of capital goods, then some liquid capital passes directly into "real" capital goods without passing through the competitive market where new issues of securities are offered and sold. In itself this is of no particular moment. For, insofar as the particular corporations which pay out in dividends less than their total net incomes would be able to attract funds from the capital market in any case, no change in the direction of real capital investment is involved. For *those* corporations merely an intermediate step in the process is eliminated. If, however, by not distributing the whole of their net earnings, certain corporations thereby place themselves in command of liquid capital funds which they would not be able to secure from the competitive market, the end result is different. Certain enterprises in which the marginal productivity of capital is comparatively low are expanded at the expense of others where the productivity of capital would have been higher. To this extent "misdirected" capital investment results in the sense that resources are mobilized towards the construction of capital goods here when capital goods elsewhere would have yielded higher returns.[23]

If corporations invest their non-distributed earnings not in capital goods but in the purchase of marketable securities, either with the intention of stabilizing the dividend rate or as a reserve against contingencies, the effect is somewhat different. The securities purchased may be either new issues or those already outstanding. If new issues, then the undistributed earnings of the particular corporations are made available in the capital market and there is no reason to suppose that misdirected capital investment is more likely to result than if the earnings were paid out and the recipients purchased the new issues. If, however, the corporations buy old issues, as is more likely, they must buy them from someone, and the question resolves itself into the disposition of the proceeds by the sellers. The latter may either buy new issues, increase their outlays on consumption, or increase their balances at the banks. There would seem to be no special presumption in favor of any one possibility over the others.

If corporations neither purchase capital goods nor buy securities with their undistributed net incomes they must presumably hoard cash by building up their bank balances. Which one of the many possibilities that might ensue as a consequence here will depend upon the action taken by the banking system. Probably "hoarding" is the least likely of the three possibilities.

It does not necessarily follow, therefore, that merely because corporations do not pay out in dividends the full amount of their annual earnings that real capital investment will result equal to the sum earned but not paid to shareholders. It depends on how the funds are applied. Nevertheless it seems probable that actually much the greatest portion of undistributed net income is used by the corporations concerned in purchasing capital goods. If this be true, the practice of corporate reinvestment undoubtedly results in greater savings and investment than would occur were the full annual earnings paid out to stockholders. For while no doubt some

[23] This must not be interpreted to mean that the market for new issues (including of course additional issues by already established corporations) is entirely faultless in performing its selective functions. Anyone familiar with the facts would hardly subscribe to any such belief. We have indeed alluded to the difficulty already in Ch. VIII, sec. III.

shareholders would use their larger dividends for the purchase of new securities probably a very much larger number would use their larger cash incomes to increase their purchases of consumption goods.[24] In other words, one probable result of the practice of reinvesting corporate earnings is to reduce the proportionate expenditures on consumption goods and to increase those on investment goods. According to the particular theory of the trade cycle to which one subscribes this may be regarded as desirable or otherwise. We are only concerned to point out that aggregate real investment is likely to be increased during boom periods over what it would be if corporations paid out dividends approximately equal to their earnings.

Let us now examine the argument that the policy of "plowing back" earnings is essential to the maintenance of dividends in depression, and therefore assists in the maintenance of consumers' outlay.

If during depression dividend payments decline less than corporate incomes, consumers' outlay will be maintained at a higher level than if dividends completely paralleled corporate incomes. Cash resources in the hands of shareholders are more likely to be spent in consumers' goods markets than if held by the corporation. In this way therefore the increased outlay on consumption goods (over what would otherwise prevail) tends to maintain employment and hasten revival. If corporations however pay dividends in excess of earnings it must mean that they are either drawing down cash balances already in their possession or disinvesting. In considerable measure they probably do both. The reduced volume of operations lessens the need for working capital and to this extent enterprises may safely reduce cash holdings without sacrificing working capital needs. On the other hand, unless their sales are made at prices which do no more than barely cover direct avoidable costs, current receipts of cash will exceed current outlays.

[24] This is the more likely if the shares are held primarily by individuals in the medium income brackets. The recent growth of widespread stock ownership with individually small holdings suggests that, in the United States at least, increased dividend payments would largely be spent on consumption goods purchases. Shareholders in the large income groups are of course more likely to invest their larger cash dividends in new issues. Some data on the proportion of total dividends received by different income groups will be found in Berle and Means, *The Modern Corporation and Private Property*, pp. 60-62.

Hence, even though they are suffering losses, some capital goods worn out in the productive process are partially retrieved in cash and not immediately replaced. Thus it is the disinvestment of real capital that provides the cash for dividend disbursements in excess of earnings. Dividend payments are maintained partly by dishoarding and partly by disinvestment, while their disbursement in excess of earnings prevents consumers' outlay from falling as much as it would otherwise. But the removal of redundant stocks of finished goods and the increasing need for purchasing capital equipment worn out but not replaced, together create a situation from which revival may more easily emerge.

Theoretically, however, the beneficial results of the above process could equally well occur even though corporations had paid out as dividends almost all their earnings during the previous boom —except for one technicality. Unless a corporation *has* a surplus credit it is not likely to pay out dividends in excess of earnings because of the legal penalties for impaired capital. The most usual and approved way of accumulating a surplus credit, of course, is not to pay out all the earnings of the boom as dividends. Hence corporations which have no surplus will not pay dividends in excess of current earnings. But the ability to distribute cash to shareholders in a depression is not necessarily connected with the size of the surplus credit. Cash is made available for dividends largely from the operation of the factors discussed in the previous paragraph: the disinvestment of capital goods and reduced working capital needs. Yet the laws being what they are and our manner of thinking what it is, probably not nearly such large dividend payments in excess of earnings would or could (legally) occur during depressions if surplus credits had not been built up during the previous boom. Theoretically, however, the beneficial effects of dividend distributions in excess of current earnings are not dependent upon the existence of earned surplus. Precisely the same results would follow if we allowed capital, in the accounting sense, to become impaired. There is no reason whatsoever to suppose that because a corporation's balance sheet records a subsidiary proprietorship account labeled "surplus" it also must have cash somewhere about in an equivalent amount.

V. SUMMARY

The retention of earnings rather than the paying of cash dividends is but one means of increasing the aggregate total investment in the corporation. Consequently the appropriate logic runs in terms of increments of investment in relation to increments of prospective earnings. If the directors are acting in the interest of the shareholders they should only reinvest earnings provided the increased capital employed within the enterprise is likely to yield returns as high as those available in alternative investment opportunities. Properly interpreted, this principle is applicable to small corporations that are expanding, where earnings are not fully realized in cash, and where bonded indebtedness is being gradually paid off.

The legal rules governing dividends aim to protect both creditors and shareholders. Neither the capital impairment rule nor the net profits rule affords much protection to either group. The widespread use of no par shares has destroyed the original identity between the maintenance of legal capital and the maintenance of original investment, while debt-paying ability is not necessarily related to the stated value of shareholders' claims. The newer statutes have made the redefinition of capital for legal purposes comparatively easy.

The statistical evidence indicates that American corporations have been firmly convinced of the wisdom of reinvesting a comparatively large fraction of their reported net incomes. The more commonly expressed explanations and defenses of this policy are of doubtful validity. The widespread use of stock dividends is part and parcel of the same general reasoning concerning appropriate dividend policies. Either corporate directorates have been almost uniformly of the opinion that the marginal yields from additional investment was above the rate of interest or they have followed the rules of thumb without much thought of their applicability to each particular enterprise.

The policy of paying dividends considerably smaller than earnings during prosperity and in excess of earnings during depression probably tends to increase aggregate investment in the upswing over what it would otherwise be. Except for the legal complications, the payment of dividends exceeding earnings or in the face of losses during a slump is not dependent upon a previous policy of reinvesting earnings; the cash distributed is made available mainly from disinvestment and reduced working capital needs. The policy, however, does tend to maintain aggregate consumers' outlay.

A SUPPLEMENTARY NOTE ON TESTING THE RESULTS OF THE POLICY OF RE-INVESTING EARNINGS

It would be illuminating to discover by a statistical analysis whether or not the very common practice among American corporations of reinvesting a fairly large fraction of their annual earnings has worked out in the best interests of the shareholders. According to the argument already advanced, this would mean that the increment in capital investment from reinvested earnings yielded increments in returns to stockholders at least equal to those available in alternative employments. Unfortunately, however, there are very serious difficulties inherent in any attempt to test the results of reinvested earnings by empirical means.

The first difficulty has already been noted and so far as the writer is able to see is quite insurmountable. That is, a board of directors in order to justify reinvestment need not expect that the additional capital will actually bring about an increase in net earnings available for stockholders above their previous level. For, if with no additional investment earnings may be expected to fall by a certain amount, the reinvestment will be justified provided it prevents them falling by an amount equal to the returns available on the same amount of free capital if invested elsewhere in the economy.[25] That is, a board of directors acting on its expectations of an admittedly uncertain future would have here an almost unanswerable reply to any stockholder who charged excessive reinvestment of earnings.[26]

[25] See *supra*, sec. I.
[26] See the statements of business men quoted by Kendrick, M. S., *The Undistributed Profits Tax*, Washington (Brookings), 1937, pp. 34, 40, *passim*.

While recognizing this inherent difficulty, investigation of the practice of reinvesting earnings along the following lines might be revealing.

One might make rather detailed studies of individual corporations over a rather long period. Here again, however, there are certain unavoidable difficulties. In the first place in order to secure a representative sample many corporations would have to be included. More serious, however, is the fact that different corporations employ somewhat different methods in computing and reporting their net earnings, hence to this extent the results are not comparable. Furthermore, over any period of time long enough to determine the wisdom of reinvesting earnings the corporation will probably have altered its capital investment through other changes. An increase in capital employed may arise from four sources: reinvested earnings, sales of stock, sales of bonds, or increase in short term liabilities. If the capital secured from bond sales earned more than its interest charges, the total increment in net income available for shareholders is not attributable to the capital from reinvested earnings. So also with limited return preferred shares. Despite these handicaps, however, a study of individual corporations through many years might yield interesting data concerning the wisdom of reinvesting earnings.[27]

[27] So far as the writer is aware no attempt has been made to apply a marginal type of analysis to individual corporations. A few studies have been made of the trend of average rates of return on total capital employed. While a declining average rate of return does not necessarily indicate marginal returns lower than those elsewhere available, there is perhaps a presumption to this effect. Dr. R. Weidenhammer has plotted the return on invested capital in the U. S. Steel Corporation from 1902-1931 ("Causes and Repercussions of the Faulty Investment of Corporate Savings," *American Economic Review*, Vol. 23 (1933), pp. 34-41). He finds an unmistakably downward trend, which suggests that the notably conservative dividend policy of this corporation has not been wholly in the best interests of the stockholders. Somewhat similar computations by Hartzell of earnings available for interest and dividends, as a percentage of total assets (revised) indicate that the average rate for the decade 1901-1910 was 12.1 per cent, for 1911-1920, 8.2 per cent, and for 1921-1930, 6.4 per cent (Hartzell, E., "Profits in the Steel Industry," *Accounting Review*, Vol. 9 (1934), pp. 326-333).

Weidenhammer (*loc. cit.*) has also calculated the return on net tangible assets for four of the leading variety chain store corporations for 1918-1931. These show a persistently declining average rate of return from 1923-1931.

Much interesting material concerning earnings rates in particular corporations for the period 1922-1933 is contained in Sloan, L. H. *et al.*, *Two Cycles of Corporation Profits*, New York (Harpers), 1936. Here for more than 135 industrial corporations there has been presented the ratio, "Cash Dividend Return on Stock Owners' Share of Invested Capital," by individual years. As might be expected there are great differences between individual companies, although a surprising number are distressingly low. A low ratio might mean any one or a combination of three things: 1. That the earning power was low and that net earnings available for distribution were therefore small; 2. That earnings were large enough to per-

A possible approach to the problem might seem to be through the use of the income tax data as published annually in *Statistics of Income* by the U. S. Treasury Department and the *Source Book for the Study of Industrial Profits*.[28] And at one time the writer was hopeful that interesting results might be derived from these figures. But for reasons which may be briefly summarized these also probably cannot be used to determine the marginal returns from increased capital investment through reinvested earnings.

The series most likely to yield useful results is that for the 2,046 identical manufacturing corporations, divided into 11 major groups and 74 minor groups.[29] But even though the minor groups often contain relatively few corporations, the figures are nevertheless group figures; hence the large returns of some corporations from increased investment may be offset by the losses incurred by others, and to this extent the comparison of increments in investment with increments in returns on a group basis may mean very little.[30] The difficulty of allowing for increments in capital employed from sources other than earnings exists here too. Finally, there is the problem of cyclical variations and unusual conditions affecting particular industries over any

mit dividends but they were mostly plowed back; 3. That the invested percentage return thereon understates the true earning power. In considering this last, however, it should be borne in mind that not a few prominent corporations have in recent years veered more to the practice of under- rather than over-stating capital investment. Unfortunately Sloan's study does not present data which would permit a testing of the results of reinvesting earnings for particular companies.

[28] Epstein, R. C., and Clark, F. M., *A Source Book for the Study of Industrial Profits*, U. S. Department of Commerce, Washington, 1932. Professor Epstein has made considerable use of it in his *Industrial Profits in the United States*, New York (National Bureau of Economic Research), 1934, where some of the material from the *Source Book* is reprinted as an appendix.

The *Source Book* contains considerable information on 2,046 identical manufacturing corporations divided into eleven major groups, and 664 identical trading corporations, divided into three groups, and for certain purposes these are broken down into 99 sub-groups. The 2,046 manufacturing corporations were in continuous existence from 1919-1928, and the same corporations are included in the same group for each year. They were corporations of large and moderate size, whose investments ranged from $250,000 to more than $50,000,000; in 1928 more than 90 per cent of them possessed capitals of more than $500,000. Unfortunately, although the tables for certain items cover the period 1919-28, the dividend tables cover only the period 1923-28. This is a serious handicap in any effort to determine the results of reinvested earnings since the period is quite short; however, the results in terms of earnings after 1930 are probably not difficult to guess.

[29] See previous note.

[30] The *Source Book* at page 58 gives the *number* of corporations showing negative net incomes among the 2,046 manufacturing corporations. For the years 1924-28 the greatest number of corporations showing negative net incomes was 76, in 1928. Unfortunately, however, the total dollar amounts of the losses are not given and hence cannot be deducted.

five year period.[31] All things considered, it is doubtful if the group data can be employed to test the results of reinvested earnings.

It would seem, therefore, that about all one can do statistically is to observe what fraction of their annual net incomes American corporations have customarily plowed back into their businesses.

Various computations of the aggregate and proportionate amount of reinvested earnings have appeared from time to time. For the period 1910-1919 Dr. Knauth in 1922 estimated that while corporate savings fluctuated considerably from year to year they constituted roughly one quarter of total savings and about 4 per cent of the national income.[32] In 1929 Professors Ebersole, Burr and Peterson by rather complicated statistical methods estimated the amount reinvested by all corporations from 1916-1927 as something over $30 billions, or 43.7 per cent of the net income available for dividends.[33] Dr. Fabricant has recently published figures compiled from the income tax returns which seem to indicate that for the period 1919-1933 inclusive, net cash dividends paid by all corporations were 110.7 per cent of aggregate net income after payment of income and profit taxes.[34] In other words, cash dividends paid were greater than income available for dividends. But since taxable net income would probably tend to be smaller than net income available for dividends as reported to stockholders, and with losses the other way about, it seems unlikely that dividend payments in excess of earnings from 1930-1933 exceeded the total reinvestment of earnings for 1919-1929.[35] Net income reinvested was probably positive for the 15-year period.

[31] Presumably, of course, a board of directors in deciding what proportion of the year's net income to pay out in dividends entertains some "expectations" concerning cyclical changes, technological changes, etc., over the proximate future. That is, the members of the board can hardly be assumed to be unaware of such matters and their probable impact upon the particular enterprise; but this is not to say, to be sure, that their expectations are perfect.

[32] Knauth, O. W., "The Place of Corporate Surplus in the National Income," *Journal of the American Statistical Association*, Vol. 18 (1922), pp. 157-166.

[33] Ebersole, J. F., Burr, S. S., Peterson, G. M., "Income Forecasting by the Use of Statistics of Income Data," *Review of Economic Statistics*, Vol. 11 (November, 1929), pp. 171-196. A rather elaborate corrective technique was here used in an effort to reduce the rough figures for the various years to a comparable basis and to remove under- and over-statements.

Unadjusted figures for corporate savings are given in the *Statistical Abstract of the United States*, e.g., for 1936 at p. 252. Interesting data are presented for a three-year period (1927-29) by Paton, W. A., *Corporate Profits as Shown by Audit Reports*, New York (National Bureau), 1935, especially Ch. VI.

[34] The excess seems to have been roughly $5,450 millions. See National Bureau of Economic Research *Bulletin* no. 50 (April 18, 1934), p. 10, for the years 1919-30, and *Bulletin* no. 55 (April 11, 1935), p. 7, for the years 1931-33. These figures exclude tax-exempt corporations and life insurance companies.

[35] Ebersole *et al.* (*op. cit.*, p. 178 note), report the following concerning the degree of understatement of earnings as reported for income tax purposes: "For

For the 2,046 identical manufacturing corporations the percentages of net income (*before* income and profits taxes) paid out in cash dividends were respectively, 55, 50, 55, 72, 65 per cent for the years 1924-28.[36] The total amount reinvested by these corporations during the five years was 3,605.23 millions of dollars, or 33.02 per cent of the net income available for dividends, i.e., net income after income taxes.

In the table on p. 266 there is shown the proportions of net income available for dividends reinvested by 35 minor groups.[37] It will be observed that the range from lowest to highest is considerable.[38] What inference is to be drawn from these figures, however, is not clear. Certainly there is no obvious connection between the proportion of earnings reinvested and the behavior of net income. If anything a high proportion of reinvestment shows some tendency to be associated with stationary or declining earnings.[39] But the converse is not especially apparent. The only obvious fact is the very wide differences between the groups, presumably indicating the diversity of conditions surrounding each industry. For the reasons already noted, however, the figures here given must be interpreted with caution.

Hence with the information now available it appears impossible to show statistically just what have been the results (in terms of subsequent earnings) of the very common practice among American corporations of reinvesting a large percentage of their annual net incomes. While misdirected capital investment in particular instances has doubtless occurred, it seems impossible to demonstrate statistically that this

104 industrial corporations with identical names included in the quarterly index of corporation profits, the total net income shown in returns with the same names was 90.2, 87.3, 85.9, and 90.0 per cent, respectively, of the total published profits for years, 1923-1926." But for all corporations a 10 per cent understatement seems excessive. There would seem to be no reason to doubt the validity of the dividend figures, however.

Fabricant cites figures compiled by the Standard Statistics Company for 418 large industrial corporations which indicate that reinvested earnings for these corporations during 1927-1929 exceeded cash dividends and losses 1930-1933 by 1,226 millions. *Loc. cit., Bulletin* 55, p. 7, note.

[36] Epstein, *op. cit.*, p. 243. Paton, *op. cit.*, p. 6 reports that for 699 relatively small corporations in the years 1927-1929 only 57 per cent of earnings available for dividends was paid in cash.

[37] For the 11 major groupings the range is considerable, extending from 22.37 per cent for Lumber to 60.35 for Leather. But because the variation in the component minor groupings is large the composite figures in some cases are not very representative and are not here given.

[38] For Meat Packing and Weaving Woolens, two other groups examined, there was no positive reinvestment of earnings for the years 1924-1928.

[39] If true, this may possibly be explained as follows: Corporations with poor earnings will probably find it difficult to raise funds in the capital market. Consequently if the directors believe the enterprise must have capital they are likely to reinvest a large fraction of whatever earnings the corporation succeeds in making.

Industrial Groups	Number of Corporations	Net Income (after tax) Available for Dividends (in millions of dollars)					Percentage of Net Income Reinvested 1924-28
		1924	1925	1926	1927	1928	
1. Wire and Nails	20	8.26	8.20	8.56	7.10	10.52	13.01
2. Professional and Scientific Instruments, including optical goods	23	23.16	42.97	44.05	39.61	44.10	14.73
3. Carpets, including carpet yarns, rope and cordage	18	8.82	8.32	6.36	7.33	4.90	16.3
4. Flour, Feed and Grist Mills	32	9.37	5.57	5.80	6.85	6.93	17.4
5. Misc. Chemicals and Chem. Products	26	79.03	83.72	113.28	112.52	138.84	17.53
6. Blank Paper	35	21.38	16.81	16.78	16.97	17.90	22.97
7. Petrol. Refining and Products	52	229.61	380.45	423.90	217.67	474.70	26.70
8. Textile Mach. and Parts	18	7.28	10.29	9.77	11.44	10.64	26.81
9. Silk Weaving	17	5.60	11.73	6.76	3.79	4.27	27.68
10. Factory Mach. other than Textile, Printing and Electrical	23	12.50	20.63	20.34	17.38	22.49	27.72
11. Glass	18	17.33	16.87	14.98	10.66	14.01	29.12
12. Misc. Leather Products	29	5.98	6.45	4.83	9.06	3.73	29.4
13. Tools	30	7.03	10.31	12.24	9.87	15.19	30.73
14. Bolts and Nuts	15	2.25	3.57	3.92	3.14	4.89	32.75
15. Paints	42	13.13	15.05	15.22	12.83	16.06	32.93
16. Ceramics	48	14.07	15.25	16.00	13.45	12.00	33.50
17. Tobacco	23	74.29	83.60	89.77	95.60	97.06	33.9
18. Crude Chemicals and Fert.	9	8.37	10.56	9.99	11.05	14.10	36.17
19. Cardboard Boxes	33	4.17	4.92	4.77	6.68	5.77	37.89
20. Publishing Newspapers	20	39.06	32.05	50.95	57.47	67.86	38.06
21. Motor Vehicle and Parts	32	216.34	321.50	323.10	254.67	269.44	39.12
22. Publishing Books and Music	17	6.62	6.34	5.82	5.15	5.82	39.69
23. Engines and Parts	11	6.58	3.01	4.85	5.59	3.98	39.94
24. Dairying and Dairy Prod.	26	11.15	15.16	15.99	16.33	17.17	40.7
25. Office Machinery	13	8.97	13.26	13.11	16.89	19.02	40.88
26. Rubber	26	36.85	102.91	51.18	39.58	4.80	41.87
27. Misc. Lumber Products	28	19.55	19.56	17.25	7.14	13.48	42.9
28. Misc. Paper Products	23	8.03	7.95	8.52	6.19	7.54	43.42
29. Portland Cement	21	23.92	26.77	26.81	23.12	24.70	43.54
30. Elect. Machinery, Appliances and Supplies	54	106.26	111.93	124.90	100.61	124.22	44.10
31. Toilet Preparations	9	2.97	2.84	3.01	3.18	3.60	44.87
32. Stationery	20	2.36	3.09	3.33	5.02	5.13	48.38
33. Pianos and Organs	11	4.94	5.76	5.74	3.66	2.95	49.15
34. Misc. Stone and Clay Products	27	18.23	23.87	25.31	23.64	27.99	50.47
35. Boots and Shoes	25	19.75	18.90	18.35	23.27	21.42	69.2

result has been general. Perhaps one suspicion is about as good as another so far as the statistical evidence is any guide.

REFERENCES: CHAPTER IX

BURTCHETT, F. F.—*Corporation Finance*. Chs. 32, 33.
DEWING, A. S.—*Financial Policy*. Book IV, Chs. 8, 9.
FIELD, K.—*Corporation Finance*. Ch. 27.
GERSTENBERG, C. W.—*Financial Organization and Management*. Ch. 27.
HOAGLAND, H. E.—*Corporation Finance*. Chs. 31, 32.

BONBRIGHT, J. C.—"Theory of Anglo-American Dividend Law: Surplus and Profits," *Columbia Law Review*, Vol. 30.
EPSTEIN, R. C.—*Industrial Profits in the United States*. New York. 1934.
MASON, P.—"Profits and Surplus Available for Dividends," *Accounting Review;* March, 1932.
PATON, W. A.—*Corporate Profit as Shown by Audit Reports*, New York, 1935.
PREINREICH, G. A. D.—*The Nature of Dividends*, Lancaster, Pa., 1935.
WEINER, J. L.—"Theory of Anglo-American Dividend Law: American Statutes and Cases," *Columbia Law Review*, Vol. 29.
WEINER, J. L.—"Theory of Anglo-American Dividend Law: The English Cases," *Columbia Law Review*, Vol. 28.

Chapter X

FLUCTUATIONS IN INCOME THROUGH TIME: THE BUSINESS CYCLE PROBLEM AND THE INDIVIDUAL ENTERPRISE

I. The Business Cycle Pattern. II. Oscillations in Money Flows and Business Profits. III. The Business Cycle and Capital Investment. IV. Adaptations to the Cycle by the Single Enterprise. V. Summary.

The three chapters immediately preceding have considered the problems of what is meant (ideally) by saying that business enterprises endeavor to maximize net returns from the employment of their resources, how the results of business operations for any expired period are measured by accounting techniques, and what reasoning may appropriately be followed in determining whether dividends should be paid to shareholders or the aggregate investment in the enterprise should be augmented or diminished. For the most part our remarks in those chapters are applicable to business enterprises regardless of the presence or absence of cyclical variations in output, employment, real and money incomes, prices, etc., within the economy as a whole. It so happens, however, that all capitalistic economies of which we have knowledge are characterized by oscillations from periods of depression to periods of prosperity. Any business enterprise operates within an unstable framework of this character. As a consequence we need to examine the repercussions of the trade cycle phenomenon upon the single business enterprise.

I. THE BUSINESS CYCLE PATTERN

1. The meaning of the term "business cycle." 2. Business cycle patterns.

1. *The meaning of the term "business cycle."* The "business cycle" is a term which has come to be applied to those fluctuations in prices, output, incomes, employment, business profits, etc., excluding seasonal and secular variations, which are empirically observable through time. In one sense the term is unfortunate since it suggests a regularity of pattern more or less continuously repeated. This implication is not strictly borne out by economic analysis. All economists know that each cycle has certain unique characteristics which tend to differentiate it from others. Furthermore, it is clear that there is no *one* business cycle except in the sense of some average of a number of individual indices. As Professor J. M. Clark has emphasized, any statistically established cycle is a composite which distorts individual differences in the underlying data, e.g., an index of pig-iron production would not portray exactly the fluctuations in output of each and every blast furnace. Any index which purported to portray *the* business cycle would necessarily distort somewhat the fluctuations in its component parts representing different phases of economic activity. Again, whichever index of "the business cycle" one chooses will be mainly determined by the purposes for which he wishes to employ it. A stock market speculator will have a somewhat different statistical interest than an unemployment relief board. Accordingly, then, as one's immediate interest centers in prices, output, industrial profits, employment, etc., he will tend to mean slightly different things by the business cycle. Nevertheless, because it is convenient to have a portmanteau term by which to designate those more or less synchronous fluctuations in almost all branches of economic activity, and because there is more than a suggestion that they result from common causes, the term business cycle is perhaps warranted. It must be remembered, however, that our use of the phrase in no way implies the existence of a

statistically determinable pattern which is retraced without change in each and every alternation from prosperity to depression.

2. *Business cycle patterns.* With respect to any time series portraying changes in economic data, two most important facts are amplitude and timing. Neither, however, is more than a relative term in business cycle analysis. When we speak of the amplitude or timing of the fluctuations of a particular series we must have in mind some other series which serves as a basis of comparison. On *a priori* grounds there is no reason why we might not select arbitrarily almost any one statistical series and use it as a frame of reference. Thus, for instance, we might take pig-iron production and compare other series with it as to timing and degree of fluctuation. More recently Professors W. C. Mitchell and J. M. Clark have introduced the concept and developed statistically a "reference cycle" as a sort of benchmark with which other series are compared. The reference cycle is a composite statistical series portraying the movements of "general business activity." [1] For our purposes it is sufficient to note merely a few general statistical relationships or patterns as an introduction to our major interest—the significance of the cycle for the individual enterprise.

As between different industries, the construction trades show a pronounced tendency to lead general business in both downward and upward movements, although, as is to be expected, there are important differences between industrial, commercial, and residential construction. Leads and lags between the production and sales of consumers' goods and producers' goods are not clearly marked, although there appears to be some slight tendency for the production of the former to precede changes in the production of the latter. As one would expect, the production of consumers' goods, generally speaking, attains its peaks and troughs somewhat before the prices of consumers' goods.

Turning from timing to the amplitude of the fluctuations in different series, it is rather well established that construction and

---

[1] The construction of such an index is fraught with difficulties which cannot be dealt with here. See, however, W. C. Mitchell's article on "Business Cycles" in *Encyclopaedia of the Social Sciences*, Vol. III, pp. 92-106; also Clark, J. M., *Strategic Factors in Business Cycles*, New York (National Bureau), 1934, pp. 7-13 *passim*. Much of what follows in the present section is based on Clark's volume.

producers' goods in general show much greater fluctuations than the reference cycle of general business activity.[2] Again, the physical production of goods oscillates considerably more than amounts paid out as income to the factors of production, i.e., wages, salaries, dividends, rents, royalties, etc. On the other hand, business costs fluctuate relatively less than business income. In the field of prices, retail prices fluctuate relatively less than wholesale prices; and as between durable and non-durable goods price changes are greater in the former. As a general proposition the farther back from consumers' goods markets we go the greater the amplitude in the fluctuations in prices. For example, using July, 1929, as a base, raw material prices at wholesale in the United States fell to 50.6 (February, 1933) while manufactured goods had fallen only to 68.7 at the same date. Taking July, 1929, as a point of departure, one of the outstanding characteristics of the period 1929-1934 is the manner in which particular prices diverged sharply from the relationship they bore to one another in that base period. The "fanning-out" is very marked, indicating that the degree of price change is by no means constant between different groups of prices through the cycle. If space permitted, many other interesting relationships between prices, production, and other matters might be treated.[3] But these would take us too far afield.

II. OSCILLATIONS IN MONEY FLOWS AND BUSINESS PROFITS

1. Money receipts and outlays during an upswing. 2. Money receipts and outlays during a downswing. 3. The behavior of reported net income.

It is convenient to commence our analysis of the impact of the business cycle upon the individual firm by examining its effect upon money receipts and money outlays.

[2] For an explanation of this fact running in terms of the "acceleration principle" see Clark, *op. cit.*, pp. 33-44.

[3] See Mills, F. C., *The Behavior of Prices*, New York (National Bureau), 1936; also "Changes in Prices, Manufacturing Costs and Industrial Productivity, 1929-

1. *Money receipts and outlays during an upswing.* The most immediate effect of a change in the level of business activity upon the individual enterprise (apart from a change in the market price of its shares) is a change in the rate of absorption of its product by buyers.[4] Per unit of time more or fewer units are being taken by buyers in the market. If, at the same price, buyers now purchase more units than previously, a movement towards prosperity has begun, if fewer units, a shift in the direction of depression.[5] The demand curve for the product of the firm has shifted to the right in the first (prosperity) and to the left in the second (depression). A shift in the demand or average revenue curve means necessarily a changed marginal revenue curve, and, assuming no immediate change in the cost data, a change in price will be necessary in order to equate marginal cost and marginal revenue.[6] If the new demand curve parallels the old an increase in the rate of absorption due to cyclical changes will lead to a rise in selling prices, a decrease to a reduction.

Assuming for the present no change in the marginal cost curve, the effect of a shift in the demand curve to the right will be an increase in the flow of net money receipts into the enterprise

1934," National Bureau of Economic Research, Bulletin 53, December 22, 1934; Bulletin 61, November 9, 1936, "Production during the American Business Cycle of 1927-1933," by Mitchell, W. C., and Burns, A. F., is also revealing.

[4] In the particular business enterprise not all changes in the rate of absorption of its product are traceable to the business cycle. Two other possibilities must be noted. In the first place the competitive position of this enterprise in its industry might improve without any change occurring in the aggregate demand for the product of the industry as a whole. This firm has merely come to take a larger proportion of a constant aggregate amount of sales per unit of time. This firm sells more while others sell less. On the other hand because of a change in consumers' tastes there may be an increase in the total demand for the products of all the firms in the industry. In other words, consumers prefer this industry's product to that of others more than previously. In formal language: in the first case there is movement of the demand curve of the firm to the right while those of other competing firms move to the left; in the second, the demand curves for all the firms of a particular industry move to the right while elsewhere in the economy there is a movement of demand schedules to the left.

[5] For enterprises selling under conditions of pure competition a change in demand would immediately reveal itself by a change in price. See *supra,* Ch. VII, sec. VI.

[6] In considering the wisdom of a change in price those in charge of the enterprise will have to take into account the probable consequences of an immediate price change upon the demand curve for the product at subsequent points in time. A raising of the price of the product may create a prejudice against the firm, and

per unit of time. A portion of the larger *gross* money receipts will be required to finance the production of the now larger output consequent upon the shift in the demand curve to the right.[7] But except in circumstances to be noted below, net money receipts will tend to be greater.

There are some reasons for believing that during a boom demand curves of individual enterprises not only shift to the right but undergo a change in elasticity as well. Mr. R. F. Harrod has recently introduced in this connection what he calls the "Law of Diminishing Elasticity of Demand." His contention is that as a boom progresses the time, trouble, and annoyance to the purchaser of discovering where lower prices and superior quality are to be had remains constant while the significance of small savings decreases because of his now larger income. As a consequence, his willingness to shift to another seller offering a slightly lower price, or to forsake a particular seller because he has raised his price, is decreased. The demand curve for the product of the individual firm during a boom therefore tends to become more inelastic over a certain range in the neighborhood of the prevailing price.[8] Conversely, of course, during a slump, reduced incomes tend to render demand schedules more elastic. Mr. Harrod's argument seems plausible and to account partially for certain buying habits observable in everyday life.

hence react unfavorably on subsequent sales, by suggesting that the firm is "profiteering." Similarly, it is a common contention of business men that price reductions during depression are to be avoided if possible because of (1) the difficulties encountered in subsequently raising them without creating ill-will, and (2) the suggestion to the buyer of inferior quality. In part these problems are business men's own creation since, by refusing to alter prices, they lead buyers to expect stable prices for certain products. Such considerations, however, no doubt weigh with business men and affect their price policies; and in so far as they do, business men recognize "costs" (resistances) other than those appearing in the accounting records. The cost curves have in a sense changed. For an ingenious theoretical treatment of some of these questions see Smith, H., "Discontinuous Demand Curves and Monopolistic Competition, A Special Case," *Quarterly Journal of Economics*, Vol. 49, pp. 542-550.

[7] Observe that we are still assuming no change in cost conditions, merely an increase in output.

[8] Harrod, R. F., *The Trade Cycle*, Oxford (Oxford Press), 1936, pp. 18-22. Mr. Harrod's argument is not restricted to cyclical changes entirely but includes secular changes in the direction of growing affluence. See p. 87. The "law" has been qualified and partially restricted in its application by Mr. R. F. Bretherton and Mr. H. W. Singer in the *Economic Journal*, September, 1937, and March, 1938, respectively.

If with growing prosperity the demand curve both shifts and becomes steeper then the rise in price, assuming the enterprise always seeks to equate marginal cost and marginal revenue, will be greater than if only a shift had occurred.[9] Mr. Harrod believes that this principle accounts for much of the rise in prices observable during a boom.

During a period of rising business activity an increase in demand for the product of the firm will almost certainly be accompanied by an upward shift in its marginal cost curve, and hence any given output requires a greater money outlay than before.[10] Whether the rise in money outlays will be proportionate to the increase in money receipts will depend upon the relative price movements of products and inputs. The well-known tendency of wage rates to lag somewhat behind increases in product prices tends to cause money receipts to exceed money outlays.[11] On the other hand, raw material prices are likely to move more rapidly than finished goods prices, thus setting up an opposite reaction. Although here any generalization is open to qualification, it seems reasonable from the information available that during a boom money outlays *would* tend to lag behind money receipts for most enterprises *if* their purchases of raw materials and rates of production were governed entirely by their current sales of products. As is well-known, of course, during a boom enterprises commonly anticipate rising raw material prices and consequently buy forward, i.e., carry larger stocks, and also produce in excess of current sales. As a consequence outlays may keep pace with the rising receipts and even exceed them. In the latter instance the firm would probably be borrowing from banks. What we have just said concerning the flow of money receipts and outlays is

[9] Any reader can easily demonstrate this to his own satisfaction by drawing a simple diagram.

[10] What we have in mind here is that, insofar as some components of the marginal cost curve are direct money cost outlays, a rise in their purchase price will raise the marginal cost curve. It is not necessary to assume that the new and higher marginal cost curve will parallel the old. In fact this probably will not be true.

[11] Especially towards the end of the boom the rise in labor cost per unit of product tends to exceed the rise in wage rates because of a decline in diligence on the part of employees. Conversely, during depression labor costs fall more than wage rates because of an opposite change. This tends to modify the statement in the text above.

not at odds with the commonly noted fact that corporate balance sheets frequently show a declining cash position as a boom progresses. The size of the cash fund need have no connection with the rate of *flow* of cash in and out of the enterprise per period of time, provided both synchronize.[12] Cash balances tend to decline during prosperity because of forward buying, a tendency to carry somewhat larger inventories, and larger receivables.

2. *Money receipts and outlays during a downswing.* Much of what we have said already concerning the flow of money receipts and outlays during a period of rising business activity may be inverted for a decline and a depression. Demand curves tend to shift to the left and to become more elastic, and prices tend to fall. Whereas before there was anticipatory buying of inventories and accumulation of stocks, during a downswing in business, individual firms have a strong incentive to liquidate inventories. Sales fall off but purchases decline still more. The flow of money receipts tends to exceed the flow of money outlays and cash accumulates. If the firm has previously borrowed from the banks or merchandise creditors, these tend to be paid off. Similarly receivables are liquidated and new on-account sales decline. Whilst prices are falling there is little to encourage buying of raw materials or the hiring of laborers. The value of cash balances appreciates; the emphasis is upon the desirability of "keeping liquid," that is, accumulating idle cash. The effect of this policy upon the economy as a whole and, therefore, the business enterprises contained in it, is decidedly unfortunate since it is deflationary in a high degree. Yet there is no real difficulty in understanding why each business enterprise—from its own point of view—should regard such a policy as the essence of wisdom.[13]

[12] The cash balance obviously is related to the *relative* flow of cash receipts and outlays.

[13] The reason why an increased desire for liquid as opposed to non-liquid assets is highly deflationary is that it is quite impossible for business enterprises *generally* to hold relatively fewer assets such as merchandise, materials, machinery, etc., unless consumers are willing to increase their purchases of these assets and thereby surrender cash to business concerns. Although it is impossible for *all* firms to hold relatively fewer assets of this type and relatively larger cash balances they may *try* to do so none the less. The consequence of a general effort to "unload," however, is to force down prices for these assets, which, in turn, may create a further desire to liquidate, leading to still lower prices. Business concerns *as a whole* can-

3. *The behavior of reported net income.* The foregoing dis-cussion of alterations in demand has been concerned mainly with the cyclical flow of money receipts and money outlays. We must now examine quite a different thing—the behavior of net income as determined by accepted accounting procedures. During a period of expansion moving towards a boom most enterprises will report larger net incomes even though the increased rate of money receipts is paralleled by a proportionate or even larger increase in money cost outlays.[14] For as we have argued already in an earlier chapter, accounting net income is computed on the assumption that certain types of assets—mainly durable and depreciable assets —have been correctly valued for all time when acquired. As a consequence, if a proportion of this original purchase price is charged against gross income of a period in which the selling price of the product has been rising, without adjustment for the greater money values now being consumed in production, the net income figure will tend to increase.[15] Net income is also exaggerated by the usual treatment of inventories. These are purchased at one price level and after an interval appear as finished goods. By the time they are sold, however, prices are often higher and they are recorded in gross income at this higher price. Costs are charged at a lower price level than that at which gross income is recorded. The result is a rising net income figure. The more rapid the rise in prices and the longer the production period the greater the increment in net income that will result from this practice. All the foregoing, moreover, is accentuated during a boom by the twin practices of forward-buying of raw materials and manufacturing to stock. Although the firm will show a rising net income figure in its accounting statements, a larger fraction of its gross income

not liquidate their non-cash assets quickly; but they may certainly try to do so and thereby produce a price deflation.

The price deflation and increase in liquidity preference may cause some enter-prises to fail. Something further is said on this point in Ch. XII, sec. V.

[14] Even if the rise in gross income in the accounting sense were accompanied by a proportionate rise in *all costs*, net income as an aggregate would none the less increase and by the same proportion.

[15] Some light on the degree to which net income figures are affected by basing depreciation charges on an original cost basis rather than on the higher price levels prevailing during the period in which income is being charged with de-

will be necessary to maintain physical inventories at a constant level. By no means can all the increase in net income be made available to the shareholders as cash dividends.

During a decline in business activity the enterprise will tend to report a considerably smaller net income per period or even losses. We have already indicated that cash balances will tend to increase; but not all costs in the accounting sense necessitate a cash outlay. As often emphasized, certain costs such as depreciation, obsolescence, etc., are treated as largely independent of the volume of current operations. When such fixed expenses are charged against a reduced gross income from sales the result is a smaller net income figure. Furthermore, the common rule of "cost or market, whichever is lower" in inventory valuation serves to accentuate the decline in net income conversely with its exag-

preciation is given by the following figures prepared by Solomon Fabricant for the National Bureau of Economic Research. See *Studies in Income and Wealth*, New York (National Bureau), 1937, Vol. I, p. 129.

DEPRECIATION CHARGES EXPRESSED IN TERMS OF ORIGINAL COST AND REPRODUCTION COST, 1919-1935

All corporations in the United States
(millions of dollars)

Year	(1) Depreciation charge in terms of original cost	(2) Depreciation charge in terms of reproduction cost	Difference (1) minus (2)
1919	1,620	2,620	—1,000
1920	1,940	3,330	—1,390
1921	2,200	2,770	—570
1922	2,490	2,780	—290
1923	2,620	3,260	—640
1924	2,700	3,190	—490
1925	2,860	3,250	—390
1926	3,270	3,670	—400
1927	3,350	3,740	—390
1928	3,600	3,890	—290
1929	3,870	4,250	—380
1930	3,990	4,180	—190
1931	4,000	3,920	80
1932	3,690	3,240	450
1933	3,500	3,110	390
1934	3,360	3,300	60
1935	3,420	3,410	10

geration during an interval of rising prices. Inventories on hand at the close of the period will be written down to market prices which are less than purchase costs, which means a loss on holding them chargeable to the period.

Were the enterprise able to reduce accounting costs in proportion to the decline in gross income there would be no need for it ever to show a loss on current operations—net income would always be positive. For the reasons already mentioned, however, accounting costs in relation to gross income decline less than proportionately during depressions and rise less than proportionately during booms. The accounting statements therefore tend to exaggerate both the rise and the fall in net income.

Professor John B. Canning has emphasized repeatedly that these exaggerations of net income during booms and of losses (or declines in net income) during depressions are mostly illusory, since they arise in large measure from the arbitrary way in which past outlays for relatively durable assets are allocated through time. He has written:

> The large net income figures found by the accountants in years of large volume of output are characteristically grossly overstated; the red ink that appears in the income balances of low-volume years—because of the arbitrary treatment of "fixed expenses"—is, more often than not, just ink. There is no kind of expense that, unconditionally, and in economic reality, is a fixed expense with respect to annual operating income; there are only arbitrarily fixed *allocations* of certain expenses.[16]

If the writer understands him correctly, Canning's main point is that because of cyclical variations accountants' gross income shows wide fluctuations corresponding to variations in sales of goods to consumers at varying prices. These sales entail certain costs. What the accountant ostensibly is endeavoring to do is to allocate against the income of any period the cost of acquiring that period's income. As a consequence, there is little or no justification for the arbitrary allocation of a constant figure—representing certain elements in cost—against a fluctuating income. It is much more rea-

16 Canning, J. B., "A Certain Erratic Tendency in Accountants' Income Procedure," *Econometrica*, Vol. I, No. 1, pp. 56-62, at pp. 56-57.

sonable to argue that the charge should be a fluctuating amount related to the size of the income. This would mean that depreciation and similar charges would be greater during a boom and correspondingly smaller during depression, with the result that reported net income for most enterprises would be decidedly more stable from period to period than it is when current practices are followed.[17]

The equal allocation of certain expenses between good years and bad is probably employed because of its arithmetical simplicity as much as anything else. Now there can be nothing but applause for simplicity, providing it is not purchased at too high a cost in terms of unfortunate consequences in other directions. The accounting practice of equal allocation of the purchase price of an asset over its expected life in accounting periods is very unfortunate in its effects because business men are influenced in a good many ways by the size, positive or negative, of reported net income. It is rather like looking at a thermometer; one is inclined to feel much hotter or colder after reading the temperature than he was before, even though he was previously conscious of being warm or chilled. So a business man is likely to be more elated or depressed after reading the accountant's statement of net income than he was before. If this were all, the matter might be dismissed as harmless and of no consequence. But insofar as business men and others are affected in their judgments and actions by the reported net income the matter is more serious. For instance, we often read in the columns of the stock market commentators that the fall (or rise) in share prices for the day was caused by unfavorable (or favorable) reports of "first quarter earnings." Now these usually appear about 8 to 10 weeks after the quarter is ended. Any damage is surely over and done with for that quarter. Only insofar as the reports of that quarter presage things yet to come should share prices be affected. And the information presented on this problem is almost negligible.

[17] Canning offers certain suggestions by which the "erratic tendency" might be eliminated. But these cannot be dealt with here. See *ibid.*, pp. 59-60.

III. THE BUSINESS CYCLE AND CAPITAL INVESTMENT

1. The inducement to invest. 2. The inducement to invest during an upswing. 3. Decreased inducement to invest during a downswing.

From the broader point of view of the economy as a whole perhaps the most important characteristic of the business cycle is the marked fluctuation in the volume of investment from one phase to another.[18] Now investment in the modern world, apart from public undertakings, is mainly carried out by and through the individual business enterprise. As a consequence, in the present study we must examine the impingement of the trade cycle upon investment by business firms.

1. *The inducement to invest.* In an earlier chapter dealing with promotion we argued that for a new enterprise to be undertaken there must be a reasonable presumption that the rate of return upon the investment will exceed the rate of interest. Since the rate of interest was taken to indicate the returns available upon free capital invested in other opportunities there would be no inducement to bring a new concern into existence unless the expected returns upon capital therein were at least as great as the rate of interest. Logically the *sine qua non* of investment is a prospective yield greater than or at least equal to the rate of interest.

This requirement applies, however, not only to the creation of new enterprises, but also to the purchase of assets by those already established. Mr. J. M. Keynes has recently developed this idea at length and with precision by introducing the concept of "the marginal efficiency of an asset." [19] The marginal efficiency of an asset is first of all a rate in the sense in which the rate of interest is a rate and may be explained as follows. Let us assume that a

[18] Whether fluctuations in the rate of investment in the economy are primarily responsible for the cycle fortunately we need not examine. Investment here is used in its economic sense of the purchase of new capital goods.

[19] Keynes, J. M., *The General Theory of Employment, Interest and Money*, New York, 1936, Ch. 11 *passim*.

machinery equipment company will accept orders for a particular kind of machine at a supply price S. Assume further that as a consequence of possessing this machine a particular enterprise estimates it will add to its net receipts an amount indicated by the series $R_1 + R_2 + R_3 \ldots R_n$. In other words, the R series represents the added net income the firm in question expects to secure from possessing the machine rather than not possessing it. Now there will always be some rate of discount which will make this R series equal to S, the price at which a new machine may be purchased; and that rate of discount which equates the two is the marginal efficiency of that kind of asset to the firm in question at this particular point in time.[20] Stated otherwise, we might say that the marginal efficiency of any kind of asset to a particular firm is the expected rate of return upon its cost. Now for the individual firm the rate of interest is determined by factors beyond its control. In order for investment to take place the persons in charge of the firm must believe that the marginal efficiency of the asset in question exceeds the rate of interest; if the two are just equal it is a matter of indifference whether the asset is purchased or not. Alternatively stated, investment in an asset presupposes a rate of return upon its cost exceeding the rate of interest.

In the real world neither the rate of interest nor the marginal efficiency of different kinds of assets remains constant through time. Fluctuations in the former, however, are probably of a much smaller order of magnitude than variations of the latter.[21] Furthermore, from the point of view of the individual enterprise the rate of interest may be taken as a datum from which it may reason.[22]

---

[20] Symbolically $S = \dfrac{R_1}{1 + e} + \dfrac{R_2}{(1 + e)^2} + \dfrac{R_3}{(1 + e)^3} \cdots \dfrac{R_n}{(1 + e)^n}$, where the R's and S are given and e, the marginal efficiency of the asset, is the unknown to be found.

[21] The reasons why fluctuations in the rate of interest are confined within a certain rather narrow range are not easy to specify. In part, they are to be found in institutional factors pertaining to the organization of the banking system; but this does not provide a sufficient explanation. For our purposes it is enough to note the empirically established fact.

[22] Small changes in the rate of interest with an unchanged marginal efficiency of capital are probably quite unimportant in altering business men's decisions to invest. See in this connection, *American Economic Review*, Vol. 28 (1938) *Supplement*, pp. 73-76, Henderson, H. D., "The Significance of the Rate of Interest"

The marginal efficiency of different kinds of assets on the other hand is neither given nor stable. In the first place, it is an estimate, tinged with great uncertainty, which each enterprise will have to undertake for itself; it may not be read from the financial pages of the morning paper. Being essentially an estimate and not a calculation which can be made precisely, it is peculiarly open to all those influences which affect human judgments concerning the future course of events. Let us now examine the fluctuations during different phases of the business cycle of the marginal efficiency of different kinds of assets or of capital goods in general, and indicate their effect upon the volume of investment.[23]

2. *The inducement to invest during an upswing.* A period of rising business activity is often said to be characterized by a buoyant optimism. So far as the individual enterprise is concerned such a designation is not unwarranted. The flow of cash receipts is likely to be encouraging; because of the change in demand schedules product prices are firm or rising; and the net income as reported by the accounting statements will tend to be increasing. How do these affect the marginal efficiency of assets?

Let it be recalled that the marginal efficiency of an asset is that rate of discount which equates its supply price with the present value of the prospective increments in income to the enterprise resulting from its addition to the combination of assets already in its possession. Since the supply price will be given if the asset is to be purchased from outside the firm, it follows that boom conditions exert their primary influence upon the marginal efficiency of different kinds of assets through raising the estimates of the probable additions to the net income stream. The rising selling prices, the apparently large and growing demand for the products, the encouraging statements of net income, all point to the conclusion that net income will be increased substantially by the addition of more assets.[24] Otherwise expressed, there is much in the

in *Oxford Economic Papers* No. 1 (October, 1938), pp. 1-13, and Meade, J. E., and Andrews, W. P. S., "Summaries of Replies to Questions on Effects of Interest Rates," *ibid.*, pp. 14-31.

[23] In what follows we shall speak sometimes of the marginal efficiency of capital but this is merely a shorthand expression for the marginal efficiency of particular assets of which there are innumerable kinds.

[24] If raw material prices are rising and are expected to continue to rise, then this is a further reason for buying now before they go higher.

situation to give business men the impression that the rate of return upon the cost of particular assets will be high. The marginal efficiency of capital is estimated at a high level. This applies not only to durable assets but also to working capital types of assets as well, i.e., inventories, supplies, etc.

What of the rate of interest, the other determinant of investment? Here also changes favorable to investment are likely to be taking place. In the first place, and especially during the early phases of revival, the rate of interest is likely to be low. Perhaps more important, though, is the increased willingness of the banks and long-term investors to view business requests for free capital in a favorable light. In other words, at the same (nominal) rates of interest their willingness to lend and advance capital on long and short term is greater.[25] This situation results only in part from the increased supply of investible funds concomitant with the boom itself. In no small measure it arises from the somewhat lower estimates of the importance of the risk factor by lenders.[26] The latter tend to minimize the risks of investment because of the favorable external business situation, i.e., rising prices, favorable earnings statements, a declining rate of business failures, etc. The risk to lenders of non-performance by the borrowers appears to be less and tends to be so calculated by them.[27] Furthermore, insofar as they require a "safety factor," i.e., a margin within which the earnings of the borrower may decline without endangering their promised returns or principal, lenders are likely to estimate the probable returns from increased investment in the enterprise only slightly less optimistically than borrowers. Thus the supply

[25] Where competition between lending agencies is not severe and custom plays a large role this may be almost the only change from depression to prosperity. Many country banks in the United States, for example, almost never change their rates of discount but their willingness to advance funds to borrowers is by no means constant throughout the cycle.

[26] Keynes, *op. cit.*, pp. 144-145, emphasizes that under a system of borrowing and lending there is added to the inherent risks of enterprise a further risk arising out of the borrowing and lending relationship *per se*. This latter may be counted by both the borrower and the lender and hence act as an impediment to investment which would be non-existent were persons to invest only their own funds. See also Breit, M., "Ein Beitrag zur Theorie des Geld- und Kapital-marktes," *Zeitschrift für Nationalökonomie*, Band VI, Heft 5, at pp. 654-655.

[27] "Lenders" should here be interpreted to include purchasers of shares of stock as well. Nothing of the legal borrower-lender relationship is implied above.

conditions of free capital are favorable to investment by business enterprises.

The conjunction of the above factors—a relatively high marginal efficiency of capital, a low rate of interest, and an increased willingness by lenders to make commitments [28]—is such as both to encourage business enterprises to undertake investments, and to create a situation in which it is comparatively easy for them to acquire funds with which to carry these projects toward fruition. Idle cash already in the enterprise will be converted into other assets while short-term borrowing and security sales will be undertaken in order to acquire still more assets. As a consequence replacements, improvements, extensions, inventory purchases, the buying of supplies, etc., are likely to go forward at a rapid rate. In short, investment by business enterprises will be at a high level.

3. *Decreased inducement to invest during a downswing.* If the upswing is characterized by an estimated high marginal efficiency of capital, a confidence in those estimates, and consequently a willingness to make commitments (i.e., to invest), the downswing and depression are marked by opposite tendencies. Whereas previously the returns upon cost were estimated to be favorable to investment, depression conditions emphasize the wisdom, from the point of view of the individual enterprise, of holding off, of doing nothing. Falling prices, mounting losses, less than capacity operations, etc., all serve to emphasize that the marginal productivity of existing assets has fallen to a low ebb. There is a further point here. During the boom the estimates of the marginal efficiency of capital were not only high but imbued with considerable certainty. During the depression, on the other hand, business men regard their computations with marked uncertainty and great skepticism. Perhaps as much as anything else the prime factor weighing with business men during a depression is their own lack of confidence in their own computations and estimates. They are likely to appraise the marginal efficiency of capital at a very low level indeed. Rather than considering new commitments they are

---

[28] Insofar as the prices of goods remote from the consumer fall farther than consumers' goods they tend to raise the marginal efficiency of capital since one of its determinants, S, their supply price, is reduced. Conversely, as the boom progresses and such prices rise farther and faster than final goods, the marginal efficiency of capital is reduced.

impressed with the danger of not being able to meet obligations already incurred.

The disposition of lenders likewise undergoes a change for the worse. They are acutely aware of the dangers of default which seem to be more imminent with the now reduced volume of production and falling prices. Furthermore, they are inclined to regard any schemes for the profitable employment of capital with marked skepticism. What was formerly considered ample security is now treated with obvious disdain. Consequently what few loans are made are contracted at onerous terms, and in large measure represent lenders' efforts to salvage some of their previous commitments. Few new loans are negotiated and the renewals granted are merely the unwilling choice from among several discouraging alternatives.

The net result of the foregoing is a tendency for the business enterprise to hoard cash. Let us consider for a moment why this should be the case. We have already indicated that one characteristic of the depression is a marked fall in the marginal efficiency of capital relative to the rate of interest. This means that the incentive to make investments in either working capital assets or in durable assets is almost negligible. As a consequence as inventories are gradually sold off (since only very rarely do sales fall to zero), they are not replenished but instead the cash is hoarded. Again, machinery and equipment are worn out and become obsolete but are not replaced.[29] This also tends further to augment available cash. Apart from the sharp decline in the marginal efficiency of capital there are other incentives to liquidity operating with increased force during depression. The fall in prices means a rise in the purchasing power of money, which is to say its value appreciates while the value of other assets declines in terms of money. Finally, against an uncertain future in which creditors may press for payment and other unfortunate contingencies may develop, a large cash balance provides perhaps a most comfortable assurance. The order of the day is the quest for liquidity.

[29] It is unusual too for output by the enterprise to drop to zero; some production persists. Insofar as goods manufactured are sold for a price exceeding the direct money cost outlay incurred in their production, cash balances will be increased.

IV. ADAPTATIONS TO THE CYCLE BY THE SINGLE ENTERPRISE

1. Position of the individual enterprise in the cycle pattern. 2. The problem of price policy. 3. Accounting cost and price policy. 4. Accounting net income and the volume of investment.

Our discussion of the business cycle and the individual enterprise has concerned itself so far with the flows of money receipts and expenditures, the fluctuations in reported net income, and finally, factors affecting the volume of investment purchases. There is a strong temptation to conclude a chapter of this kind with a discussion of remedies for the cycle itself. Since any proposed remedies must bear a close relation to the causes believed responsible for the cycle and since the latter cannot be dealt with here, the temptation to propound remedies is easily resisted. Furthermore, this volume is primarily dealing with the individual enterprise, and a single firm cannot invoke cures for ills deep-seated in the economy; the best that any one concern can do is to maintain a constant awareness of the business cycle as such and endeavor to make the best available adaptations to it. That is to say, the individual enterprise can hope to accomplish little more than to organize its affairs and operations so that the unfavorable impact of the cycle upon its activities will be reduced to a minimum.

1. *Position of the individual enterprise in the cycle pattern.* In an earlier section of the present chapter we pointed out that *the* business cycle in any statistical sense was necessarily a composite of a number of individual series showing leads and lags and varying amplitudes of fluctuation between one another. Any individual enterprise finds itself situated at some particular position within the economic system as a whole: its place may be such that it is far removed from consumers' goods markets in the structure of production; it may be producing a luxury good for sale to persons in a certain high income group; or again, the demand for its product may be entirely a derivative from the demand for

ₒome other product.[30] One of the first and most useful things the individual firm can do in adapting itself to the business cycle is to discover exactly its position in the general economic framework and upon what other industries or particular income groups the sale of its output depends. This is not altogether simple and in practice certain difficulties are bound to be insolvable. Nevertheless individual business enterprises seemingly could do a good deal more along these lines than they do at present. An enterprise selling fur coats at retail would expect a much closer correlation between its sales and the sales of passenger automobiles than between its sales and, say, freight car loadings. A much wider use of the almost innumerable statistical series now published at frequent intervals might be made by individual concerns. As it is, probably the great mass of them are conscious of little more than the Dow-Jones stock price averages. So far as possible the individual enterprise should endeavor to discover one or several series which seem to approximate in amplitude the fluctuations in its own sales and prices but which tend to precede the latter in timing by an interval sufficiently long to permit adjustments.[31] The emphasis should be mainly on prices and sales since, despite advertising and sales promotion in general, these factors are the least subject to control by the enterprise. The adjustments in costs and purchases must be made to the expected changes in prices and sales rather than the other way about.[32] Of course it must not be inferred that by the use of such techniques we believe that the business cycle can be "ironed out" for the individual enterprise. The contention is merely that with a very moderate cost outlay many business firms could make very much better adaptations to cyclical movements than they now make. Finally, the basic difficulty inherent in all cyclical forecasting must not be forgotten, namely, that if producers and buyers in general did behave as

[30] A vertically integrated enterprise may occupy several stages of production but the crucial stage for cycle problems is where the product is sold to outsiders. For the rate of absorption of the product here will tend to govern the rate of output at the lower stages.

[31] A useful volume has recently appeared giving the sources at which various statistical series may be secured and at what intervals. See Davenport, D. H., and Scott, F. V., *An Index to Business Indices*, Chicago (Business Publications), 1937.

[32] See in this connection, Stevens, W. M., *Financial Organization and Administration*, New York (American Book Co.), 1934, Chs. 18-19.

the forecast suggests they should, the forecast would inevitably prove wrong as to timing and amplitude. If *everyone* were to believe that the price of wheat would be higher three months hence by more than its storage costs, its price would almost certainly increase immediately. The three months' lag would not hold. In the present stage of development of cyclical forecasting, however, no such unanimity of faith is even approximated.

2. *The problem of price policy.* Apart from endeavoring to anticipate changes in sales and prices sufficiently early to make profitable adaptations to them there is the whole question of price policy and its effect on sales. Here we have in mind that ever-growing group of enterprises operating under conditions of monopolistic competition.[33] The problem of price policy and the business cycle has been treated at some length in recent economic literature and only a bare mention of a few elements of the subject may be made here.

One thing seems reasonably clear: if an enterprise, even a monopoly, maintains a constant price for its product in all phases of the business cycle the fluctuations in sales will be greater than if prices were raised during booms and lowered during depressions. Furthermore, if we assume that the marginal cost curve for the firm shifts upwards by some amount during booms and shifts downward during depression then a change in price is called for if the firm is to maximize its profits. Given the external demand situation for the product, the firm should adjust output and price in such a manner as to equate marginal cost and marginal revenue. The only case in which no change in price would be required in order to maximize profits would be one where the demand curve was completely inelastic over almost its whole range—an admittedly atypical situation. If the demand curve has any slope whatever a change in the marginal cost curve should be accompanied by a change in the selling price of the product if profits are to be maximized. This contention, however, is based on one assumption which is vigorously denied by many business men, viz., that the price charged for the product in one period has no effect upon the shape and position of the demand curve in subsequent time.

[33] Enterprises producing and selling under conditions of nearly pure competition have no control over their prices whatsoever.

There is perhaps some truth in the argument of men of affairs that a price reduction during depression adversely affects the demand for the product at a later date. On the other hand it is doubtful, in the writer's opinion, if the effects are anything like so disastrous as is frequently imagined. All *a priori* considerations point to this conclusion.

For the economy as a whole, of course, an excellent case can be made for the desirability of price variations. For despite all the developments which have occurred it is hardly disputable that a free enterprise system must rely on price changes as a medium through which changes and adjustments can work themselves out. Furthermore, the problem of adjustment to any given change in the economy is greatly increased if some prices are rigid and others flexible. For the degree of change in flexible prices tends to be the greater because certain other prices are inflexible and therefore not available as an adjusting mechanism.

3. *Accounting cost and price policy*. The price policies followed by business concerns during depression and prosperity are no doubt seriously affected by the accounting statements of cost and net income. The accounting statements, even in a somewhat refined form, unfortunately do not make the distinctions necessary to the proper determination of output from the economic point of view. At any point in time the aim of the enterprise is to maximize profits in the sense previously defined in Chapter VII. Given the economic data within which it has to operate, the enterprise should equate marginal cost and marginal revenue. But as we have already emphasized in an earlier chapter, marginal cost means incremental cost, i.e., those costs which are incurred as a consequence of producing more or less. By no means do all costs or expenses in the accounting sense belong in this category if we confine the analysis to short-run problems. In the short period, such as a business depression, the prime costs incurred as a consequence of producing as opposed to not producing are wage costs, material costs, power costs, and some depreciation.[34] These alone offer a resistance to production; the others tend to remain at approximately the same level regardless of the volume of output.

[34] Essentially "user cost" in Mr. Keynes' sense and as previously described.

The accounting records, however, do not distinguish between costs which are a reason for not producing and selling in the short run and those which are irrelevant for that purpose. The consequence is that business men, guided by what the accounting records seem to show their average *total* unit costs to be, feel that to produce and sell for a price below that figure involves them in a direct out-of-pocket loss. It is not so. The enterprise may lose more (in the accounting sense) or make smaller profits and be worse off economically by refusing than by accepting business which more than covers the direct cost outlays. The other costs tend to persist in any case, and anything received from the sale of the product over the costs directly incurred in its production will assist in the coverage of these unavoidable costs. If certain costs such as management salaries, obsolescence, some depreciation, etc., are unavoidable, in the sense that they must be borne if the enterprise expects to continue in business, then they are in no way a bar to price reductions or to accepting orders which do not cover total average cost. Insofar as the enterprise determines its pricing and production policies on the basis of what the accounting records *seem* to say about costs, and therefore what prices may be profitably accepted, the concern will be operating less profitably than it might.

A similar kind of error occurs in periods of rising business activity. Here again the important thing is not average cost but marginal cost. To continue to accept business and expand output because the price received exceeds total average cost is to go beyond the point at which profits are maximized. The significant thing is to compare the increment in income with the increment in cost incurred in its acquisition. Reasoning along these lines would cause many concerns to curtail their output at a point short of that often reached during the excesses of the boom.

The determination of output and prices on marginal principles rather than average would produce a further result with desirable consequences. If business enterprises fixed their prices in such a way as to equate marginal cost and marginal revenue, prices generally would rise more during the boom and decline more during depression. This would increase the flexibility of the economic system and adjustments could be carried through more easily.

Furthermore, as we argued in the previous section, fluctuations in physical output would be less, as would changes in the volume of employment.

This emphasis on a marginal cost—marginal revenue type of analysis to determine prices and output—must not suggest that it could be applied with the precision of the theoretical reasoning. Inevitably there would be a band or range of indifference and uncertainty in the equating of marginal cost and marginal revenue rather than the exactitude of pure theory. All we are contending for here is the superiority of the marginal approach over the average cost type (especially the latter in the accounting sense), from both the point of view of the individual enterprise seeking to maximize its own profits and from the point of view of the general welfare.

4. *Accounting net income and the volume of investment.* The influence of accounting reports upon the amount and timing of investment by the enterprise is perhaps less direct than upon price and production policies but no less real. The reportedly high net incomes of boom periods no doubt tend to give business men an exaggerated impression of the probable level of the marginal efficiency of capital in their respective enterprises. They estimate that the productivity of additional plant, equipment, supplies, etc., will be greater than any information drawn from the past and present situation actually warrants. Net income seems to bear a very high ratio to original investment and this high ratio suggests that further commitments will be very profitable likewise. But a considerable portion of this high return arises, as we have shown, from the methods of computation employed. The tendency towards overinvestment in the sense that the expected returns will not be forthcoming is accentuated.

During a downswing and depression, on the other hand, errors in computation in a reverse direction are likely to develop. The accounting reports showing losses or low earnings tend to emphasize the low returns being secured on original cost and therefore the probable low marginal efficiency of capital. The result is that business enterprises are inclined to make few capital goods purchases even for replacement purposes. At the same time, however, insofar as the prices of capital goods are declining and there is a reasonable presumption that the depression will not last forever, the marginal returns securable from additional capital investment are probably increasing. Were the accounting statements less inclined to exaggerate the gravity of the depression situation by employing methods of calculation which are less arbitrary in their allocation of original cost between accounting periods, probably more business men would realize that the marginal efficiency of capital had not fallen to such a low level as they imagine. As a result investment would be better maintained and the economy as a whole would be better off. Something of this kind to be sure does occur towards the end of a slump period and is one of the main factors making for revival. It would be all to the good, however, if it could be not so long delayed, or, better still, if capital goods purchases could proceed at an almost steady and even rate. But in no small measure the accounting methods now in vogue work against such an achievement by giving business men a false impression of the amplitude of the variations in net income.

V. SUMMARY

The business cycle is a statistical composite in the sense of being an average of numerous individual indices representing different aspects of economic activity. The amplitude and timing of different statistical series in comparison with some composite index of "general business activity" vary considerably: construction tends to lead on both downswings and upswings and the amplitude of the fluctuations is also greater; physical output varies more than income to the factors of production; retail prices fluctuate less than wholesale, etc. For any given enterprise its particular position in relation to all these changing relationships—prices, output, employment, etc.—is of profound significance.

An upswing manifests itself to the single enterprise in the first instance probably in an increased rate of absorption of its product by buyers. Demand curves probably become more inelastic as the boom progresses. If enterprises were not prone to buy-forward and to manufacture in excess of current sales it seems likely that the flow of money receipts would increase faster than the flow of money outlays. Unless sales drop to zero during a downswing there is a tendency for cash to accumulate within the firm. However, the obligations to creditors incurred during the preceding boom prevent many concerns from accumulating idle balances as large as they would like. The preference to hold liquid assets over non-liquid assets certainly increases. The usual accounting methods of computing income tend to exaggerate the degree to which profits increase in booms and decline during slumps.

The determinants of investment tend to be the marginal efficiency of capital and the rate of interest. The marginal efficiency of assets of different kinds is peculiarly susceptible to all kinds of psychological influences because it is essentially a matter of expectations. During an upswing persons make optimistic computations of probable yields to be had from new investment and have confidence in these estimates. Those with funds to invest also take a rosy view and are willing to purchase securities to finance new capital investment. If the upswing is characterized by an estimated high marginal efficiency of capital, a confidence in such estimates and a willingness to make commitments, the downswing is marked by opposite tendencies. Instead of adding to the stock of capital goods those worn out tend not to be replaced at once. Hoarding and a decline in investment are characteristic.

The individual business enterprise can only adapt itself to the business cycle, not eliminate it. A thorough understanding of where it fits into the general cycle pattern will tend to minimize the harm the cycle can impose upon the enterprise. A more careful attention to a marginal cost-marginal revenue type of analysis by business firms would probably mean more flexible prices and hence easier economic adjustments at the same time that profits would fall less or losses would be reduced. The price policies of business concerns are probably unduly influenced by what the accounting records seem to depict as costs. Not all accounting costs are a bar to production and sale during a slump. The accounting computations of profits and losses probably generate alternate waves of over-optimism and over-pessimism and as a consequence react upon the volume of investment unfavorably.

REFERENCES: CHAPTER X

BURTCHETT, F. F.—*Corporation Finance*. Ch. 36.
CLARK, J. M.—*Strategic Factors in Business Cycles*, New York (National Bureau), 1934.
DEWING, A. S.—*Financial Policy*. Book IV, Ch. 1.

CRUM, W. L.—*Corporate Earning Power in the Current Depression*, Cambridge, Mass. 1935.
GUTHMANN, H. G.—"Industrial Working Capital During Business Recession," *Harvard Business Review*, Vol. 12.
HARROD, R. F.—"Imperfect Competition and the Trade Cycle," *Review of Economic Statistics*, Vol. 18 (1936), pp. 84-88.
KEYNES, J. M.—*General Theory of Employment, Interest and Money*, New York. 1936.
LACHMANN, L. M.—"Uncertainty and Liquidity Preference," *Economica*, August, 1937.
LUNDBERG, E.—*Studies in the Theory of Economic Expansion*, London, 1937.
ROSENSTEIN-RODIN, P. N.—"The Coordination of the General Theories of Money and Price," *Economica*, Vol. 3.
SHACKLE, G. L. S.—*Expectations, Investment and Income*, Oxford: Oxford University. 1938.
SLOAN, L. H., et al.—*Two Cycles of Corporation Profits, 1921-1933, 1934-1944*, New York, 1936.

Chapter XI

THE EXPANSION OF BUSINESS ENTERPRISES

I. The Meaning of Expansion. II. The Justification of Expansion and Its Alternative Forms. III. Alternative Forms of Expansion. IV. Expansion and the Financial Plan. V. Summary.

~~~~~~~~~~~~~~~~

Probably most persons who are responsible for bringing new enterprises into existence look forward to the day when the new enterprise will grow and expand beyond the scale of operations at which it is initiated. Although many concerns grow very little and then by almost imperceptible degrees, it is also true that others often expand enormously and beyond the fondest hopes of their promoters. In some respects the expansion of business enterprises raises no special economic questions that we have not at least alluded to in earlier chapters. On the other hand, the expansion of business corporations often takes a variety of forms that are called forth by the peculiarities of special situations and these are worth examining. But before considering these let us first dispose of certain preliminary matters that will assist in clarifying the subsequent discussion.

I. THE MEANING OF EXPANSION

1. Legal and economic senses of expansion. 2. The distinction between added assets and means of acquiring assets.

1. *Legal and economic senses of expansion.* The question first arising in any discussion of enterprise expansion is what is usually meant or implied by the term "expansion," and more especially in what sense we propose to use it. In ordinary speech one uses the term loosely to mean various things: a rise in the total sales

295

per period of time, an increase in the total production facilities, a larger physical output, a greater total capital employed, etc. In everyday usage expansion has no very precise meaning. Our concern, however, is not mainly with the "proper" meaning to be given to the term expansion *per se;* it is rather to discover, if we can, what we mean by saying an enterprise is expanding. Very naturally this will be partially, if not wholly, determined by our concept of the enterprise.

In an earlier chapter we endeavored to point out that an enterprise or firm has both economic aspects and legal aspects. On the legal side we emphasized that an enterprise consists entirely of an aggregation of asset items (in the private acquisitive sense) in which certain persons possessed definable rights. From this point of view a firm would be said to have expanded when the sum total value of the aggregation of capital items had increased. Otherwise expressed, we might say that an enterprise expands when the total assets it employs become greater.[1] The particular methods by which the increase in assets is brought about is of interest in some connections but not especially so in seeking an answer to the question whether expansion has or has not occurred. While from this point of view one ought logically to designate *any* increase in the firm's total assets an "expansion," there is a general disposition to restrict the term to more or less *permanent* increases in total assets. That is, we would not ordinarily say an enterprise was expanding (or contracting) because at certain seasons of the year the total assets employed temporarily increased (or decreased).[2] Thus, from the legal point of view an expansion represents a more or less permanent increase in the aggregation of capital items employed by the firm.[3]

[1] In order to determine if expansion has occurred, asset totals must necessarily be compared at specific points in time. If the comparison is to mean anything the same methods of valuation must be used at the two dates. It would be meaningless to determine asset values at one date on an original cost less depreciation basis and at another on a discounted earning power basis. This removes the difficulty involved in deciding whether "write-ups" in the accounting values of the assets are properly termed expansion of the enterprise. For the problem of expansion it makes little difference what valuational methods are used so long as they are consistently employed.

[2] On this basis any enterprise is *always* either expanding or contracting in some degree, for the total of assets is not a constant from day to day.

[3] It should be noted that the distinction is not between increases in durable or

From the point of view of economic analysis we emphasized that a firm is a production unit within which the application of certain economic resources is determined by some individual rather than by the price system. Viewed from this angle, an enterprise would be said to expand when the total resources over which the co-ordinator exercised control increased. Mr. Coase has expressed this by saying that the total transactions organized within the firm have increased.[4] But it would be difficult to conceive of cases where the total transactions organized within the firm increased without more resources falling under the control of the co-ordinator. More transactions mean additional assets.

Thus we see that both from the legal and economic points of view expansion comes to have a very similar, almost identical meaning. This is not surprising because the very idea of enterprise expansion is essentially economic in character and is only involved at law and accounting indirectly and inconsequentially. Henceforth when we use the term expansion we shall mean a more or less permanent increase in the total assets employed by the enterprise.[5]

2. *The distinction between added assets and means of acquiring assets.* Having now indicated what we propose to mean by enterprise expansion, we are in a position to pass on to the more important questions associated with it: the economic justification of expansion, why expansion may prove profitable, the alternative forms it may assume, etc.

In order to avoid a confusion which might otherwise creep in, we must first draw a rather obvious distinction. In considering

fixed assets and increases in "working capital" assets, but between increases in total assets which are more or less permanent and those more or less temporary. Some enterprises have almost no "fixed" assets at all but they most certainly are capable of expansion in a very real sense.

[4] "A firm becomes larger as additional transactions (which could be exchange transactions co-ordinated through the price mechanism) are organized by the entrepreneur and becomes smaller as he abandons the organization of such transactions." Coase, R. H., "The Nature of the Firm," *Economica*, August, 1937, p. 393.

[5] One needs to say "more or less" permanent since an enterprise may decide, say after a few years, that the expansion was originally (or is now) unwarranted and therefore contract. Also we need to be careful not to insist that the additional resources be "owned" by the firm since the legal relationship may be a lease contract. Not a few important railroads in the United States are held together by leasing rather than ownership arrangements.

enterprise expansion one may focus his attention either upon the changes occurring in the quantity and nature of the assets added and their interrelations, or upon the financial arrangements by which these assets come under the control of the enterprise. Although they are likely to be closely intertwined in any particular business enterprise expansion, it is none the less useful to make the distinction for purposes of analysis because they are logically quite distinct. To illustrate briefly: we may say that a particular corporation ought to expand in order to secure the advantages of large scale production, or because existing production facilities are so overcrowded by the large demand that unit costs are unnecessarily high. This is perfectly reasonable and but one of many ways of saying that more capital invested in the enterprise will give a higher productivity. Yet all this says nothing about the relative merits of financing the expansion through the sale of bonds, preferred shares, or common shares, or by long-term or short-term leases. Nor again, having decided the wisdom of expansion in the sense of adding to the total assets employed by the firm, have we said anything about the desirability of special devices of legal ownership such as holding companies, etc. These latter questions, while related, are yet logically separable from the productivity of additional assets. In what immediately follows, the economic question of the productivity of capital will be our first concern. The financial and legal questions we shall postpone for a little.

II. THE JUSTIFICATION OF EXPANSION AND ITS ALTERNATIVE FORMS

1. Expansion warranted if returns exceed costs. 2. Expansion a change in the scale of production. 3. Economies of an increase in scale: a. factors making for a decline in cost of production, b. other advantages of an increase in scale. 4. Advantages of special forms of increased scale: a. vertical integration, b. horizontal integration, c. lateral integration. 5. Qualifications to the advantages of larger scale. 6. Technological change and alterations in the scale of production.

1. *Expansion warranted if returns exceed costs.* We have argued frequently that the economic objective of the enterprise is

to maximize returns to the owners, which for the corporation means the shareholders. How are we to apply profit maximization to the problems of expansion of business enterprises?

Let us recall that by expansion we mean a more or less permanent increase in the total assets employed in the enterprise. Now the acquisition of assets involves a cost to the owners of the enterprise. An increase in the total assets employed by the firm—an expansion—is logically justified provided their acquisition adds to the present worth of the net income stream accruing to the shareholders. It must add more to prospective receipts than to probable costs. If the additional assets are procured by the sale of bonds, for example, the costs are mainly two: first, the interest cost during the life period of the loan; and second, any added risks to the shareholders incurred as a consequence of the borrowing operation. It might be thought that the effective interest rate at which the corporation acquired the free capital through the sale of the bonds will include full allowance for risk elements. In a sense this is true; but it includes an allowance for the inherent risks of the loan *as viewed by the lender* which is not the same as the risks and their valuation to which the borrowers, the stockholders, are exposed. So long as the shareholders' investment is more than sufficient, even at sacrifice prices, to provide for the repayment of the bondholders' principal the risk to the bondholders is negligible. But from the point of view of the stockholders it is otherwise. To them the danger of having to surrender a part of their claims in favor of the superior claims of the bondholders is a very real risk upon which *they* will place quite a different valuation. Consequently, the risks as viewed by the two parties are not likely to be the same. If, on the other hand, the assets are acquired by increasing the outstanding common shares, they will be purchased either by the present stockholders, by persons not now shareholders, or, what is most probable, partly by existing shareholders and partly by outsiders. In any case, from the point of view of the enterprise as it now stands, the question at issue in determining the advisability of expansion is this: Will the amount added to the income of the existing shareholders exceed the sacrifices incurred in its acquisition, including in the latter any contingencies growing out of the admission of new shareholders?

It is abundantly clear at the outset that both the added income and the added costs of expansion can be no more than estimates. Except under very unusual circumstances neither one can be determined with precise accuracy.[6] Probable costs are usually somewhat easier to calculate than probable increased income because in some measure the former can be reduced to specific contractual terms, e.g., by a bond indenture, a leasing arrangement, etc. To estimate the probable increased income is more difficult because the problem contains more variables. First is the question what kinds of assets will add most to income granted certain assumptions concerning demand, prices, etc. Second, assuming some increased capital can be employed to good effect, how fast does its marginal productivity decline as more is added? Some expectations on these points are indispensable before one can pass upon the wisdom and degree of expansion. In any actual business enterprise, of course, the problem is likely to present itself in a less formidable guise than we may have implied. Assuming the urge to expand is not based on irrational considerations, it probably arose out of a more or less definite realization by the management that certain specific assets would add a good deal to stockholders' net returns. Practically speaking, the thought to expand the enterprise sprang from the apparently high marginal productivity of capital; particularly certain kinds of assets. The question then becomes how do these expected added returns compare with the costs of securing them.

The economic justification of the expansion of a business enterprise, therefore, is that the increment in returns will exceed the increment in costs. Unless this relationship between costs and returns is believed to exist, an increase in the total assets employed is unwarranted.

Let us now consider why added returns may exceed added costs, i.e., why expansion may prove profitable to the owners.

2. *Expansion a change in the scale of production.* Since an expansion is a more or less permanent increase in the total assets employed, it means a change in the shape and position of the firm's marginal and average cost curves. That is, almost invariably, the

[6] Special cases such as a firm making a product under a cost plus contract to the government, e.g., war supplies, sometimes occur. But these are not typical.

aggregation of fixed factors of production, to which more or fewer variable factors are applied in order to increase or decrease the rate of output, is increased. Such an alteration in the combination of the agents of production employed is to be kept distinct from using certain fixed factors with varying intensity. A change in scale means a change in the firm's whole cost schedule, while

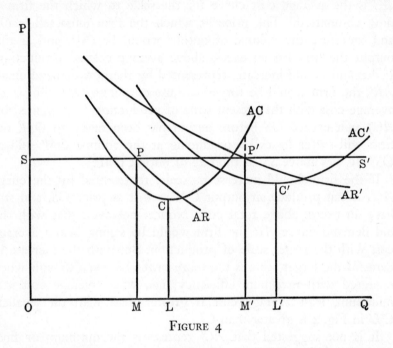

FIGURE 4

the former refers to the variations in cost with variations in output, the *scale* being given, i.e., the combination of fixed factors to which the enterprise is committed for the time being.[7] In one case the cost curves are completely changed; in the other there is a movement along the curves.

It is worth pointing out that in order for an expansion of the scale of production to be warranted, i.e., to prove profitable to the enterprise, the larger scale need not be more efficient than the smaller in the sense that when operated at its most conomical rate of output (the point of minimum average cost) average costs

[7] See *supra*, Ch. VI.

are less. This is most clearly seen by taking a special case in which, either by public authority or agreement among producers, *the price is fixed*. In Fig. 4 assume that the price, regardless of demand, must be *OS;* then the only relevant point on all the demand curves is their intersection point with *SS'* in the diagram. In Fig. 4 assume that the original demand curve is *AR* and that *AC* is the average cost curve for the scale to which the firm is now committed.[8] The price at which the firm must sell is *OS* and therefore the volume of output would be *OM*, and at this output the firm has an excess above average cost of production. If demand should increase, represented by the new demand curve *AR'*, the firm would be forced to raise output to *OM'*. But since average cost with the present scale of production (represented by *AC*) will exceed *OS* before output has been raised to *OM'* the firm will suffer losses by producing at the volume *OM'* sold at *OS; AC* lies above *SS'* at the rate of output *OM'*.

If the firm should increase its scale, represented by the curve *AC'*, it can produce an output *OM'*, sell it at price *OS*, and still have an excess above total cost. Notice, however, that with the old demand curve *AR* the firm would be selling below average cost with the larger scale of production. But with the increase in demand the larger scale is the more profitable even though when operated with maximum efficiency, i.e., when average cost is a minimum, least average cost is greater than with the smaller; *C'L'* in Fig. 4 is greater than *CL*.

It is not suggested that *AC'* represents the optimum or final adjustment of scale to the given conditions. Quite possibly either a larger or smaller scale than that indicated would be more profitable. Furthermore, competitive forces over time would probably bring further adjustments, particularly if entry to the industry is unrestricted. The case chosen is admittedly unusual, since we have assumed the whole way through that the price at all times must be *OS*. Under the circumstances the firm has to make such adjustments as the demand situation requires. The same possibility of an association of an increase in scale with an increase in least average cost is quite conceivable even if we drop the assumption of a given

---

[8] Since the marginal cost curves are irrelevant for this problem they are not drawn on the diagram.

and unchangeable price. It is perhaps unnecessary, however, to present the more complicated diagrams which this case requires.[9]

3. *Economies of an increase in scale.* While to be profitable an enlargement of scale need not be accompanied by a reduction in least average cost, as we have just shown, the two are not infrequently associated. In such a case economies of large-scale production are said to exist. Let us look into this.

The phrase "economies of large-scale production" is a loose one embracing several quite different things which need to be separated out for analytical purposes. In the first place there are those gains from larger-scale operations which are quite independent of the particular form of enterprise organization. That is, economies may arise from an increase in scale quite apart from those special advantages often associated with, say, vertical or horizontal integration. Again one ought to distinguish economies, advantages, and gains which are essentially technological in nature—that is, they inhere in the methods by which the commodity is produced or the service rendered—and those which are a concomitant of the growing size of the enterprise *per se*. For example, the production of the commodity on a larger scale often brings a decline in average cost, even assuming the supply prices of all input factors remain unchanged; but a larger enterprise may force down somewhat the prices at which it buys input factors from supplying firms.

In the present section we shall examine the reasons why as an enterprise increases its scale there may be net economies. The special advantages of integration will be reserved for discussion until the next section.

a. *Factors making for a decline in cost of production.* We might perhaps label these the pure advantages of large-scale production, since they were no doubt mainly in mind when the phrase was coined.

If there be economies of large-scale production in this narrower sense they will manifest themselves in the association together of

[9] A number of complications arise since the marginal cost curve may intersect the marginal revenue curve either to the right or the left of the point of least average cost. A full treatment would have to include both possibilities.

an increase in the scale of production and a downward shift in the cost curve for the enterprise over the most relevant or crucial range. Referring back to Fig. 4, the economies of large-scale production would show themselves diagrammatically in the case where $C'L'$ were less than CL. It would also be likely that for some considerable range on either side of C' the curve AC' would be less than CL. In order for the enlarged scale to be more profitable to the enterprise it would also have to be true that the excess of aggregate receipts over aggregate costs would be greater with the new and larger scale than with the old and smaller scale. This would be most likely to be true as a consequence of a shift in the demand curve to the right.

It is worth emphasizing, however, that for a small volume of production the enlarged scale will be less economical than the smaller scale. That is, even though $C'L'$ will be less than CL in Fig. 4 when there are net economies of large-scale production, large portions of AC' will lie above AC for reduced volumes of output. Thus it is unnecessary, and in fact impossible, for the cost curves representing the larger scale to lie below those for the smaller scale *throughout their whole range*. It suffices if within the limits of variations in output most likely to be required in practice, the cost curve for the larger scale will lie below that of the smaller scale. This indeed coincides with everyday experience. At the bottom of a depression, for example, when most enterprises are operating at a very small volume of production small scale enterprises are often more profitable (or less unprofitable) than the larger concerns which only gain their advantages of size with a high rate of output. Something of this sort is said to hold true of the steel manufacturers in the United States.

What factors or causes may produce a dropping of the cost curve as a consequence of an enlargement of scale?

One of the most important reasons is that certain cost elements do not increase proportionately with the extension of productive capacity. There is a certain lack of complete divisibility in some productive services which means that as the scale of production is augmented their aggregate cost either remains constant or increases less than proportionately.[10] This is sometimes expressed by saying there is a certain "lumpiness" (as opposed to granularity) in the conditions of supply of productive agents to the firm. Moreover, for technological reasons the purchase cost of certain types of capital goods does not increase nearly so rapidly, within limits, as the increase in their productive power. This is particularly true of prime-movers, yet applies to other kinds of machines and equipment as well.[11] This "lumpiness" situation is no doubt quite important. If we might imagine for a moment that all productive services were available to the enterprise in infinitely small amounts, there would appear to be no reason why a very small production unit might not secure the full technological advantages that are in fact available only to large units.

Again, there are the well-known and indubitable advantages of increased specialization of labor and capital goods which a larger scale of production permits. These are so familiar and have been recounted so often that there is little need to repeat them here.[12]

The foregoing may bring about a decline in the cost curves with an increased scale even though the prices at which the firm buys input factors remain the same. Very often, however, an enlargement of scale is accompanied by a reduction in the prices at which the firm may purchase materials, supplies, equipment, etc., from other firms. These lower prices may represent genuine savings to the firms in question or they may merely be forced upon them by superior bargaining power. This may account in some small degree for the downward shift in the cost curves.[13]

[10] What we have in mind here is that there is under-utilization of these productive resources, human or non-human, at the smaller scale. This does not mean, of course, that at the smaller scale such resources are not worth what they cost; but only that they are capable of rendering more services without any, or with only a slight, increase in cost. This is likely to be the case with certain supervisory services and with certain capital goods.

[11] It is often pointed out as an important physical fact, for example, that the increase in the cubic contents of a container is more than proportionate to the increase in the surface area.

[12] Increased specialization of labor is not an unmixed gain since the costs of effective co-ordination are likely to rise very rapidly beyond certain limits. A recent and very excellent discussion of the advantages of increasing specialization with increasing scale is Professor Arnold Plant's paper, "Centralize or Decentralize," in Plant, A., ed., *Some Modern Business Problems*, London (Longmans), 1937, pp. 3-33.

[13] Theoretically, since such gains apply mainly to the purchase of variable fac-

b. *Other advantages of an increase in scale.* Quite apart from any effect an increase in scale may have on production costs is the increasing monopoly power often associated with greater size. As a firm grows larger its ability to influence the prices, price policies, and general behavior of its competitors in a manner favorable to itself increases. This may take various forms, but in general the change is reflected in the demand curve for the product the firm sells and not in the cost curves. Merely because of its larger size competing firms may come to regard it as the "natural" leader in initiating price changes; it may become the leader in a "follow the leader" price policy. Furthermore, as a firm grows larger the disposition of buyers toward it, as opposed to other firms, often grows more favorable. Consequently an increase in the scale of production may be accompanied by beneficial changes in its demand schedule, rendering it more elastic at lower prices, less elastic as higher prices, and perhaps shifting it to the right as well. Thus in addition to changes on the side of cost are those on the side of demand, which also serve to increase the firm's net profits.[14]

4. *Advantages of special forms of increased scale.* The foregoing discussion of the advantages of large-scale production has been essentially general in character and in this respect widely applicable almost regardless of the particular form an increase in the scale of production may happen to assume in special cases. In particular industries and individual enterprises these general advantages of large-scale production are often supplemented and reinforced by peculiarities in the technology of production or the nature of competition. Our general statement is necessarily insufficient to explain completely all those increases in the scale of pro-

tors of production, they should be a function of the volume of purchases and independent of the scale of production. That is, if a firm of smaller scale were to buy the larger quantities it would secure price concessions too. In practice, however, there are reasons for believing that they are not equally available to large-scale and small-scale firms. On the other hand, being a large buyer sometimes works to the disadvantage of the enterprise; supplying firms are enabled to raise the price, or in competitive markets the purchases of the larger firm are so great as to raise it.

[14] A good discussion of large-scale production from a somewhat different point of view than that in the text above is Professor Myron W. Watkins' article on the subject in the *Encyclopaedia of the Social Sciences*, Vol. IX, pp. 170-180.

duction to be found in real life. Vertical, horizontal, and lateral integration deserve special consideration on this score.

a. *Vertical integration* refers to an extension of the firm's activities forward to finished goods markets or backward toward the earlier stages of production, or possibly both. In terms consonant with our previous discussion, vertical integration means that costs may be reduced by extending backward toward the earlier stages of production, or alternatively, gross income increased by pushing forward toward ultimate consumers' markets. In either case net income is expected to increase as a result. In an important sense forward integration suggests that the marginal productivity of capital in the enterprise is greatest in the marketing and sales branches of the concern. As an enterprise integrates forward the demand schedule with which it has to deal is no longer the same; and even though additional capital investment is required before the firm may deal with this different group of buyers, it is believed that the increase in gross income will exceed the increase in costs. When, on the other hand, a firm integrates backward, the demand situation is likely to remain unchanged but certain operations formerly performed by other enterprises are now undertaken by this firm itself. In almost all cases integration is likely to mean an increase in the proportion of fixed to total factors of production employed by the enterprise.

Mr. E. A. G. Robinson has pointed out that forward integration is more likely to be encouraged by trade depression while backward integration is stimulated by a boom. During depression the firm is apt to feel that the final sellers of its product do not do all they might to maintain sales, i.e., that the firm itself could do so better. During a boom, on the other hand, the inability to secure enough raw materials, supplies, products, etc., at "reasonable" prices is likely to emphasize the advantages of bringing these production stages within the enterprise.[15]

The reasons why vertical integration should often prove especially desirable are not easy to delineate; but some few observations may be offered. Apparently vertical integration is most likely to appear in connection with two quite different types of products

[15] See, Robinson, E. A. G., *The Structure of Competitive Industry*, New York (Harcourt, Brace), 1932, Ch. VIII, *passim*, especially p. 129.

although for decidedly unlike reasons, viz., enterprises producing a specialized quality product and those producing a standardized product by mass production methods.[16] Enterprises turning out a specialized and quality product not infrequently find it difficult to secure proper raw materials or suitable market outlets for their wares. If the raw materials required are inclined to be scarce and available at only a few sources, an enterprise may seek to protect itself from interruptions in supply by backward integration. Certain highly developed products may require such special marketing skills that about the only suitable procedure is for the manufacturing concern to integrate forward and control the market outlets. No special training is required to sell canned goods at retail, but the same does not hold for, say, office equipment machinery. Products that require "servicing" are often in this category. On the other hand, firms producing standardized products suitable to mass production methods and difficult to differentiate as between producers are also likely to integrate vertically and probably the incentive to do so is somewhat stronger. For here competition in sales is on a price basis and larger profits are to be gained mainly by taking advantage of the great economies to be achieved from continuous production. How far these arise from peculiar technological characteristics of production, as in iron and steel, oil, meat packing, chemicals, etc., is not entirely clear offhand, but this is apparently an important factor.[17] Again, too, vertical integration backward may offer advantages insofar as the enterprise may thereby insulate itself from the greater amplitude of price fluctuations characteristic of goods more remote from final consumers' markets. In some ways there is about as much to be lost as gained on this score since such prices may fall well below cost at times. Finally, insofar as monopoly power is a function of size, this must not be left out of account.

b. *Horizontal integration* undoubtedly has as its primary aim an increase in the degree of monopoly possessed by the single firm,

[16] See Wiedenfeld, Kurt, "Industrial Combination," *Encyclopaedia of the Social Sciences,* Vol. III, pp. 664-674, from which this account has been drawn in part.

[17] It is quite astonishing how frequently vertical integration is discussed in terms of the iron and steel industry, which in so many respects is technologically quite unique. Much of the gain of continuous steel production lies in the saving of kinetic energy.

although it may achieve certain economies incidentally.[18] But on abstract grounds there would seem to be few real gains in a horizontal type of integrated enterprise which could not be equally well achieved by a number of independent concerns. The one notable exception perhaps is afforded by economies in management costs insofar as the firm makes incomplete use of management services. Very frequently, too, managerial policies developed for a single manufacturing or sales unit are applicable to many without appreciable modification, e.g., chain stores, branch banking, etc., and this permits certain gains. But on the whole horizontal combination probably draws its greatest gains from augmenting, consolidating, and extending the market range of whatever monopoly power the enterprise has already achieved. This may be no more than allowing full scope and play to consumer preference already in existence as is so often the case in retail establishments, e.g., having all the store units look alike. But it may extend further.

c. *Lateral integration* is the term now commonly applied when an enterprise takes on certain products not previously dealt in but which require the same productive equipment or the same marketing organization as those now constituting its main business. The production of certain products is often unavoidably seasonal or otherwise highly fluctuating, and during off-seasons the equipment may well be turned to producing other products with a different seasonal variation. Again, an enterprise may find it profitable to take on new products which utilize the same market outlets or cater to similar needs. It is not difficult to understand why a harvesting machinery company should drift into the manufacture of farm tractors and other types of farm equipment.

Although these three, vertical, horizontal, and lateral integration, are probably the most common, special types or forms may often develop in response to peculiar technological or competitive situations. As Mr. E. A. G. Robinson has observed, they may assume

---

[18] "Even when control is not fully achieved and competition continues to rule the market, a horizontal combination offers the advantage of better adaptation to existing market conditions: production is concentrated in lower cost plants and the losses accruing from shutting down of other plants are more than offset by the reduction in unit costs incident to the operation of the better equipped or more advantageously situated plants at full capacity." Wiedenfeld, *loc. cit.*, p. 672.

"as many different shapes as the old man of the sea." Abstract theoretical analysis is not of much use here since the technical peculiarities of production are so likely to dominate the form. And without special knowledge thereof generalizations are of little use.

5. *Qualifications to the advantages of larger scale*. Before passing on to other matters, however, two general comments on large-scale production and combinations seem warranted.

In the first place, while either or both simple large-scale production and integration may offer certain advantages and gains which give a special impetus to enterprise expansion, these may not proceed at an even rate from small or moderate-sized enterprises to quite large firms. The increase in efficiency and profitability per unit of investment is not necessarily proportionate to the increase in the scale of production. In fact a good deal of evidence suggests the contrary; in many industries, in-between-sized firms appear to be decidedly less profitable per unit of investment than quite small firms or very large firms. Seemingly such enterprises combine the disadvantages of both without the peculiar superiorities of either; they are too large to achieve the flexibility of adjustment and simplicity of co-ordination of small concerns, and not large enough to secure the full technical and monopolistic advantages of large enterprises.

Secondly, although there may be advantages of large-scale production, including those peculiar to integration, these obviously do not persist without limit. If the association of increasing size of enterprise with increase in monopoly power were not so close as it is, the advantages of larger size would not be nearly so great as they often appear to be. Observation suggests that after a not very distant point in the increase in the size of the firm the costs of effective co-ordination and cohesion rise very rapidly and in some measure are not attainable at any cost.[19] In actual affairs these are

---

[19] Professor P. Sargent Florence has argued to the contrary in his *Logic of Industrial Organization*, London, 1933. But partly for the reasons given by Mr. Robinson and partly for others, the present writer cannot agree. See Robinson, E. A. G., "The Problem of Management and the Size of Firms," *Economic Journal*, June, 1934, pp. 242-257. The issue is well stated in Mr. Robinson's own words: "I should be prepared to agree that in some circumstances it [the firm] may be very large indeed; that for some products which are consumed rarely and not in large amounts the optimum size might be greater than would be afforded by the whole world market. But I should certainly hold that for every type of product there

likely to be overborne over a certain range by the added revenues from growing monopoly power: the ability to influence the prices and policies of competitors and supplying firms in a direction favorable to the now larger enterprise. At just what point a firm forfeits more in the form of diminished managerial efficiency and effective control than it gains in technical economies and increased monopoly power will depend upon conditions of production and the competitive market situation within which the firm operates. In both respects there are obviously large differences between industries.

6. *Technological change and alterations in the scale of production.* We have called expansion a more or less permanent increase in the total assets employed by the enterprise. And our discussion of it, including the treatment of the economies of large-scale production and integration, has been on the assumption of a given state of technological knowledge and given prices of the factors of production. In the real world, of course, these are not constant and unchanging through time. As a consequence they are often a common cause of enterprise expansion superimposed upon, or independent of, anything discussed heretofore.

Inventions and technological improvements in general are frequently responsible for an increase in the size of the individual enterprise. Such changes may widen the market through improvements in transportation, so that the demand situation with which the firm has to deal is changed, or alternatively, a new invention may offer such superior advantages that, even though the demand curve is unmoved, profits will be increased by adding to the capital investment, securing lessened costs, and selling more units at lower prices. While an invention to be significant must lower costs or improve the product, it must be kept logically distinct from the reduction in cost securable from larger-scale production where the technique of production is given. Diagrammatically they both

is in a given state of technique some size at which the technical and other economies of larger scale production are outweighed by the increasing costs of the co-ordination of the larger unit, or by a reduced efficiency of control due to the growth of the unit to be co-ordinated. The point at issue between Professor Florence and myself is whether, in conditions of perfect organization, management costs will rise as output increases, or managerial efficiency will diminish." *Loc. cit.*, pp. 247-248. Empirical evidence, however, is probably more pertinent here than theoretical reasoning.

look the same; but the operative causes are quite different. A technological improvement could lower the cost curves in an enterprise which had previously exhausted the full possibilities of large-scale production.[20]

Similarly, a change in the relative prices of the factors of production, or a decline in the purchase cost of certain capital goods, may well induce an expansion of the enterprise in the sense already defined. If labor costs rise while interest rates remain the same, the firm may well find it advisable to substitute capital goods for labor services to such a degree that the total assets employed are augmented. Whether particular productive operations are performed by machinery or human labor is largely a matter of relative costs and these are not unchanging through time.

III. ALTERNATIVE FORMS OF EXPANSION

1. Leasing arrangements. 2. Purchase arrangements. 3. Mergers and consolidations. 4. The holding company as a mode of acquiring assets.

Our discussion of the criteria of enterprise expansion, why it may yield returns in excess of its costs, etc., was purposely general in character. That is to say, our analysis was based almost exclusively on economic considerations in the narrower sense and was intentionally independent of special ownership devices for acquiring control of additional assets, and unconcerned with the relative merits of different financing methods often available to an expanding corporation. The advantages of larger scale and the wisdom of expansion generally do not depend for their validity upon the use of any special legal forms or unique security contracts. Since, however, corporate expansion often occurs under quite different legal and technical arrangements and since these, according to circumstances, have somewhat different advantages from the point of view of the shareholders, a full treatment of corporate expansion must also include a discussion of them. Let us first consider

[20] An invention serves to lower the cost schedule usually for all scales of production, although it is sometimes true that the invention is of such a character that it can be adopted only by those enterprises operating on the larger scale.

the alternative legal arrangements by which the corporation may secure control over additional assets.

From a broad point of view there are only two methods by which an enterprise may obtain additional productive resources: by an ownership arrangement or a rental arrangement, although, of course, each may take numerous forms. What the growing enterprise requires from an economic viewpoint is productive services either from human beings or from capital goods. But it may actually *own* shares of stock or a rental contract. In other words, the chain of connections between the enterprise and additional agents capable of yielding productive services may be direct or circuitous in varying degrees.

1. *Leasing arrangements.* A corporation frequently expands by renting additional production facilities under long- or short-term contract. Furthermore, since a lease is a contractual agreement between two parties it may contain whatever terms, conditions, and stipulations to which the two parties may care to agree. Hence in the very nature of the case no very useful generalizations concerning their contents can be formulated. The more important provisions, however, are usually those relating to the amount of the rental and its mode of payment, e.g., fixed or variable; the responsibility for repairs and improvements; the renewal arrangements; purchase options, etc. No great imagination is required to visualize the almost innumerable variations in these provisions possible from one contract to another. Nevertheless, there are often some general advantages to a corporation of leasing assets as opposed to owning them.[21]

Perhaps the prime advantage of a leasing arrangement is its comparative ease and speed of negotiation. The firm may acquire the use of more assets almost at once. Also additional long-term security financing is frequently not necessary as in an ownership arrangement. A lease, moreover, raises no question concerning the perpetuation of the control of the corporation by the existing shareholders—providing the lessee does not default on its obligations to the lessor—because no new shareholders are admitted by

[21] Sometimes, especially in railroads, the lessee corporation is the majority stockholder in the lessor corporation, which may lead to many legal complexities.

the lease itself.[22] Contrariwise the lease is not all pure gold. Despite, or perhaps because of, the development and proliferation of legal talent, disputes over the meaning of the lease contract are an ever imminent contingency. No matter how carefully drawn, the possibility of costly disputes and uncertain judicial interpretation is always present. Furthermore, there are the opposing virtues of frequent versus infrequent renewals. Over a long time conditions may change drastically and a fixed rental for assets having a diminished usefulness may prove a severe drain on cash resources. But short term leases with frequent renewals may place the firm in a poor bargaining position *vis-a-vis* the lessor. Whether on net balance a lease is a good arrangement or a poor one will depend upon the alternatives available in the instant case.

2. *Purchase arrangements.* Let us now consider the other possibility that the firm acquires the additional assets for expansion under an ownership rather than a leasing arrangement.

In some instances an expanding corporation has the choice of either buying capital goods already in existence or ordering their construction anew. Under perfectly competitive conditions it would be a matter of indifference to the firm which method was employed; for a new capital good yet to be constructed would cost more than one already in existence by just that amount which measured its superior ability to render valuable service, due allowance being made for the waiting period necessary for its completion. But in the real world two factors in particular usually make it not a matter of complete indifference whether the firm orders a new asset or purchases an old one. In the first place, capital goods, even of the same general class, are not identical with one another; there is some considerable product variation. Two factory buildings available for purchase at the same price are rarely equally satisfactory from the point of view of the prospective buyer, although of course there is always some combination of prices at which the firm would just as soon have one as the other. So, also, in considering the relative merits of purchasing an existing building (or any piece of productive equipment) as opposed to having

---

[22] If additional working capital must be raised in order to maximize the productivity of the leased assets it may be necessary to sell securities. Thus indirectly the lease may force the sale of additional shares.

a new one constructed it will usually be true that when integrated with the existing productive combination they will not yield quite identical services to the enterprise. The poorer integration with existing facilities may more than outweigh the lower purchase cost of the second-hand asset. While it is always possible to "modernize" and refurbish an older building it is never quite the same, quite apart from its shorter life span, as a new building. Every city dweller has observed this.

In the second place, the market for capital instruments, both new and second-hand, is far less perfectly organized than the markets for most consumers' goods. New machinery and equipment of a particular type is often not exactly the same when ordered from two different producers, and for that reason may not be equally satisfactory to the expanding corporation. The second-hand market, on the other hand, is often a market in which there are relatively few sellers and a paucity of buyers. As a consequence the prices at which equipment may be purchased are often a function of relative higgling ability. For all these reasons a particular corporation in the process of an expansion necessitating certain assets may find that it has a very restricted choice between ordering their construction afresh and buying them in the second-hand market. Nevertheless, it ought not to be assumed without investigation that new construction is the only possibility; substantial savings are often to be had from taking advantage of the imperfections of the market for capital goods already in existence. Which is the preferable alternative in any particular instance will, of course, depend upon the relative costs compared with the relative returns. And without a number of specific assumptions or actual data from a particular case no useful deductions or valid generalizations can be drawn.

3. *Mergers and consolidations.* A special case involving a resort to the "second-hand" market for capital goods is the combination of two enterprises by merger or consolidation. In a merger one of the several corporations brought together retains its legal existence while the others disappear. In a consolidation two or more corporations disappear as legal entities and a new corporation takes their place.

If one enterprise is to expand by absorbing another through a merger arrangement it must be because, all things considered, it is more profitable to acquire an already existing enterprise than to secure additional assets for expansion by alternative methods. Why might this be the case? Perhaps one of the prime reasons for mergers between formerly competing corporations is an attempt to increase the degree of monopoly power possessed. Assuming that each had some monopoly power before, it may well be that through a merger their combined monopoly power is something more than the simple sum of the monopoly power of each considered alone. A merger for such reasons may occur either in an industry which is undergoing a general expansion, or in one the demand for whose product is declining. A particular corporation may expand profitably through a merger even though the industry as such is shrinking in importance both relatively and absolutely. Moreover, when the industry is contracting, two independent enterprises may recognize the wisdom of combination through merger, whereas were the industry expanding, separate existence might appear to be more profitable for each. In other words we must not assume that expansion is warranted only when the whole industry is growing.

Both merger and consolidation involve the question of the valuation of business enterprises as a unit. The essential uniqueness of this problem as contrasted with the valuation of particular items of equipment, i.e., assets, is what meaning and weight is to be attached to so-called "going concern value." In other words, in determining how much an enterprise is worth as a unit, it is usually emphasized that in addition to the value to be attached to the individual assets considered independently of one another something must be counted in for the particular juxtaposition and integration in which they stand as a whole.[23] While this question involves peculiar complications and problems, especially from the legal point of view, we may offer a few comments as to why the aggregation of assets considered as a whole may have a greater value than a

[23] It must be recognized that such going concern value may be negative as well as positive. If the assets stand in such a relation to one another that their value as individual items is reduced because a cost outlay must be made in order to separate them out to make available whatever useful services the assets are capable of rendering, the going concern value is negative. Used automobiles of ancient vintage are often worth considerably more as "parts" than as automobiles.

mere summation of them considered individually. If there be such an excess it must arise from whatever cost outlays would be required to achieve a similar productive combination. A business enterprise which has been in existence for some time very often acquires a smoothness of operation which is not immediately to be had by placing specific buildings, machines, raw materials, and labor in a certain physical relationship with one another. If this be true then an already established organization which has passed through this "breaking-in" stage may have a greater value as a unit than the sum of its individual parts. At a time when the demand for the product is brisk and existing productive facilities seem woefully insufficient there may be much to be said for acquiring another enterprise by merger rather than suffering the unavoidable delays and costs attached to enlarging the enterprise by other means.[24]

Merger and consolidation are but two methods of bringing together two or more enterprises which previously have maintained a separate existence. In general, neither one possesses any special advantages over the other in the abstract. But given the full details with respect to two or more enterprises which are to be brought together, the circumstances will usually indicate the more desirable procedure in the instant case.

If the particular corporations to be amalgamated have badly arranged capital structures, that is, the financial plan represents an unfortunate combination of security contracts, or if neither financial structure lends itself well to considerable extension, a new corporation in which a suitable plan may be more easily worked out is often much the better arrangement. On the other hand, one of the corporations may have an unusually favorable charter granting important rights and immunities which could not be secured by a new corporation, and, if so, it may be worth making substantial sacrifices in order to maintain that corporation in existence. Conversely, the charters of the separate corporations may all be too restrictive to allow full scope to the contemplated activities

[24] It is not surprising that mergers are more common during boom periods when the costs of delay, confusion, and foregone income appear especially great. We have already dealt with this problem of "breaking in" a new enterprise in Ch. VI, *supra*.

of the enlarged enterprise and therefore a new corporation possessing these powers may be preferable to a drastic charter revision
of one of the existing corporations. Again, differences in state laws
may govern the decision in important respects. If the corporations
to be amalgamated are of about equal size, a new corporation is
more likely to be formed than if one is considerably larger than
the others. For in the latter case a merging arrangement will not
complicate the financial structure of the acquiring corporation
nearly so much as when its size is doubled or more than doubled.
If new financing is required over and above that directly incidental
to the combination of the enterprises a new corporation may
greatly simplify the problem. Obviously the number of fact situations which may develop in these and other ways are so numerous
and so diverse that useful generalizations are quite impossible.

Broadly speaking the really bothersome problems of amalgamation are not those of the relative merits of merger contrasted
with consolidation. Rather they consist in working out valuations,
terms of purchase, exchange ratios between securities, etc., which
the different parties in interest will consider sufficiently "fair" to
warrant acceptance. Not infrequently a deal of time and money
will be spent in attempting to present a plan of amalgamation
which has the indispensable virtue of workability; and except in
rare instances of comparative simplicity the plan first proposed
will not be the one ultimately to achieve final adoption. Here, as
Professor Dewing has observed in another connection, it is "expediency tempered with justice rather than justice tempered with
expediency" which more accurately describes the proceedings.

4. *The holding company as a mode of acquiring assets.* As noted
earlier in the present chapter an enterprise may secure control
of the assets requisite for expansion not directly by lease or purchase but indirectly through the ownership of securities. That is,
instead of the corporation owning additional machines, tools, buildings, etc., it may own shares of stock which permit it indirectly
to command the uses to which such capital goods will be put, even
though it possesses no direct ownership rights therein. This familiar legal situation is known as a holding company-subsidiary
company arrangement. On what grounds may one explain corporate expansion by this method?

The advantages of expansion through the use of one or more subsidiary corporations are mostly financial and legal rather than economic in nature. The purchase of enough voting shares in another corporation to assure the election of one's own choice of directors is an alternative to merger or consolidation in acquiring additional assets for expansion. Being a simple purchase or exchange of stock it frequently avoids those complications and dissensions so often associated with amalgamation. Should the acquisition subsequently prove unwise it is somewhat easier to return to the *status quo ante* than if the two enterprises were united by merger or consolidation. From the point of view of the expanding corporation the arrangement is therefore more flexible than outright fusion. Still restricting our discussion to holding companies as an alternative to amalgamation, a holding company has the great advantage of requiring a smaller investment by the shareholders than does a merger. More assets may be controlled with any given investment or any given aggregate of assets can be controlled with a smaller investment.[25] Very often to organize a holding company is a simpler, and therefore a better arrangement than to consolidate two or more corporations; that is, the corporations to be brought together are united by having at least a majority of their voting shares vested in a new corporation, a holding company, organized for the purpose. In this manner it is only necessary to reach an agreement among the voting shareholders of the companies concerned rather than all the security holders; the bonds, preferred stocks, etc., of the underlying companies are left undisturbed. Such an arrangement is often a half-way house to complete fusion.

As contrasted with merger or consolidation a holding company is frequently less satisfactory from a legal point of view. To be in the position of dominant stockholder in another corporation is sometimes unenviable, and, on occasion, has been the basis for

[25] It must not be inferred that an expanding corporation can always purchase voting control of whatever companies it desires at a reasonable figure. The voting stock of the latter may be closely held and not for sale at any but very high prices. Furthermore, the shareholders may band together and insist upon purchase of *all* the shares or none at all. Not a few corporations have discovered that when they tried to "buy up" control of another enterprise they got no more than a minority interest therein at a high cost. If such contingencies are real an expanding corporation may be better advised to forget all about the "advantages" of holding companies and make a direct offer for merger or consolidation.

costly lawsuits.[26] Furthermore, recent modifications of the tax laws have reflected the growing public disfavor of holding companies *per se*. And this attitude seems likely to continue. Yet despite these limitations the holding company remains popular with business interests.

We have so far considered holding companies as a medium of expansion under conditions where merger or consolidation is the alternative; that is, we have considered the merits and demerits of holding companies when already established enterprises are to be acquired in the expansion process. But enterprise expansion often assumes a holding company form when there is no intention of absorbing other firms already in existence.

There are often very cogent practical reasons for vesting the ownership of newly-to-be-acquired assets in a subsidiary company and having the expanding corporation own shares of stock rather than specific capital goods. In other words, subsidiary companies are often used when there is no resort to the "second-hand" market in capital goods at all. In general such an arrangement is usually invoked because of conditioning legal circumstances rather than anything else. In many states the treatment accorded domestic and foreign corporations is not equally favorable. If domestic corporations are favored in various ways, e.g., taxation, regulation, filing of reports, etc., and if an enterprise expects to do business in a particular state, it may be well worth the added cost to organize a separate corporation which from the legal point of view handles the business within the state while the expanding corporation retains complete control of the subsidiary through ownership of all its outstanding securities.[27] Again, if the nature of the enterprise expansion involves the assumption of important risks, such as torts, enhanced danger of business failures, etc., the corporation may try to segregate and limit these so far as possible by separate incorporation of those parts of the business especially so exposed. How far contingent liabilities of this nature may be isolated will depend upon the whole factual situation and the court in question; but

---

[26] See Berle, A. A., *Studies in the Law of Corporation Finance*, Chicago (Callaghan), 1928, Chs. 3, 8.

[27] Such arrangements are particularly likely to be necessary in the case of public utilities.

there is little doubt that the possible protection or insurance is usually worth the cost.[28] A non-legal reason for separate incorporation is often the hope of not emphasizing to competitors, the public at large, and buyers of the product in particular that a common business interest is here present.[29]

The really prime *financial* advantage of holding company-subsidiary company arrangements is the enlarged scope within which the so-called principle of "trading-on-the equity" may be applied. Very briefly, this principle is that if one can obtain additional capital at a fixed cost in interest or dividends less than he can make that capital earn the rate of return upon his own capital will be increased.[30] The principle may be applied within a single enterprise with good effect; when a corporation sells bonds at, say, a 6 per cent rate while the average rate of return upon the borrowed capital is 8 per cent, the excess above interest charges goes to the shareholders. But a holding company form of organization brings out the full potentialities of the principle. This may be illustrated by a simplified example. Assume a corporation with an average rate of return upon the total capital employed of $100,000 (book valuation) is 10 per cent. Assume further that the enterprise has been financed one half by the sale of fixed return securities at a 6 per cent rate and one half by common shares.[31] In this instance the annual net earnings of $10,000 would be allocated $3,000 to prior claimants and $7,000 to common shares. On the par value or original investment the common shares have a yield of 14 per cent.[32]

Suppose now that we vest the ownership of these common shares in another company, a holding company, and receive in exchange therefor $40,000 in 6 per cent bonds and $40,000 (par value) in

[28] See Latty, E. R., *Subsidiaries and Affiliated Corporations,* Chicago (Foundation), 1936.

[29] The foregoing does not in any sense pretend to be a complete catalogue of all the fact situations that give rise to holding companies. See in this connection, Field, W. J., "Some Uses of Holding Companies," *Journal of Land and Public Utility Economics,* January and May, 1932.

[30] Perhaps the best discussion of the principle is still to be found in Lyon, H., *Corporation Finance,* Cambridge, Mass. (Houghton Mifflin), 1916, pp. 50-82.

[31] The fixed return securities may be all bonds, all preferred stocks or some combination of the two.

[32] If the common shares were traded in on the market they would almost certainly sell above par. But by how much it is impossible to say.

common stock. Notice that for purposes of exchange the $50,000 par value common shares of the original company are assumed to have a value of $80,000. This value might be more or less, and would depend in part upon the judgment of the organizers as to how much they thought "outsiders" would consider "fair" or "reasonable." If the original company pays dividends to the full amount of its common stock earnings the income of the holding company will be $7,000. Assume that the organizers of the holding company are able to sell its bonds to investors at par, $40,000. Bond interest charges absorb $2,400 of the holding company's income, leaving $4,600 for the common stock which is a yield upon par value of 11.5 per cent. But while the return is 11.5 per cent on the par value of the holding company shares it is greater on the original investment. Let us assume that the common shares in the first company represented an investment of $50,000. Now by organizing the holding company and selling its bonds to others this original investment has been reduced to $10,000, although now represented by $40,000 (par value) common shares of the holding. company. The return, therefore, is $4,600 on $10,000 which is 46 per cent. The original common shareholders still maintain complete control of the original company because indirectly they may vote all its shares. And of their original investment they have but $10,000 still committed and that yields a return of 46 per cent. Thus the holding company arrangement has done two things: first, reduced the cash investment necessary to retain control; and second, increased the return on that smaller investment.[33]

It is at once obvious that this financial device does not reach its fullest development with merely one underlying company and one holding company. As a mode of expansion a holding company might well assume control of several subsidiaries.[34] And as a matter

[33] We have assumed that the holding company incurs no expenses but these could be very small and may be disregarded in a first approximation.

[34] This is particularly likely to be the case in horizontal integration. When applied to expansion, however, it must not be assumed that the corporations taken over could be purchased at a price equivalent to the original investment in their common shares. This would modify the possible increase in the rate of return upon one's own capital; but it would not remove it so long as the shares could be purchased at a price at which the yield thereon exceeded the rate of interest at which the holding company could secure free capital.

of fact such a scheme would probably contemplate the inclusion of several subsidiaries sooner or later. Furthermore, in an upward direction there is no reason to stop with one holding company. So long as fixed return securities may be sold to others on suitable terms, the investment necessary to control may be reduced and the rate of return upon that investment increased. The continued success of the whole scheme is obviously dependent upon the earnings of the underlying companies not falling below those amounts assumed in drafting the financial plans of the successive holding companies. If the earnings of the underlying companies fall, then of course the rate of return upon cost will decline inversely to its former rate of increase. Practically, of course, limitations to the holding company structure begin to appear after perhaps the third or fourth step in the pyramid because of the cost of maintaining separate corporate entities, and the enhanced difficulty of selling fixed return securities to outsiders. On the other hand, however, it is unnecessary to own 100 per cent of the shares of the one or more holding companies organized; some of these shares might be sold to outsiders, too.[35]

Thus the financial gains of holding companies may be very real and there is no mystery surrounding their popularity from this point of view. We have already mentioned their advantages from the legal side. On strictly economic grounds—that is, from the point of view of increasing total real income or diminishing total real costs within the whole economy—holding companies have very little to commend them.

Thus for a variety of reasons associated with special factual situations an expanding enterprise may find it necessary or desirable to secure access to additional assets in a variety of ways. No one method such as leasing, combination, holding company, etc., is clearly superior under *all* circumstances; but in any particular instance there is ordinarily one arrangement which offers the maximum of net advantages.

[35] For a more elaborately worked out example of the financial possibilities of holding companies, see *Control of Power Companies*, Sen. Doc. 213, 69th Cong. 2d. Sess. (1927), pp. 172-175.

IV. EXPANSION AND THE FINANCIAL PLAN

1. Expansion and the sale of security contracts. 2. Alternative outlets for the sale of additional securities in expansion.

In section III we were concerned with alternative legal and financial devices by which an expanding corporation might bring additional assets under its control. But expansion involves problems of another sort too. Almost inevitably expansion of a corporation involves a greater or smaller change in its financial plan. That is, quite apart from the matters just discussed, are the questions of the most suitable kind of security contracts to sell in order that assets may be acquired and the most desirable channels through which to sell them.

1. *Expansion and the sale of security contracts.* In an earlier chapter on promotion we discussed the relative merits of bonds, preferred shares, and common shares as a means of raising capital. Not much need be added here to our general observations at that point since essentially the same considerations apply to a corporation which is expanding as to one just being formed. There are some few differences though. An expanding corporation will find it much easier to employ the facilities of the organized capital market than a new enterprise. For the former has already established itself as a going concern with an earning power and therefore can make certain representations to prospective security buyers on the basis of past performance. It has a record of past earnings, its products and trade position are perhaps well known and an investment banking house runs a much smaller risk of being unable to sell the firm's securities. An established concern, moreover, will often find it safer and easier to raise free capital by the sale of bonds or preferred stock because in the first place it can judge in part from experience the probable degree of fluctuation in its earnings and hence what regular contractual commitments may be safely undertaken, and in the second, investors will be more willing to purchase with an assurance that the obligations

will be met. Similarly, non-voting securities are often salable in a growing and profitable corporation yet quite undisposable for cash by an enterprise which is just commencing. But by and large the same merits and demerits apply to the different types of security contracts in both new and expanding corporations. Very often, to be sure, the particular methods by which the assets are secured will dictate rather narrowly the lines of extension of the financial plan. Here again the idiosyncrasies of each case are likely to be more controlling than the advantages of particular types of contracts in the abstract.

2. *Alternative outlets for the sale of additional securities in expansion.* If additional securities are to be sold for cash an expanding corporation has often the choice of several avenues of distribution.[36] An underwriting agreement with an investment banking house is a common method by which the corporation secures cash at once and can proceed with the expansion plans directly.[37] Although investment bankers charge for this service, of course, it may be well worth its small cost to the corporation at such a time and later.[38]

An alternative to underwriting by investment bankers is the direct sale of additional securities to existing stockholders. This method of sale is usually restricted to cases where cash is to be raised by the sale of common stock, although occasionally other types, e.g., preferred stock, are so sold. Selling to present shareholders has the advantage of maintaining essentially the same group of holders while avoiding underwriting fees and similar costs. Unless quite special inducements are offered the plan is only feasible in most instances if the number of new shares to be sold is a com-

[36] Very often, of course, securities are exchanged for assets directly. This is particularly common in mergers, holding companies, etc.

[37] Nowadays corporations often finance an expansion *in the first instance* by short-term borrowings from the banks with the understanding that more permanent financing will be undertaken later. That is, the sale of the security contracts may follow rather than precede the undertaking of the expansion plans. This possibility must be kept in mind in all that we say here concerning security sales to finance expansion. Very often, especially in consolidations, mergers, purchase of subsidiaries, etc., this will be the method adopted because a public offering of securities before anything is done may partially destroy the success of the whole plan by broadcasting it to the world at large.

[38] See Willis, H. P. and Bogen, J. I., *Investment Banking*, New York (Harpers), 1936, *passim*.

paratively small fraction of those already outstanding. Most share-holders will ordinarily not be anxious to increase their holdings by much more than, say, 10 per cent, and some not at all. In order to make the plan attractive and to assure full subscription, "rights" are issued permitting present stockholders to acquire the new shares at a price considerably below current market quotations. This gives the rights a value and any holder not wishing to exercise his right will presumably sell it to someone who will. In this way a well-established corporation may secure funds for expansion at comparatively low cost and with the incidental advantages already mentioned.

Occasionally a corporation will offer shares of stock to em-ployees or customers for purchase, but almost never because it is the cheapest way in which to raise the funds. Usually the prime motive is something different: either to enlist the loyalty of em-ployees, a form of employee relations; or to bind customers more firmly to the enterprise than would otherwise be the case. The generally very disastrous results of both employee and customer ownership during the great depression, however, have apparently disillusioned most corporations as to their supposed merits.[39] Under certain conditions such schemes may not be entirely without ad-vantages.

V. SUMMARY

From either the legal or economic point of view, business enter-prise expansion means an increase in the total assets employed within the firm. For comparative purposes the assets must be valued by the same method at the two different dates. The discus-sion of expansion needs to differentiate sharply between the changes in the amount and composition of the assets and the financial and legal means by which these assets are brought under the control of the enterprise.

Expansion is justified provided it will produce an increase in the present worth of the net income stream accruing to the share-holders. The risks as viewed by lenders and borrowers of the addi-

[39] The policy was particularly disastrous among public utility enterprises.

tional capital probably will not be the same. From another point of view expansion involves an alteration in the scale of production. It is not necessary, however, that the expansion of scale be accompanied by net economies of larger scale production in the technical sense for a shift to a larger scale to be warranted. Net economies of scale are the consequence of imperfect divisibility of the factors of production, the advantages of specialization, and an increase in the degree of monopoly power. There are often special advantages of an increase in scale that takes an integrated form. The advantages of larger scale do not always proceed smoothly by small gradations, and if monopoly power were not also increased it seems likely that the optimum scale with a given technique of production would not be overly large. Inventions typically produce a change in the optimum scale.

There are only two ways an enterprise may acquire additional assets: by an ownership arrangement and by a renting arrangement. Leases have certain relative advantages in some circumstances over outright purchase. The expanding firm has a choice between the purchase of used capital goods—either single items or whole enterprises as in amalgamation—or new capital goods. Generalizations here have little validity because the facts peculiar to each situation are likely to be controlling. The holding company arrangement is often used both where new capital goods are being added and where already existing enterprises are being taken over. The advantages of the holding company are principally legal and financial rather than economic in character. On the legal side limitation of liability, segregation of assets, and conformity to state laws are perhaps most important. On the financial side the private gains are limitation of investment to assure control and the added scope in which to apply the principle of trading on the equity.

The relative merits of the different types of security contracts are not altered by an expansion project, although an expanding corporation has greater opportunity to use the facilities of the organized capital market. A growing corporation as contrasted with a new corporation may sell securities to existing shareholders, customers and employees. The motives in selling to customers and employees, however, are not primarily those of obtaining the added funds in the cheapest manner.

REFERENCES: CHAPTER XI

BURTCHETT, F. F.—*Corporation Finance*. Chs. 37-40.
DEWING, A. S.—*Financial Policy*, Book V, Chs. 1, 2, 7, 10-12.
FIELD, K.—*Corporation Finance*. Chs. 16-21.
GERSTENBERG, C. W.—*Financial Organization and Management*. Chs. 29-31.
HOAGLAND, H. E.—*Corporation Finance*. Chs. 33-37.

EPSTEIN, R. C.—"Profits and the Size of the Firm in the Automobile Industry," *American Economic Review*, Vol. 21.
LATTY, E. R.—*Subsidiaries and Affiliated Corporations; a study in stockholders' liability*, Chicago, 1936.
LIVERMORE, S.—"The Success of Industrial Mergers," *Quarterly Journal of Economics*, Vol. 50.
Securities and Exchange Commission, *Report on the Study, etc. of Reorganization Committees*, Part VII, Washington (Government Printing Office), 1938, Appendix B, II "Corporate Merger and Consolidation," pp. 526-556.
WATERMAN, M. H.—"Financial Policies of Public Utility Holding Companies," *Michigan Business Studies*, Vol. 5.

Part Three

BUSINESS REORGANIZATION AND ENTERPRISE IN THE MODERN ECONOMY

Chapter XII

THE CAUSES OF BUSINESS FAILURE

I. The Concept of Failure Applied to the Business Enterprise. II. Economic Change and Business Failure. III. Incompetence and Business Failure. IV. Fortuities and Business Failure. V. Cyclical Fluctuations and Business Failure. VI. Summary.

~~~~~~~~~~~~

Any discussion of the causes of a particular state of affairs broaches difficult problems. In a degree these difficulties are of a philosophical sort, and to that extent of course are precluded from consideration here. But one very obvious distinction borrowed from philosophical discussion and adopted into common speech is here relevant: the distinction between immediate causes and underlying causes. If we review in our minds the problem of causation as it relates to a particular event we are at once aware of this distinction. If for example *A* shoots *B*, and *B* dies, and our problem is what caused *B*'s demise, we may say that the immediate cause of *B*'s death was the destruction of his brain cells by a bullet from *A*'s pistol. And we may say that the "cause" of *B*'s death was that he was shot by *A*; for many purposes this is a sufficient explanation. But for other reasons we may wish to probe more deeply and inquire what caused *A* to shoot *B*. This opens up a whole train of events of which the firing of the pistol by *A* was only the end term. We may discover, perhaps, that *B* was annoying *A*'s wife, and that *A*'s psychological make-up being what it was, this induced *A* to shoot *B*. We may go even further of course and inquire why *A*'s reaction to the event was of this violent sort. This may lead us into an analysis of *A*'s whole upbringing and past experiences until finally the lines of investigation run out into the whole fabric of society. We may pursue this analysis to almost any degree that seems appropriate for the purpose in hand; there is theoretically no limit. Yet after we are all through we can only say that the immediate cause of *B*'s death was a bullet entering his head, but that behind that event lay a multitude of situations and events which tended to bring it about.

And so it is with the "causes" of business failure: some are immediate and some are more remote. Any discussion of these causes must recognize the distinction.

I. THE CONCEPT OF FAILURE APPLIED TO THE BUSINESS ENTERPRISE

1. Failure in the economic sense and withdrawal of productive capacity. 2. Business concept of failure. 3. Immediate cause of failure.

Perhaps before proceeding further with the discussion of the causes of business failure it might be well to indicate what we propose to mean by failure as applied to business enterprises.

1. *Failure in the economic sense and withdrawal of productive capacity.* An examination of the theoretical literature in economics reveals that its authors have apparently not thought it necessary to define "failure" or scarcely even to employ the term. One reads of the withdrawal of firms from an industry but usually there is no indication of whether failure is taken to be synonymous with withdrawal or antecedent to it. For the broader problems of economic adjustment the important thing is withdrawal of productive capacity, and perhaps for that reason the departure of particular firms which yet leave productive capacity behind has been slighted. Nevertheless, for our purposes the concept of failure becomes important.

If a new enterprise is brought into existence, it is presumptive evidence that those supplying the capital believe that the net returns thereon in this opportunity are greater than those elsewhere available, due allowance being made, of course, for risk and uncertainty elements.[1] On the basis of these prospective returns

[1] No doubt many enterprises are annually promoted into existence where even the most cursory investigation would show the folly of expecting any positive return on the capital invested. Almost incredible ignorance and optimism plus a strong urge to be one's own boss, as e.g., in the retail trade, seem to be mainly

money capital is invested, real capital goods come into being, and the financial structure of the corporation is reared. If it be granted that new enterprises come into existence because of a prospective return to invested capital here greater than the then going rate, it is perhaps less difficult to indicate what we mean by failure. In the narrow economic sense failure means simply that the returns to capital invested in the opportunity that the promotion was designed to exploit have in fact so fallen short of those expected that, instead of the realized returns being *greater* than those that were elsewhere available, they have actually proven to be *less*. Otherwise expressed, we might say that costs being computed on an alternative opportunity basis *at the time the enterprise began*, costs are in excess of returns.[2] In diagrammatical terms average total cost is in excess of average revenue. The enterprise is a failure in the sense that had this state of affairs been expected or anticipated the firm would not have been brought into being. Hence economically speaking there has been misdirected capital investment; the enterprise is a failure.

Failure in this sense, however, does not necessarily mean that the resources will be withdrawn from the industry and that production will cease. Whether or not this result will follow will depend upon the degree to which it is possible in the instant case to disinvest the capital entirely or adapt it to the production of alternative products or services. Many capital goods are technologically so highly specialized that they are not adaptable to uses other than those for which they were designed. In this instance the unfortunate circumstance of returns less than those anticipated when the commitment was made is not a sufficient reason for ceasing production. If the alternative to continuing the production of this product is to sell the equipment for scrap, the returns currently secured may be relatively quite high on such scrap value. In that instance the best of the available alternatives is to continue on with the manufacture of the original product; the liquid funds obtained from selling the equipment for scrap if invested in some-

responsible for such promotions. These ventures as well as fraudulent promotion schemes will not concern us here.

[2] This amounts almost to saying that the rate of return on past historical outlay cost has been less than the going rate of interest. Indeed for practical purposes this does well enough for a first approximation.

thing else will yield a smaller return than that obtainable from using the assets here. The income from production and sale of the product must of course be greater than the direct cost outlays incurred, for otherwise the return on the specialized equipment is zero or negative. But the returns may in some instances fall a good deal before this situation is encountered.[3]

It is worth noting, however, that failure in this economic sense of an excess of average total cost above average revenue through historical time need not be accompanied at once by financial difficulties, such as a poor credit rating, an inability to meet cash obligations as they mature, etc. That is to say, an enterprise may be a failure in the economic sense defined and yet neither receivership, bankruptcy, nor liquidation follow as a result. Moreover, as we have just indicated, a business enterprise may be a failure in the economic sense (or for that matter in the legal sense too) without a withdrawal of capital equipment from the industry. If the capital equipment is highly specialized and has a small net scrap value a whole succession of enterprises may come into being and pass out of existence before the specialized capital goods are withdrawn from production. Notice also that this statement holds regardless of whether we interpret the term "enterprise" or "firm" in its economic sense or in its legal sense.[4] This fact has important economic consequences in that a comparatively long time interval may be required before needed adjustments within a particular industry can be brought about. If the capital goods are compara-

[3] This is a matter of common observation familiar to everyone. For instance, most street railway companies in the United States now earn a negligible return on the basis of past historical capital investment. Yet the equipment being highly specialized in the form of tracks, cars, wires, etc., it is next to impossible to adapt it to other uses and its scrap value net after disinvestment costs is very small. As a consequence such enterprises continue to operate so long as they succeed in securing an income from selling transportation service greater than the direct out-of-pocket costs involved in producing that service by an amount at least equal to a fair return on the net scrap value of the equipment. When the returns fall below that the tracks are torn up and the cars sold for kindling wood and scrap iron.

[4] In Chapter II, it will be recalled, we stressed the unit of co-ordinating ability as the mark distinguishing one firm from another from the point of view of economic analysis. From the point of view of the law we have a new enterprise when one legal entity gives way and is succeeded by another: thus, for instance, when a new corporation carries on after another has been formally liquidated to satisfy creditors' claims.

tively durable, and are not soon rendered hopelessly obsolete by great technological improvements, many years may elapse before the misdirected capital investment will cease to exert its influence on the conditions of supply.

To attempt to summarize: from the point of view of economic analysis failure means an excess of average costs (in the sense of historical outlay cost) over average receipts; but failure in this sense need not necessarily cause the firm in question to cease operations or default on any of its obligations. Many a firm is a failure in the economic sense and yet neither withdraws from business nor acquires a poor credit rating. Finally, even though financial difficulties do lead to default, and certain well-known legal consequences ensue, the capital goods may none the less continue in production for a considerable time interval, and thereby affect the price and total output of the commodity concerned.

2. *Business concept of failure.* While the foregoing distinctions are important for many problems, some of which we will wish to consider in subsequent portions of this chapter, we must not neglect the fact that in the business world the term "failure" applied to business enterprises has a rather precise and comparatively restricted meaning. In ordinary language when we say that a business enterprise has "failed" we mean usually that it has become involved in certain legal consequences because it has been unable to meet certain claims upon it to pay money. In the real world business concerns operate in a legal system which insists that obligations to pay money between persons must be respected. This is of course but one aspect of the whole complicated institution of private property, and partly what we mean when we refer to property as a "bundle of rights," e.g., the right to bring legal action to secure the payment of money due. In the business world the word failure has this very definite meaning, namely, that some person or persons have instituted legal proceedings against the enterprise with the intention or hope of obtaining payment of their claims. And while recognizing the economic distinctions alluded to above it seems advisable to employ this more clear-cut concept of business failure here rather than to depart too far from ordinary usage. Hence in the ensuing discussion where we

use the term failure without qualification we shall mean simply that the enterprise has come to a point where it is unable to meet the cash claims upon it.

3. *Immediate cause of failure.* It is at this juncture that our preliminary remarks about immediate and underlying causes are relevant to the problem of business failure. If failure means the inability of the enterprise to meet creditors' claims upon it, then the immediate cause of failure is simply and solely not enough cash. Neither competition nor depression, overcapitalization or mismanagement, or anything else is *immediately* responsible for failure; failure results from the prime fact of insufficient cash. This simple fact deserves emphasis because it is so often overlooked in discussions of the "causes" of business failure. There is more than a grain of truth in the common statements of business executives that their enterprises failed because of insufficient working capital, i.e., they could not pay their debts because they had not cash to do so. To be sure the explanation only focuses attention upon the end term in a whole series of events and to that extent adds very little to one's comprehension; but there is a very real sense in which it is true. The inability to pay debts, failure, is of course approached by degrees and there are sometimes technical legal questions as to precisely when failure exists.[5]

While there would be general agreement that the immediate

[5] It is sometimes the practice in discussions of this kind to indicate four stages of financial difficulty: (1) financial embarrassment, meaning difficulty in meeting pecuniary obligations as they mature but not as yet any actual default; (2) financial insolvency, meaning inability to meet debts as they mature; (3) total insolvency, meaning an excess of total liabilities over total assets; (4) confirmed insolvency, meaning that at law there has been adjudication of the facts and that legal steps are under way for the satisfaction of creditors' claims (bankruptcy, receivership, assignment). See Gerstenberg, C. W., *Financial Organization and Management*, New York (Prentice-Hall), 1934, pp. 728 ff.; or Burtchett, F. F., *Corporation Finance*, New York (Harpers), 1934, pp. 820 ff.

In the legal literature insolvency in sense (2) is termed insolvency in the equity sense, while (3), total insolvency, is said to be insolvency in the bankruptcy sense. An enterprise insolvent in the bankruptcy sense would necessarily be insolvent in the equity sense also. On the other hand it is perhaps worth pointing out that rather different valuation principles are employed in the latter than in the former. Inability to pay debts as they mature may simply mean that there is an unwillingness to convert other assets into cash on short notice because they will fetch less than their "true value" in some sense. In the bankruptcy sense, however, there is the implication that even at "fair values" the liabilities exceed the assets.

cause of failure was insufficient cash to meet the claims of creditors it is not satisfactory to leave the discussion with this simple assertion. The really important question is what factors (causes) bring business enterprises into a position where they are unable to pay their debts as they mature. In any given case, of course, the specific causes will be in some measure unique, involving purely chance elements and accidental combinations of circumstances. But in the writer's opinion it is very easy to overestimate the degree to which each instance of failure is a law unto itself and to underrate the degree to which general causes are present and regularly operative. Hence in what follows we shall endeavor to make our analysis essentially general in character in an effort to emphasize these similarities.

For purposes of discussion we shall distinguish three types of causes of business failure: economic change and development, incompetence, and accidental or fortuitous happenings. It is not suggested that these are completely separable in every instance of failure; but merely that they are different *kinds* of things which are logically distinguishable for purposes of analysis.

II. ECONOMIC CHANGE AND BUSINESS FAILURE

1. Types of change in the economic data: a. the introduction of a new commodity. b. the introduction of a new method of production. c. the opening of a new source of supply. d. a change in the organization of the industry. 2. Economic change and the adaptability of the enterprise.

It has been the achievement of the mathematical economists to demonstrate that the whole price system (i.e., the prices of finished goods, of intermediate goods, the factors of production, personal and corporate incomes, etc.) is a system of mutual interdependence. The incomes of producers are not independent of the prices of the products, the costs of production, or the outlays of the consumers. For our present purposes this simply means that any change anywhere in the economic system is not without *some* significance for the other parts of the system. To be sure the effects of certain changes are so diffused that they pass almost unnoticed by the individual enterprise; or again, for any one firm the change may be so far removed from its scene of operations that (for all practical purposes) it may be safely disregarded.

But from time to time and often in a quite unpredictable manner significant and important changes develop in the economic data with which the enterprises in a particular industry have to deal. Generally speaking these changes are the more damaging the greater the rapidity with which they occur and the greater the adaptations they necessitate. While it is impossible to catalogue all such changes which may ultimately lead to business failure it is convenient to discuss them under certain broad classifications and, with respect to each, to indicate how they may induce business failure. For the time being we omit from consideration those cumulative fluctuations in output, employment, prices, etc., known as the business cycle, although, as will be indicated presently, cyclical variations may reinforce the effects and hasten the results of other dangers. Broadly speaking we might classify significant changes according to whether they reacted primarily upon demand factors or supply factors. But since these are to a considerable degree interwoven it seems preferable to carry forward the discussion under the following headings: (a) the introduction of a new commodity; (b) the introduction of a new method of production; (c) the opening of a new source of supply; (d) a change in the organization of the industry.[6] It is not suggested of course that for certain purposes it might not be advisable to subdivide these more minutely.

1. *Types of change in the economic data.* (a) *The introduction of a new commodity.* A new commodity almost invariably carries with it certain dangers for existing enterprises. Every new commodity is a partial substitute for some already established commodities. The new commodity of course need not be wholly new but merely such an improvement upon some existing commodity

---

[6] This classification of developmental changes has been adapted from Schumpeter, J., *The Theory of Economic Development*, Cambridge, Mass. (Harvard), 1934, especially Chs. II and IV.

that the demand for the older one declines sharply.[7] Countless examples are ready to hand: the introduction of rayon and its effect upon silk and cotton goods; steel furniture as opposed to wooden; the radio and its effects upon the phonograph and piano industries; fuel oil and coal; retreaded automobile tires as a substitute for new ones; and many others.[8]

When a new or improved commodity appears the producers of the old product must make adaptations if they are to compete effectively under the new conditions. But unfortunately this is not always easy. As repeatedly emphasized the capital goods used by a particular industry tend to be highly specialized; and if the new product requires a quite different type of capital equipment the necessary shift may be quite impossible. For example, if fuel oil and electricity are sharply reducing the demand for anthracite coal as a domestic fuel there is practically no opportunity to disinvest the capital represented by breakers, shafts, etc., and transform it into electrical generators or oil refineries. In practice it would be necessary to scrap the existing plant and equipment, raise large amounts of free capital, and attempt to enter an industry unfamiliar to the existing management. But if the enterprise is already suffering reduced earnings because of the new product it will probably find difficulty in obtaining liquid capital sufficient to carry out the change.[9] If the prospect is for a declining demand for the old product and if a shift to the production of the new is out of the question, then perhaps the only salvation for the individual concern is to bend its efforts towards obtaining

[7] It must not be assumed that new products react unfavorably upon *all* established enterprises but chiefly upon those directly competitive with the new product. The effect upon other industries may be decidedly favorable insofar as these products are complementary to the new good or used jointly with it. The automobile was perhaps unfortunate for the railroads but beneficial to rubber growers and cement producers. Many more products are complementary than is commonly recognized.

[8] Many of the most important new products are intermediate goods used in the process of manufacture. See the interesting list of "fifty typical" new products of manufacture in *Recent Economic Changes*, New York (McGraw-Hill), 1929, pp. 112-113.

[9] The organization of the capital market is such that much emphasis is placed upon past earnings records. This emphasis augurs ill for the sale of securities by an enterprise whose earnings have been falling off because of the appearance of a new product.

a larger share of the shrunken total demand. In this way it may be possible to maintain net earnings at a level high enough to avoid failure. But by definition this type of adjustment is not possible for *all* firms in the industry; not all can have an increased fraction of a declining total demand; necessarily some must be unsuccessful and failure ensue.[10]

It is of course not true that a shift over to the production of the new product is an impossible adaptation. Sometimes with a moderate capital investment it is possible to supply the new demand.[11] But the appearance of a new product will almost certainly require some adaptation, and if the enterprise is to retain its earning power the change had best be undertaken. Usually there is sufficient time to make the change over; only occasionally does a new product completely sweep the field at once. But even where change is possible, and there is time to carry it out, some firms will doggedly persist in the old ways with the net result that they ultimately fail. Such a trusting Micawber-like faith is difficult to understand although there can be little doubt of its existence. It will remain a mystery, for instance, why with the appearance of the radio as a commercial success more phonograph producers did not shift over to radio manufacturing. Yet cases of this sort are extraordinarily common.

b. *The introduction of a new method of production.* Whereas the introduction of a new product reacts primarily upon the demand for the product of already established enterprises a new method of production affects the conditions of supply. It is not the "newness" of the method which is significant, to be sure, but that it reduces cost by recombining the agents of production in a manner hitherto not used; and the recombination may or may

[10] In some industries it is conceivable that no enterprises need necessarily fail because of a declining total demand for the product. If the individual firms can contract their scale of operations sufficiently, the same number may remain although each is smaller. In practice this is very unlikely to occur except in agriculture.

[11] Apparently such readjustments are most easily carried out in the "service" industries provided not too much capital equipment is highly specialized. For example, not all vaudeville houses went out of the entertainment business with the appearance of the cinema; perhaps the great majority became moving picture houses. So also some carriage manufacturers became automobile producers; but not many.

not be the result of an invention in the strict sense.[12] Whatever
the reason, it allows those producers which adopt it a competitive
advantage over their rivals, and the latter must either install the
new methods or suffer losses and perhaps ultimate failure. On the
other hand even if all firms in the industry make the change to
the new methods, trouble may still arise. For even though the new
method reduces costs and selling prices, the demand for the product may be insufficiently elastic at the lower prices to permit all
producers to market their increased output at a profit. Excessive
productive capacity for the industry as a whole may easily be
the net result. Under such conditions a serious competitive strug-
gle may evolve which will only be brought to an end by the
elimination of certain firms.

There is perhaps a greater likelihood of the required adaptations
being carried out in the case of an improvement in the methods
of production than when the change is a new product. In the
first place, the producers are more likely to be aware of the
character of the change and the necessity for making it; and
second, the financial barriers to be overcome are perhaps less
serious. Typically only those firms which prior to the appearance
of the new technique were showing relatively low earnings are
likely to have trouble in financing it. A technological change of
this sort is often just the final blow necessary to drive certain
firms from the industry; they cannot finance the purchase of the
new equipment and their competitive position is greatly weakened because they do not possess it. For example certain railroads
in the United States have recently improved their passenger service by speeding up the trains and installing stream-lined equipment. This has apparently been very popular and no doubt gives
such roads a competitive advantage. But this new equipment is
quite costly, and it seems doubtful if many of the smaller and
less prosperous roads will be able to install it. Insofar as the latter
compete with the others between common terminals it seems rea-

[12] See, for example, the interesting description of the changes in the glass bottle
industry in recent years in Lynd, R. S. and H. M., *Middletown*, New York
(Harcourt, Brace), 1929, pp. 39-48. For an interesting list of new production
processes see *Recent Economic Changes*, pp. 114-115. Many of these are of course
highly technical and not understandable by the layman at a glance.

sonable to suppose that they will lose traffic. For roads which are already on the borderline of failure this may be just sufficient to push them over.

c. *The opening of a new source of supply.* A new and cheaper source of supply may prove disastrous for the producers in a particular geographical region. The new source may be "discovered" as in the extractive industries, or it may be brought about by developments and changes under human control. The opening of the newer coal mines in the North Central states, coupled with a shift in the center of population, has been damaging for the older eastern producers. Likewise the development of the very rich copper deposits in South Africa has threatened copper producers the world over. More recently pulp and paper producers in eastern Canada and the northern United States are being menaced by a reputedly much cheaper product made from Georgia slash pine.[13] For the paper industry, which has already been overdeveloped and suffering from low earnings, this may force many more enterprises to the wall. At other times the new source of supply is made possible by the reduction of tariffs or the cheapening of transportation costs.[14] The trunk line railroads in the United States meant the gradual extinction of many local manufactures; while in more recent times swifter transportation and better refrigeration have permitted fresh fruits and vegetables from the south and far west to be marketed at low cost during the winter months in the more densely populated northern regions, all of which is not without significance for canning and preserving concerns. Changes of this character are continually taking place.

The degree to which the older enterprises will be able to meet the competition from the newer sources of supply will depend upon a variety of factors. If the industry is extractive in character, there may be no possible way for the older producers to avoid a

[13] It is said that "alpha" cellulose now costing around $70.00 per ton f.o.b. the mill can be produced from southern slash pine for $36.00. The saving on newsprint is somewhat less. See *Proceedings* of the Second Dearborn Conference of Agriculture, Industry and Science, Dearborn, Mich., 1936, pp. 212-218.

[14] It is said, for example, "The operation of the Panama Canal and the realignment of rates since the war have resulted in moving Chicago 336 cents away from the Pacific coast per ton of staple goods, while moving New York 224 cents nearer." *Recent Economic Changes*, p. 26.

sharp reduction in income, and in time failure may be inevitable.[15] If on the other hand the reason for the lower costs in the new region is cheaper raw materials, a better labor supply, or nearness to markets, then the older firms may be able to shift their plant location.[16] But here again the ability to do so will depend upon how much free capital the firm can command in order to carry out the change. Some textile concerns have shifted their plants to the southern states in recent years, but not all; some have failed and ceased production entirely. If the new source of supply has been the result of tariff changes, and if there are marked differences between foreign and domestic costs, then perhaps most firms in the industry will fail.[17]

d. *A change in the organization of the industry.* Perhaps the most common change of this type is an alteration in the optimum size of enterprise for the given industry. Such a change need not be the result of any technological improvement; for instance, it may very well be the consequence of a secular growth in the demand for the product. The growth of the annual demand for automobiles has doubtless worked to the disadvantage of the smaller firms and in favor of larger enterprises, and this apart from the important improvements in production methods which have been characteristic of the automotive industry. There is much evidence to indicate that the scale of production has been increasing rather generally in industry in the United States since 1900.[18] Many industries have passed through a stage of mergers and, if the more or less typical pattern is followed, certain firms are usually left out of this movement. Not infrequently their com-

[15] If the new price established be less than the direct costs of production of the older firms they will of course be wise to cease operations immediately. But even if this be not the case, earnings may be so sharply reduced that they find difficulty in meeting creditor obligations.

[16] For a description of changes in the geographical location of industry see *Recent Economic Changes*, pp. 206-216; also Garver, F. B., Boddy, F. M., Nixon, A. J., *The Location of Manufactures in the United States, 1899-1929.* Minneapolis (University of Minnesota), 1935.

[17] If, for instance, the high protective tariff in the United States on watches and woolens were abolished their prices would probably fall drastically and many firms would fail. The desirability of so doing is not here under review, of course, except to observe that the necessity for tariff protection is commonly grossly exaggerated.

[18] The figures from census data are conveniently available in a chapter by Willard L. Thorpe in *Recent Economic Changes*, pp. 167 ff.

petitive position is so weakened that failure ensues.[19] So also if the larger size of enterprise assumes an integrated form. If some enterprises are integrating vertically or horizontally within the industry this may almost force the remainder to take similar steps in order to compete effectively.

2. *Economic change and the adaptability of the enterprise.* In the preceding paragraphs an attempt has been made briefly to indicate certain common types of recurrent economic change. The mere existence of change is in itself clearly insufficient to cause failure; rather it is the inability of the enterprise to adapt its operations to the changed economic data with sufficient speed and thoroughness to avoid a serious decline in earning power. In some cases, it would appear that there is almost no possibility of adaptation to the changed conditions; in others, adaptation is possible but extremely difficult to carry through because of the specific character of the capital goods and the company's inability to finance the change. In yet others the management apparently could make the change were it alert and not bound by habit and tradition. Nevertheless it seems undisputable that significant economic changes of the type described are almost certain to leave some enterprises with drastically reduced earning power. Whether profits will be reduced sufficiently to impair seriously the debt-paying power of the enterprise cannot be answered in general terms; the financial structure, the character of the industry and a variety of other factors are all relevant. But it is not difficult to find instances where earning power and debt-paying ability will be injured long before the enterprise will have failed. Hence while the immediate cause of failure will be the often alleged cause of a "shortage of working capital," i.e., an inability to meet creditors' claims, this shortage will itself be the resultant of reduced earnings consequent upon important changes within the industry or in other parts of the economy. The underlying cause of failure was a change in the economic conditions within which the firm operated and its inability or refusal to adapt to them.

[19] It is not to be inferred that mergers are uniformly profitable for the enterprises merged. But it seems undeniable that firms which do not alter their size suffer unfortunate consequences competitively. This may not necessarily be the result of any technical superiorities of the larger firm on the side of production; it may be merely an increase in their degree of monopoly power.

III. INCOMPETENCE AND BUSINESS FAILURE

1. The meaning of incompetence and its recognition. 2. Evidence of incompetence. 3. The misapplication of working capital. 4. The mismanagement of fixed capital. 5. Errors of financial judgment. 6. Summary.

While economic change and development and the inability of business enterprises to adapt themselves to them are potent causes of business failure, it is quite clear that not all business failures can be so explained. From the evidence available it seems reasonable to suppose that many failures would occur annually even if significant economic and technological changes were absent. Important differences certainly exist between persons with respect to all kinds of abilities and there is no reason to suppose that managerial ability is any exception; in other words, there are persons better and less well qualified for the tasks which business management must perform. And this relative incompetence or inefficiency in management must be accorded a prime place in any list of the causes of business failure.

1. *The meaning of incompetence and its recognition.* Unfortunately, however, the exact meaning of incompetence when applied to business management is not entirely clear. Perhaps all too frequently we have a tendency to say that failure in a particular instance was the result of incompetence and to cite as evidence the fact of failure itself. We allege incompetence, it seems, because no other clearly discernible cause is observable; incompetence tends to become a cover-all term of uncertain meaning. This is unsatisfactory. If incompetence is a cause of business failure, as it doubtless is, then it ought to be recognizable before failure occurs, and not be merely a tag which we affix after the event. Unfortunately it is often difficult to define or recognize incompetence except in the most extreme cases. To be sure we are often able to sense incompetency or inefficiency subjectively; but this is unreliable and inconclusive. What we should like is some means

by which incompetence could be reduced to objective criteria which could be broadly applied. Yet there seem to be well-nigh insuperable obstacles to the attainment of this ideal. For almost the only objective tests which can be developed are those derivable from the financial and operating statements—ratios, relations, etc. —and by no process of abstract reasoning can we derive "ideal" or "optimum" ratios which are widely applicable. The best that can be done with this method is to develop numerous ratios, either averages for the industry or drawn from the most successful concerns, and compare with these the relations obtaining in the particular enterprise under examination in the hope that the contrast may suggest some useful deductions on management efficiency. But it is usually impossible to read off the result from the figures and predict with certainty how soon, if ever, the particular concern will fail because of the degree of incompetence indicated. That is, how great a deviation from the statistical norm or ideal is permissible without drastic consequences? No easy answer is possible. But there is yet a further difficulty. Frequently, perhaps usually, not all the ratios will point in the same direction; some will be favorable, others less so, and perhaps a few will be alarming. Will the favorable relations indicating favorable conditions be sufficient to offset the otherwise drastic consequences of the unfavorable, or if not, to what extent, and by how much? To answer such questions precisely, we must obviously possess some means of determining the relative importance of the different ratios. But here again no objective criteria are available, nor conceivably could they be developed; human judgment will inevitably play a large role, and the individual prognosticator will probably not find it easy to state why in one instance he pronounces management inefficiency and incompetence sufficient to cause insolvency, and in another not. The problem is not like predicting at what steam pressure a given boiler will burst; no equally objective measures of pressures and resistances are possible.

The foregoing remarks of course are not intended to discredit the widely used methods of ratio analysis of business records. Rather the aim has been merely to point out certain characteristic limitations inherent in the very nature of such relationships. They fall short of perfection to be sure, but in many ways they are far superior to the alternative of unaided intuition.

2. *Evidence of incompetence.* If management incompetence is present in a business enterprise it ought to manifest itself in an observable manner. The most obvious indication of managerial incompetence, of course, is an apparent inability to make the enterprise earn as large a net return under the given circumstances and conditions as might reasonably be expected. Incompetence of management is usually first suggested by the fact that the enterprise does not show net profits as large as would seem possible. But the net profits figure is the resultant of many management decisions and policies. In order to determine in just what directions the management has been incompetent one must look more closely.

The management of any enterprise has at its disposal a certain aggregate of assets which has been procured from the proprietors (which may be the same real persons as the management although not necessarily) and from creditors. These assets are for certain purposes conveniently divisible into working capital assets and fixed capital assets. The economic function of the management is so to employ these assets that returns to the owners are maximized through time. But an incompetent management would be one which failed to achieve this end and its failure to do so might be charged either to a misuse of working capital, fixed capital, or both. In other words, mismanagement consists in an injudicious application of the available assets. But there is another aspect of incompetence which might or might not be a properly labeled incompetence of management. This has to do with the manner in which capital was procured. It is sometimes said, for example, that an enterprise failed because of an inappropriate capital structure which imposed heavy fixed charges. The responsibility for this state of affairs is, however, to be charged in the final analysis to the owners (in a corporation, to the stockholders) who authorized the creation of such a capital structure.[20] Now the man-

[20] In certain very large corporations the adoption of the financial plans of the management may be almost automatic and such errors are definitely chargeable to them; that is, the shareholders are largely dormant. Yet technically the shareholders are finally responsible and they certainly bear the consequences.

agement charged with the day-to-day operation of the enterprise may or may not constitute the same persons as the owners. If not, then it might be quite inaccurate to charge the former with incompetence leading to failure since the financial plan set up by the shareholders may be so ill-balanced that no operating management, however efficient, could avoid failure. There are thus two aspects of incompetence which, for analytical purposes at least, ought to be distinguished: first, mismanagement in the use of fixed and working capital available for the earning of an income, second, financial errors and mistakes of judgment chargeable to the owners of the enterprise. In the following discussion of incompetence and its manifestations this distinction is preserved, although, admittedly in practice, they are often intertwined.

3. *The misapplication of working capital.* The misapplication of fixed and working capital assets may manifest itself in a variety of ways and they are not completely separable. None the less let us first consider mismanagement of working capital.

We have emphasized earlier that the problems of working capital are in the last analysis problems arising from the imperfect synchronization of cash receipts and outlays plus those originating from the fact that the enterprise will find it advisable to hold cash as a convenient hedge against uncertainties and contingencies whose precise nature cannot be predicted or which cannot be contracted out for a price to someone else. The problem of uncertainty will greatly vary in seriousness from enterprise to enterprise; and since we have already treated it in an earlier chapter we shall not repeat what was there said.[21] Working capital problems, therefore, are essentially problems originating in the imperfect synchronization of cash receipts and outlays within the firm, and these do not remain constant during different phases of the business cycle.

In the balance sheet sense, working capital consists of receivables, inventories, cash, and marketable securities if any.[22] If the management is not making an efficient application of this working

---

[21] See *supra*, Ch. VI, sec. III.

[22] For some enterprises it would be necessary to exclude inventories if they are of a sort that are not salable without tremendous markdowns on comparatively short notice. A dealer in tombstones or real estate tracts would hardly have his inventories classified among the current assets by an outsider.

capital it ought to show itself in observable ways. Perhaps the most commonly employed ratio to test efficiency in this respect is the current ratio which is presumed to indicate the ability of the firm to meet its creditor obligations over the next period.[23] Several refined versions of this relationship have been developed. The so-called "acid test" ratio, which is the ratio of cash and receivables to current liabilities, is regarded as more significant since the ability of the firm to realize on its inventories may be problematical. The receivables are often subjected to further analysis. They may be expressed as a ratio of sales and if this ratio shows a tendency to rise it is evidence either that a significant number of bad accounts is being included in receivables, in which case the figure for aggregate receivables is open to suspicion, or that the management is lax or inefficient in collecting from its customers.[24] The inability to collect from customers is in time fatal because in the going concern the cash receipts from customers are a most important source of cash with which to pay the creditors. In addition to receivables the inventory likewise may be subjected to more detailed analysis. The ratio of inventory to total current assets, particularly if very high, may suggest over-purchasing. Perhaps more significant, however, is the ratio of inventory to sales. If this ratio shows a tendency to rise it sug-

[23] The current ratio is simply the ratio of current assets to current liabilities. With respect to the liabilities, current usually means obligations to pay cash within the next twelve months. Likewise the current assets are those which will or could be turned into cash (e.g., marketable securities) over the same interval. Perhaps because of its greater familiarity than other ratios there is a disposition to keep up a good current ratio as long as possible. At least one study indicates that ". . . only in the final year before failure did current assets fail to exceed current debt by the presumably safe margin of a 100 percent, as indicated by a 2 to 1 ratio." Smith, R. F. and Winakor, A. H., "Changes in the Financial Structure of Unsuccessful Industrial Corporations," *University of Illinois Bulletin*, Vol. 32, No. 46 (July 16, 1935), p. 38. However, the tendency was for current assets to become less liquid; the proportion of cash and receivables to total current assets declined. *Ibid.*, p. 39.

[24] It is sometimes possible to estimate the number of slow accounts by comparing the average collection period with the terms of sale commonly granted. For example, if the average credit sales per day (annual net sales divided by 365) are X, and the terms of sale are net 30 days, then if all customers paid promptly the average total accounts receivable should not exceed 30X. If the total accounts receivable were for example 60X it would indicate that on the average all accounts were a month past due. This is more difficult to apply where sales are partly on account and partly for cash unless the proportions are known.

gests that the management is not moving its goods as rapidly as formerly, or that included in inventories is a substantial proportion of unmarketable merchandise. Finally, the ratio of current debt to inventory may be significant as an indication of the degree to which a concern is buying forward, or, on the other hand, to which it is failing to pay its creditors on time.

The foregoing ratios and relationships may throw some light on the incompetence of management in handling working capital. As previously observed, however, it is impossible to lay down absolutely ideal ratios which are applicable in all industries and trades.[25] But it may very well be possible to state that, compared to other enterprises in the industry which are showing good earnings, this enterprise is mismanaging its working capital, and that if current policies are continued failure will develop. The reasons for the alarming statistical showing as to working capital may of course be many and various. The firm's advertising policies may be bad, its product of poor quality, its credit department ill-managed, or any number of things, either alone or in combination. Whatever the reasons, the management may properly be designated as less than adequately competent in its handling of working capital. The gross mismanagement of working capital will lead sooner or later to a default on creditors' claims, i.e., failure.

4. *The mismanagement of fixed capital.* Mismanagement or incompetence in the use of fixed capital assets is perhaps less convincingly demonstrable.[26] Perhaps the most obvious evidence, however, is a high average production cost per unit of output which cannot be charged, seemingly, to anything specific such as poor plant location or the working of low grade ores. If fairly computed production costs are not relatively high there would seem to be no reason to charge the company's difficulties to incompetence in handling fixed capital.

[25] For an interesting tabulation of some of these ratios in different industries see Foulke, Roy A., *Behind the Scenes of Business*, New York (Dun and Bradstreet, Inc.), 1937.

[26] In recent years some companies have deliberately followed the practice of writing down their fixed asset values to purely nominal amounts. In such cases of course it is almost meaningless to work out ratios between fixed asset figures and others.

The ratio of sales to fixed assets may throw some light on the use made of fixed capital assets. If this ratio shows a tendency to decrease, it suggests that the management is either accumulating plant and equipment in excess of its needs or ability to make use of these assets, or that unused or unusable equipment is included in the asset figures. The latter suspicion may be confirmed by a low ratio of maintenance expenditures to fixed capital in comparison with similar ratios in other firms in the same industry.[27] The ratio of sales to fixed assets may also be compared with similar concerns in the same field with enlightening results, although here again due allowance must be made for explainable differences. A high operating ratio, i.e., the ratio of operating expenses to operating income, suggests an inefficient management although it is not conclusive in itself. If the ratio of fixed assets to total assets shows a tendency to increase it suggests that the firm is possibly using up its working capital in financing plant extension and may soon encounter a shortage of working capital sufficient to cause default on debt payments.[28] If because of a change in production methods requiring more capital goods per unit of output, i.e., more capitalistic methods of production, the corporation must increase its investment in fixed assets, then in most instances an increase in working capital will also be required. That is, even though the plant extension has been cared for by long-term

[27] This ratio must be used with caution if the inferences are not to be misleading. Guthmann argues that because construction costs fluctuate considerably the plant turnover ratio may not reveal the relative efficiency of two managements, but merely show that one plant was constructed during a period of high cost and the other at a period of low. This is possible to be sure. But it would not invalidate a decreasing rate of plant turnover as an indication of increasing inefficiency. More important is Guthmann's other suggestion as to the necessity of making sure that the two plants are designed to render the same services. See Guthmann, H. G., *Analysis of Financial Statements*, New York (Prentice-Hall), 1936, pp. 158-160.

[28] Apparently the decline in the proportion of working capital assets to total assets is likely to be more or less continuous for several accounting periods prior to failure. "Comparison of the Current Ratio and the ratio of Working Capital to Total Assets showed that while the general trend of each ratio for the Average Company was downward, a more distinct trend was to be observed in that of Working Capital to Total Assets. Thus the trend of the ratio of Working Capital to Total Assets revealed an uninterrupted decline from .284 in the tenth year before failure to .061 in the final year before failure." "A Test Analysis of Unsuccessful Industrial Companies," *University of Illinois Bulletin*, Vol. 27, No. 48 (July 29, 1930), p. 53.

financing the firm may encounter a shortage of working capital if no provisions have been made to augment it too. The attempt to finance plant enlargements or improvements by depleting working capital assets will almost certainly cause difficulty eventually in meeting current obligations to pay cash.

5. *Errors of financial judgment.* As noted above, the mismanagement may be almost entirely errors of financial judgment chargeable to the stockholders and/or their representatives, the directors. The management, in the sense of the persons in charge of production, sales, etc., may have very little to say about such questions as changes in the financial plan, the distribution of dividends, etc., which are either decided by the stockholders or the board of directors. In any case whether or not the persons directly involved are identical this type of incompetence should be kept logically distinct from the other. The voting stockholders may be anxious to reap the full advantages of "trading-on-the-equity" and as a consequence bond the property to such an extent that even a moderate decline in net earnings creates difficulty in meeting bond interest charges.[29] In all other respects the concern may be managed effectively and efficiently, but the heavy fixed charges make default and failure inevitable. The fault here is not necessarily that the enterprise was overexpanded but that the manner in which the capital was procured was faulty. Before failure occurs, evidence of too great trading on the equity may be discernible in a high ratio of funded debt to fixed assets. Much the same relationship is indicated by the ratio of net worth to total fixed assets. If these ratios appear high in comparison to firms similarly situated in the industry the enterprise is likely to be vulnerable and failure may develop easily.

The payment of dividends when the working capital position

[29] The practice of concentrating the voting power in the hands of a small group of shareholders by the use of one or more types of non-voting shares perhaps tends to encourage overtrading on the equity. In some well-known cases the voting shares represent little or no capital contribution other than services of problematical value. Hence the owners of these shares have every reason to take all possible risks from overborrowing since if the borrowing should increase net income they, being residual income claimants, will gain; if, on the other hand, the borrowing should cause the corporation to fail they, having contributed little or nothing, would stand to lose only an equivalent amount.

does not warrant the distribution of cash may cause serious diffi-culty. It should never be forgotten that the payment of dividends means an outlay of cash which must come either from working capital or be borrowed for the purpose. Apart from legal tech-nicalities the advisability of parting with cash may have little or nothing to do with earnings as shown by the statement of profit and loss. Many a concern was technically in a better position to pay dividends in 1933 than in 1936 even though in 1933 it was recording losses while in 1936 it was showing substantial profits. In 1933 cash reserves were in many cases more than ample for the needs of the business while in 1935-36 all available cash was required for the maintenance of operations at a high level. The declaration of dividends is a matter for the board of directors and here as elsewhere incompetence and bad judgment may show themselves. It is of course not unknown for a board of directors to declare a dividend in an effort to convince prospective security buyers of the strong position of the company.[30] But if the security sales fail to come off the enterprise may find itself so short of cash that it is forced to default shortly thereafter.

Although overcapitalization is sometimes mentioned as a cause of failure it seems clear that overcapitalization *per se* could not cause failure *unless* the enterprise were so capitalized as to create a heavy burden of fixed charges. In other words, an injudicious combination of bonds and shares might cause default because of the heavy annual interest charges, but not overcapitalization alone. It is the types of security contracts employed in the financial plan that cause the trouble, not the total face value of the security contracts outstanding. Overcapitalization which consisted entirely of proprietorship claims, e.g., nothing but common and preferred stocks, could not of itself cause a corporation to fail even if the total outstanding shares far exceeded in face value the assets paid in to the corporation. The return to the shareholders per share might be very small but there is no reason why this fact alone would cause failure. To be sure, if the directors sought to pay dividends on this capitalization far in excess of what the earnings

---

[30] Dewing mentions several cases where railroads paid dividends when neither earnings nor cash position would warrant in order to maintain their bonds as legal investments for savings banks. See *Financial Policy of Corporations*, p. 609.

and cash position would warrant, trouble would almost certainly develop. But the difficulty is essentially an attempt to pay too large dividends, not overcapitalization. An undercapitalized corporation could bring itself to the same position by unwise dividend disbursements.

6. *Summary*. The foregoing discussion of incompetence as a cause of business failure has sought to point out the meaning of incompetence and to suggest various objective criteria by which it may be recognized before there is any actual default to creditors. Our treatment of ratio analysis does not do justice perhaps to that technique, but there are many volumes on the subject providing full coverage. We must reiterate however our earlier cautions on the limitations of such analysis: first, there seems to be no method by which one can develop logically any "ideal" or "optimum" ratios which are generally applicable; secondly, in order to draw conclusions as to the proximity of business failure in a particular instance one would require a weighting scale for rating the relative importance of the different ratios because all of them are not likely to point in the same direction. Notwithstanding these inherent limitations, ratio analysis is doubtless superior to the alternative of unaided intuition.

IV. FORTUITIES AND BUSINESS FAILURE

In the very nature of the case accidental, unpredictable, nonrecurring, or fortuitous happenings do not lend themselves to generalization as a class. People can and do generalize about volcanic eruptions but it seems difficult to know what useful generalizations might be formulated concerning floods, earthquakes, tornadoes, and wars. They have very little in common except their inscrutable behavior. Events of this character may very easily cause business enterprises to fail; acts of God and the like cause the enterprise to fail, destroy it typically, because they wipe out of existence most of its physical assets. The assets are simply demolished while the claims against the assets remain; failure is inevitable. The risks of some of these uncontrollable events which may cause severe loss may be shifted over to others at a cost by means of insurance and are frequently so handled. Others, on the other hand, are not insurable or not insurable at what seems to the firm a reasonable cost. Civil disturbances, the untimely death of an important individual, a bank failure, the sudden insolvency of a large trade creditor, etc., are fortuitous developments against which insurance is not usually carried.

Events such as those just mentioned either individually or in combination may cause business enterprises to fail. But as we have already suggested it is not possible to say much about them other than to note their occurrence. They are undoubtedly the least important group of causes of business failure.

Possibly one ought to include under fortuitous developments as a cause of business failure such a matter as the unfortunate maturity date of a bond issue. During a severe depression the organized capital market may be so disturbed that it is impossible to refund maturing obligations even at very high rates of interest. Since one cannot predict the low point of a depression twenty or fifty years in advance, a maturity date of a bond issue which coincides with a deep depression is mostly accidental. Many a corporation in the United States, for instance, was forced to default on a maturing bond issue in 1932 simply because there was little or no possibility of selling new securities with which to refund. A year or two on either side of the maturity date would have meant comparatively clear sailing instead of failure; failure was partially or almost wholly fortuitous.

V. CYCLICAL FLUCTUATIONS AND BUSINESS FAILURE

1. The trade cycle as a contributing and as an independent cause. 2. The downswing and cash receipts. 3. The downswing and cash outlays. 4. Cash flows and debt-paying ability.

In the foregoing sections we have assigned business failure to the three causes of economic change and development, incompetence, and fortuitous events. We set up this classification in order to simplify our analysis and we would admit readily the wisdom of further subdivision in a more extended treatment. Throughout we carefully avoided any specific mention of the phenomenon of the business cycle. Anything we have said thus far would presumably be applicable to business enterprises which operated in a world which was not characterized by those fluctuations in prices, production, business profits, employment, etc., which we call the trade cycle. Yet it is common knowledge that business failures are more numerous in periods of declining business activity and periods of depression than during intervals of rising activity and genuine boom. It is important, therefore, that we round off our discussion of the causes of business failure by devoting some attention to the business cycle.

1. *The trade cycle as a contributing and as an independent cause.* The relationship of the trade cycle and all it implies to the question of the causes of business failure lies mainly in two directions. In the first place the business cycle undoubtedly increases the force with which other unfavorable developments react upon the business enterprise. For instance, if a particular firm is finding difficulty in adapting its productive organization to a shift in demand, a technological improvement, a new and cheaper source of supply, etc., the advent of a business depression accompanied by high money rates and diminished consumers' spending will inevitably make the problem of adaptation that much harder. Or again, if an enterprise is operated with a certain degree of incompetence that incompetence may show itself with special emphasis in a period of falling business activity when the problems of business management are both more numerous and more difficult. In other words business cycle changes, especially downswings and depressions, reinforce the effectiveness of other causes in bringing about business failures.[31]

In the second place, however, business fluctuations bring about certain difficulties for business enterprises quite apart from the three type causes we have already mentioned. In some measure

[31] During periods of rising business activity the adverse effects of certain operative causes of business failure are partially offset by the favorable developments of the boom itself.

the trade cycle is an independent cause of business failure. Let us look into this.

2. *The downswing and cash receipts.* We were at some pains to point out in an earlier section that the immediate cause of business failure is insufficient cash to meet obligations as they mature. Moreover in Chapter VI we sought to emphasize that the problem of working capital in the business enterprise was essentially a problem having its basis in the imperfect synchronization of cash receipts and cash outlays. The adaptation of the business enterprise to the imperfect synchronization of cash receipts and cash outlays is an ever present difficulty; but it is likely to become especially severe during a downswing. In other words, during a decline and depression the necessity for maintaining debt-paying ability tends to increase at the same time that the difficulties of doing so are likely to be enhanced.

A falling off in general business activity is typically characterized by declining prices and a rise in liquidity preference by both individuals and business enterprises. And these are necessarily related. A decline in prices accompanied by a belief that prices will fall still further means that the value of money in terms of other assets is appreciating; therefore, there is an incentive to prefer money to other forms of wealth. From the point of view of the individual with limited resources there is a strong inducement to postpone purchases until he feels reasonably certain that prices are unlikely to fall much further or are soon likely to rise. From the point of view of the business enterprise this means a falling off in its rate of sales and by the same token a decline in its rate of cash receipts. The reduction in the rate of consumers' outlay occasioned by the belief that the fall in prices is not yet over means a diminution in the sales of business enterprises and also their cash receipts. Similarly, if business concerns look forward to a further fall in prices they too have an incentive to decrease their merchandise and inventory holdings and to possess cash instead. But it is manifestly impossible for *all* business enterprises generally to decrease their inventories and to hold cash under circumstances where ultimate consumers have a reduced incentive to purchase. It is simply impossible for *all* business enterprises to flee to cash and away from merchandise and other assets likely to fall in price unless consumers are willing to increase their purchases by a considerable fraction. But we have already shown that individuals as well as business concerns have an incentive to postpone buying until the fall in prices has run its course. Under the circumstances the net result is likely to be a fall in prices all round without any marked increase in the rate of flow of goods into the hands of consumers. Selling prices are marked down, inventories are revalued, but there is very little gain in the unit sales of business enterprises. But what of all this in relation to working capital problems during a downswing?

If selling prices fall, and unit sales increase less than proportionately, then cash receipts from sales must likewise decline, for cash receipts are the product of the number of units sold times the price at which each was sold. The rate of cash receipts is very likely to fall off. Cash receipts will also be reduced for another reason: during a downswing in business activity the number of uncollectible accounts is likely to rise; persons lose their jobs, their incomes are decreased, and their ability to pay falls. That is, not only does the current cash income from sales tend to fall off but also cash receipts from on account sales of earlier periods decline likewise. Consequently for most business enterprises there is likely to be a falling off in the rate of cash receipts per unit of time.

3. *The downswing and cash outlays.* Let us now consider the matter of cash outlays. We have shown that during a decline in business activity the rate of flow of cash receipts per unit of time is likely to decrease. This need cause no difficulty in and of itself provided there is a corresponding decline in the rate of cash outlays. Even though cash receipts do decline the business enterprise may none the less continue to meet its obligations provided only that the necessary cash outlays fall proportionately or more than proportionately.

Regardless of the fact that a firm's customers may tend to pay their accounts and notes more slowly or to default thereon in larger proportion, the enterprise none the less must pay its obligations to creditors promptly in order to avoid failure. The unfortunate fact that others do not pay the firm does not permit the firm to reduce its payments correspondingly; creditors must be paid or failure will ensue. During any interval of time the cash payments of a business enterprise are of two sorts: first, cash payments required to liquidate obligations incurred in previous periods but not payable until this period; second, cash outlays necessary during the current period because of current operations. It is important to bear this distinction in mind for purposes of analysis. The first will include payments for merchandise previously purchased, payments to short-term creditors such as commercial banks, interest on long-term indebtedness such as bonds, taxes of various kinds, and perhaps other items. In large measure these payments are the consequence of decisions made in past periods and they have to be met even though the decisions are now seen to have been in error. If the firm had known that selling prices were going to fall, it certainly would not have bought such large stocks of merchandise and contracted to pay for it now at the higher prices of an earlier day. The firm will probably be forced to sell its merchandise at lower prices than it had anticipated but it will be forced to pay for it at the purchase price. Previous commitments of this character are typically unalterable and the enterprise will be forced to make whatever cash outlays they require.

Cash outlays on account of current operations, however, are of a different stripe. While the firm may cease production of any immediately salable product entirely, that is, reduce production of what it sells to zero, it is not usually true that all cash outlays will be thereby avoided. In most enterprises it is usually necessary to keep a certain skeleton working force employed and drawing wages and salaries even though the plant, in the popular sense, is not operating at all; the office and sales forces usually remain at work as do the more non-replaceable plant employees. In other words, there is usually an irreducible minimum below which cash outlays cannot be reduced quite apart from any obligations incurred in previous periods. Such cash outlays are unavoidable if the enterprise is to remain in existence. Although there is this more or less fixed minimum of cash outlays in any enterprise, even with zero plant output, it is often the case that current sales require cash outlays larger than this basic minimum. It is typically true that even in a downswing sales do not fall to zero and that these current sales require current cash outlays.[32] Moreover if such sales are not entirely from stock some fabrication of salable product will be unavoidable. Hence the firm will be forced to make cash outlays on this account. Cash expenditures over and above the basic minimum, however, are matters of business judgment and discretion; they are not fixed and unalterable in the same manner as accounts payable. The management has to decide where and how much to cut and trim the cash outlays occasioned by the simple fact that the firm is trying to stay in business.

In summary, then, the cash outlays which a firm will be called upon to make during a downswing in business arise from two sides: first, those occasioned by past managerial decisions which the firm must meet to avoid failure; secondly, those made necessary by the fact that the firm is endeavoring to remain in existence and carry on in the current period. The first group allows the enterprise little or no choice; the second is partially discretionary but partially predetermined also by the nature of the business venture.[33]

4. *Cash flows and debt-paying ability*. The crucial question for failure is the comparison between the decreased rate of flow of cash receipts and the decreased rate of flow of cash outlays. If the former decreases more than the latter the firm will be embarrassed by insufficient cash. The danger of this happening is undoubtedly greater during a downswing and depression for reasons we have already indicated. If it should occur, the firm is likely to fail unless it can succeed in obtaining additional cash resources to augment

[32] As a general proposition the decline in unit sales will be the greater the farther removed is the enterprise from consumers' goods markets. The "acceleration" principle comes in here. Also the more durable goods will suffer a greater decline than less durable goods. It is worth noting, too, that the decline in prices is less, according to empirical studies, in capital goods and durable consumption goods. These industries are more quasi-monopolistic and price rigidities are more common.

[33] The distinction sought for in the text above might be alternatively expressed as follows. The first group includes cash outlays necessary to pay off liabilities (in the balance sheet sense). The second group includes cash outlays which involve the exchange of cash for some other type of asset. This alternative formulation brings out the distinction reasonably well but less completely and sharply than that we have employed above.

its diminishing balance. The alternative methods of raising cash during a slump are certainly not numerous. Although in boom times the firm will ordinarily borrow from the banks or sell more securities, in a depression the security markets are not receptive and the commercial banks likewise are not eager to grant new credits or extend existing loans. The firm may find that the ordinary sources from which a depleted cash account might be increased are not open. If cash receipts continue to lag behind cash outlays, despite all possible parings of the latter, the firm may have to resort to its last alternative, namely, an endeavor to convert some of its assets not ordinarily intended for sale into cash. But here again difficulties abound. As we have argued in an earlier chapter, the market for used capital goods is far from perfectly competitive; prospective buyers are apt to be few and the prices bid are likely to be but a small fraction of the worth of the assets to the selling firm under more favorable business conditions. Furthermore, during a slump, the number of prospective buyers will be further diminished because few, if any, enterprises will be acutely conscious of an immediate deficiency in productive capacity.[34] The marginal productivity of additional capital goods seems to them quite small; any bids they offer will be predicated almost exclusively on possible future needs rather than on current requirements. Hence the amount of cash to be realized from this source on short notice is not usually very large. Thus, if cash receipts decline more than cash outlays, if the enterprise cannot sell more securities nor borrow from the banks, and if, finally, it cannot convert other assets into cash, then there can be but one final result: the enterprise will have to default on its obligations; it will have to fail.

A period of declining business activity, therefore, is very apt to create working capital problems of sufficient acuteness to induce failure. In general these will be the more serious the more rapidly the recession proceeds; a slow decline creates fewer difficulties because there is more time in which to make adjustments to it.[35] If

[34] Our earlier remarks in Chapter X, sec. III, 3, may be referred to in this connection.

[35] It might be inferred from what we have said that cyclical working capital

changes are completely sudden and unforeseen there is no opportunity to make any adaptations whatsoever.

It might be argued, to be sure, that effective management of working capital is of just such a character that the course of development described in the previous section is not permitted to occur. In view of the patent fact that not *all* business enterprises fail in a depression, such a contention has a certain validity and pertinence. On these grounds we might, perhaps, have included all the foregoing as a subdivision under the main heading of managerial incompetence. Regardless of the sequence of treatment, however, the main point is sufficiently clear: a downswing in business activity accompanied by a price deflation and a quest for liquidity that is fairly general creates unusual difficulties in the management of working capital assets to maintain debt-paying ability. While all business enterprises do not fail during a depression the scramble for cash and its accompaniments may force some of them to default to their creditors, that is to fail.

VI. SUMMARY

Failure in the narrow economic sense means essentially a failure in expectations: the returns to invested capital have fallen short of those anticipated at the time the enterprise was brought into existence. Failure in this sense by no means guarantees the withdrawal of productive capacity or any immediate difficulty in paying creditors' obligations. In business parlance failure means inability to pay maturing cash claims and the obvious immediate cause is insufficient cash balances. The underlying causes which usually work together may be classified as economic change, incompetence, fortuities, and the trade cycle.

New commodities, new production methods, new sources of supply, alterations in the structural organization of industry, and other changes are continually occurring in a capitalistic economy and these impinge upon particular corporations with varying

problems are confined to downswings and depression. This of course is not true. Yet while there are special working capital problems of a boom, they are not so serious nor so difficult to adjust to for the enterprise.

force. Change itself is unimportant, but the inability of the enterprise to adapt itself to the changes in the data sufficiently to maintain earnings and debt-paying ability may often cause failure. Specialized capital goods and the difficulties of obtaining new investment to finance the needed adaptations are perhaps the most serious obstacles to successful modifications.

Incompetence will first manifest itself in the inability of the enterprise to earn profits. But this is only the end result; the mismanagement must lie in the handling of working capital and/or fixed capital assets. Ratio analysis of financial and operating statements is useful in determining the kind of incompetence and its degree. Two inherent limitations of ratio analysis must be borne in mind: "ideal" ratios cannot be determined by abstract reasoning and there is no ideal system of weighting the relative importance of the different ratios. Nevertheless ratio analysis is much superior to casual and unorganized observation. Sometimes the incompetence is to be found not so much in the day-to-day operations of the business as in major decisions of financial policy: the combination of bonds and shares, dividend practices, etc.

Fortuities are probably the least important cause of business failure and in the nature of the case generalizations concerning them are impossible.

The business cycle reinforces the effectiveness of the other causes of business failure because slumps enhance the difficulties of successful adaptation. On the other hand the downswing of the cycle by its effect upon the flow of cash receipts relative to cash outlays may magnify the problem of maintaining debt-paying ability. The diminished flow of cash receipts from current and previous sales is not always offset by corresponding diminutions in inescapable cash outlays. New borrowings and sales of assets in order to raise cash are frequently impossible to negotiate. Although not all concerns are similarly pinched the general deflation and rise in liquidity preference may force some enterprises to default to creditors.

REFERENCES: CHAPTER XII

Burtchett, F. F.—*Corporation Finance.* Chs. 42, 43.
Field, K.—*Corporation Finance.* Ch. 28.

GERSTENBERG, C. W.—*Financial Organization and Management*. Ch. 23.
HOAGLAND, H. E.—*Corporation Finance*. Ch. 41.

————

GUTHMANN, H. G.—*Analysis of Financial Statements*, New York. 1935.
MERTON, R. K.—"Fluctuations in the Rate of Industrial Invention," *Quarterly Journal of Economics*, Vol. 49.

Chapter XIII

SOME ECONOMIC ASPECTS OF COR-PORATE REORGANIZATION

I. The Distinction Between Readjustment and Reorganization. II. The Valuation Problem in Corporate Reorganization. III. The Reduction in the Face Value of the Claims Against the Assets. IV. Summary.

In the preceding chapter we sought to elucidate the more important underlying causes of business failure. In this connection we emphasized the very important consequences flowing from the fact that under modern industrial conditions capital goods tend to assume specialized forms from which only quite specific services may be derived. We emphasized further that the value of such specialized capital goods in uses other than those for which they were designed was typically only a very small fraction of their purchase cost. Likewise important is the fact that such specific capital goods often possess great durability; frequently a long time interval must elapse before they exhaust their ability to render the particular services for which they were designed. Consequently, for the reasons cited, when business enterprises fail, either in the economic or in the business sense, it does not necessarily imply a corresponding withdrawal of productive capacity from industry. On the contrary, when business corporations fail, especially large concerns in the industrial sphere, the resulting adjustments are not the withdrawal of capital goods as physical items representing productive capacity, rather they are adjustments altering the amount and character of the claims against such capital goods as assets. The *value* of the assets will be recomputed and revised downwards; and likewise of course, the face amount of the claims against the assets will be scaled down correspondingly. In other words, nowadays when industrial corporations fail they are not as a rule broken up and liquidated but are reorganized instead. As we have just said, the adjustments following upon failure are typically adjustments involving the rights and claims of different groups against the enterprise; only incidentally and partially is there a breaking up and transfer to alternative uses of the capital goods from which the claims against the enterprise derive their value. The assets are revalued, the claims against the assets are written down, but the particular working relationship in which the capital goods stand with reference to one another—the productive capacity in the physical sense—typically remains unaltered. If the nature of capital goods were such that disinvestment were as easy as investment, then business enterprises as such would always be liquidated when failure occurred.[1] But as we have been at some pains to point out this is simply not the fact situation. As a consequence the failure of a large business enterprise is much more likely to be followed by reorganization than by liquidation.

We must not create the impression, on the other hand, that when business enterprises fail they are *always* reorganized. Where only a small fraction of the total investment is represented by capital goods with a high degree of specificity, the alternative of liquidation is the better choice. Financial enterprises, such as banks, insurance companies, brokerage and investment houses, etc., are typically liquidated rather than reorganized; so, too, with concerns in the wholesale and retail trade. While such enterprises often do possess some capital goods of a specialized sort they are usually a small proportion of the total assets. More important perhaps as a factor inducing liquidation rather than reorganization is that the total value of the assets considered as individual items in separation is not greatly different from their value in the particular combination in which they happen to stand with reference to one another at the time of failure. An insurance company's investments in bonds, mortgages, etc., derive little or none of their worth from the fact that they happen to be contained in one portfolio; on the

---

[1] If disinvestments were easy, then an enterprise would cease operations as soon as it was discovered to be a failure in the economic sense, i.e., to be yielding a return less than the going rate of interest. But in most cases inability to secure a return on historical investment equal to the going rate does not mean that the best choice of the available alternatives is to cease operations. It is usually impossible to retrieve the original commitment in full and in liquid form. See Ch. XII, sec. II.

other hand, a railroad line is something more than a pile of steel rails, wooden sleepers, tie-plates, and six inch spikes. In the first instance little or nothing is lost by disassembling the assets and selling them item by item; in the second to break up the relationship in which the component parts stand to one another is to sacrifice most of their value. Liquidation is called for in the one but reorganization in the other.

I. THE DISTINCTION BETWEEN READJUSTMENT AND REORGANIZATION

In the preceding chapter we distinguished between failure of an enterprise in the economic sense and failure in the business sense. From the point of view of economic theory an enterprise is a failure if the rate of return actually derived from the capital investment is less than the rate available on alternative investments at the time the enterprise was brought into existence. Alternatively, in terms of a cost-income analysis, we may express the same idea by saying that average revenue is less than average cost where the latter includes a return on the invested capital equal to that available on alternative employments for capital at the time of promotion. Failure in the everyday business sense, on the other hand, means default, or impending default, on obligations to pay cash as they mature.

This distinction between the economic and business sense of failure allows us to demarcate more precisely than is usually possible corporate readjustment from corporate reorganization. Corporate reorganization in the technical usage follows upon failure in the business sense of inability to meet obligations to pay cash claims as they mature. Failure in the business sense may lead either to liquidation or to reorganization; and because the firm cannot meet its obligations as they mature it has no choice in the matter and must accept whatever consequences the law provides. Creditors' claims are superior to owners' claims and therefore the proprietors must step aside to allow creditors to pursue their legal remedies. The important consequence of failure in the everyday business sense is that it sets in motion certain legal processes leading to certain changes which the owners of the enterprise must accept regardless of their own wishes in the matter. In other words, the processes and changes are not optional with the proprietors but obligatory.[2]

Corporate readjustment, on the other hand, differs from corporate reorganization in that in readjustment the changes which result from the process are those initiated by the shareholders of their own choosing and not forced upon them because of actual or impending default on obligations to pay cash. The stockholders of a corporation may have good or insufficient reasons for desiring the readjustment; this is less important than the fact that they are the group which decides that something ought to be done. In readjustment no legal machinery is placed in operation because nothing has occurred which gives rise to an action at law or in equity. The corporation has violated no statute or contract. The nature of the readjustment, however, may be the modification of contracts by consent of both parties.

Readjustment is frequently called for as a consequence of failure in the economic sense defined and it may take either one or both of two general forms: first, a revaluation of assets to recognize the degree to which the enterprise is a failure economically; second, a modification of the contractual rights of security holders and/or a restatement of the value of the security holders' claims against the corporation. During the years 1930-1935 many corporations recognized that the stated book values of their assets were considerably in excess of what those assets were worth on any valuation based upon prospective earnings. Many boards of directors felt that under the circumstances the proper procedure was to reduce the value of the assets to a more reasonable figure. Depending upon the amount of the balance in the surplus account, such write-downs

---

[2] The above may not be an entirely realistic description of the course of events in some cases. So-called friendly receiverships in equity as well as 77B and Chandler Bill proceedings have been initiated frequently by those in charge of the enterprise; but here it appears to those in charge to be preferable to hurry along the legal process rather than to allow the regular course of events ultimately to set it in motion. In actual practice, of course, the owners often influence the final plan of reorganization even in cases where the value of their claims is quite small; but in the final analysis this simply means that creditors do not exert their powers to the full extent.

in the value of the assets did or did not necessitate some restatement of the corporate capital. In other corporations the value of the assets was not written down but the corporate capital in the legal sense was restated at a smaller figure in order to write off an accumulated deficit. The motives leading to such corporate readjustments were many: a desire to reduce the annual accounting charges for depreciation sufficient to permit the reporting of net profits; a wish to begin (legal) dividend payments to shareholders as soon as possible without first restoring impaired capital resulting from past losses; and perhaps, in some cases, nothing more than a wish to present financial statements more in harmony with the facts.[3] Here we have instances of corporations which are a failure in the economic sense of the returns falling short of original expectations but where there is no default of obligations to creditors. Depending upon all the relevant considerations it may or may not be appropriate to readjust the value of the assets and the stated value of shareholders' claims.[4]

A different kind of corporate readjustment, as distinguished from corporate reorganization, is that in which shareholders' or creditors' contractual rights are altered by negotiation and subsequent agreement. These, too, typically result from failure in the economic sense. Many corporations at the time of their formation included cumulative preferred stock in their capitalization. When the financial plan was drafted, doubtless the earnings of the corporation were expected to be sufficient to pay these cumulative

[3] By writing down the book value of the assets against surplus created by restating the book value of shareholders' capital the shareholders merely accept as a capital charge now what would otherwise be expense debits against the accounting gross income of future periods. As a consequence the net income for these subsequent periods will be larger than if each had to bear its proportionate amount of the original purchase cost, or of original valuation, of depreciable assets. Some corporations during the great depression reduced the book value of their depreciable assets far below any discounted earnings valuation; the figures written into the fixed asset accounts were purely nominal.

[4] In strict logic one ought to include under corporate readjustment any upward revaluation of assets and corresponding credits to net worth accounts. These are less common and the motives for so doing less compelling than in the case of downward revisions. If the value of the assets is considerably understated the fact will show up in larger earnings anyway and there is little gain to the enterprise in reflecting this higher valuation on the books by other than a master valuation account such as good-will. Yet logically writing down the value of assets to recognize changed conditions is but the obverse of writing them up.

preferred dividends at regular intervals. As matters have worked out, however, the directors have not felt it safe or wise to declare these dividends, and accumulations have run up into sizable figures. Now so long as these past accumulations are unpaid the common shareholders cannot receive any dividends on their holdings. Since the preferred shareholders are not creditors of the corporation no legal consequences will follow even if the cumulative preferred dividends are never paid. But since both the preferred and the common shareholders are often anxious for the early resumption of dividend payments an adjustment may be worked out whereby the preferred shareholders receive something other than the full liquidation in cash of their accumulated back dividends. Or again, during trying times for the corporation, the preferred shareholders may agree to exchange their cumulative shares for non-cumulative preferred shares. Adjustments in the capitalization and the financial plan of this sort are very common. Such changes are not forced upon the shareholders by reason of default to creditors; they are initiated by all shareholders or suggested by one group thereof and accepted by another. Cases are not unknown, moreover, in which corporations have negotiated a moratorium from creditors on sinking fund clauses, or on interest payments, without any actual default first occurring.

To all changes such as these, involving the restatement of proprietors' capital, the modification of shareholders' contractual rights, exchanges of shares, the abrogation of creditors' contract clauses by negotiation, and perhaps others, *which are initiated voluntarily by the proprietors, or their representatives, and are not the consequence of legal proceedings* having been initiated by reason of actual or impending default on obligations to pay cash, the present writer would apply the phrase corporate readjustment. Where the changes—in the financial plan, the valuation of the assets, and the shareholders' equity—are not a matter of choice with the proprietors but are forced upon them because of legal procedure established for dealing with cases of actual or imminent nonpayment of debts he would apply the term corporate reorganization. Admittedly the distinction is not absolutely clear-cut in all instances; but it is sufficiently precise to be useful for most problems.

II. THE VALUATION PROBLEM IN CORPORATE REORGANIZATION

1. The factors determining liquidation value. 2. Asset values in reorganization. 3. Reorganization and investment expectations.

If a business enterprise has failed in the business sense there at once arises the important question of whether it ought to be liquidated or reorganized, and if the latter, what form the reorganization ought to take. At first thought it might appear that the choice between the alternatives of liquidation or reorganization is one turning upon the particular facts in each case and concerning which one can formulate no widely applicable generalizations. In the present writer's opinion this view is erroneous; certain broad logical principles seemingly can and should be applied in all cases of business failure. Let us examine this further.

When a corporation has failed, the important question is whether it ought to be liquidated or reorganized, and if the latter, what form the reorganization ought to take. Yet on what economic considerations does this decision turn? Surely it depends upon the value of the assets in their present combination as contrasted with their value in the dismembered state; in other words, upon the relative value of the non-cash assets in liquidation and in reorganization.[5]

1. The factors determining liquidation value. What the assets of a failed corporation will bring if separated out and liquidated depends essentially upon three considerations: (a) on the degree to which the capital goods (machines, buildings, equipment, etc.) are specialized in character or are capable of being adapted to alternative uses; (b) on the degree to which their significance and utilization, and hence their value or worth, are independent of or intimately bound up with the particular combination in which they

[5] An enterprise will usually pay cash claims upon it as long as possible, i.e., until default is unavoidable. Money being the value denominator the asset cash raises no problem of valuation at all. The really difficult problem is the money value of the non-cash assets.

now stand with reference to one another; (c) on the costs of liquidation.

a. If the assets consist largely of heavy equipment items, e.g., a steel-rolling mill, an oil refinery, or an hydro-electric plant, then they are almost incapable of being moved physically or of being adapted to other uses at all. Moreover the market for such second-hand capital goods is very imperfectly organized: the degree of product differentiation is so large that even other enterprises in the same industry can integrate them only imperfectly with their existing productive equipment; frequently too, buyers are so few as to produce a condition of oligopsony. If, on the other hand, the capital goods are such as an ordinary factory building, containing comparatively light and shiftable machinery (e.g., electric motors) with relatively many uses, they will have a high sales value. In the one case, the high degree of specificity of the capital goods and the prohibitive costs of physical transfer make their value in alternative uses almost zero; in the other, their more general character and smaller physical bulk give them a value apart from their present situation.

b. The degree to which the assets are closely integrated with one another into a pattern also tends to determine their liquidation value. Financial enterprises (banks, insurance companies, brokerage and investment houses) as well as wholesale and retail trading concerns typically have assets whose value in separation is not greatly different from their value in the particular combination in which they happen to stand at the time of failure. Obviously the same thing would not be true of the high tension transmission lines of an electric power company, the mains of a gas company, or the assembly line of an automobile manufacturer. In the latter cases the physical relation in which the capital goods stand to one another is the major reason for whatever value they have and that relationship cannot be undone without a heavy cost outlay. Matters such as these tend to be all-important in determining what the assets of a failed corporation will bring if disassembled and sold in piecemeal fashion.[6]

[6] The two characteristics of specialized uses and separability are, of course, not entirely unrelated: capital equipment that is highly specialized is often closely integrated with other capital goods from which it cannot be separated easily or

Not all the assets of a failed corporation, of course, will be of the capital goods type; there are the working capital assets also. In the main these are separable, much as the assets of financial enterprises, without great loss of value. Receivables, inventories, and the like, are usually less difficult to evaluate and in any given case one can compute their liquidation value within narrow limits.[7]

c. Our interest in the value of the assets of a failed corporation in liquidation centers upon their value net of any liquidation costs. The costs of liquidation will include labor and capital costs of disassembly plus any legal costs (e.g., a referee in bankruptcy), that are inevitable in the process. Such costs are not, however, a fixed sum but will vary with the methods employed. A very rapid liquidation may mean that less is received for the assets than if time is taken to find purchasers to whom the assets have greatest worth. Moreover, a hurried dismemberment by destructive methods, e.g., dynamite and crowbars, may be cheap if only the costs of dismemberment are considered, but may be very costly on a net basis if whatever alternative use value the capital equipment possesses is destroyed thereby. In general we assume that those methods of liquidation are employed which will yield the maximum value sum.

Let us designate this maximum value obtainable from liquidation by the symbol L. For any enterprise which has failed L can and must be computed before the relative wisdom of liquidation or

cheaply. In some measure also it would appear that there is an inverse relationship between the degree to which capital goods have alternative uses and are separable without substantial loss in value and the degree to which the enterprise is engaged in productive operations where the economies of large-scale production bulk large, especially if the latter are mainly physical in character. I do not believe the relationship holds all the way through, however, in the sense that where we find the one we invariably find the other.

[7] Complications may arise where the assets include securities sufficient to control subsidiary companies. Here the value of the stock interest will be determined by the relationship between the parent and the subsidiary and by the possibility of selling the controlling interest to another corporation. If the subsidiary is but an integral part of productive organization of the failed corporation, e.g., manufactures parts for, or is merely the marketing agency of its parent, then the worth of a controlling stock interest therein is mainly dependent upon the fate of the parent corporation. On the other hand, a public utility holding company controlling numerous operating companies in different sections of the country, does not add very much to their value over and above what they possess independently. Here a controlling stock interest can often be sold to another corporation regardless of what happens to the parent.

reorganization can be determined.[8] For as we have already argued, if the value of the assets in reorganization (which we will designate by R) is greater than L the corporation ought to be reorganized; if not, it ought to be liquidated so far as purely economic considerations are at stake.

2. *Asset values in reorganization.* In determining the value in reorganization of the assets of the failed corporation it must be emphasized at the outset that the figure we want is the value in reorganization of the assets *as they now stand.* It is this amount, which we may call R, which must be compared with their net liquidation value, L. But how compute the value in reorganization of the assets as they now stand?

Let us commence with a very simple problem familiar to everyone. Let us suppose that my automobile has been badly damaged in a collision. I am at once confronted with the problem of deciding whether it is better to have it repaired and placed in good running order, or to sell it to a junk dealer for the best price I can obtain. Clearly I cannot answer the question until I know three things: (a) the highest junk price I can obtain for the automobile in its present wrecked state; (b) how large a cash outlay is necessary to place it in a condition such as I desire; and (c) the value of the reconstructed car to me when repaired. With respect to all three we assume that the complete circumstances of time and place are given. In regard to (b) it is quite clear that the amount I can spend to place it in good running condition is not a fixed sum but to some extent a variable. Nevertheless we can suppose that I regard certain minor items, more in the nature of improvements than replacements, as "not worth their cost" to me, and that therefore I will not have them done. But that apart from these assume that the indispensable minimum cash outlay I will have to make for repairs is $125. Let us assume further and with respect to (c) that when these necessary repairs have been made the automobile will have a value to me exactly equal to the best purchase I can make in the used-car market for $200. Clearly, unless the best

---

[8] When we say that the liquidation value of the enterprise can be computed we do not mean to imply, of course, that it can be computed right down to the last dollar. All we mean is that L can be computed with reasonable accuracy; probably in most cases the margin of error in the estimates will not exceed 10 per cent.

price I can obtain for the car in its present wrecked state is something more than $75, it will pay me to have it repaired rather than to sell it for junk. For, by investing $125 in it, I can obtain a reconstructed car having a value of $200, from which it follows that to me the value of the car in its present wrecked state is not less than $75. If on the other hand an equally good substitute automobile is purchasable for $180, then the junk value plus my necessary investment must yield an automobile worth *more than* $180 before it will pay me to order the repairs.

An almost exactly similar problem is presented when we are trying to determine the value in reorganization of the assets of a failed corporation. It is this sum which, when compared with L, indicates the alternative merits of reorganization and liquidation.

An enterprise which has failed will almost invariably require additional capital investment as a part of the reorganization plan. From one point of view the very essence of reorganization is the investment of more capital, although according to the circumstances the amount needed may be great or small. In some cases perhaps to replenish working capital resources which have been dissipated in the interval immediately preceding failure is sufficient. In others, new machinery, the modernization of existing plant, etc., must also be undertaken if the reorganized enterprise is to compete effectively. Now the investment of additional capital as part of the process of reorganization is in all respects the same as any other problem of capital commitment. The same principles apply. In our discussion of promotion, dividend distribution, expansion, etc., we emphasized that the appropriate analysis for capital investment runs in marginal terms. The same reasoning holds with respect to reorganization. There is a certain optimum amount which under the circumstances it will pay to invest in reorganizing the enterprise. Call this amount M. The determinants of M are two: first, the marginal efficiency of capital [9] investment in the enterprise to be reorganized; second, the rate of interest. So long as the marginal

---

[9] It might be advisable for the reader to review what was said about the concept of "the marginal efficiency of capital" in Ch. X, sec. III, and also concerning the marginal principles of capital investment in Ch. IX, sec. I. Perhaps it is sufficient here to repeat that the marginal efficiency of an asset is the (anticipated) rate of return upon its cost.

efficiency of additional investment is greater than the rate of interest (the rate of return on capital in alternative uses), increments of investment are warranted. Alternatively stated, we can say that in the reorganization process additional capital should be invested up to that point at which the prospective rate of return on the last small unit of investment is equal to the rate of interest. This is the optimum amount of money, M, which it will pay to invest in the reorganization process. So much and no more is economically warranted.

Let us now assume that if the optimum amount of capital is invested the reorganized enterprise as a whole will have a value on the basis of its prospective earning power of an amount V. That is to say, the value of the assets of the failed concern as they now stand, plus the additional investment which it is worthwhile undertaking, will give the reorganized enterprise a *total* value designated by V. But if this be true, it is obvious at once that in reorganization the value of the assets of the failed concern *as they now stand* is indicated by the expression $(V-M)$. This residual we may designate by R; that is, $(V-M)$ equals R. As in the case of L, R must be interpreted as net after the deduction of any reorganization expenses. Now if we know that the value in reorganization of the assets of the failed concern is R, and that their value in liquidation is L, it follows obviously that if R is greater than L reorganization is the better alternative; while if L is greater than R liquidation is the proper choice.

We have endeavored to show that the value of R is a derivative of V, the value of the enterprise as a whole if the optimum amount of new investment is committed to it. What opportunities exist for the profitable investment of capital in the reorganization process will of course depend upon the whole factual situation surrounding each instance of failure. In some cases further investment will be waste of resources because the earning power of the reorganized corporation will still be very low. If that be true, dissolution in the most economical manner will best serve all interested parties. In other cases, however, the marginal efficiency of capital investment will be distinctly above the going rate of interest and the enterprise can be reorganized with considerable profit. In the last analysis reorganization is called for only on the belief that R is greater than L.[10]

3. *Reorganization and investment expectations.* We ought to emphasize, perhaps, that the decision to reorganize, evidencing a belief that R is greater than L, must be made on the basis of anticipated returns on capital investment rather than upon definite certainties. As in all cases of capital investment in the real world the prospective yield is tinged with uncertainty. Yet when a business enterprise fails an aura of gloom may so spread about the proceedings that persons take an unwarrantedly pessimistic view of the probable returns on additional investment. The vulgar phrase "throwing good money after bad" epitomizes the very common mental reaction of many persons towards new investment in a failed enterprise. Broadly speaking, in order to secure funds for reorganization the prospective returns on the additional capital there invested will have to appear notably greater than those available in alternative opportunities.[11] Unwarranted pessimism is as typical of reorganization as optimism is of promotion. Security holders and others, however, are probably not yet accustomed to consider capital investment incident to corporate reorganization as essentially the same as any other type of capital investment. There seems to be a tendency to regard them as quite unrelated and dissimilar problems. By and large this attitude is quite illogical.

[10] Throughout the whole of the present section we have talked about the value of the assets as a whole in reorganization as opposed to liquidation. Strictly speaking this is an oversimplification. Assuming that R is greater than L we should then consider each individual asset item and ask whether it is worth more as a part of the reorganized enterprise than the cash derived from liquidating it. Some assets probably should be liquidated even though by and large *the enterprise* ought to be reorganized. But the exposition in the text would have been greatly extended if the discussion had been carried through in this more accurate manner. Any reader can supply the necessary amendments or qualifications that the more precise formulation imposes. If we wish we may designate by the symbols $r_1, r_2, r_3, \ldots r_n$ the worth of the individual asset items in reorganization, and by $l_1, l_2, l_3, \ldots l_n$ their worth in liquidation. On this basis we have: $L = l_1 + l_2 + l_3 + \ldots + l_n$ and $R = r_1 + r_2 + r_3 + \ldots + r_n$.

[11] Something analogous is to be found in the simple example of a wrecked automobile earlier cited. The customary attitude here is one of undue suspicion of the effectiveness of the repaired automobile; people tend to feel that the accident may have caused undiscoverable damage to the car which will mar its usefulness and hence lessen its worth. Something of the same sort seems to characterize the attitude of persons contemplating additional capital investment in an enterprise that has failed. The analogy cannot be pushed too far however.

There is a further point however. Since R must be based upon estimates, it is impossible to demonstrate the absolute correctness of any single computation. Outwardly equally competent persons are likely to hold different views as to just how large R is; and in the reorganization process there may be considerable bickering between groups of claim-holders over this very question, e.g., shareholders insisting they have an equity that bondholders refuse to recognize.

III. THE REDUCTION IN THE FACE VALUE OF THE CLAIMS AGAINST THE ASSETS

1. The principle of absolute priority. 2. Some difficulties in the application of the rule of absolute priority. 3. Summary.

Our discussion so far has centered upon the relative values of the assets of a failed corporation in reorganization and liquidation. There is also, however, the problem of readjusting the claims against these assets.

Failure in the business sense is itself evidence that the total face value of the shareholders' and creditors' claims against the assets is greater than the value of the assets as they now stand; not all claims can be paid in full. This statement holds true, of course, on the assumption that the assets are evaluated in the only way relevant for present purposes: that is, on the basis of discounted earning power. It is of slight interest to a bondholder, concerned with interest and principal sums, to know that on an original cost less depreciation basis the value of the corporation's assets is more than the debts if these assets will not earn enough to pay his contractual interest. If original cost less depreciation were alone relevant the financial problems of the railroads of the United States would have long since disappeared, as in fact they have not. Failure of an enterprise means, *inter alia*, that the face value of the claims against the assets is greater than their value on a discounted earning power basis. The claims consist of two broad types: creditors' claims and ownership claims; and as already pointed out, it is only when creditors' claims go unpaid that certain well-known legal consequences ensue.

1. *The principle of absolute priority.* If an enterprise has failed, which implies that the total of the claims is greater than the value sum of the assets, then, regardless of whether reorganization or liquidation is called for, not all claims can be met in full. Let us suppose, however, that R is greater than L, that is, that the assets as they now stand have a greater value in reorganization than in liquidation, and that therefore reorganization will proceed. Notwithstanding this fact, the value sum R is less than the total face value of the claims against the assets. On what principle should the claims be reduced to an equality with the asset values, R?

Let us designate the total face amount of the claims by the symbol E; these claims will consist of creditors' claims, C, and owners' claims, O, so that, $E = C + O$. Now if R is less than E it is quite clear that some means must be invoked by which the two can be equated for, in the last analysis, the total amount available for partition among the claimants is no greater than R as the assets now stand. The problem is, By what procedure should the various individual items constituting E be reduced so that their diminished total is just equal to R? [12]

If all claims against the assets were on an equal footing, then each claim would merely be reduced by the proportion $\dfrac{E - R}{E}$. Yet by law and agreement the C claims rank ahead of the O claims.

[12] A considerable literature has grown up on this question of alternative principles for reducing E to R. Much of it is controversial and not always have the disputants focused their argumentation on precisely the same issues. The following works are especially worth studying, however, and the ensuing discussion in the text has benefited greatly from the ideas therein contained. Bonbright, J. C., and Bergermann, M. M., "Two Rival Theories of Priority Rights," *Columbia Law Review*, Vol. 28, pp. 127-165; unsigned note, "The 'Fair' Plan under Section 77B," *ibid.*, Vol. 35, pp. 391-404, 549-565; Frank, Jerome, "Some Realistic Reflections on Some Aspects of Corporate Reorganization," *Virginia Law Review*, Vol. 19, pp. 541-570, 698-718; Barrett, E. B., "'Fair Plan' under Section 77B, Applicability of the Boyd Case," *Michigan Law Review*, Vol. 34, pp. 992-1002; Foster, R. S., "Conflicting Ideals for Reorganization," *Yale Law Journal*, Vol. 44, pp. 923-960. There is a good and easily accessible discussion of the "fairness" problem in corporate reorganization in Bonbright, J. C., *Valuation of Property*, New York, 1937, Vol. 2, pp. 864-870. The earlier cases and approaches to the problem are discussed in Rosenberg, J. N., Swaine, R. T., and Walker, R., *Corporate Reorganization and the Federal Court*, New York (Baker, Voorhis), 1924. This volume reprints certain earlier published law review articles by these writers.

The appropriate logic, therefore, in reducing E to R would seem to be to commence with the O claims and, in reverse order of their relative priorities, to lop off claims until E were reduced to R. If all the O claims were wiped out and E were still greater than R, then it would be necessary to follow the same procedure with the C claims until ultimately the diminished E were equal to R.[13] This scheme just outlined for scaling down claims, made necessary because E is greater than R, has come to be known as the rule of absolute priority.[14] It seems to accord with the legal principles usually followed for partitioning property between superior and inferior claimants. Contracting parties are presumed to know what they are doing; hence when shareholders admit creditors (e.g., bondholders) as prior claimants to assets and earnings the presumption is that they know what this means.[15] Therefore, if the corporation

[13] Since the total face amount of the claims in particular orders of priorities is, in practice, often quite large—e.g., there may be an issue of preferred shares amounting to several millions of dollars—it may be necessary to apply a less than 100 per cent reduction within a particular group in order to equate E to R; all claimants in any one group stand on an equal footing and must be treated alike. But as between groups surely the logical principle in scaling down claims is to wipe them out completely in inverse order of their priority until those left are no greater than R.

[14] Bonbright and Bergermann, who seem to have christened this doctrine the absolute priority rule, were at the time of writing willing to allow an exception in the case of first lien bonds carrying such a low rate of interest that before failure they typically sold below par. They argued that (*op. cit.*, pp. 156-157) to give these bondholders par for their claims would produce the somewhat paradoxical result that they were better off after the reorganization than if no failure had occurred; for in reorganization they would get par for their claims while without failure their bonds consistently sold below par because of the low contractual rate of interest.

To the present writer, however, this seems an illogical mode of reasoning running contrary to the whole spirit of the absolute doctrine. Even though the bonds have a low face rate of interest they would gradually appreciate to par as their maturity date approached if the enterprise remained a going concern. But according to the contract, default on the interest automatically advances the maturity date of the principal precisely as if the ultimate maturity had been reached. Hence there is no reason why first lien bondholders should have their claims scaled down simply because the corporation had itself brought about the maturity date *de facto* somewhat earlier than anticipated originally. Ultimately the bondholders would get par if the enterprise stayed out of the courts. They should get the same, if they are first claimants, when it fails.

[15] We do not mean to imply that in certain contractual relations special safeguards will not be necessary to minimize the dangers of sharp dealing: the complications of modern bond indentures are probably a case in point. There is no reason to suppose, however, that shareholders as a class are more apt to misunderstand their pledges than are bondholders their rights. In fact the presumption is,

fails it is only reasonable to insist that the absolute priority rule should be the general principle adhered to for paring claims against assets and earnings. In solvent enterprises this is certainly the rule followed: operating losses are charged against the owners' claims, not the creditors', and everyone accepts the practice as a matter of course; symmetrically, therefore, one has a right to expect the same policy when concerns fail. As one legal scholar has written: [16]

Reorganization has supplanted liquidation as the normal consequence of the failure of large corporations. It is offered as an alternative to the sacrifice of going concern values which usually exceed liquidation values. Yet creditors' and even preferred stockholders' rights are normally conceived of as rights and priorities in liquidation. This is both the abstract legal conception, and the natural implication of the financial documents and sales literature whether used to obtain mercantile credit or to sell securities with liens and preferential rights. The expectations of priority are created both with reference to what may be realized in the event of corporate failure and as sanctions to minimize the risks of failure. The promoters and managers identified with the junior stock are to be kept from rash solicitation or use of capital by the fear that whatever losses occur must wipe out their own investment stake. In supplanting liquidation as the corporate day of judgment, reorganization must offer equivalent opportunity for realization of these rights and expectations of priority—yet the attempt to insist on strict enforcement of priorities usually interferes with the conservation of going concern values. The incompatibility of these two desirable objectives gives rise to conflicting ethical attitudes and ideals—one punitive and the other practical. These ideals manifest respectively the basic human passions of vengeance and avarice. Each ideal has had its own typical champions.

The rule of absolute priority for scaling down claims in corporate reorganization is apparently generally accepted as "fair and reasonable" by most legal writers. The one notable exception seems to be Mr. R. T. Swaine who has propounded an alternative principle known as the "relative priority of income rule." In contrast with the absolute rule the relative rule would insist that fairness is achieved in reorganization plans provided the parties in interest are left undisturbed in the order of their priority of claims

if anything, the other way about for the reason that bond contracts are much more complicated.

[16] Foster, R. S., *loc. cit.*, pp. 925-926.

on income. That is, those having a first claim on income before failure will be given a first claim on income in the reorganized enterprise, and so on down the line. Strictly applied this would mean that no group of claimants would ever be wiped out entirely in a plan of reorganization although what some would receive would have little or no value at all because the earnings of the reorganized corporation would never amount to enough to yield them anything. The relative rule would countenance the conversion of first and unconditional claims (e.g., first mortgage bonds) into first contingent claims (e.g., income bonds) even though common shareholders were given, say, option warrants under the same plan.[17]

In addition to the fact that the relative rule in practice is likely to preserve rather than eliminate stratified capital structures, it is premised throughout on the assumption that it is socially desirable to accord debtors (shareholders) lenient treatment at the expense of creditors. Yet the justification for such an assumption is by no means self-evident. It could scarcely be argued that, *as a class*, bondholders are better able to bear losses than shareholders. Indeed a good case could be made for the reverse. The proverbial "widows and orphans" are more likely to own bonds than shares. Moreover those who urge the virtues of the relative rule often emphasize the essential similarity of bondholders and shareholders as joint adventurers taking risks. Yet these same persons would certainly be unwilling to grant that bondholders should receive more than their

[17] For a detailed statement of the relative doctrine see Mr. Swaine's articles: "Reorganization of Corporations: Certain Developments of the Last Decade," *Columbia Law Review*, Vol. 27, pp. 901-931; and "Reorganization of Corporations" in Ballantine, A. A. (ed.), *Some Legal Phases of Corporate Financing, Reorganization, and Regulation*, Chicago (Callaghan & Co.), 1931, pp. 133-230. The relative priority rule has been described by a legal writer as follows: "The greatest departure from the orthodox rule is the so-called relative priority theory. This rejects any necessity of satisfying claims in full and treats reorganization as a revitalization of the corporation in which all interested parties share the burden of rehabilitation. Priority is recognized by preserving in the new structure the old security ranking, so that each interest holder receives his *pro rata* share of that new security issue which replaces his previous one, with an approximately equal income claim, but possibly of a less secured character; and the providers of new cash receive whatever more is necessary to attract their capital." Unsigned note, "The 'Fair' Plan in Corporate Reorganization: II," *Columbia Law Review*, Vol. 35, pp. 550-551; notes omitted.

contractual rights where the corporation has proven wonderfully successful instead of a dismal failure.

2. *Some difficulties in the application of the rule of absolute priority.* Although the principle of absolute priority in scaling down claims against the assets is theoretically precise and, in the writer's opinion, eminently reasonable, we must not overlook certain difficulties that may arise in its application.

The first of these difficulties is that V, from which R is derived, is necessarily based upon expectations as to the earning power of the reorganized enterprise through future time; consequently, within a certain range, different claim-holding groups may hold conflicting views as to the value of R, and in the nature of the case, it is impossible to demonstrate the absolute "correctness" of any one value for R. An extremely "conservative" view of the earnings of the reorganized enterprise will mean the exclusion of certain claimants in reorganization that would be admitted where V (and hence R) are appraised more optimistically; consequently in drafting the reorganization plan it may be proper to grant them contingent claims and await developments rather than to blot them out entirely. Should the pessimistic forecasts prove correct their contingent claims will then be worthless but they will prove of value if the reorganized corporation should be more profitable than anticipated.[18]

A second difficulty in rigidly applying the absolute priority rule in practice is associated with the acquisition of indispensable new investment. It is the investment of additional funds, M, that renders V greater than R; moreover if no funds can be raised from any source, the amount available for partition among the claimants against the failed corporation is L, which is by assumption less

[18] As is common knowledge, shareholders in real cases of reorganization are apt to insist that the assets of the failed corporation are worth more than creditors will admit and that under any "reasonable" valuation they have an equity that should be recognized. Under equity receivership reorganizations there was no satisfactory means of resolving such disputes; but under 77B and Chapter X of the Chandler Bill the court has power to decide. The basic source of such disputes, however, is that R is based upon the expectations. It seems to the present writer that whatever virtues Mr. Swaine's relative priority doctrine possesses spring from the fact that R is based on estimates and therefore its value is speculative rather than certain.

than R. Since persons are often hesitant about investing in an enterprise that has once failed, the contributors of new money may drive a hard bargain and insist that they be given claims against the reorganized corporation *greater* than the amount of the new capital they invest, i.e., M. In value terms, the total claims against the reorganized corporation available for allocation are, of course, exactly equal to V, the value of the enterprise after the new capital has been invested to reorganize it. Now if investors did *not* demand concessions because they are putting funds into a corporation that has already failed once, they would be satisfied with claims against the reorganized enterprise of an amount M, which would leave for the old claim-holders an amount R.[19] But if those who provide the new capital to carry through the reorganization insist on favors they will demand new securities with a value greater than M; but this means that the old claim-holders will obtain from the reorganization something less than R. Theoretically, if those who supply the new money acted in concert they could force the old claim-holders to accept claims against the reorganized corporation of an amount less than R by as much as $R - L$, i.e., give them no more than L. Without new capital the alternative to reorganization is liquidation and therefore those holding claims against the failed corporation will gain through reorganization provided they get anything more than they would receive in liquidation, i.e., if they receive claims against the reorganized corporation having a value greater than L. Because there are alternative means of raising cash, that is, no monopoly exists among holders of cash balances, the old claim-holders probably will not have to concede as much as $(R - L)$; but they may well have to sacrifice something in order to get new capital. If sacrifices do have to be made in order to call forth new investment, they should be exacted from those in the lower orders of claimants. As we have already observed the old claims, C and O, are arranged in a hierarchy and therefore if in reorganization they are to receive less than R (because of the insistence of those putting up the new money), the sacrifices should be imposed on the principle of absolute priority.

[19] We assume, of course, that in reducing E to R, claims are eliminated according to the principle of absolute priority already discussed.

In the case of reorganization, of course, the sources from which the new money is to be raised will tend to determine the kind of sacrifices imposed on the old claimants in favor of the suppliers of new funds. If those who invest new money have had no previous connection with the venture they may insist that the securities they receive shall occupy an exclusively first claim on earnings and assets. On the other hand, an appeal to *existing* claimholders to provide the necessary cash may well take the form of offering them more for their old claims than they ought to receive under a strict application of the rule of absolute priority, i.e., more than their proper share of R. For example, to secure new investment for reorganization, a group of shareholders may be given new shares having a value substantially greater than the sum of the new cash they contribute and the value of their interest in R. In many a case of reorganization in the real world, of course, cash will be derived from both new investors and existing claimholders and as a consequence both types of sacrifice will be made by the existing claim-holders.[20]

These genuine and by no means negligible difficulties often encountered in applying the absolute priority rule to actual cases of reorganization must not suggest that we regard it as impractical or unworkable. On the contrary, since claims have to be scaled down in reorganization, it is essential that the ideal that

---

[20] The point may be made clearer and more precise as follows: Granted $E = C + O$, let $C = (c_1 + c_2 + c_3)$ and $O = (o_1 + o_2 + o_3)$, where the small letters designate the respective classes of creditors and owners in order of priority. As before let $V = R + M$. Since the enterprise has failed, we know that $E > R$. Let us assume in the instant case that $E > R$ by the amount $(o_2 + o_3)$; in other words, if we like, that the second preferred and common shareholders have no equity in the assets. Then it follows that $R = (c_1 + c_2 + c_3 + o_1)$ or more briefly $R = (C + o_1)$ and, of course, $R - C = o_1$. Now if the creditors find it unnecessary to make any concessions in order to get the first preferred shareholders to put up all the new money, M, the first preferred shareholders would receive claims against the reorganized corporation of a value $(M + o_1)$. But in the case under discussion we assume that first preferred shareholders need urging in the form of more attractive terms, hence they are offered claims against the reorganized corporation of an amount greater than $M + o_1$. But if the preferred shareholders get more the creditors must get less; therefore the creditors will obtain claims against the reorganized enterprise of something less than $(c_1 + c_2 + c_3)$. How much less will depend upon their ability to raise cash from other sources; but in any case they will not, if they are rational, sacrifice more than the amount $(R - L)$.

the principle formulates be given explicit statement and accorded general acceptance by the courts. We can work out the niceties of particular reorganization plans effectively only if, conceptually, we have an ideal towards which we are striving. Since under the newer reorganization statutes judges and others are forced to pass upon the "fairness" of reorganization plans, it is extremely important that they have common concepts of fairness that are clear and precise as ideals. Otherwise only chaos will result. The absolute priority doctrine seems to provide both a simple and reasonable ideal that can be set against actual plans of reorganization for comparison and judgment. If because of practical considerations—such, for instance, as the inherent difficulty of determining V and its derivatives precisely and the direct money cost of attempting to do so [21]—the absolute principle is only approximated, not fully achieved, in real world cases of reorganization, we must accept such compromises as reasonable and defensible because of the inherent complications of the whole problem of corporate reorganization.

3. *Summary*. As between the alternative standards of fairness of absolute priority and relative priority it must be confessed that, so long as fairness alone is under consideration, the weight of argument is definitely on the side of the absolute rule. The absolute rule conforms with legal precepts and the understanding of the parties at the time the contracts were drafted. There would seem to be no compelling reason for establishing a unique rule for creditor-debtor relations merely to deal with the problem of corporate reorganization. The relative priority rule would seem to be a rule useful to stockholders and other junior claimants in times of disaster, but not a rule that they would wish to embrace in times of success. Logically or ethically it is difficult to make a case for such an arrangement. On the grounds of fairness one must espouse the rule of absolute priority.

Absolute justice, however, is something rarely achieved completely in the world as we know it. Full justice is only one of

---

[21] It may be observed in passing that where V is so much a matter of expectation and judgment increased cost outlays to determine its amount yield very little increase in the precision of the estimates after a certain rather early point.

several conflicting ideals. And it is at this point that the arguments of the practical man acquire force and relevance. Every right-thinking man desires justice as opposed to injustice. Yet he would be a rare man indeed who would insist that *absolute* justice must be meted out wholly without regard to the costs and sacrifices involved. The problem of corporate reorganization surely is a case in point. In order to raise additional capital, to reduce the costs of reorganization, and to hasten the whole procedure, strict justice must probably be tempered with expediency. The consequence is that, while one may espouse the absolute priority doctrine as the ideal of fairness in dealing with reorganization problems, he could also admit certain modifications of it to cope with the exigencies of practical affairs.

None of the foregoing must be interpreted to mean that we are urging the abandonment of the absolute rule as the ideal of fairness. On the contrary that ideal needs to be given full recognition by the courts. If because of a conflict with other ideals which must also be partially realized absolute fairness is not attained in each and every instance of reorganization, we must not infer that the ideals have been abandoned; rather, we must recognize these compromises as inevitable in view of the ramifications of the problem. Complete justice according to the absolute doctrine could doubtless be closely approximated in practice; but, beyond a certain point, one may question whether closer approximations are worth the increasing sacrifices (costs) that they impose in other directions.[22]

---

[22] What we are here contending for is not some form of compromise between the absolute priority rule and the relative priority rule, but only a partial tempering of strict justice with expediency. A compromise between the two rules, in the sense that in actual cases of reorganization both the absolute and relative rules are applied as criteria of fairness, is a bad arrangement. As Bonbright and Bergermann have shown (*op. cit.*), p. 163, it becomes a club by which reorganization managers may inflict sacrifices on proprietors and creditors in any manner desired. The absolute rule should be the ideal openly followed in judging the fairness of plans, and security buyers should be able to purchase their investment contracts with that understanding. Bonbright and Bergermann in the article cited, however, are of the opinion that the courts, in fact, have countenanced compromises in many cases. Yet it should be noted that they wrote in 1928 and therefore were dealing with equity procedure and not with section 77B and the Chandler Bill Cases under which judicial approval of fairness was and is expressly required.

IV. SUMMARY

We use the term readjustment for all changes in the recorded values of assets and alterations in the rights and privileges of security holders that are initiated voluntarily by the owners and are not the sequel to failure in the business sense earlier defined. Reorganization, on the other hand, is the consequence of actual or impending default on obligations to pay cash to creditors where the resulting changes in the financial plan, the valuation of the assets, etc., are not a matter of voluntary choice with the owners but are forced upon them.

Whether a failed corporation should be liquidated or reorganized depends upon the relative values of its assets as they now stand in liquidation and reorganization. The value of the assets in liquidation will be determined by the degree to which they possess alternative uses and are woven into a carefully integrated combination, and the costs of liquidation. The value of the assets in reorganization, on the other hand, is a derivative from the value the reorganized enterprise will possess if the optimum amount of new capital is invested in it. Its aggregate value minus the new investment committed to it, $(V - M)$, is the worth in reorganization of the assets of the failed corporation as they now stand. The relative values of R and L determine the choice between liquidation and reorganization.

Failure in the business sense is *ipso facto* evidence that the face value of the claims against the assets is greater than the worth of the assets. Consequently some principle must be invoked for reducing the claims to an equality with the assets available for partition. The rule of absolute priority—that claims should be eliminated in inverse order of their relative priorities until those remaining are just equal to R—seems to accord with general legal principles and the understanding of the parties at the time the contracts were drawn. The alternative rule of relative priority is based more upon considerations of practicality and expediency than any demonstrated logic or adherence to accepted legal principles. The rule of absolute priority, however, is not without some complications in application. The fact that V is a matter of expectations rather than certainties and that some sacrifices may be necessary to induce indispensable new investment may bring it about that the absolute rule cannot be completely realized in real cases of corporate reorganization. Nevertheless the absolute rule is the ideal which actual plans of reorganization should be made to approximate. This is all the more necessary where, as under the newer statutes, judges and others are required to pass upon the "fairness" of reorganization plans submitted to them.

REFERENCES: CHAPTER XIII

DEWING, A. S.—*Financial Policy*, Book VI, Ch. 1.
GERSTENBERG, C. W.—*Financial Organization and Management*. Chs. 34, 35.
HOAGLAND, H. E.—*Corporate Finance*. Ch. 42.

BONBRIGHT, J. C. & BERGERMANN, M. M.—"Two Rival Theories of Priority Rights," *Columbia Law Review*, Vol. 28.
BUSCHECK, A. J.—"A Formula for the Reorganization of Public Service Corporations," *Columbia Law Review*, Vol. 32.
NICHOLS, G. F.—"A Rationale of Corporate Reorganization," *Journal of Business of the University of Chicago*, Vols. 8, 9.
SPAITH, C. B. & WINDLE, J. K.—"Valuation of Railroads under Section 77 of the Bankruptcy Act," *Illinois Law Review*, Vol. 32.
Unsigned note—"Purposes and Financial Plans of Industrial Reorganizations," *Harvard Business Review*, January, 1929.
Unsigned note—"The Development of the Doctrine of Fairness," *Harvard Law Review*, Vol. 45.

Chapter XIV

LEGAL ASPECTS OF CORPORATE REORGANIZATION

I. The Critical Problems of Corporate Reorganization in Practice. II. Corporate Reorganization through Courts of Equity. III. Corporate Reorganization under Section 77B of the Bankruptcy Act. IV. Corporate Reorganization under Chapter X of the Chandler Act. V. Summary.

〰〰〰〰〰〰〰〰〰〰

Up to this point our discussion of corporate reorganization has been almost entirely theoretical in character. We have mainly concentrated upon those problems and decisions which are inherent in corporate reorganization *per se* rather than upon an analysis of the statutes and legal procedures under which corporations in the United States have been rehabilitated in practice. Primarily, we have sought to emphasize that the valuation question is of crucial importance in determining whether reorganization or liquidation is the appropriate sequel to business failure. Indeed, the valuation problem so dominates the whole atmosphere of corporate reorganization that, from one point of view, all other questions are subsidiary. The much-discussed question of "fairness" of reorganization plans, for example, is only meaningful on the assumption that an accepted valuation of the assets shows that not all claimants can be paid in full. Regardless of statutory provisions it is difficult to imagine that the time will ever come when the valuation question will cease to dominate the drama of corporate reorganization; so also the derivative problem of fairness seems likely to remain.

Yet we cannot reasonably abandon the problem of corporate reorganization by simply drawing attention to certain perennial problems of which it is composed. Since corporate reorganization involves a readjustment of property rights, the legal system must provide a forum in which these adjustments can be carried out. In the United States this forum was for a long period that of the equity courts. But since 1934 the bankruptcy courts, first under section 77B and now under Chapter X of the Revised Bankruptcy Act of 1938, have largely displaced those of equity; traditional and customary procedure has yielded to codification by statute.[1] Although reorganization under equity has had much the longest historical record of experience it does not necessarily follow that we should devote proportionately more attention to it. Indeed, from the point of view of present-day reorganization problems much of that experience is of antiquarian interest only. For our purposes equity procedure in corporate reorganization is pertinent insofar as it serves to broaden our understanding of current procedures. It so happens, moreover, that both 77B and the Chandler Bill represent Congressional attempts to remove long-standing weaknesses in reorganizations under equity. Consequently we shall find an examination of the older equity procedure a useful introduction to the analysis of 77B and the Chandler Bill. Although there are certain similarities between equity procedure and 77B, nevertheless the change from equity to 77B was much more drastic, from almost any point of view, than the change from 77B to the Chandler Bill. The Chandler Bill, although introducing a number of important alterations and extensions, is, notwithstanding, constructed on the same general pattern as 77B. Thus, by way of contrast between the old and the new, there is merit in giving more than passing attention to corporate reorganization under courts of equity even though it is now outmoded.

The reorganization of corporations under these three arrange-

---

[1] By reorganization in equity we mean, of course, that system whereby courts of equity by the appointment of a receiver were able to maintain intact the asset fund of a failed corporation against the onslaught of creditors pending the preparation of a plan of reorganization by which the assets could be sold at a receiver's sale as a unit and free from the claims of creditors. See *supra*, Ch. V, sec. I.

Reorganization under 77B means reorganization under the Corporate Reorganization Act (sections 77A and 77B of the Bankruptcy Act) enacted June 7, 1934 (48 Stat. 911), amended August 20, 1935, 11 U.S.C.A. sections 206, 207.

By reorganization under the Chandler Bill we mean corporate reorganization under Chapter X of the revision of the Bankruptcy Act of 1898 and acts amendatory and supplementary thereto, approved June 22, 1938, Public—No. 696—75th Congress, Ch. 575, 3d Session.

ments might be treated in various ways. Perhaps the simplest would be to describe in turn the procedure under each and leave it to the reader to draw his own inferences and comparisons. As a means of presenting an intelligible, straightforward narrative there is much to be said for this method, especially from an author's point of view. And several such excellent descriptions are available. Yet for certain other purposes it is not entirely satisfactory. There is a tendency, perhaps, to stress technical details of procedure and to overemphasize form at the expense of substance and reality. For better or worse this will not be the form of exposition adopted here. Rather we shall endeavor to take certain crucial and practical problems which any reorganization procedure under existing legal institutions must meet, and to evaluate, if possible, the degree of success with which these problems were or are solved by the method under consideration. In other words, instead of describing in detail the successive steps in reorganization under equity, 77B, and the Chandler Bill we shall try to organize our discussion of these procedures around certain basic problems by indicating just how and with what results these problems were (or are) dealt with by the three methods. But before this comparative approach can be essayed, however, we must first consider what these problems are.

I. THE CRITICAL PROBLEMS OF CORPORATE REORGANIZATION IN PRACTICE

When we pass from theoretical constructions to corporate reorganization in the workaday world certain practical problems arise to which any legally established reorganization machinery must yield a solution. Some of these problems are both private and quasi-public in character. To be sure there is over-lapping since very few problems of corporate reorganization are entirely private or wholly public. By private problems we mean those that arise directly out of the necessarily conflicting interests of the different groups of claim-holders against the failed enterprise. By public problems, on the other hand, we mean problems of reorganization where the solution reached has important repercussions on the general welfare. The problems of corporate reorganization, therefore, extend beyond the mere private squabbles between owners and creditors over the assets of a failed corporation. This must be borne in mind during the ensuing discussion even though we do not continually reiterate it.

As already argued, if we wish to compare the relative merits of corporate reorganization *via* receivership in equity, under 77B, or under Chapter X of the revised Bankruptcy Act, we may conveniently do so by asking just how and with what success did each yield a solution to certain practical problems. What are these problems? We submit that the following five are of primary importance and that the way these problems are handled in practice largely condemns or commends the reorganization system being scrutinized.

First is the crucial problem of deciding whether reorganization or liquidation should follow upon business failure. Since the claimants on the assets of the failed enterprise, the contributors of new capital, and the general public will be harmed if an enterprise is reorganized that ought to be liquidated, this problem is of paramount significance. Consequently one needs to examine the reorganization machinery from this point of view: To what extent and by what methods does the machinery bring this question into the open and facilitate the formulation of a prompt and satisfactory answer? Does the machinery, for instance, make it easy for certain groups to insist upon reorganization even though the value of the assets of the failed enterprise to the claimants would be greater in liquidation? The choice between liquidation and reorganization has a significance extending beyond the purely private interests of the claim-holders against the failed corporation and those who invest new capital. If capital resources and other agents of production are retained in (or directed to) one use when their productivity in another would be greater, there is a genuine, if statistically unmeasurable, reduction in the community's real income. Moreover, unwarranted reorganizations delay the adjustment of excessive productive capacity to a shrunken demand, and tend thereby to produce depressed conditions throughout a whole industry. Indeed, one might argue with some force that petitioners for legal assistance to carry through a reorganization ought to be required to submit convincing evidence that reorganization and not liquidation is the appropriate remedy in the instant case. In other words, on broad economic considerations perhaps the presumption ought to be that the enterprise should be liquidated, thereby placing the burden of proof to the contrary squarely on the petitioner. This does not mean, of course, that very few enterprises that failed would actually be reorganized, only that it ought not to be taken for granted without demonstration that reorganization will follow failure as day follows night.

Second is the important question of the way in which the particular reorganization machinery functions to make it relatively easy or comparatively difficult to procure the necessary new capital to carry through the reorganization, assuming it to be warranted. Unnecessary obstacles here are a serious indictment, since, as we have seen, new investment is usually indispensable in the rehabilitation of a failed concern. Mere statutes or legal machinery cannot assure, of course, that the necessary funds will be forthcoming; but by making it possible to give the new capital contributors an exclusively first claim on assets and earnings through the displacement of previous liens and claims, new investment may be greatly encouraged. Similarly, if the direct outlay costs of the reorganization process are kept to a minimum consistent with other desirable objectives, and if it is unnecessary to pay certain claimants in cash, new funds will be more readily forthcoming because less will be needed and more of it will go for productive purposes rather than to foot the bill for previous errors. In various ways the reorganization machinery may so function that prospective investors are encouraged, not warned off, and have emphasized to them the favorable returns available on new investment.

Third is the problem of dissenting minorities in corporate reorganization. This very practical problem arises out of the conflict of two generally accepted and commendable principles. First, except on a special showing, persons should be allowed to make such use and disposition of their own property as their own wisdom (or lack of it) seems to dictate. Second, where differences of opinion arise in matters of policy the accepted mode of reaching an agreement is by the principle of majority rule. In the main, the law has been careful to block the many attempted inroads upon the rights of individuals to deal with their own property. Yet, on the other hand, it is doubtless true that under certain circumstances strictly to uphold the legal rights of one individual or a small group will damage others composing a much larger group. The problem of resolving differences of opinion, where individual judgments are almost certain to differ, well emphasizes the unavoidable conflict occasioned by the juxtaposition in reorganization of the competing ends of "justice" and "expediency." Some means of reaching a workable decision and of forcing that decision upon the dissenters there must be, unless one is willing to accept the prospect of well-nigh unending debate. Yet one cannot deny that a simple and unrestrained form of majority rule in corporate reorganization can easily become a vehicle that crushes aside justice (in any acceptable sense) instead of carrying it along. Such a result is indeed facilitated where, as is so often the case, a sizable proportion of the parties in interest have little or no opinion one way or another, e.g., the small shareholders in a large corporation. Certainly no "ideal" solution to the problem of dissenting minorities in corporate reorganization can be formulated off-hand; but the way the problem is handled provides a useful point of comparison between reorganization procedures.

Fourth there is the problem of obtaining some independent and disinterested review of the plan of reorganization as finally evolved in order that its fairness, its feasibility, and its general appropriateness in view of all the known facts may be appraised. Some persons would perhaps deny that the legally established machinery ought to make any provision for such a review. Yet the arguments bolstering this position are almost exclusively founded on the assumption that only the rights of private property holders are involved in corporate reorganization and that therefore the parties in interest and in conflict should be allowed to work out their own solution without intervention. But as already argued public as well as private interests are at stake; hence an independent review is not only proper but, at least in large, quasi-public corporations, necessary. Even if we grant that only private interests are involved, a good case could be made for an impartial review on the argument that a reorganization plan evolved out of conflict is apt to consist of a bundle of compromises not satisfactory to anyone as a whole plan nor carrying much assurance of success. Consequently there should be the opportunity, at least, for some competent but disinterested party to examine the plan and to suggest changes therein.

There is another side to this question of independent review that does not pertain to the actual plan of reorganization so much as to the whole proceedings. At least in democratic countries national governments ostensibly strive to promote general welfare through the exercise of legislative, judicial, and executive functions. Consequently they have a general obligation to prevent the established procedures for the reorganization of corporations from being used by special groups for their own profit and aggrandizement. In other words, the reorganization forum is presumably designed to provide a prompt, inexpensive, and equitable method of dealing with failed corporations; it would be a strange and intolerable end result if it actually so functioned that, say, investment bankers, corporation lawyers, and corporate executives were able to sequester for themselves a large fraction of the available assets at the expense of creditors and shareholders. Since such dangers have not in the past been entirely illusory there is need for an independent supervision of the reorganization proceedings as a form of insurance against the reorganization machinery being bent towards the pursuit of private ends not in accord with its purposes.

Finally, there is a very obvious problem of keeping down the direct and indirect costs of corporate reorganization to a minimum figure consistent with other desirable objectives. Obviously there is a conflict of ends here since a minimum cost of reorganization is incompatible with, say, the objective of maximum fairness or other desirable attributes in reorganization.[2] Nevertheless it is possible to keep down certain costs of reorganization without

[2] The point sought for above may be made clearer by an analogy. Suppose that one wishes to travel from *A* to *B* by automobile and is interested in making the trip quickly, cheaply, and safely. Speed, economy, and safety are conflicting ends. The greater the speed the less safety and economy. Similarly, greater safety can be had only at a sacrifice of speed, but perhaps with no sacrifice of economy. For a given journey there is probably some combination of the three that provides the optimum rate of travel in the sense that, having in mind the three objectives, no other combination would be equally satisfactory.

sacrificing other desirable objectives and so far as possible the legally established reorganization machinery should minimize these, for whatever costs of reorganization there are must be paid either from the assets of the failed corporation or from the new capital contributed for its reorganization. Either way the amount claim-holders in the aggregate can receive is reduced. The direct costs of reorganization have usually consisted primarily of legal, financial, and court fees paid for services.[3] The indirect costs, on the other hand, have usually been the unfortunate consequences in terms of lost business, decline in competitive position, a lowering of the working morale, etc., occasioned by the often long interval between failure and successful reorganization. The reasons for such a lag are many but need not be gone into at this point; it is now sufficient to emphasize the importance of curtailing the costs of reorganization to the necessary minimum.

It seems to the writer that the five "problems" just listed and briefly discussed are the more important of those that any established procedure of corporate reorganization will have to meet and solve. As a consequence the manner in which the three different systems of corporate reorganization—equity, 77B and the Chandler Bill—have yielded solutions thereto and the adequacy of these solutions provide convenient criteria by which to compare the three arrangements as a whole. Let us now endeavor to apply our criteria.

II. CORPORATE REORGANIZATION THROUGH COURTS OF EQUITY

1. Background of equity reorganization. 2. The decision between reorganization and liquidation. 3. New capital investment and dissenting minorities. 4. Independent review of the reorganization plan. 5. Costs of reorganization in equity. 6. Conclusions on equity reorganization.

1. *Background of equity reorganization.* It is a little surprising that notwithstanding the simplification of incorporation under

---

[3] In no small measure, of course, these direct costs have been occasioned by the efforts of the different conflicting interests to secure relatively more for themselves by a reorganization plan which favors *their* group at the expense of others.

general statutes over the past century there was no parallel legislation that facilitated the reorganization of failed corporations.[4]
In other words, while corporations grew in number and importance there was no corresponding simplification of the procedure
for either liquidating them or reorganizing them when they had
proven unsuccessful. The consequence was that the courts had to
bend old forms and devices to new uses. Out of this necessity
evolved the procedure of reorganizing corporations under the
protective cloak of courts of equity.

Historically viewed the use of federal equity receivership [5] as
a means of enabling corporations to be reorganized grew out of
a recognition of the general public's interest in the failure of certain types of corporations. When some of the early railroads failed
(in the business sense earlier defined) it was recognized that, notwithstanding the rights of creditors in their debtors' property,
there existed also the superior considerations of the public interest.[6] The public interest demanded that the railroads be maintained intact as operating units and not dismembered by creditors
in their efforts to collect their claims. The private squabbles between debtors and creditors in a failed railroad had to be sub-

[4] More accurately there was no parallel legislation which was successful. The
individual states could not make laws which would allow a majority to bind a
minority to an arrangement because of the federal constitutional clause *re* abrogation of contracts. Some state statutes merely sanctioned receivership in equity
courts, while some others (Pennsylvania, Illinois, and Minnesota) have enacted
the reorganization sections contained in the Uniform Business Corporations Act.
This last is patterned on an English statute of 1870. See Finletter, Thomas K.,
Principles of Corporate Reorganization in Bankruptcy, Charlottesville, Va.
(Michie), 1937, pp. 28-29.

[5] Our earlier remarks on receivership in Chapter V might well be reviewed at
this juncture.

[6] Garrard Glenn, an eminent authority on the subject of creditors' rights and
related matters, states that the first use of receivership in connection with a failed
corporation (a railroad) was by a state court in Georgia in 1846. A portion of
that decision as reported by Glenn is interesting. In sustaining the appointment
of a receiver the court said: "The facts of the case under consideration were
novel and peculiar. Here was a road extending through six Counties, and one
hundred miles in length. What disastrous consequences would have resulted if
each judgment creditor had been allowed to seize and sell separate portions of
the road, at different sales, in the six Counties through which it passed, and to
different purchasers! Would not this valuable property have been utterly sacrificed—the rights and interests of the creditors, as well as the objects and intentions of the Legislature in granting this Charter entirely defeated." (*Macon and
Ry v. Parker* (1851), 9 Ga. 377, 393 ff.) as given by Glenn, G., "The Basis of
Federal Receivership," *Columbia Law Review*, Vol. 25, pp. 434-446, at pp. 441-442.

ordinated to the broader interests of the general weal. The railroads were thought to supply services so intimately connected with the general welfare that no stoppage in the flow thereof was deemed tolerable. As a consequence the law sought a means of maintaining the properties intact as a functioning unit and found it in the device of a receiver in equity. As one writer has phrased it, "Using old equitable forms which were designed to convert the properties of an insolvent debtor into cash for distribution among its creditors, they [the courts] evolved a proceeding which achieved the opposite results of preserving the properties intact and of readjusting the debts of the insolvent debtor."[7] In theory the appointment of a receiver in equity was a creditors' remedy and not a procedure for the relief of insolvent debtors. Yet when first used in connection with the reorganization of failed railroads, which were clearly affected with a public interest, it must have been recognized that the receivership form was a convenient means of protecting that interest.[8] By allowing the properties of the failed railroad to come into the hands of a court officer, the receiver, continuity of operations was assured and creditors were estopped from pursuing their legal remedies until the property could be sold for their benefit as a unit. Generally speaking, the sale of the property at the receiver's sale was to a new corporation that would continue to carry on the same economic functions. Because of the size of the properties to be sold as an entirety usually the only bidder at the receiver's sale was the reorganization committee, frequently self-designated, which ostensibly represented the claimants in the assets of the failed enterprise and whose bid, if accepted, was at once assigned to the new corporation which thereby ac-

[7] Finletter, *op. cit.*, p. 1.

[8] The keepers of inns, wharves, grist mills, turnpikes, have long been recognized as engaged in occupations that are "affected with a public interest." But nowadays the phrase is by no means restricted in its scope to such enterprises. Its meaning and extension are constantly changing and an enormous literature relating to it exists. The following two articles provide a good introduction to the subject. Robinson, G. H., "The Public Utility Concept in American Law," *Harvard Law Review*, Vol. 41, pp. 277-308. McAllister, B. P., "Lord Hale and Business Affected with a Public Interest," *ibid.*, Vol. 43, pp. 759-791. Most of the standard texts on public utilities also treat the subject briefly, for example, Mosher, W. E., and Crawford, F. G., *Public Utility Regulation*, New York and London (Harpers), 1933, Ch. 1.

quired the assets of the failed corporation free and clear. In the language of the day, the plan of reorganization was declared operative. Such, in very brief outline, was the procedure that evolved for the reorganization first, of railroads and then, subsequently, for other corporations, through receivership in equity. The following description by a legal scholar is remarkable for its brevity and clarity: [9]

A corporation finds itself in financial embarrassment. It has a floating debt, several classes of bond and note issues (some secured, others unsecured), and several classes of outstanding stock. A friendly equity suit is instituted in the Federal Court, the basis of jurisdiction being diversity of citizenship. The complainant, a creditor, alleges that the corporation is financially embarrassed, and asks that the assets be marshaled, liquidated and distributed, and that receivers be appointed to continue the business pending the sale of the property. The defendant admits the allegations of the complaint, consents to the relief sought and thereupon the Court appoints receivers who take possession of the defendant's assets and continue the business. . . .

The creditors and stockholders are enjoined from bringing suits against the defendant or interfering with the receivers; and, where the defendant's assets are located in districts beyond the jurisdiction of the court, ancillary receivership suits are instituted.

Self-constituted committees of the various classes of creditors and security-holders are formed, generally by leading representatives of such classes, or by bankers who issued the securities—now and then by small holders. The committees . . . seek the deposit with them of the classes of securities they assume to represent. . . . If the committees conclude that the business is worth saving, they negotiate with one another as to the terms of a reorganization. . . . At last the committees agree. A reorganization plan is prepared. . . . Representatives of the respective committees are selected to act as a joint reorganization committee, or bankers are selected to act as reorganization managers. . . .

The receivers offer the property for sale. . . .

There is rarely any competition at the sale, for the property is so vast that there is no one to purchase it except the old security-holders. The reorganization committee buys in the assets. It pays actual money only to the extent of furnishing the cash distributive share, as fixed by

[9] Rosenberg, James N., "Corporate Reorganization and the Federal Court," *Columbia Law Review*, Vol. 17 (1917), pp. 523-537 at pp. 523-526. An apology is in order for such a long quotation but it summarizes so very well the basic steps entailed in the procedure by which corporations were organized through courts of equity that perhaps it is excusable.

the court, to the security-holders who do not assent to the reorganization. . . .

. . . If the bid is accepted, the bidder assigns his bid to the new corporation, formed pursuant to the plan. . . . Business goes on without a moment's interruption; and the only visible change is that whereas the old establishment bore the name "Eastern Traffic Company," the handsomely engraved letterhead of the newly-created entity is "Eastern Traffic Corporation."

Most large corporations that were reorganized prior to 1934 in the United States, were reorganized under arrangements and procedures very similar to these. Indeed, it has been said that in the twenty years preceding 1916 more than fifty per cent of the country's corporations were reorganized on this basis.[10] It is reorganization through this machinery that we have first to examine and appraise in relation to the criteria suggested in the previous section.

2. *The decision between reorganization and liquidation.* We argued above that the most crucial problem to be met and solved in corporate reorganization was the choice between liquidation and reorganization. How was this problem handled by the equity system of corporate reorganization?

The use of receivership in equity as a device applied to failed corporations grew up, as we have just seen, in connection with business enterprises affected with a public interest, especially railroads. For these corporations there was usually no question of the necessity of continuing the economic service regardless of the losses imposed upon those possessing claims against the failed corporation. By and large the railroads were monopolies in the sense that no very adequate substitute was available that would serve the same end or purpose, i.e., reasonably rapid and economical transportation. Hence when railroads failed they more or less had to be reorganized out of regard for the public interest. It so happens, however, that on economic grounds too the assets of most railroads were of such a character, and stood in such a physical relationship one to another, that they were clearly worth more to the claim-holders in reorganization than in liquidation. Much

[10] See Paul D. Cravath in Stetson, F. L., *et al., Some Legal Phases of Corporate Financing, Reorganization and Regulation*, New York (Macmillan). 1917, p. 154.

the most important asset of a railroad as a railroad—that is, apart from any assets the railroad may own, e.g., lands and forests, not used and useful in providing transportation service—is its road-bed on a right of way together with appurtenant stations, yards, etc. Now these are highly specific capital goods whose alternative use is limited and which in liquidation bring next to nothing in cash proceeds.[11] Consequently, quite apart from questions of public interest, it is probably true that most corporations reorganized through equity proceedings in the earlier days were, as a matter of fact, actually worth more in reorganization than in liquidation. The correct choice between liquidation and reorganization was made, but not because there was any formal posing of the problem, but merely because the enterprises to which equity reorganization was first applied happened to be of a sort that used highly specialized capital goods in an octopus type plant.[12]

As time passed and the corporate form of business organization became more common the use of receivership in equity was not restricted to failed corporations that were affected with a public interest and therefore had to be reorganized. The procedure was gradually extended to other corporations where the public welfare was much less clearly involved. How then was the problem of the choice between reorganization and liquidation presented and answered?

The choice between liquidation and (attempted) reorganization under the equity system was presented *de facto* when a petition was filed for the appointment of a receiver. It was firmly established as a legal matter that no creditor or group thereof had a

[11] Not always of course: the Delaware, Lackawanna & Western Railroad not so many years ago sold a stretch of its road-bed through a semi-mountainous region to the State of Pennsylvania which converted it into a state highway.

[12] By an octopus type plant we meant a plant such as required by water companies, power and light companies, gas companies, telephone companies, telegraph companies, and the like, including railroads of all kinds, where there must be a physical extension of the capital equipment over a considerable area in order to render the service. Such enterprises are sometimes said to be "natural monopolies" in the sense that competitive conditions would be intolerably wasteful because of the costly duplication of facilities, and often less satisfactory to consumers as well because of the limited extent of the service, e.g., telephone and telegraph companies. In general, enterprises requiring an octopus type plant are likely to be natural monopolies and for that reason alone are apt to be "affected with a public interest."

right to have a receiver appointed; in logic and in fact the petition was always addressed to the discretion of the court, and the latter was expected to determine the answer on the basis of all the relevant data. Thus the decision as to the relative merits of reorganization and liquidation really rested with the court to which the petition for the appointment of a receiver was addressed.[13] If the court saw fit to grant a receivership, then the parties in interest could go ahead and try to reorganize the failed corporation, but not otherwise. For, if the receivership petition were denied, the parties in interest in the failed corporation had really almost no alternative but to liquidate the assets in bankruptcy since there was no way of restraining the claim-holders from dismembering the assets and thereby destroying the working combination in which they stood. Hence it was that the choice between liquidation and (attempted) reorganization ultimately and finally rested with the court of equity which had to grant or deny the receivership petition. What considerations influenced the court to grant or deny the petition for the appointment of a receiver is therefore important.[14]

For corporations not affected with a public interest it must be recognized that the appointment of a receiver is historically and logically the remedy of a judgment creditor. At least in the theory of the law the appointment of receiver in equity has been regarded

[13] Note the following: ". . . a remedy of this kind should only be granted when the court is satisfied from the papers before it that the curative purpose for which the remedy is sought may be accomplished, and that a remedy equally adequate and appropriate to the circumstances cannot be elsewhere found . . . there has not been made out on the papers before me the probability of the successful issue of a conservation receivership, and hence, the reason for the interposition of the equity does not exist . . . there is outside of equity an adequate and, as I believe, a more appropriate and effective remedy for the situation." *Municipal Financial Corporation* v. *Bankus Corporation*, 45 Fed. (2d) 902, at 906-907, as quoted by Finletter, *op. cit.*, p. 15.

[14] Note the following somewhat picturesque language used by a legal writer: "The problem which presents itself to the business man and the lawyer when a concern is in difficulty, is whether it is desirous to liquidate and destroy, or to build and construct. Bankruptcy ordinarily, if I may use a rather easy phrase, is the undertaker. The equity receivership is the physician who desires to cure the patient. In bankruptcy nearly every case ends in liquidation. . . . The underlying thought, the compelling motive of equity receivership is to save the business." Mayer, J. M., "Federal Equity Receiverships," in *Six Lectures on Legal Topics* (Association of the Bar of the City of New York), p. 165, as quoted by Stevens, Robert S., *op. cit.*, p. 769.

as an aid to, and not a denial of, the right of collection, although the latter may be temporarily delayed in its action. But if receivership is a creditors' remedy, and if receivership is intended to hold the assets together as a unit, it would seem to follow that creditors would only be benefited by receivership in circumstances where the assets would realize more for creditors' claims if sold as a unit than if dismembered and sold piecemeal. What does this mean however? If the assets will bring more sold as a unit than if dismembered and sold item by item, it must mean that the value of the assets is greater in reorganization than in liquidation.[15] Hence, on economic grounds, the justification for the appointment of a receiver by the court is the court's belief that the assets of the failed corporation are worth more to all claimants in reorganization than in liquidation. Here, then, is where the crucial decision between reorganization and liquidation is raised and answered: when the court is forced to grant or deny the petition for the appointment of the receiver.

In considering petitions for the appointment of a receiver for the assets of a failed enterprise, can one say that the judges thought of the problem from the point of view of the economic considerations just mentioned? One would like to be able to give an unequivocal answer, but this is impossible. Doubtless the judges gave some thought to the question from this point of view, but under the existing machinery it was not placed squarely before them as the question at issue. Rather, perhaps, they were inclined to consider the more narrowly legal problems raised and to take the position that little harm could come from the appointment of a receiver (since he could always be dismissed and liquidation ensue if the facts warranted) and possibly some positive good might result. The often costly delays of such a policy were not sufficiently recognized. Especially under the consent receivership scheme (friendly receivership proceedings), the courts were perhaps too prone to accept the creditor's allegations and the corporation's reply at their face value when a thoughtful examination by the court of the economic questions basically at issue

---

[15] As we have already emphasized, if the assets of a large corporation are to be sold as a unit there will typically be only one prospective buyer, namely, the claim-holders in the failed enterprise.

would have shown whether the assets of the failed corporation were worth more in reorganization or more in liquidation, and hence whether the petition for the appointment of a receiver should have been granted or denied. Doubtless the most serious criticism of this aspect of corporate reorganization in equity is that the basic question of asset valuation was not squarely posed at all.[16]

3. *New capital investment and dissenting minorities.* The two problems of the treatment of dissenting minorities, and the means available for raising additional capital as part of the reorganization plan, may be conveniently treated together in a discussion of reorganization in equity.

One of the gravest difficulties of corporate reorganization in equity was the absence of any acceptable means by which even a very large majority could impose their agreement upon a dissenting minority. We have repeatedly emphasized that equity receivership was based on the theory that the sale of the assets as a unit would bring more to all claim-holders, especially creditors, than piecemeal liquidation; but a sale for the benefit of creditors there must be under the equity arrangement.[17] Consequently, the

[16] Some evidence of how seriously the courts considered the valuation problem in passing upon requests for the appointment of receivers is offered by a study of equity receiverships in California by a special U. S. Senate committee. This committee wrote as follows: "In the bills in equity praying for the appointment of receivers for the period examined, the value of the assets of the companies for which receivers were appointed, was alleged to amount to $473,313,877.39, and the debts were $161,051,114.11. The recklessness with which the assets were alleged in the bills of complaint, and the total disregard of any reasonable scale of values set up on the books of the companies at the time of the application for the appointment of receivers, are shown in the final reports of those officials of the court where they are given a book value of $199,977,648.13—a decrease of $279,336,229.26, or 59 per cent in process of receivership, revealing either an utter contempt for the truth of the allegations set out in the petitions, which were verified under oath, an attempt to prove solvency in order to secure the appointment of receivers, or wasteful and incompetent management. The evidence adduced does not favor one of those theories of decline over the other." *United States Senate, Report No. 365,* 73d Congress, 2d Sess., Washington (Government Printing Office), 1934, p. 2.

[17] There is one case, *Phipps* v. *Chicago, Rock Island & Pacific Ry. Co.,* 284 Fed. 945 (C.C.A. 8th, 1922), which held that if the plan of reorganization treated all creditors fairly, there was no necessity of going through the formality of a judicial sale and that, instead of cash, dissenting creditors could be forced to accept securities as allotted to them under the reorganization plan. This case involved no mortgage liens, however, and the only creditors so affected were unsecured creditors. While the case elicited considerable comment and some high

only available means of dealing with dissenting minorities was to allow them to share proportionately to their interests in the pro-ceeds from the sale of the corporation's assets as a unit. Yet, for reasons already noted, almost the only bidder at the final sale of the assets as an entirety was the reorganization committee repre-senting the majority of the claimants.[18] In other words, the major-ity was in the position of having to buy out the interests of the minority. In order to clarify the procedure let us suppose that by some miracle the reorganization committee succeeded in ob-taining 100 per cent approval of its reorganization plan by all claimants. The reorganization committee would then hold all the claims against the assets and, at the court-supervised sale thereof, could merely tender the claims in payment and (provided there were no other bidders) it would thereby acquire the assets as an entirety free and clear of all encumbrances. It could then proceed with whatever arrangements constituted the plan of reorganiza-tion. No cash apart from court costs would have to be paid. If, on the other hand, there were a dissenting minority, the reorgani-zation committee could not acquire the assets free and clear until some provision had been made for the dissenters. Since the dissent-ers, by definition, did not agree to the reorganization plan, and since under the equity arrangements there was no way of forcing them to do so, the only alternative was to pay them off in cash. But how much are they entitled to receive?

In equity reorganizations the sale of the assets as a unit took place at the so-called receiver's sale. And it was customary also for the equity court to fix a reservation price for the assets as a whole, called the "upset price," which was the minimum bid the court would allow to be accepted. Consequently, any bid of this amount or greater was acceptable to the court.[19] The upset price

hopes at the time (see Rosenberg, James N., "Phipps v. Chicago, Rock Island & Pacific Ry. Co.," *Columbia Law Review*, Vol. 24, pp. 266-272) it seems to be now agreed that the case did not establish an accepted precedent. See Gerdes, *op. cit.*, Vol. I, pp. 57-59.

[18] One reason why no other bidders appeared was that they were unable to qualify by posting bonds or cash with the court in sufficient amount. But such a provision was probably necessary to keep out irresponsible bidders. See Tracy, J. E., *Corporate Foreclosures, Receiverships and Reorganizations*, Chicago (Cal-laghan), 1929, pp. 216-218.

[19] We may postpone for a moment a consideration of the manner in which the court fixed the upset price.

being given and also the proportion of the total claims constituting the minority, it then became a simple matter to determine how much cash had to be paid over to the minority.[20]

Yet this necessity of paying dissenters to the reorganization plan in cash presented two serious difficulties: first, it meant that no plan of reorganization could be carried through unless a very large percentage of the claim-holders agreed to the plan. In any sizable reorganization even 95 per cent agreement still meant that a large cash sum had to be paid out to dissenters as a condition of acquiring the assets free and clear. In the second place, the necessity of making this cash payment to dissenters meant that just that much more free capital had to be raised as part of the reorganization plan. Indeed this last really created a virtual stalemate which greatly hampered the preparation of the plan and at the same time made it more difficult to secure approval of a plan by a large majority. One could not tell how much cash had to be raised until the percentage of agreement and the upset price were known. On the other hand, no very definite plan could be proposed and gain general acceptance so long as the amount of cash to be raised was indeterminate. To secure acceptance to a plan the amount of cash to be raised, and therefore the assessments on claim-holders, had to be known; but the amount of cash to be raised as part of the reorganization plan was unknown unless the percentage of agreement to the plan and the upset price were given. Each presupposed that the other had been determined. As might be imagined, the net result of such a dilemma was not a happy one. The power of minorities to prevent the adoption of a reorganization plan was out of all proportion to the value of their claims against the assets of the failed corporation. The con-

---

[20] Suppose, for instance, that the upset price were fixed at $10,000,000 and that the mortgage bondholders' claims (all one class) had a principal amount of $15,000,000 and accrued interest of $900,000. Assume also that the reorganization committee had secured 95 per cent approval among the bondholders; in other words, the relevant dissenters were 5 per cent. The reorganization committee would then have to pay out cash to the dissenters of $500,000 on principal and $30,000 on account of interest. The property is sold for less than the amount of the mortgage. We are here assuming that all the assets fell under the mortgage which would not be the case always. See the cases discussed by Tracy, *op. cit.*, pp. 307-326, for more complicated examples. In our example we neglect any deduction for the expenses of the receivership which would of course have to be paid before the property could be delivered free and clear.

sequence was that, at least for relatively large reorganizations, the reorganization committee more or less had to get investment bankers to agree to underwrite the uncertain cash requirements, for in no other way could it be assured that the cash would be forthcoming. Without the necessary cash to pay off dissenters the plan was doomed to failure, but the amount to be paid to dissenters was uncertain until the plan was announced, consequently some outside party had to guarantee to provide (within limits) whatever cash would ultimately be required; the outside party was usually an investment banker.[21]

4. *Independent review of the reorganization plan.* Under the equity form of corporate reorganization courts did not from the first hold to the view that they were concerned with the fairness of the plan of reorganization ultimately prepared and carried through.[22] But as time passed equity courts came to recognize more and more that some independent consideration of the fairness of the plan of reorganization was necessary and that, indirectly, it could be exercised by the court.[23] By what procedures and methods did equity courts exercise this function?

Since under the equity arrangements there had to be a sale of the assets of the failed corporation, and since the court had to confirm such sale, the court could, in effect, block any plan of reorganization of which it disapproved by refusing to confirm

---

[21] If the receiver continued the operations of the property and took in more than enough to pay current operating expenses then there was sometimes enough cash from this source to pay dissenters. Receivers often leave debts instead of cash, however. Sometimes a reorganization committee could borrow at commercial banks on the deposited securities. A final method was to levy an assessment on depositing bondholders. See Tracy, *op. cit.*, pp. 249, 310-311.

[22] "Whether there shall be a new organization formed of stockholders, bondholders, or creditors, with what respective interests, and upon what terms, is one that should be left for the determination of the persons interested, without interference in any way by the court or its officers. The court in these cases is a harbor of refuge, not a repair shop. It will hold the property of the corporation safe from outside attacks, and in proper cases will keep its business going, so that whatever value there may be in the business, qua business, may be preserved for all concerned; but it will not undertake, either by itself or by its officer, to reorganize the old corporation, or to create a new one, or to solicit subscribers to some syndicate of prospective purchasers." *Chable* v. *Nicaragua Canal Construction Co.*, 39 Fed. 846 (C.C.N.Y. 1894) at 848.

[23] Perhaps one of the best discussions of the cases dealing with fairness is to be found in Payne, Philip M., *Plans of Corporate Reorganization*, Chicago (Foundation), 1934, Ch. V.

the sale. As already explained the courts adopted the practice of fixing a minimum price, the upset price, at which they would confirm the sale of the assets.[24] Consequently in fixing the upset price the courts were in a position to grant or deny approval of the plan of reorganization. Yet in fixing an upset price a court was inevitably expressing a judgment or opinion as to the value of the assets. In a sense, therefore, it might be said that the courts expressed the results of their independent review of the reorganization plan by stating their own figure of the minimum value of the assets. It must be confessed, however, that this was more the form than the substance of the actual proceedings in equity for the reason that only rarely was the upset price fixed by the court after a careful appraisal of the value of the assets on an earning power basis.[25] The courts recognized that even though they might fix a "reasonable" price, in some sense, there was no assurance either that any buyer would be forthcoming who would pay that price, or that if the reorganization committee were willing to do so that it would be able to raise the requisite cash for dissenters. The choice before the court in effect reduced to selling the assets as a whole at a price that would allow the reorganization plan to be carried through or ordering piecemeal liquidation. In most cases the reorganization committee was almost certain to be the only bidder, and if the court felt that reorganization was prefer-

[24] Bonbright, *op. cit.*, Vol. II, p. 849, cites Joseph L. Weiner to the effect that the first mention of fixing upset prices was in 1885. The court was not bound to fix an upset price, however, nor having fixed one was it bound to confirm a sale at that price if subsequent knowledge indicated it to be too low. *Ibid.*

[25] Bonbright quite correctly emphasizes that, "It is much simpler to tell *why* the courts have fixed upset prices than to discover *how* they have fixed them." *Ibid.*, p. 850. Following Weiner, he goes on to state that there are at least four views on how the upset price ought to be fixed by the court. First, a merely nominal figure that will tend to force the dissenters to join in the proposed plan because what they will receive by remaining out is so much smaller. Second, a figure based on what the assets would bring if liquidated, since if no plan of reorganization were worked out the assets would have to be liquidated. Third, a figure that would pay cash to the dissenters in an amount equal to the value of the securities received by the assenters under the reorganization plan. Fourth, the upset price should be fixed at as high a figure as will permit the plan to be carried through. As a practical matter, however, the choice probably lies with a figure somewhere between the nominal valuation of the first view and the maximum the reorganization committee can pay, the fourth; two and three are not likely to receive very serious consideration.

able to liquidation it almost had to fix the upset price at a figure within the reorganization committee's ability to raise cash for dissenters. Such a solution certainly left something to be desired; but with the reorganization machinery available, both the court and the reorganization committee were narrowly restricted in their choice of alternatives.

Although the final sale of the assets had to be at a figure the reorganization committee could pay, the court none the less had some power over the reorganization plan. In the first place, within the limits of the committee's ability to raise cash for dissenters, the court could vary the upset price so as to encourage or discourage a particular plan. By fixing a relatively low price the court almost forced dissenters to come in with the majority since the cash settlement would be so small; conversely, by a relatively high price the court could offer support to the dissenters. Moreover, quite apart from the actual upset price figure, the court had considerable discretion in its power to entertain objections to the plan, to refuse to order a sale of the property, and by other means.[26] Indeed as time passed the courts came more and more to recognize the upset price as merely an incident to allowing an acceptable plan of reorganization to come into operation, and the emphasis shifted from the upset price as such to the fairness and feasibility of the plan itself. This point of view seems first to have been applied in 1918 in the important case of *Grasselli Chemical Co.* v. *Ætna Explosives Co., Inc.*[27] In the Ætna case the judge not only appointed a reorganization committee to work out a plan, but when after a reasonable time they had not reached a definite agreement he actually dictated the general outline of a plan which he deemed fair. This plan became the reorganization plan and was

[26] ". . . progressive Federal judges, who, though having no express power to impose a plan of reorganization approved by a majority upon a reluctant minority or to protect a minority from a tyrannical majority are, in part at least, accomplishing these results by indirection, i.e., through refusing, for example, to sanction a sale to a reorganization committee when the plan of reorganization proposed by the majority is unjust and through refusing minority interests the right to intervene in the suit when their purpose is merely to obstruct." Rosenberg, James N., "The Ætna Explosives Case—A Milestone in Reorganization," *Columbia Law Review*, Vol. 20, pp. 733-740 at p. 733.

[27] C.C.A. 1918, 252 Fed. 456. See Mr. Rosenberg's article mentioned in the previous note.

accepted unanimously by all parties in interest. Such a result was a far cry from the not uncommon view of earlier periods that the court had no concern with the plan of reorganization worked out by the contending parties.[28] Yet how far the power of the courts extended if some creditor chose to stand on his strict legal rights and to oppose a court-dictated plan is not entirely clear.[29]

No discussion of independent review of corporate reorganization plans under the equity procedure would be complete without mention of the so-called rule of the Boyd case.[30] The question fundamentally raised by the Boyd case was the propriety and equitableness of a reorganization plan which allowed shareholders of the failed corporation to participate in the reorganization at the same time that (some) creditors are denied any right to participate. Boyd, an unsecured creditor of the Northern Pacific *Railroad* Co., who had been paid nothing when that company's property passed in reorganization to the Northern Pacific *Railway* Co., sought to enforce his unpaid claim against the latter. Boyd contended that the transfer of the assets to a new corporation was fraudulent where stockholders were allowed a chance to partici-

[28] In the article mentioned, Mr. Rosenberg shows that the courts had been gradually working towards a greater and greater concern with the fairness of the reorganization plan as a whole, citing in particular *Guaranty Trust Co.* v. *Missouri Pacific R.R. Co.*, 238 Fed. 812. Mr. Rosenberg argued that the procedure in the Ætna case was based on a sound equitable principle that he states as follows: "Once the *res* comes into the Court's possession, the Court has the power, and having that power is under a commensurate duty to see to it that the *res* shall leave the Court, according to principles of justice. This means that a Court cannot content itself in allowing a sale of the assets and a purchase by the highest bidder, nor can it consent blindly to a dismissal of the suit. A sale when made as part of a reorganization is hardly a sale at all . . . if any such steps are taken it is within the Court's power and, perhaps, even incumbent upon the Court to inquire whether the consummation of those steps will mean an equitable disposition of the *res*." Rosenberg, *op. cit.*, p. 739. It should be noted, however, that Mr. Robert T. Swaine, an at least equally eminent authority on equity reorganizations, could not agree with the view taken by Mr. Rosenberg. See his article, "Reorganization—the Next Step: A Reply to Mr. James N. Rosenberg," *Columbia Law Review*, Vol. 22, pp. 14-27.

[29] Mr. Swaine in the article cited in the previous note quotes at length from *In re Prudential Outfitting Company* (D.C. 1918) 250 Fed. 504 at 507 where Judge Learned Hand said: "The dissenting creditors must be paid in cash their own proportion of the bid, which is their inviolate right. They are protected by the power of the court to fix an upset price, aided in the case of bankruptcy by the statute itself. Any admissible plasticity of reorganization lies in the court's power over that feature of the proceedings."

[30] *Northern Pacific Ry. Co.* v. *Boyd*, 228 U.S. 482 (1913).

pate while unsecured creditors were omitted entirely.[31] The Supreme Court held for Boyd. The court was careful to point out that Boyd need not have been paid in cash, saying:

His interest can be preserved by the issuance, on equitable terms, of income bonds or preferred stock. If he declines a fair offer he is left to protect himself as any other creditor of a judgment debtor, and, having refused to come into a just reorganization, could not thereafter be heard in a court of equity to attack it. If, however, no such tender was made and kept good he retains the right to subject the interest of the old stockholders in the property to the payment of his debt. If their interest is valueless, he gets nothing. If it be valuable, he merely subjects that which the law had originally and continuously made liable for the payment of corporate liabilities.

The effect of this decision upon plans of corporate reorganization was doubtless considerable because it re-emphasized that stockholders' claims were inferior to creditors' claims and rights, despite the complexity of reorganization problems, and that the courts, if a case were brought, would enforce the rule. The case seems to give support to the doctrine of absolute priority discussed in the previous chapter. Reorganization plans prepared subsequent to the Boyd case were careful to give due regard to the rule there laid down.[32]

5. *Costs of reorganization in equity.* Speed and economy in equity reorganizations were mainly notable by their absence. The direct costs of receivership, especially where ancillary receiverships were required because not all the property of the failed corporations was in one judicial district, were very high indeed. The compensations paid to such receivers were in general liberal, while fees for legal counsel to the receivers were on a similar scale.[33]

[31] The stockholders received new stock in the *Railway* company by paying in $10 per share in the case of the preferred and $15 in the case of the common. Since the par value of the shares received was greater, presumably the old shares of the railroad company had some value under the plan. Hence shareholders got something while unsecured creditors were excluded.

[32] Tracy states that following the Boyd case it became the practice to insert in the decree of the foreclosure a clause to the effect that any sale to another corporation as part of a plan of reorganization must contain a fair offer to unsecured creditors if stockholders are allowed to participate in the reorganized (successor) corporation. The court was allowed to pass upon the fairness of the offer to unsecured creditors. *Op. cit.*, p. 341.

[33] That the costs of equity receiverships were enormous even though one includes only the direct costs thereof, i.e., fees to receivers and their attorneys, is

Had receivership been typically short-lived, a high time rate for receivers and their lawyers would not have been so expensive; but for reasons already indicated receiverships not infrequently lasted several years.[34] The necessity of getting a high percentage agreement to any proposed plan of reorganization before it could be carried through almost inevitably meant protracted delays. Apart from the moneys paid to receivers there were the fees paid to the various protective committees and their counsel as well as

amply illustrated by the study made of such proceedings in southern California by a special Senate committee in 1933. In 267 equity receiverships administered the ratio of the amount paid to all creditors on all liabilities was 4.41 per cent; and the ratio of the amount paid to general creditors to the amount of the unsecured claims approved was 5.50 per cent. Nevertheless the amount paid in fees to receivers and attorneys was 106.09 per cent of the amount paid to general creditors, and 29.50 per cent of the amount paid to all creditors. See *Hearings on Investigation of Bankruptcy and Receivership Proceedings in United States Courts,* pursuant to S. Res. 78, 73d Congress, 2d Sess., Washington (Government Printing Office), 1934, p. 872. In the opinion of the committee that examined into these cases little benefit resulted, for they reported: "Most of the receiverships into which we made enquiry were found to have been inefficiently operated. The receivers were, for the most part, inexperienced. In some cases attorneys without executive training or any considerable knowledge of business were appointed receivers, and the effect was nothing more than the imposition of a highly expensive superstructure upon the business." *U.S. Sen. Rept. No. 365, 73d Congress, 2d Sess.* (1934), p. 5.

[34] Some evidence on how long receivership proceedings lasted is offered by Dr. W. E. Warrington's study, *The Nature and Extent of Losses to Bondholders in Corporate Reorganization and Liquidation, 1919-1928,* Philadelphia (University of Pennsylvania), 1936. From the appendices of this volume which give the duration of receivership for almost all the cases studied the following table has been compiled. The simple arithmetic average, however, is not as meaningful as it might be since there is considerable variation between cases. Moreover, the table is not to be interpreted too strictly since some figures as given by Warrington are necessarily approximations. The figures follow:

Type of Corporation	No. of Cases	Average Period of Receivership
Steam Railroad	20	2.9 yrs.
Electric Railroad (Liquidation)	23	4.7
Electric Railroad (Interurban)	59	3.8
Electric Railroad (Urban)	29	5.3
Electric Light, Gas and Power Co.	16	2.5
Iron and Steel Producers	10	3.5
Oil Producers and Refiners	15	2.9
Pulp and Paper Manufacturing	10	3.9
Coal Mining	5	1.8
Real Estate and Land Development	3	1.3
Meat Packing and Food Products	7	4.3
Steamship and Navigation	6	4.3
Sugar Growing and Refining	4	2.0

those paid to the reorganization committee. Such committees were self-appointed and on occasion there was more than one committee for a given group of claimants, which meant duplication of effort and expense until they joined forces. It is significant that such committees fixed their own compensation, and persons are not prone to undervalue their own contributions. This tendency of particular groups of professional reorganizers and their attorneys to fix liberal payments for themselves was probably not a necessary consequence of reorganization in equity, but none the less it was a noteworthy characteristic of large equity reorganizations in practice.[35]

The necessity for forming a new corporate entity in order that the assets of the failed corporation might be freed from previous liens and encumbrances was not an economical arrangement for accomplishing the purpose. Yet the courts, except in one case of doubtful validity, had no other means of clearing the assets of pre-existing claims or of determining the amount to which dissenters to the reorganization plan were entitled. The not inconsiderable costs of incorporation and of engraving new bond and share certificates was an expense added to the already serious diffi-

[35] The Securities and Exchange Commission attempted to determine the size of the fees collected by protective and reorganization committees by a sampling process. Its questionnaire was answered by 152 committees where reorganization was completed up to December 31, 1934. In a few (18) committee members received no fees. The S.E.C. was able to tabulate the data for 104 committees where creditor securities were involved with the following results: the face amount of the securities deposited was $247,097,578 and the fees paid to committees were $1,432,717, or 0.58 per cent of the securities deposited. Of the 104 committees, 46 were for creditor securities issued by industrials, and 39 by utilities. From one point of view the face amount of the securities deposited does not sufficiently indicate the costs to the security-holders of committee services since the market value of the securities would typically be less than their face value by a considerable margin. See Securities and Exchange Commission, *Report on the Study, etc., of Protective and Reorganization Committees*, Part I, p. 199.

The fees collected by legal counsel to such committees were also tabulated. For 96 committees for creditor securities, similar to but not necessarily identical with the 104 committees discussed in the previous paragraph, counsel fees were 0.63 per cent of the face value of securities deposited. *Ibid.*, p. 222.

If the Commission's sample is typical of equity reorganization committees, then it would follow that committee and counsel fees together averaged about 1.21 per cent of the face value of the securities deposited. To judge from the cases examined in detail by the S.E.C., however, the range of deviations from the average was considerable,

culties of raising new capital to carry through the plan of reorganization.

The direct expenses of reorganization just alluded to were probably less in the aggregate than the indirect costs in the form of lost business, decline in working efficiency, and general indirection in the conduct of the affairs of the enterprise. Even though some reorganization plan was likely to follow receivership eventually, the protracted delays and uncertainties of receivership inevitably meant a decline in the competitive position of the corporation. In the final analysis these indirect costs had to be borne by the claimholders in the failed enterprise. While such indirect costs are probably difficult to measure in any instant case there is no doubting their reality. And there seems to be little question but that the equity form of corporate reorganization was not of a type to minimize them.

6. *Conclusions on equity reorganization.* If one attempts to summarize the defects of the equity procedure of corporate reorganization on the basis of the foregoing necessarily brief digest he might do so as follows:

The fundamental economic question of the comparative wisdom of liquidation and reorganization was not *expressly* posed anywhere in the proceedings although doubtless the equity courts did consider it, *inter alia,* in granting or denying the petition for the appointment of a receiver. The equity arrangements did not facilitate the raising of additional capital which is almost always a necessary part of any economic rehabilitation of a failed concern. Because dissenters had to be paid in cash, almost unanimous consent to any reorganization plan was necessary before it could be carried through. Only in comparatively late years did the courts consider it part of their duty to pass upon the fairness and feasibility of the reorganization plan. Even then equity courts had only an indirect means, through the upset price, of giving force to their views on the fairness of reorganization plans; the fairness doctrine of the *Boyd* case, although, of course, subsequently a recognized rule, was not one originally formulated by equity courts but imposed upon them from above. Finally equity reorganization was time-consuming and costly from the point of view of all parties in interest.

These were the defects and weaknesses of corporate reorganization in the United States that the amendments to the Bankruptcy Act were designed to remedy.

III. CORPORATE REORGANIZATION UNDER SECTION 77B OF THE BANKRUPTCY ACT

1. Background of 77B. 2. The decision between reorganization and liquidation. 3. Dissenting minorities and 77B. 4. New capital investment and 77B. 5. Independent review and the "fairness" problem under 77B. 6. Speed and economy in reorganization under 77B. 7. Conclusions on 77B.

1. *Background of 77B.* Periods of falling prices and general financial stress and strain have typically called forth strong protests from debtors and a demand that something be done to relieve their plight. The years following 1929 were no exception. It cannot be said, however, that there had been no realization of the faulty procedures for reorganizing failed corporations before the great depression; the law journals prior to 1930 are strewn with articles emphasizing the weaknesses of equity reorganization.[36] But doubtless the depression gave added impetus to the reform movement, with the result that in 1933 and 1934 respectively Amendments 77 and 77B to the Bankruptcy Act of 1898 were enacted. Section 77 applied to railroads engaged in interstate commerce while 77B applied to business corporations generally with the exception of certain types organized under special laws.[37] It is to be observed, therefore, that the amendments drew a distinction between railroad corporations under the Interstate Commerce Commission and other corporations. Moreover, corporations other

[36] See, for instance, the articles of Rosenberg, James N., *et al.*, reprinted in *Corporate Reorganization and the Federal Court*, New York (Baker, Voorhis), 1924.

[37] Section 77B states in the first sentence that its provisions are available to any corporation which could become a bankrupt under section 4 of the Bankruptcy Act; section 4 reads in part, "Any person, except a municipal, railroad, insurance, banking corporation or a building and loan association, shall be entitled to the benefits of this Act as a voluntary bankrupt." Section 77B was not confined entirely to corporations in the very narrow sense. See Finletter, *op. cit.*, pp. 103-111.

than railroads affected with a public interest and under the jurisdiction of regulatory authorities, e.g., state commissions, were given special treatment under section 77B.[38] Thus there was a clear attempt in the amendments to recognize a distinction that the equity courts had long sensed and used, namely, that some enterprises were much more clearly affected with a public interest than others, and on that account required special treatment in reorganization.

Before passing to an examination of the more important sections of 77B,[39] relative to our primary interests, we may note why the reorganization amendments were made a part of the Bankruptcy Act. Historically bankruptcy legislation in the United States had been used to liquidate assets for the benefit of creditors, not at all for the purpose of rehabilitating failed corporations. The reason for changing corporate reorganization procedure by amendment to the Bankruptcy Act was simply that it seemed to be less open to constitutional objections than other federal legislation that might have sought the same end.[40] For reasons already noted state legislation to revise reorganization procedure was impractical.

2. *The decision between reorganization and liquidation.* At first glance 77B appears to have done very little to emphasize the crucial economic importance of the choice between reorganization and liquidation. From one point of view 77B merely recognized and codified the procedure which had grown up for the appointment of receivers by courts of equity. For instance, everyone was familiar with the fiction of the "consent" receivership whereby a corporation itself took the initiative, *via* a friendly creditor, in procuring the appointment of a receiver for its assets. Consequently 77B recognized the fact, and made it possible for the

[38] Section 77B (e) (2) provided that such corporations might not have a plan of reorganization confirmed without first allowing the appropriate regulatory commission to examine the plan and file objections and proposed amendments thereto which the judge was bound to consider. Also it was provided that, "In case the debtor is a public utility corporation wholly intrastate in character no court shall approve any plan of reorganization if the regulatory commission of such State having jurisdiction over such public utility certifies that the public interest is affected by said plan, unless said regulatory commission shall first approve of said plan as to the public interest therein and the fairness thereof." *Ibid.*
[39] We shall be mainly concerned with 77B and only incidentally with 77.
[40] See Finletter, *op. cit.*, pp. 21-34; Gerdes, *op. cit.*, Vol. I, pp. 87-92.

debtor corporation itself to commence proceedings looking towards the appointment of a legal protector of its assets against the onslaught of creditors. Creditors, of course, could still take the necessary steps if for some reason the debtor corporation neglected to do so; but 77B did away with the useless fiction represented by the consent receivership.[41] As in equity proceedings, however, the petition for court protection was addressed to the court's discretion. What were such petitions required to allege and how did the courts decide between granting and denying them; and were the relative values in liquidation and reorganization of the assets of the distressed corporation given full weight in the decision?

A petition for relief under 77B had to allege (a) that the debtor was insolvent in the equity sense of being unable to meet its debts as they matured; (b) that there was a need for relief under the act; (c) that the debtor desired to reorganize.[42] These provisions, attended of course by good faith, had to be met regardless of whether the debtor or its creditors filed the bill. A creditor's petition had really to demonstrate, in addition to the matters required in a debtor's petition, that the corporation had committed an act of bankruptcy, or that equity receivership or liquidation proceedings in bankruptcy were pending. Thus creditors' petitions were really more stringent in their requirements than those of the debtor itself. But 77B went further than this. Having shown that the corporation needed relief such as 77B contemplated, the petition

---

[41] Three creditors having provable claims against the debtor amounting to $1,000 more than the value of any security held by them were entitled to file a petition. Secured creditors could file only if they were "unsecured" in the amount just indicated.

[42] These requirements probably require a further word of explanation. Being unable to pay debts as they mature does not include a case where the corporation has cash but, in order to maintain its competitive position in the industry, prefers not to pay creditors but to use the funds to buy materials, supplies, and the like. See *First National Bank of Cincinnati* v. *Flershem*, 290 U.S. 504 (1934). This case seems to indicate that before relief will be granted the corporation must have exhausted its cash resources and borrowing ability so that default on obligations is imminent. See Finletter, *op. cit.*, pp. 53-59.

Demonstrating a need for relief under the act simply meant a showing that unless court protection were granted, creditors would dismember the assets in their attempts to collect their claims, presumably to the harm of the debtor. The theory was, apparently, that the debtor, being merely temporarily embarrassed, was entitled to relief.

must then show that there was a reasonable prospect of a feasible reorganization being carried through. Although 77B contained no specific provision to this effect, at least one authority contends that the whole tenor of the amendment implied it. Professor T. K. Finletter argues that 77B was intended solely for the purpose of effecting a reorganization, hence, "Unless it can be shown that the probabilities are that this purpose will be achieved, the reorganization court, as in equity, will refuse to assume jurisdiction." [43] If this contention is correct, then we are really getting down to important economic questions such as the relative values of *R* and *L*, in the language of the previous chapter. For what meaning ought to be attached to a feasible plan of reorganization? Certainly no plan of reorganization is "feasible" where the assets would be better liquidated than continued in their present relationship one to another in reorganization. As Finletter has written,[44]

A petitioner, therefore, who is unable to satisfy the court that the properties of the debtor are worth reorganizing and there is a reasonable probability that a plan can be put into effect, has not demonstrated his good faith in the legal sense. To do so he must prove that the court is undertaking a responsibility which will probably accomplish the end for which it is intended. . . . Operating statements and other evidence which will show the fundamental worth of the business must however be presented as otherwise the court cannot know whether liquidation is the proper remedy.

Indeed such a point of view seems to have been expressed by the United States Supreme Court in a recent case where it was said, "However honest in its efforts the debtor may be, and however sincere in its motives, the District Court is not bound to clog its docket with visionary or impracticable schemes for resuscitation." [45] And, furthermore, it is said that in the Southern District of New York the Federal judges adopted a rule that petitioners must show why suitable relief for the debtor was not available under section 12 of the Bankruptcy Act of 1898 which dealt with

[43] *Op. cit.,* p. 63, notes omitted. He goes on to add that specific basis for the contention above could be drawn from the good faith clause and from the clause requiring that the debtor allege a desire to reorganize.

[44] *Op. cit.,* pp. 64-65, notes omitted.

[45] *Tennessee Publishing Co.* v. *American National Bank,* 299 U.S. 18 at 22 (1936).

compositions.[46] These averments seem to indicate that under 77B the courts did consider the relative wisdom of reorganization as contrasted with liquidation in considering the petitions addressed to them. Doubtless the individual judges did not take a uniform attitude towards the pleas of the debtors, some being more lenient than others. Since the question at issue was the relative worth of the assets in reorganization and liquidation, and since the former especially was a matter of judgment, honest differences of opinion were clearly possible. Hence where one judge would deny a petition because, perhaps, he felt R was less than L, another judge, apparently equally competent, might grant the petition because he felt a "reasonable" appraisal showed R to be greater than L.[47]

In view of the foregoing we might reasonably conclude that 77B was an improvement over equity procedure in that there was a greater likelihood that the court would consider the valuation problem, the relation between R and L, in granting or denying petitions.[48] The act might have gone further, in the writer's opinion, and expressly required petitioners to submit positive evidence that reorganization *was* the proper solution to the debtor's problems. Such a provision would have made it easier for the courts to reach a proper decision by bringing the crucial economic problem squarely into the proceedings. Yet notwithstanding the absence of a statutory requirement of this kind, it would appear that 77B in practice was a definite improvement over equity procedure in the

[46] See Finletter, *op. cit.*, p. 71, note. He adds that "such a showing is of course important in determining whether liquidation or rehabilitation should be ordered."

[47] See in this connection the cases discussed by Spaeth, C. B., and Friedberg, J. F., "Early Developments under Section 77B," *Illinois Law Review*, Vol. 30, pp. 137-177 at p. 165 ff.

[48] If the court decided to grant the petition then it might either appoint a trustee in bankruptcy or continue the debtor in possession. In general a trustee in bankruptcy under 77B performed the same functions as an equity receiver. See Finletter, *op. cit.*, Ch. IV. In a good many cases the debtor was continued in possession and in that instance held very nearly the same relation to the court as would a trustee. The Securities and Exchange Commission reports that in 1936 out of 810 proceedings instituted which it examined the debtor was continued in possession in 67 per cent (543 cases) thereof. S.E.C. *Report on the Study and Investigation, etc., of Protective and Reorganization Committees*, Part II, Washington, 1937, p. 523, note. Many persons feel that to continue debtors in possession was a bad practice but the argument is certainly not clear-cut either way. Under section 77 a trustee had to be appointed.

amount of attention devoted to the question of the relative valuation of the assets.

3. *Dissenting minorities and 77B.* Section 77B practically did away with the problem of getting a large percentage agreement to a plan of reorganization and the affiliated problem under equity of raising cash to pay dissenters. In the first place, no dissenters were entitled to be paid in cash: they were bound by statute to accept whatever terms the majority had agreed to. The percentage agreement necessary to secure confirmation of the reorganization plan by the court was two-thirds of the creditors and a majority of the stockholders. The acceptance of the plan by creditors, of course, was not by all creditors regardless of status, but by classes of creditors. Creditors whose claims were not affected by the plan or whose claims were to be paid in cash did not have to consent to the plan of reorganization.[49]

The approval of the shareholders, by classes if such there were, was not necessary where the debtor was found to be insolvent, that is, the value of the creditors' claims exceeded the value of the assets, for in that instance the value of the shareholders' equity would clearly be a negative quantity. Since the same principle applied to creditors in the order of their priority, it is quite clear that 77B, at least nominally, took a stand in favor of the absolute priority doctrine for scaling down claims rather than the alternative rule of relative priority. It is equally clear, however, that the significance to be attached to this stand depended upon how strictly or how generously the courts appraised the total asset values available for division between the claimants. For the first time, perhaps, the courts were faced with the problem of evaluating enterprises, not for ratemaking purposes, "a fair return on a fair valuation," but on the basis of the prospective earning power. As a consequence, original cost less depreciation figures, or fancy engineering appraisals based upon unexpired physical service life regardless of the *value* of those physical services, are quite beside the point. The only relevant consideration is what can the assets

[49] Section 77B (b) (5) contained a rather complicated provision to cover situations where two-thirds of the creditors of a particular class did not assent to the plan; in effect, the judge was to pass upon the terms allotted them as to fairness, protection, etc. This provision need not concern us in what follows.

be made to earn through future time. Having decided to reorganize rather than to liquidate, evaluation on an original cost basis is senseless and none but prospective earning power is left. That some legal writers and some judges have seen this goes almost without saying, but whether the principle was generally recognized by the courts in determining whether or not stockholders had any equity in the asserts, and hence were entitled to vote upon a plan of reorganization, is not so clear.[50] Yet even if the courts did use prospective earning power as the basis of valuation for this purpose, there would still be room for varying degrees of optimism in estimating the prospective income stream. Consequently where some judges would allow that the stockholders had an equity, and therefore had to approve the plan, other judges if acting in the same case would deny that there was anything for shareholders.[51]

4. *New capital investment and 77B.* Section 77B facilitated the task of raising additional capital as part of a reorganization plan in two ways. In the first place, it was not necessary to pay dissenters to the plan in cash and therefore, as contrasted with reorganization in equity, it decreased the amount of cash that had to be raised. We have noted heretofore that section 77B permitted two-thirds of the creditors in amount of any class to impose an arrangement for the settlement of their claims upon the remaining one-third. If the plan adopted called for no immediate cash payment to creditors, no dissenter had a right to demand (nominal) liquidation of the corporation—via a receiver's sale at or above an upset price fixed by the court—to determine the size of his cash settlement. We emphasized earlier that the cash settlement to dissenters complicated and partially stalemated reorganizations in equity; hence its removal alone, by the 77B amendment, was a

[50] Finletter is certainly under no misapprehensions as to what is relevant in determining value for this purpose. He writes, "In the case of productive properties the earning capacity of the assets should be the base of the valuation. . . . The economic worth of productive property is measured by its capacity to earn. An economic valuation of productive assets would therefore equal the sum of all future earnings of the property discounted as of the date the valuation is made. Such an economic valuation is, it is believed, appropriate to proceedings under the reorganization acts." *Op. cit.*, pp. 498-499. See also *ibid.*, pp. 499-506, where he develops the point and cites cases to show that some courts have recognized the view taken.

[51] See the cases discussed by Bonbright, *op. cit.*, Vol. II, pp. 884-889, which show varying degrees of liberality in the treatment of shareholders.

notable step towards rapid and economical reorganization. But with respect to the problem of raising capital there was also a marked advance because if dissenters were not paid in cash, the total cash necessary to carry through a plan of reorganization was definitely reduced.

Section 77B contributed to the solution of the capital-raising problem in corporate reorganization, however, in another way: it made more accessible the sources through which cash could be raised. That is, not only did 77B decrease the cash required in reorganization but it simplified the supply problem. In general, a corporation in the process of reorganization has three main sources from which cash might be raised: first, by the sale of new securities; second, by the cash sale of a portion of its assets; i.e., a transformation from one asset form to another; third, by a moratorium on cash payments to creditors whereby cash balances accumulate gradually.[52] Under the equity system the chief means of raising cash in reorganization was by the sale of securities of the successor corporation to the security-holders of the failed corporation partly in exchange for their old securities and partly for cash; such cash payments usually being termed "assessments." In some measure, however, the equity system used the other two methods also. Yet with respect to all three the ease of their employment was much less under equity procedure than under the statutory provisions of 77B. In the first place, 77B being an amendment to the Bankruptcy Act required that "A plan of reorganization . . . (1) *shall* include provisions modifying or altering the rights of creditors generally, or of any class of them, secured or unsecured, either through the issuance of new securities of any character or otherwise; (2) *may* include provisions modifying or altering the rights of stockholders generally:" [53] Since two-thirds of the creditors could bind a whole class thereof and since no judicial sale was necessary to displace liens or otherwise modify rights, it was comparatively easy to raise cash by selling new securities having a first claim on assets and earnings, by converting securities with fixed income claims into

[52] If creditors agree to postpone their claims for a certain interval during which the enterprise continues to operate, then cash receipts will exceed cash outlays, which means that cash balances will become larger.

[53] Section 77B (b) italics supplied.

contingent claims, or by postponing maturity dates of bond issues and reducing their contractual interest rates. Whereas under equity it was almost impossible to give new capital contributors rights in assets and earnings more than equal to those retained by the first claimants in the failed corporation, under 77B it was comparatively easy to give them exclusively first claims because pre-existing liens and contracts were easily modified. In the less serious cases of business failure a temporary moratorium on interest payments and, perhaps, an extension of principal maturities was sufficient to take care of cash needs. Yet, under equity, such comparatively simple adjustments required the same complicated and expensive procedure of receivership and judicial sale to raise capital as reorganizations where new capital was needed in large sums. Section 77B made it easier to adapt the remedy to the seriousness of the new investment requirements.

5. *Independent review and the "fairness" problem under 77B.* Under section 77B the court was obliged to pass upon the "fairness" of the reorganization plan, and the judge might not confirm a plan unless "it is fair and equitable and does not discriminate unfairly in favor of any class of creditors or stockholders, and is feasible." [54] Yet notwithstanding this clause there was nowhere in 77B any statement that would indicate precisely the meaning to be given the phrase "fair plan of reorganization." Since shareholders were excluded where they had no equity, i.e., where the enterprise is insolvent, one might infer an attempt to codify the rule of the *Boyd* case. Yet since the plan *must* modify or alter the rights of creditors and *may* alter the rights of shareholders, the philosophy of the *Boyd* case was certainly not followed all the way through.[55] At least one writer argues that under 77B the plan must meet two tests as to fairness: (1) the order of priority of the claims is recognized; (2) each creditor or shareholder is given the full worth of his interest in the debtor's assets.[56] But where no criteria

---

[54] 77B (f) (1).

[55] Some modification of creditors' rights was doubtless necessary to make the amendment a part of the Bankruptcy Act.

[56] See Gerdes, *op. cit.*, Vol. II, p. 1739. But note the following by R. S. Foster in "Conflicting Ideals for Reorganization," *Yale Law Journal*, Vol. 44, pp. 923-960 at p. 958.

"The assumption of solvency, however, will make it difficult to accomplish the desired scaling down of creditors' claims. Both reorganization acts enjoin the

of fairness and feasibility were established by the statute, probably each court judged each plan of reorganization according to its own individual and shadowy standards. Certainly some courts felt that 77B was intended to deal leniently with debtors, and with this major premise there would be a tendency to find an equity for shareholders on the barest evidence.[57]

Under 77B the court was not required to pass upon the reorganization plan until it had been accepted by the requisite percentages of stockholders and creditors. That is, to some extent committees, similar to those employed in equity proceedings, continued under 77B to propose plans and to secure assents thereto.[58] Even though assented to by the required percentages, the court had to consider the plan as to fairness and feasibility on its own account and either confirm it or reject it. At the hearing any interested party might enter objections to the plan or propose modifications thereto. Yet there seems to be little doubt but that the court would be influenced in its decision by the fact that the required percentages of creditors and shareholders had already approved the plan; for, from the court's point of view, acceptance was presumptive evidence that the plan was fair. However, with the continuance of the committee system such an inference was not entirely warranted.

preservation of the equity, if any, of junior creditors in language substantially identical with that applicable to stockholders. While it is possible to bind an entire class of creditors to terms accepted by two-thirds in amount, this is only in case the plan is found to be "fair and equitable." Objecting junior creditors may point to the assumption of solvency as indicating one hundred per cent equity for them, no matter how trivial the participation offered to stockholders. Dissenting bondholders may use the same argument in case anything is offered to junior creditors, and use it even more persuasively in case equities of both junior creditors and stockholders are recognized. They will insist that the standard of fairness under the amendments to the bankruptcy act must be that hitherto laid down by the Supreme Court as applicable to equity reorganizations."

[57] The provisions governing the proposal of plans of reorganization seem to be more favorable to shareholders than creditors, assuming the debtor is solvent. A plan could be proposed by the debtor, or by 10 per cent of the shares of any class or 5 per cent of all shares; the corresponding percentages for creditors were 10 and 25. Section 77B (d). See also Barrett, E. B., " 'Fair Plan' under Section 77B, Applicability of the Boyd Case," *Michigan Law Review*, Vol. 34 (1936), pp. 992-1002.

[58] Deposit agreements could be reviewed by the court if the latter so desired. Indeed, in practice they were often submitted to the court in order to exempt them from the Securities Act of 1933. Under section 77 the control of committees by the Interstate Commerce Commission was substantial.

Thus while 77B recognized the fairness problem in reorganization it cannot be said that it did very much more than this; the criteria for judging fairness were not stated in the amendment and allowing judicial approval after, rather than before, submission to the parties in interest probably encouraged the courts to take a passive rather than an active part in the whole fairness question.

6. *Speed and economy in reorganization under 77B.* Section 77B speeded up the process of reorganization and reduced the costs thereof because it did away with most of the time-consuming and (therefore) costly features of equity reorganizations. The very much smaller percentages of creditors and shareholders required to impose a plan of reorganization upon the enterprise (assuming judicial approval thereof of course), meant that much less time was needed to reach an agreement. It was usually unnecessary to form a new corporate entity and by stamping the outstanding securities with the contractual changes agreed to, the costs of engraving new securities, etc., were avoided. Costs were reduced and the effectiveness of the reorganization machinery was increased by giving the bankruptcy court jurisdiction over the debtor's property wherever located; nothing comparable to ancillary receiverships in equity remained. Section 77B also gave the court much greater control over the expenses of committees charged against the debtor's estate than was ever had under equity: the judge had to measure each charge against the estate as to its "reasonableness" in relation to the service rendered to the reorganization.[59]

7. *Conclusions on 77B.* In summary one could urge that 77B was a marked improvement over the equity system of corporate reorganization in the way in which it handled the problem of raising new capital. The question of the choice between reorganization and liquidation in terms of the economic considerations involved was not expressly posed but there is some evidence that the courts took it into account in administering 77B. Section 77B was less expensive and swifter in its operations than equity proce-

[59] Technically the court had no control over private agreements between security holders and committees except insofar as they related directly to the reorganization. Yet indirectly the court could control these too by refusing to confirm a plan where improper charges are involved. See Finletter, *op. cit.*, p. 315.

dure and to this extent was an improvement. Possibly the amendment was least satisfactory in its handling of the fairness problem and the technique of independent review. The abuses under the committee and deposit agreement system were largely untouched; and probably many creditors and shareholders were asked to approve plans of reorganization prepared by such committees which they understood only vaguely. Yet the court was not required to pass upon the fairness of the plan until after acceptance by the parties in interest, a sequence which probably emphasized the private rather than the public interests at stake, and perhaps also encouraged automatic judicial approval of plans privately agreed to.

IV. CORPORATE REORGANIZATION UNDER CHAPTER X OF THE CHANDLER ACT

1. Background of Chapter X. 2. The decision between reorganization and liquidation. 3. Dissenting minorities and capital investment. 4. Independent review and the "fairness" problem under Chapter X: a. The independent trustee provision. b. The independent trustee and the preparation of the plan of reorganization. c. The adoption of the reorganization plan. 5. Speed and economy of reorganization under Chapter X. 6. Conclusions on Chapter X.

1. *Background of Chapter X.* Section 77B was enacted into law in some haste in order to promote business recovery by relieving distressed debtor corporations.[60] It is therefore not surprising that sober reflection and experience should subsequently suggest the desirability of certain changes in the 77B procedure. Indeed something of the kind seems to have been envisaged at the time, for section 211 of the Securities and Exchange Act of 1934 directed the Securities and Exchange Commission to make a study of cor-

---

[60] As already observed, the defects of equity reorganizations had long been a subject of comment. All that is meant above in the text is that 77B was rushed through in the early days of the Roosevelt administration together with many other measures, and that probably it received less careful attention than it might have received in less strenuous times. On the other hand, it is a fair guess that nothing would have been done to correct the weaknesses of equity reorganization had there not been a serious economic depression.

porate reorganization and protective committees and to report its
results and recommendations to Congress.[61] Hence the changes in
reorganization procedure introduced by Chapter X of the Chandler
Bill were based upon the experience gained under 77B and upon
the Securities and Exchange Commission's comprehensive study
of reorganization practices. Indeed Chapter X of the revised Bankruptcy Act of 1938 which deals with corporate reorganization is
in a sense the Commission's bill. The parallelism between the Commission's recommendations and the provisions of Chapter X is very
marked.[62] On the other hand, a comparison of the amendment to
the Bankruptcy Act of 1898, dealing with the reorganization of
interstate railroads (Section 77), and Chapter X suggests that certain of its provisions were used as a model in drafting the new
reorganization statute.

Since the Securities and Exchange Commission's report so largely
parallels the philosophy embodied in the provisions of Chapter
X, the findings and recommendations of that study will bear brief
review before we consider the changes introduced by the statute
itself.

The Securities and Exchange Commission has been primarily
charged with protecting the interests of investors, and by and large
its study of reorganization practices as exemplified in important
cases sought to show how investors' interests were jeopardized, or
even disregarded, under prevailing procedures.[63] In the main the
Commission emphasized the dangers, especially in large reorganiza-

[61] The Securities and Exchange Commission's comprehensive study appeared
at various dates from 1936 on as *Report on the Study and Investigation of the
Work, Activities, Personnel and Functions of Protective and Reorganization Committees.* Seven volumes have appeared up to the present (early 1939) and an
eighth is scheduled soon. It should be noted that the Commission's study employs
a broader concept of reorganization than that employed in the present work:
reorganization in their usage also included what we have called readjustment.

[62] The S.E.C. conclusions and recommendations will be found in *ibid.,* Part I,
Washington (Government Printing Office), 1937, pp. 897-916. The so-called *Lea
Bill* (H.R. 6968, 75th Congress) was also sponsored by the S.E.C. but failed of
passage. It dealt in the main with the solicitation of proxies and deposits. For a
discussion of the practices with respect to deposit agreements which required
correction in the view of the Commission see Part II of their study and Fortas,
Abe, "The Securities Act and Corporate Reorganizations," *Law and Contemporary Problems,* Vol. 4 (1937), pp. 218-240.

[63] Certain abuses of equity reorganization discussed by the S.E.C. but corrected
by 77B are omitted from consideration here.

tions, of strategically situated groups such as investment bankers and/or the management gaining control of the reorganization and deriving emoluments therefrom at the expense of the bona-fide claim-holders against the failed corporation. On the basis of the cases studied the Commission felt that investors' interests were especially endangered by two not uncommon practices: first, continuing the debtor in possession in the bankruptcy proceedings, i.e., not appointing a trustee, or appointing as trustee someone who had been previously connected with the failed corporation; second, the domination of security holders' protective committees by persons with similar affiliations. In other words, the Commission felt strongly that investors' interests in reorganization could only be protected properly if the whole proceedings were taken out of the hands of those who had been closely affiliated with the corporation before failure. Coupled with all this was the Commission's insistence that "full disclosure" throughout the whole proceedings would be wholesome.

On the positive side the Securities and Exchange Commission's report took the position that the reorganization of failed corporations is not simply a matter of private concern. Public interests are involved too; and therefore a public officer should play an active role in the proceedings and an expert public body should be allowed to comment upon reorganization plans before they are adopted.[64]

These few sentences of course do far less than justice to the exhaustive reports of the Securities and Exchange Commission on reorganization. But perhaps they at least suggest the underlying ideas and principles upon which the revised reorganization statute, Chapter X of the Chandler Bill, was drafted.

2. *The decision between reorganization and liquidation.* On first reading, Chapter X appears to do very little more to bring the important economic question of the choice between reorganization and liquidation squarely into the judicial proceedings than did the law and practice under 77B which it superseded. Either the debtor or its creditors may file a petition, and creditors' petitions, as under

---

[64] These remarks strictly apply only to the views of the Commission with respect to large, quasi-public corporations.

77B, must allege more facts than debtors' petitions.[65] Petitions must state substantially the same matters as before but in addition there must now be included "the specific facts showing the need for relief under this chapter and why adequate relief cannot be obtained under chapter XI of this Act" (sec. 130 [7]). Since Chapter XI deals with compositions by corporate debtors with unsecured creditors it is apparently the intention that Chapter X will be employed only to reorganize corporations where the problem is complicated by the presence of secured claims and different classes of creditors. Petitions must, of course, be filed in "good faith," and Chapter X endeavors to define good faith negatively. Section 77B did not define "good faith," but court rulings thereunder inevitably clarified the concept and such negations have been codified under Chapter X. Thus, section 146 states that a petition is not to be interpreted as filed in good faith if the creditors have obtained their claims for the purpose of filing a petition, or, if "it is unreasonable to expect that a plan of reorganization can be effected." Since the burden of proving good faith lies with the petitioner,[66] courts could, if they wished, insist upon definite evidence that the failed corporation ought to be reorganized in the interests of all parties rather than liquidated. To take such an attitude would be an easy way of introducing this important question specifically into the proceedings. Whether the courts will use section 146 to this end remains to be seen. It is worth noting in passing, however, that section 137 of Chapter X allows any creditor, indenture trustee, or stockholder (if the debtor is solvent), to file an answer to the petition controverting the facts there alleged. There was no similar provision in 77B. It may be, therefore, that under Chapter X creditors will have a greater opportunity to urge the virtues of liquidating the failed corporation rather than reor-

[65] Chapter X also allows an indenture trustee to file a petition; this was not possible under 77B.

Creditors must have claims of at least $5,000 in order to file a petition, not $1,000 as under 77B. Over and above the information and allegations of a debtor's petition creditors must allege one or more of the following: an act of bankruptcy, that an equity receiver has been appointed, that an indenture trustee is in possession of the debtor's property, or that mortgage foreclosure proceedings are pending. See sec. 131.

[66] See *In re Philadelphia Rapid Transit Co.*, 8 F. Supp. 51; *id.*, 73 F. (2d) 1022; *In re Grigsby-Grunow*, 77 F (2d) 200.

ganizing it, and if so, the court will have to consider the evidence and rule on the question.

Chapter X contains another provision not to be found in 77B, however, which may also force the court at least to consider the probable wisdom of liquidation instead of reorganization. Section 167, dealing with the duties of the trustee for the debtor's property, states that the trustee "shall, if the judge shall so direct, forthwith investigate the acts, conduct, property, liabilities, and financial condition of the debtor, the operation of its business, *and the desirability of the continuance thereof* . . . and report thereon to the judge"; and the trustee is to report to the creditors, shareholders, etc., the results of this investigation.[67] If judges care to make use of this section they could in each case require positive evidence that it is desirable to reorganize the business, i.e., continue it, before allowing the proceedings to go very far. Taking section 167 in conjunction with the interpretation of "good faith" suggested by Finletter and discussed above, it might be argued that adequate statutory grounds now exist for bringing the basic economic question of whether R is greater than L directly before the court for decision.

3. *Dissenting minorities and capital investment.* Since the new principles introduced by 77B were felt to be reasonably adequate to deal with the problem of dissenting minorities and with the problem of raising new capital to carry the reorganization plan into effect, Chapter X introduces no changes in these respects. We may therefore pass at once to a consideration of the very important innovations under Chapter X affecting the preparation and adoption of the actual plan of reorganization itself.

4. *Independent review and the "fairness" problem under Chapter X.* In respect to the "fair plan" problem in corporate reorganization Chapter X takes the position (by implication) that the place to begin working towards this end is at the very commencement of the legal proceedings. In other words, instead of allowing committees and other interested parties first to work out some reorganization plan and then subsequently present it to a court for an independent judgment as to its fairness, the point of view

[67] Italics supplied.

of Chapter X is that a disinterested official should have a hand in the affair from the very first. Some such reasoning certainly seems to underlie the principle of the independent trustee and the powers and duties accorded him under the bill.

a. *The independent trustee provision.* Chapter X withdraws the discretionary power formerly allowed the bankruptcy court under 77B between appointing a trustee for the debtor's estate and continuing the debtor in possession, except in the case of small corporations. If the indebtedness of the failed corporation "liquidated as to amount and not contingent as to liability" is less than $250,-000 the court *may* continue the debtor in possession or appoint a trustee as it sees fit; but where the indebtedness is more than the specified sum the court *must* appoint a trustee (sec. 156). And to be eligible for trusteeship under the Act a person must be "disinterested" as defined negatively by the statute. According to sec. 158 a trustee is not disinterested if

(1) he is a creditor or stockholder of the debtor; or

(2) he is or was an underwriter of any of the outstanding securities of the debtor or within five years prior to the date of filing the petition was the underwriter of any securities of the debtor; or

(3) he is, or was within two years prior to the date of the filing of the petition, a director, officer, or employee of the debtor or any such underwriter, or an attorney for the debtor or such underwriter; or

(4) it appears that he has, by reason of any other direct or indirect relationship to, connection with, or interest in the debtor or such underwriter, or for any reason an interest materially adverse to the interests of any class of creditors or stockholders.

In his discretion, however, the judge may appoint an additional trustee who is "a director, officer, or employee of the debtor" (sec. 156) for the purpose of operating the business and managing the debtor's property. Thus, under the Chandler Bill, the sequestration of the reorganization proceedings from domination by former officers, directors, and investment bankers of the failed corporation would seem to be complete. Not only must an independent trustee be appointed but he is saddled with important responsibilities under the new procedure.[68]

---

[68] The wisdom of *requiring* the appointment of an independent trustee was debated in the hearings on the bill and many responsible persons took a negative view. Judge John C. Knox said, "Now, all corporations and their managements

Directly in line with the theory of removing those formerly affiliated with the corporation from the reorganization process, the independent trustee is required to "report to the judge any facts ascertained by him pertaining to fraud, misconduct, mismanagement and irregularities, and to any causes of action available to the estate" (sec. 167). That is, not only may the former management have nothing to do with the reorganization proceedings, but the trustee must determine their culpability with a view to bringing legal action against them for the benefit of claim-holders against the failed corporation. Co-operation between the trustee and the former management in ascertaining the causes of failure and in remedying the difficulties is not likely to be encouraged by such a provision.[69]

are not bad. Competition, a strike, a bad season, a variety of other circumstances may make it necessary for a corporation to come to court for assistance. A corporation and its management may be known to the court. The conditions that brought it to court may be open to anybody of intelligence and who is interested in the situation. Why, under conditions of that kind, should it be obligatory upon the court to appoint a trustee upon the filing of the petition? If disclosures and investigation indicate that a trustee is to be appointed or should be appointed, then let the appointment be made."

In *Wright* v. *Vinton*, 300 U.S. 440 at 466, the Supreme Court said, "The mortgagor is in default, but it is not therefore to be assumed that he is a wrongdoer, or incompetent to conduct farming operations. . . . The mortgagor is familiar with the property. . . . It is not unreasonable to assume that, under these circumstances, the interests of all concerned will be better served by leaving him in possession than by installing a disinterested receiver or trustee."

It has also been argued that to leave the debtor in possession is less expensive and involves fewer interruptions of its business connections. Furthermore, Professor Dodd has pointed out that, since independent trustees must be chosen, an existing management may cut corners in all directions, e.g., skimp on maintenance and repairs, in order to stave off filing as long as possible. Such methods may not work for the benefit of security-holders. See Dodd, E. Merrick, Jr., "The Securities and Exchange Commission's Reform Program for Bankruptcy Reorganizations," *Columbia Law Review*, Vol. 38, pp. 223-255, at p. 228.

[69] Indeed, it would seem to the present writer that it is very doubtful if, on net balance, creditors and shareholders will gain as much as they will lose from such a requirement. Doubtless cases of malfeasance will arise where something may be recovered; but probably in most cases no cause of action will exist or nothing can be recovered. Yet because of this provision managements will tend to be secretive and unco-operative instead of open and helpful. Such obstructionist tactics are almost certain to delay reorganization, to result in lost business during the trustee's incumbency, and, in general, to impose losses on creditors and shareholders. Professor Dodd (*op. cit.*, p. 227) also makes a good point when he writes, "Where a corporation which is in need of reorganization is actively engaged in business operations, the successful conduct of these operations will in most cases be of even greater importance to the security holders and creditors than is the possible recovery of substantial sums by litigation. Successful conduct

b. *The independent trustee and the preparation of the plan of reorganization.* Much the most important duty of the independent trustee, however, is to prepare the plan of reorganization. In this task he takes the initiative and has the final responsibility; but shareholders, creditors, or indenture trustees are all encouraged to offer suggestions and proposals.[70] The plan having been prepared within a time fixed by the judge, a hearing is held thereon at which the debtor, any stockholder, or creditor may enter objections or propose modifications. Even then, however, the plan is not offered to shareholders for approval; a disinterested party in the form of the Securities and Exchange Commission is allowed first to examine and study it. Section 172 provides that before approving any plan the judge "may, if the scheduled indebtedness of the debtor does not exceed $3,000,000, and shall, if such indebtedness exceeds $3,000,000, submit to the Securities and Exchange Commission for examination and report the plan or plans which the judge regards worthy of consideration. Such report shall be advisory only." Thus before the plan is submitted to creditors and shareholders for adoption an expert yet disinterested body may offer comments and suggestions on the specific arrangement pro-

of a business requires familiarity with that business, and, at least where the enterprise is a highly competitive one, also requires aggressiveness, willingness to take risks, and the ability to preserve profitable business relationships. Even though a management has not been able to pay a corporation's debts as they fall due, it is still in many cases in a better position to furnish these and other important qualifications for success than is likely to be the case with an outsider."

It is not easy to discover just why this provision was inserted in the statute. But it may be noted in passing that the Securities and Exchange Commission, to judge from the report, was much impressed by the suits instituted by the trustee in bankruptcy in the Kreuger and Toll affairs. Two comments, however, are in order with respect to that case: first, it could scarcely be argued that the Kreuger case gave any reasonable indication of the degree of culpability present in the typical instance of corporate failure; second, while the aggregate amounts recovered by the trustee, including certain claims against the estate that the trustee was successful in having disallowed, were large *absolutely*, they were small *relatively* to the established claims against the estate, being something less than 1 per cent it seems. See, S.E.C., *op. cit.*, Part I, pp. 909-916.

[70] For corporations with indebtedness less than $250,000 where no trustee is appointed a plan may be proposed by the debtor or any shareholder, creditor, etc. But at any time the court may designate a disinterested person to formulate a plan for a small corporation too. It is said that under 77B some courts had the trustee take the initiative in order to hurry the proceedings along. See Swanstrom, Luther D. *Chapter X: Reorganization under the Federal Statute,* Chicago (Foundation), 1938, p. 13.

posed. Since the Commission's report is to be sent to all persons affected by the plan the likelihood of an intelligent vote for or against the plan by individual shareholders and creditors is enormously enhanced.[71]

c. *The adoption of the reorganization plan.* In presenting the plan for adoption to creditors and stockholders, Chapter X reverses the order of procedure of 77B. Under the latter, it will be remembered, the claim-holders accepted the plan *before* it was presented to the judge for approval as to fairness and feasibility. Now the judge approves first and creditors and stockholders *afterwards,* which is likely to remove any pressure judges formerly may have felt to approve a plan because the interested parties were seemingly satisfied. To warrant approval by the judge Chapter X requires, of course, that the proposed plan shall be "fair and equitable, and feasible"; but it also requires that the plan shall conform to the important stipulations set out in section 216. In general, section 216 is an expression of what might be called certain principles of "sound finance" if that were not already a phrase of doubtful meaning. Nevertheless reorganization plans in their financial aspects must conform to the provisions there set forth to gain judicial approval. Let us look into these.

The reorganization plan must include "equitable" provisions for the "selection of the persons who are to be directors, officers, or voting trustees, if any, upon the consummation of the plan, and their respective successors" (sec. 216 [11]). Just what equitable provisions would be with respect to such matters probably is less easy to define than to point out inequitable provisions contained in a given plan. Doubtless experience will tend to provide criteria; but even then individual judgment will necessarily play a large part; this means that the judge's discretionary power is apt to be controlling. Less vague is the requirement that the plan *must* contain no non-voting stock and where shares are preferred as to dividends they must have suitable contract clauses allowing such

[71] Indeed one might almost safely predict that a plan to which the S.E.C. sees no objection and of which the judge approves is almost certain of adoption. On the other hand, although the S.E.C. is in an advisory capacity only, any objections it offers to a plan are likely to weigh heavily with security-holders, especially small holders, and probably will block its adoption. The potential influence of the S.E.C., assuming no diminution in its present prestige, is likely to be very large.

preferred shareholders to elect directors in the event of default.[72]
A companion provision with respect to the security contracts
seems to leave the court such wide discretionary power that it
must be quoted in full. Section 216 (12) (b) required that the
charter of the reorganized corporation must include—

(1) provisions which are fair and equitable and in accordance with
sound business and accounting practice, with respect to the terms,
position, rights and privileges of the several classes of securities of the
debtor or of such corporation, including without limiting the gen-
erality of the foregoing, provisions with respect to the issuance, acquisition, purchase, retirement or redemption of any such securities, and
the declaration and payment of dividends thereon; and (2) in the case
of a debtor whose indebtedness, liquidated as to amount and not contingent as to liability, is $250,000 or over, provision with respect to
the making, not less than annually, of periodic reports to security
holders which shall include profit and loss statements and balance
sheets prepared in accordance with sound business and accounting
practice.

In interpreting and applying clause (1) above, the Securities and
Exchange Commission is more likely to take the lead rather than
the judge unless the inequities are glaring. At least this will probably be true of the larger and more complicated reorganizations.
Of course an independent trustee, being aware of the statutory
requirements, will not ordinarily tender a plan that is obviously
defective. Consequently in the simpler cases of reorganization the
section quoted may simply give the trustee general guidance rather
than strict limitations.[73]

There are, to be sure, other requirements such that the plan
must include suitable means for carrying it into effect, for dealing
with groups that do not assent, for paying costs and expenses, etc.

[72] This section (sec. 216 [12] [a]) is far from clear, however, because where
all shares must be allowed the voting privilege, to allow preferred shareholders
merely to elect directors upon default would give them nothing they did not
have already. The clause does *not* say preferred shareholders are to elect a majority of the directorate which might have been intended. Possibly this section
together with the one quoted above might allow a court to impose such a requirement.

[73] There is a suggestion, *not* a requirement, in sec. 216 (9) that where the reorganization plan provides for creditor contracts running beyond five years these
should be retired within the useful life of the property, or in any case not less
than forty years, by means of sinking funds or otherwise.

But in the main these are identical with or very like the clauses of 77B dealing with the same matters and they need not detain us here.

Only after hearings to consider objections to the plan have been held, after the Securities and Exchange Commission has filed its report and suggestions, if it elects to do so, and after the judge is satisfied that the plan conforms to the stipulations of section 216 just discussed, is the plan offered to creditors and shareholders for acceptance or rejection. Furthermore, without the court's approval no committee or person may solicit acceptances, conditional or otherwise, of any plan before the judge has approved a particular plan for submission to creditors and stockholders (sec. 176). This prohibition aims to eliminate the not uncommon practice by which depositors with protective committees almost automatically surrendered to the latter the power to accept or reject plans on their behalf.[74] As under 77B if two-thirds of the creditors of each class and a majority of the stockholders accept the plan in writing then the plan is ready for confirmation. At this juncture the court holds another hearing—this time on the confirmation of the plan—at which the debtor, creditors, stockholders, indenture trustees, the Secretary of the Treasury, the S.E.C. may object to the confirmation of the plan. In the great majority of the cases this last hearing will probably be a formality only and the reorganized corporation, having passed through the fire, will continue on its way rejoicing.

5. *Speed and economy of reorganization under Chapter X.* Whether the changes introduced by Chapter X are likely to increase or to decrease the speed and economy with which reorganizations will be effected cannot be predicted at this early date with much confidence. The probabilities, however, are that reorganization will be less rapid than under 77B and perhaps slightly more costly too, especially if the indirect costs are counted in. The mandatory provision with respect to disinterested trustees is likely to be more expensive than the not uncommon practice under 77B of continuing the debtor in possession; and if friction develops between the former management and the independent trustee, the

---

[74] Every person (or committee) representing twelve or more shareholders or creditors under the plan is required to file with the court a full statement of whom he represents and how he came to be employed. Sec. 211.

costs in terms of lost business and a generally unvigorous conduct of the debtor's affairs may be sizable.[75] The number of hearings provided for in the proceedings as well as the number of parties entitled to be heard have been increased under Chapter X so that almost certainly more time will be required to effect a reorganization. The cost of the Securities and Exchange Commission's reports and interventions will not be charged against the estate, but it should not be assumed that on that account they are unreal or incidental. The added duties imposed upon the trustee under Chapter X will not necessarily mean increased costs because for the most part the trustee now does what others formerly did and were paid for. The new bill provides for judicial review and approval of committee's expenses and attorneys' fees before they may be levied against the estate as did 77B [76] (article XIII). Even though it should develop that reorganization under Chapter X is slower and more costly than under 77B it does not necessarily follow, of course, that the added time and expense will not be well spent. As observed earlier economy and fairness are conflicting ends in reorganization. Hence, if sufficiently better reorganization plans should result, the added cost will be more than worth while. Experience alone, however, can provide the answer here.

6. *Conclusions on Chapter X.* In summary, one might venture the conclusion that the most outstanding innovation of Chapter X is its greatly increased emphasis upon the fairness problem in corporate reorganization and its attempt to provide suitable machinery for achieving that end. The independent trustee, having him prepare the plan, allowing all parties, regardless of their size, to be heard at all stages of the proceedings, the injection of the Securities and Exchange Commission into the system, the more rigid control of committees, and finally, the whole tenor of the act—all these emphasize the fairness problem. Chapter X goes a long way

[75] Some writers feel that such apprehensions are without much foundation. See, for instance, Levi, Edward H., "Corporate Reorganization and a Ministry of Justice," *Minnesota Law Review*, Vol. 23 (1938), pp. 3-29 at pp. 10-12. But cf. Swaine, Robert T., "'Democratization' of Corporate Reorganizations," *Columbia Law Review*, Vol. 38 (1938), pp. 256-279, and Dodd, *ibid.*, pp. 225-229.

[76] Chapter X indeed allows for more parties to be recompensed than did 77B. Under 77B courts were apparently cautious about allowing reimbursement for services which, although valuable, did not *directly* contribute to the reorganization plan adopted. See S.E.C., *op. cit.*, Part I, pp. 808-809.

beyond the earlier theory that corporate reorganization is the sole concern of the parties directly in interest: the general welfare and the maintenance of standards of ordinary decency and fair dealing are emphasized throughout. That it falls short of perfection in some respects goes without saying; [77] but that it is, in general, an appropriate step in the right direction can hardly be denied.

V. SUMMARY

Corporate reorganization constitutes a readjustment of property rights, and the legal system must provide a forum within which such adjustments can be carried through. In the United States three systems have been used: reorganization through courts of equity, reorganization under 77B of the Revised Bankruptcy Act of 1898, and reorganization under Chapter X of the Bankruptcy Act of 1938. The relative success of these three systems may be compared by considering the way in which they met certain crucial problems of corporate reorganization and the adequacy of the solutions reached. These problems are the choice between reorganization and liquidation of the failed corporation; the problem of raising funds for new investment; the problem of dissenting minorities; the problem of "fairness" and independent review of the plan of reorganization proposed; and the problem of minimizing the direct and indirect costs of the reorganization process.

Reorganization under the aegis of equity courts was originally developed to deal with corporations affected with a public interest but it came to be applied to other corporations as well. The granting of receivership in equity was always discretionary with the court although as time passed the practice of "consent receiverships" became standardized for large quasi-public enterprises. The problem of the relative values of R and L was not formally posed in the proceedings but it was probably considered in many cases. The equity system was quite unsatisfactory in its handling of the problems of raising new capital and dissenting minorities. The fact

[77] See, for instance, the proposed modifications of the bill by Professor Levi in *op. cit.*, pp. 22-29.

that dissenters had to be paid in cash complicated the procurement
of new funds and necessitated a large percentage of agreement
before any reorganization plan could be carried through. The
power of the court over the ultimate plan adopted lay in the fixa-
tion of the "upset" price and, after 1913, in the due recognition
of the rule of the *Boyd* case. The direct and indirect costs of
reorganization under equity were unnecessarily high because of
ancillary receiverships, the necessity of a high percentage of agreement to any plan, the court and counsel fees, the need for forming
a new corporate entity, and the protracted delays and uncertainties attending the whole procedure.

Reorganization under 77B attempted to draft the main principles
of equity reorganization into the federal bankruptcy act. The
changes adopted were none the less very marked. Debtors were
allowed to petition directly for court protection and the clauses
relating to "good faith" and "feasibility" of petitions perhaps emphasized the basic issue of the relative values of R and L. By allowing two-thirds of the creditors and a majority of the shareholders
(where the latter had an equity) to force through a plan of reorganization, the problems of dissenting minorities and raising new
money were given a better solution than under equity. The court
was required to pass upon the "fairness" of the plan, but not until
after it had been approved by the parties in interest. By speeding
up the whole process and permitting judicial scrutiny of counsel
and committee fees, the direct and indirect costs of reorganization
were sharply curtailed. The most notable contributions of 77B to
reorganization procedure were probably its treatment of the minorities and new investment problem, although it also represented
an advance over equity in its handling of the "fairness" problem
and that of economy.

Chapter X seems to have been mainly inspired by the Securities
and Exchange Commission. It does very little to alter the solutions
afforded under 77B for handling the problems of the choice between reorganization and liquidation, the treatment of minorities,
and the procurement of new capital investment. Its main changes
relate to the "fairness" problem and the mode of preparing the
plan of reorganization. Chapter X emphasizes the importance of

the complete divorce of the reorganization proceedings from the influence of investment bankers, attorneys, and management groups formerly associated with the failed corporation. It draws a distinction between small and large corporate reorganizations, and in the latter the independent trustee dominates the proceedings by preparing the plan and generally acting in the interests of all claim-holders. The S.E.C. enters the proceedings in an advisory capacity in the larger instances of corporate failure and reorganization. By allowing more parties to be heard on more occasions during the proceedings, Chapter X probably will increase the costs and delays of the reorganization process as compared with 77B.

It should be emphasized that the order of development from equity through Chapter X has been more gradual and regular than a hurried study might suggest. In some respects the later enactments are but the codification of judicial practices developed under earlier forms. Finally, it should be observed in closing that the older view that corporate reorganizations are of private interest only has gradually yielded to the view that questions of public interest and concern are also involved.

REFERENCES: CHAPTER XIV

FIELD, K.—*Corporation Finance.* Ch. 30.

DODD, E. M., JR.—"Reorganization Through Bankruptcy a Remedy for What?" *Harvard Law Review*, Vol. 48.

DODD, E. M., JR.—"Reorganization under 77B of the Bankruptcy Act, 1934-1936," *Harvard Law Review*, Vol. 49.

FRANK, J.—"Some Realistic Reflections on Corporate Reorganization," *Virginia Law Review*, Vol. 19.

FOSTER, R. S.—"Conflicting Ideals for Reorganization," *Yale Law Journal*, Vol. 44.

GLENN, G.—"The Basis of Federal Receivership," *Columbia Law Review*, Vol. 25.

LEVI, E. H. & MOORE, J. W.—"Bankruptcy and Reorganization: A Survey of Changes," *University of Chicago Law Review*, Vol. 5.

MOORE, W. H.—"Railroad Fixed Charges in Bankruptcy Proceedings," *Journal of Political Economy*, Vol. 47.

PAYNE, PHILIP M.—*Plans of Corporate Reorganization*, Chicago, 1934.

STONE, F. F.—"The Case of the Ladies' Handbags: A Study in Receivership Procedure," *Virginia Law Review*, Vol. 24.

SWAINE, R. T.—"Corporate Reorganizations: Certain Developments of the Last Decade," *Columbia Law Review*, Vol. 27.

WEINER, J. L.—"Conflicting Functions of Upset Price," *Columbia Law Review*, Vol. 27.

Chapter XV

UNRESOLVED PROBLEMS OF CORPORATE ENTERPRISE IN THE MODERN ECONOMY

I. "The" Corporation Problem. II. The Large Corporation and the Nature of Competition. III. The Corporate Enterprise and the Maintenance of Real Investment.

~~~~~~~~~~~~~~

The discussion in the foregoing chapters has been essentially from the point of view of the single business enterprise. We have dealt with the problems growing out of the legal aspects of the corporation, the problems of promotion, the notion of maximizing returns, the computation of income to the enterprise, the distribution of dividends, and the problems of expansion, failure and reorganization. By and large, however, the discussion of these questions has been pointed towards the meaning and implications of these aspects of corporate activity as they relate to the creditors and shareholders of the single enterprise. Only incidentally and parenthetically have we forsaken this limited frame of reference to glance at the broader social implications of the problems under discussion. Yet the growth and development of the business corporation as the typical unit of business ownership organization in the occidental world has brought in its train certain other problems that pass far beyond the mere private relations of the shareholders and creditors to the individual business enterprise. These latter problems are of a wholly different order of magnitude. They concern not so much the single firm as the aggregation of corporate enterprises within the economy as a whole. The discussion of these problems begins with the acknowledged fact that the organization of production in the present economic system is on the basis of business firms (characteristically) in the corporate form and proceeds to an examination of the broader social and economic consequences that devolve from it. While there seems to be more or less general agreement as to what are the "facts" regarding the aggregation of corporate enterprises or certain types of them, there is no corresponding consensus concerning the significance of these facts for problems of broad social policy. It is not infrequently argued, for instance, that the separation of ownership from management and control in the large business corporation is one of the really compelling problems of our time calling for immediate action of a drastic sort. Other persons, however, while agreeing with the facts about the divorce of ownership and control, see no corresponding need for titanic changes at all. Indeed, disputes of this order, even where there is complete agreement on the fact situation (and this is by no means always true), are apt to grow acrimonious because the participants so often hold widely divergent views concerning the objectives towards which "society" ought to be moving, or ought to be made to move. Such conflicts tend to become conflicts of ultimate ends or ideals rather than an argument over the most suitable means of attaining or approximating accepted objectives. The discussion, in other words, moves over into the realm of social policy where the basic issue is the disagreement over the type of end result towards which social policy should be directed. Thoughtful persons, however, have always tended to disagree somewhat over ultimate "values," "ends," or objectives. And it is a commonplace observation that protracted discussion of such issues frequently serves only to bind the participants even more firmly to their original beliefs. The consequence is that the appropriate policy to be adopted towards the collectivity of business corporations in their relation to society at large is largely an unsettled problem. It is in this sense that we speak of the "unresolved" problems of corporate enterprise in the modern economy.

It is of course too late in the day for us to begin any thoroughgoing consideration of these problems and their ramifications even were we bold enough to believe that we had anything fresh to contribute to the discussion. Our only intention in these closing pages is to draw attention to a few of them by indicating their bare outlines. We shall begin with a word or two about what has come to be known as "the" corporation problem in current discourse.

I. "THE" CORPORATION PROBLEM

1. The problem. 2. The effect of the separation of control and ownership on shareholders. 3. The divorce of ownership and control and the general welfare.

1. *The problem.* A number of studies of the large corporation in the United States in recent years have demonstrated first, that the ownership of the voting shares is widely diffused among many persons no one of whom holds more than a very minute fraction of the total, and second, that the proportion of the outstanding voting shares owned by the management and/or directors is similarly quite small.[1] Largely on the basis of these twin facts it has been argued that the time has come to revise our whole thinking about the relation of shareholders to their representatives, the directors and the officers, and the position of corporate enterprise in a price and profit economy.

With respect to the first point the arguments run that if the directors and/or officers of the large corporation have only a small ownership interest in the enterprise and if the remainder of the ownership is widely diffused, the "control" group (officers, directors, and perhaps banking affiliates) has more to gain for itself by employing the assets in ways other than those which will maximize returns to the owners. The small ownership interest of the control group, in other words, means that they are less concerned to maximize dividend returns than to augment their own personal incomes by using the corporate assets in other ways.

On the second point, the relation of the corporate enterprise to the price system, the argument usually takes the following form. The traditional logic of the business enterprise is to maximize re-

[1] See, Berle and Means, *The Modern Corporation and Private Property,* Books I and IV; Gordon, R. A., "Stockholdings of Officers and Directors in American Industrial Corporations," *Quarterly Journal of Economics,* Vol. 50 (1936), pp. 622-657; O'Leary, P. M., *Corporate Enterprise in Modern Economic Life,* New York (Harpers), 1933.

turns to the owners and to pursue this aim will contribute to the general good because the maximization of profits means producing such goods and services as the consumers desire. But, the argument proceeds, in the large business corporation nowadays the control group has not the same incentive to maximize profits as formerly; therefore, there is no assurance that the operation of business corporations will be towards the maximization of returns to the owners, and hence, there is no guarantee that consumers' interests are being served. In very abbreviated terms this is essentially "the" corporation problem. The reasoning is further bolstered by emphasizing that where ownership is widely diffused the control group is capable of perpetuating itself in power through control over the proxy machinery. The group in power has a distinct advantage over any other group because it can solicit proxies from existing shareholders and charge the cost to the corporation. An outside group would have to bear the expense out of its own pockets.

If we accept this statement of "the" corporation problem we may appropriately ask what deleterious consequences may flow from the acknowledged facts. If harm results from the separation of ownership and control in the large business corporation it must adversely affect the interests of the shareholders and/or the general welfare in the community at large. Let us consider these possibilities.

2. *The effect of the separation of control and ownership on shareholders.* The harm to shareholders accruing from the separation of ownership and control would be the decrease in the value of their proprietorship claims because the corporate assets were not being employed in a manner to yield the maximum net income to the stockholders. There are numerous ways in which this might be brought about. The control group might find it convenient to be lax and inefficient in the conduct of the corporation's affairs where there was no fear of their being displaced simply because it was more pleasant to "take things easy" than to strive vigorously for efficiency. Their salaries being secure and their money incomes not being an increasing function of corporate earnings they might have no marked incentive to rout out waste and inefficiency in the conduct of the enterprise to produce larger returns. How

much inefficiency is tolerable without producing failure will depend upon whether competing enterprises are similarly conducted and how numerous they are. Generally speaking, however, the present writer would venture the guess that the degree to which efficiency can be neglected without incurring the danger of the enterprise failing is not great. The control group, in other words, is not likely to allow inefficiency to become widespread for selfish reasons.

While the control group may endeavor to maximize the returns from the assets of the corporation under their jurisdiction, they may take steps to prevent these gains from accruing mainly to the shareholders. By profit-sharing and bonus plans, which until recently were not necessarily made known to the stockholders, the bulk of the profits might be siphoned off into the pockets of the management. So long as such contracts are free and open to the inspection of all, they may be worth their cost to the shareholders, considering the higher profits they call forth. This assumes, of course, that some such incentive is necessary to promote real efficiency and this might be debated. But secret bonus schemes have nothing to commend them.[2]

Apart from reducing returns to the shareholders by bonus schemes there is the possibility that the control group may increase their own personal incomes either by buying materials and supplies at unnecessarily high prices from affiliated companies in which they have a financial interest or by selling to other companies at an unconscionably low price for the same reason. Schemes of this sort in both simple and complex forms are but one of the many versions of dishonesty. It is probably true also that they are not peculiar to large business enterprises. The nepotism rampant among smaller enterprises is frequently astounding.[3]

[2] The subject of bonus arrangements is well and thoroughly treated in Baker, J. C., *Executive Salaries and Bonus Plans*, New York and London (McGraw-Hill), 1938.

[3] The problem of profits from inter-corporate dealings with enterprises in which the control group is financially interested the present writer has discussed in another connection. See "Certain Aspects of Utility Service Contracts," *Journal of Business of the University of Chicago*, Vol. 7 (1934), pp. 106-123, and "The Public Utility Holding Company Problem," *California Law Review*, Vol. 25 (1937), pp. 517-551. These articles only relate to public utility corporations.

It might be argued also that where ownership and control in the large enterprise are separated there is a tendency to enlarge the corporation even though the marginal returns from additional investment are comparatively small. If corporate executives prefer size *per se* or if they believe that their salaries will be proportional to the size of the enterprise then they may have an urge to expand regardless of the probable returns from increments of investment. It is difficult to determine whether such tendencies are important or not.

Thus, the consequences of separation of ownership and control for shareholders *may be* significant in various ways. What is the "typical" situation or what is generally true of large business enterprises concerning the relations between the proprietors and the control group is by no means certain. In other words, while a separation of ownership and control is statistically demonstrable, there is no equivalent assurance that the harm to shareholders is a mere contingency or a downright actuality. Finally, even assuming the latter to be true—a questionable assumption in the writer's opinion—there is no consensus as to what, if anything, ought to be done about it.

3. *The divorce of ownership and control and the general welfare.* If the management and control group operates the large business corporation efficiently but sequesters to itself a substantial fraction of the resulting earnings, then the most obvious social consequence is a redistribution of income between shareholders and executives.[4] The social significance of such reallocations of

[4] The proportion of earnings going to executives has apparently been greater for small companies than for large companies. Note the following, "Large companies, however, clearly distributed a lower percentage of earnings to executives than did the small companies. In 1929 they paid on the average 3 per cent as compared with 11 per cent for the small companies; and for the entire period [1928-1936], 4.9 per cent as compared with 25.5 per cent." Baker, J. C., "Executive Compensation Payments by Large and Small Industrial Concerns," *Quarterly Journal of Economics,* Vol. 53 (1939), pp. 404-434, at p. 432. It is also stated that "Stockholders in the large companies in 1929 typically received as their share of earnings 16 times more than did the executives; in 1936, 17 times more. In the small companies the stockholders received 4 times more than the executives in 1929; 3½ times more in 1936. Over the entire period the contrast is even more marked. Stockholders in the large companies received typically 14 times more than executives, while in the small companies stockholders received only 2½ times the amount going to executives." *Ibid.,* p. 433. There are further data on this point in the same author's *Executive Salaries and Bonus Plans,* pp. 230-232.

income between persons is probably not great where the enterprise
has been efficiently operated and the contracts are known to the
shareholders. If, however, the separation of ownership and control
tends to promote an overextension of investment in those corporations, there is a social loss insofar as investment elsewhere would
have yielded larger returns. To the degree that the separation of
ownership and control encourages inefficiency in its various forms
it means wasted resources in the production of commodities. Yet
it is probably true that the wastes arising from this source are one
of the less important wastes within the economy. The social disadvantages of a separation of ownership and control are certainly
a possibility; but how significant they really are is far from obvious. It is quite possible that they are trivial.

II. THE LARGE CORPORATION AND THE NATURE OF COMPETITION

The problems occasioned by the divorce of ownership from
control in the large business corporation are overshadowed in significance by the fact that in many industries the characteristic
organization of production is on the basis of a small number of
quite large enterprises. The reasons why some industries should be
composed of a few large enterprises are many. For example, if the
technique of production is such that there are marked economies
in large scale operations, the aggregate demand for the product
may none the less be insufficient to support a large number of
firms. Where an industry is composed of a few large firms the
production policies, price policies, investment policies, etc., followed by the component enterprises, may be distinctively peculiar
and have important social consequences.

If an industry comprises a few large firms it is apparent that
their degree of control over product prices is considerable. Of
course they cannot determine the aggregate number of units sold,
but they can regulate the price at which sales transactions take
place. To firms so situated, apparently the merits of stable prices

loom large. There need be no agreement to maintain stable prices. The respective enterprises may all be convinced merely that there is nothing to be gained by price cutting.[5] Despite more or less unvarying prices, the component firms need not be securing unusually large returns per unit of invested capital. Profits may be small and yet a predilection for unvarying prices remains. The prices being determined by the producers in the industry, the amount produced and sold will depend upon people's incomes and schedules of preferences taken in conjunction with these prices. It may well be true, however, that at these prices the amount sold is less than sufficient to minimize production costs to the respective large enterprises. Consumers would purchase more units at lower prices, while an increased rate of output would reduce costs of production. At the same time, however, there is no incentive for the firms to cut prices in order to sell more because of the conviction (possibly false, possibly correct) that lower prices and increased sales would reduce profits. If this be the net end result, society has achieved an uneconomical distribution of its resources and consumers suffer a diminution in their aggregate real incomes.[6]

If an industry composed of a small number of large enterprises

[5] The difficulties of working with published prices as an indication that prices are "administered" or flexible ought not to be overlooked. In the first place, there is the fact that, although prices remain unchanged nominally, the quality of the product alters enormously. For example, a 1930 model automobile of given make is quite a different thing from a 1940 model even if both retail at the same price. Secondly, in many industries the published prices are not the prices at which a great many transactions occur because of price concessions of various kinds. It is perhaps worth noting also that such price concessions of various kinds are not restricted to large buyers by any means. Many a person, through friends, relatives, acquaintances, etc., buys certain commodities at less than the announced price. This is a commonplace. Thirdly, the published price of an article may remain unchanged at the same time that the price to the buyer fluctuates daily. For instance, most persons in the United States who buy new automobiles have an old car to "trade in." The cost of a new car to the buyer fluctuates from day to day and from dealer to dealer because of the varying "allowances" granted on the old car. Such difficulties as these are especially troublesome from a statistical point of view.

[6] See Chamberlin, E. H., *The Theory of Monopolistic Competition*, Cambridge, Mass. (Harvard), 1938, *passim* but especially Ch. V; Meade, J. E., *An Introduction to Economic Analysis and Policy*, Oxford (Oxford University), 1936, Part II; Burns, Arthur R., *The Decline of Competition*, New York and London (McGraw-Hill), 1936; Dennison, H. S., and Galbraith, J. K., *Modern Competition and Business Policy*, New York (Oxford), 1938.

maintains output at a level that keeps prices stable and if each firm could expand output with a reduction in unit costs of production, then it follows that productive capacity within the industry is excessive. Insofar as this is the fact situation there has been malinvestment of capital in the sense that the community would have been better served had some of its resources been allocated elsewhere. Notwithstanding the fact that existing enterprises may be operating typically at less than the optimum volume without obtaining excessive returns upon their investment, new enterprises may enter the industry from time to time. Such new concerns may be brought into existence because of false notions about the returns being obtained by existing enterprises or because of structural changes of various kinds (shifts in market organization, technological improvements, etc.). If new firms enter the industry there is an addition to the total productive capacity and the total sales may simply be carved up between the now larger number of firms. It may even be that the new "administered" price for the product will ultimately settle at a higher level. Instead of capacity being reduced and prices lowered the "competition" of the new firm may only increase the former and raise the latter.

There is no easy solution for this problem of a few firms of large size accompanied by excessive productive capacity, more or less rigid prices, and possibly a continued tendency towards increasing the investment within the industry. That it constitutes one of the abiding problems of corporate enterprise of real importance, however, goes almost without saying. Even the outlines of a suitable solution are hard to frame because of conflicting objectives. If one accepts the view that flexible prices are indispensable to the proper functioning of a capitalistic economy he is bound to recognize that a multitude of small firms would be technologically inappropriate as means to that end. On the other hand, one cannot assume that public regulation of product prices, new investment, and rates of output will necessarily resolve the difficulty. The criteria to be adopted by such a regulatory body as a basis for policy are by no means crystal clear.

III. THE CORPORATE ENTERPRISE AND THE MAINTENANCE OF REAL INVESTMENT

1. Capital investment via the corporate enterprise. 2. Ethical aspects of new investment through security sales. 3. Profits and real investment.

Presumably all would agree that the fundamental problem confronting capitalistic economies in the third decade of the twentieth century is that of underemployment. It ought not to need emphasis, of course, that, from the economic point of view, there is no virtue in employment *per se*. When we speak of underemployment as a problem we do not mean to suggest that there should be any conscious policy directed towards increasing employment for its own sake. The reason unemployment is important from an economic point of view is that human and non-human resources stand idle which might be used to turn out goods and services scarce in relation to the aggregate wants and needs for them.[7] The production of these commodities with the unemployed resources would augment the general welfare. Although not all students of the problem would entirely agree on the complete details of any one theory of the causes of unemployment in highly developed capitalistic economies, there would be general acceptance of the view that a high level of real investment is indispensable to a high level of employment. If this view be granted, i.e., that a high level of investment moves a capitalistic economy in the direction of full employment, let us look briefly into some of the interconnections between the volume of investment and corporate enterprise in the modern world.

1. *Capital investment via the corporate enterprise.* Two characteristics of real capital investment deserve comment in connection with the problem of maintaining a high level of real invest-

[7] The social aspects of unemployment as they show themselves in the anguish, fear, and misery of those without jobs are of course far and away the most important. But these are so familiar and self-evident that they need only to be mentioned.

ment in mature capitalistic economies. First is the fact we have frequently stressed in earlier chapters: that, in the modern world, capital investment is necessarily more or less speculative in the sense that the returns thereon cannot be predicted with certainty. In a changing economy there is always the danger that capital investment may fail to fulfill expectations. Second is the fact, almost equally important, that nowadays a large fraction of the real investment in the form of capital goods is decided upon by persons who finance such projects with funds raised by the sale of security contracts to others. In other words, those who finance the expansion of existing enterprises and the initiation of new concerns by buying their bonds and shares are typically *not* the same persons who decide where new capital goods could profitably be used. Let us examine this second point a little more closely.

The consequences of this indirect relationship may be clarified by an example. If a houseowner decides to build an extension to his dwelling he has only to compare the relative merits of spending his money for more house-room and spending it for something else. Even if he has to borrow for the purpose the decision is usually not difficult to reach; by having more house-room he will recognize that his future expenditures in other directions will be less than they would be otherwise. Consider, on the other hand, the case where he is requested to buy ten shares of common stock of a new corporation. Of the industry in which the company proposes to engage he probably has little personal knowledge. Moreover, he is likely to know little or nothing about the persons who have decided that a new enterprise is warranted in this field nor how competent they are to conduct it if one is needed. Even should he know something of both he would feel less confident about the whole commitment than if he were enlarging his dwelling. Of course, if he and others like him are sufficiently dubious of the merits of the proposed venture, no shares will be sold. The point we are striving for, however, is that the initiators of the (proposed) new enterprise must first convince themselves that a new concern is warranted and then similarly convince others to the extent of purchasing its bonds and/or shares. The promoters know, of course, that the new enterprise may not prove as profit-

able as they hope, the uncertainties being what they are. Furthermore, the promoters know that prospective buyers of the company's securities are aware that they (the promoters) cannot be
absolutely certain of the returns actually to be had from investment of capital in this opportunity. The proposition differs from
that of the man and his house. The prospective security buyer is
not dealing with the probable returns from a real capital good
whose form and shape he personally supervises. The problem that
confronts him is as follows: How sound is my judgment of the
soundness of the promoters' judgment concerning the probable
yield from the real capital goods that this enterprise proposes to
use? What he really has to do is to appraise the promoters' appraisal of the venture that they regard as an investment opportunity.

The tenuousness of this chain of relationships between those
who finance investment projects and those who search out opportunities for real investment ought to be obvious to anyone. For,
to the uncertainties inherent in real capital investment *per se*, there
are superadded the uncertainties of the inter-personal relationship
between the security buyer and the security seller. If all real investment were undertaken directly by those who had funds to
invest the only problem would be the probable yield of the capital
goods to the person making the commitment: the man and his
house type of thing. Where, however, the relationship is indirect—
one buys securities from a corporation which in turn buys the
capital goods—there is imposed upon the real risks of investment
the further risk, from the security buyer's point of view, that the
corporation will not keep its covenants, that it will be badly
managed, etc. The risk that the capital goods will not yield the
returns contemplated is inescapable in a dynamic economy. The
risk of non-performance of the terms of the security contract
springs from the security buyer and security seller relationship.
Hence, at least in the modern world, there are certain inherent
uncertainties in real capital investment, but also people's estimates
of these uncertainties are influenced by the fact that, in the main,
they are forced to rely upon the judgment and abilities of others.
And it goes without saying at this point that the appraisals people

make of these risks are not constant during all phases of the business cycle. We dealt with this point in part in Chapter X.[8]

All real capital investment in the modern economy, to be sure, is not equally exposed to this latter difficulty. Already established corporations undertake new capital investment both with and without new security sales. Where securities are offered to finance expansion programs the uncertainties are partially overborne by the demonstrated success of the enterprise in times past. Of course, past success does not logically guarantee future performance, as we pointed out in an earlier chapter; but it may allay certain doubts and fears. In highly developed capitalistic economies the State itself nowadays undertakes a deal of investment. Nevertheless if our remarks are valid they do apply to a substantial fraction of the aggregate real capital investment in an economy composed of corporate enterprises.

2. *Ethical aspects of new investment through security sales.* Because those who buy the securities that finance new capital investment are forced to rely on the representations and judgment of others concerning the probable yield from new capital goods, there is clearly an opportunity for double dealing and sharp practices. The relationship being what it is, those who request funds are in a position both to misrepresent their expectations by word and phrase and supporting data and to use the funds obtained for purposes other than those announced. This is an old problem the fundamental basis of which is probably to be found in human gullibility and cupidity. For instance, the London *Times* on March 22, 1844, carried the following: [9]

The merchant, the humbler tradesman, the small shopkeeper, and the servant—these are the people whose little all is sacrificed to the impudent impostures of our modern joint stock companies. . . . A system of falsehood marks them from the moment of their birth. They are born and cradled in falsehood. To give them an introduction into society, they are fathered upon unconscious peers and non-existent commoners. By aid of a Blue Book, some dozen merchants and lawyers

[8] Mr. J. M. Keynes has discussed the matters dealt with in this paragraph in his *General Theory of Employment, Interest and Money*, pp. 144-151.

[9] As quoted by Hunt, B. C., *The Development of the Business Corporation in England, 1800-1867*, Cambridge, Mass. (Harvard), 1936, pp. 90-92. See similar utterances in *ibid.*, pp. 106, 115, and *passim*.

are appended to the senatorial list, and when this has been done, a miscellaneous body of Tomkinses and Jenkinses is tacked on, in order that no plebeian idealist may be deterred from taking a share by the array of noble names. . . .

. . . Then do imaginary dividends dance before gloating eyes— then do gratuitous mines of copper and tin open in soils unconscious of a grain of ore;—then does one hundred per cent arise from ideal slate quarries, or visionary canals;—then do streams of wealth irrigate the long sterility of Irish bogs; and every miracle is born which avarice can beget upon credulity. Then are the hoardings of years and the pittances of poverty carried to the bourne from which they never can return.

Fundamentally the nature of the appeal has changed but little over the years. It seems to be directed towards the characteristically human urge to "get something for nothing."

The combination of human credulity and the ease with which those who offer securities for sale are able to misrepresent the probable returns from investment has called forth various measures to prevent people from being "taken in." [10] The most recent large-scale attempt in this direction in the United States has been the Securities Act of 1933 which is erected on the principle that it is socially wise to insist upon full and truthful disclosure of all "material facts" pertaining to new issues of securities. The security purchaser is to be protected from exploitation by giving him truthful information sufficient to permit an informed appraisal of its investment merits.[11] There could scarcely be any argument that the sovereign authority ought to promote fair dealing and discourage dishonesty. Consequently the ethical objectives of the Securities Act would doubtless command general assent.

[10] Note the following picturesque statement as quoted in *ibid.*, p. 115: "Whenever the fingers are burned, a cure is always lustily called for by those who have been burned the most severely, and their object in this, as in the diversion that has hurt them, is always the same—they call for the appointment of a government officer, who shall from time to time regulate how they shall hold their hands to the fire without being burned. Whether this special interference shall be crowned with success by keeping down the heat of the fire, or by increasing the distance at which the venturesome hand shall be allowed to approach it, is a perplexing difficulty which has not yet been solved." From a pamphlet published in London in 1850.

[11] Apart from publications of the Securities and Exchange Commission itself the following will be found enlightening on the workings of the Act. Blum, J. W.,

Whether the insistence upon full disclosure has the effect of diminishing aggregate real investment within the economy below the level it might otherwise have attained is indeed a moot point. The arguments here are quite unsatisfactory, being usually little more than blunt assertion and denial without much analysis on either side. Since the maintenance of real investment is of such basic importance to the attainment of a high level of employment, we may examine briefly in what ways the principle of full disclosure might conceivably work as a deterrent to investment. One cannot assume, of course, that the volume of new security sales is matched by an equivalent investment in real capital goods. Refunding issues, investment trust issues, holding company issues, and the like need not call forth any new investment in new capital goods, although they *may* do so in a round-about way.[12] Our concern here is with real investment and our remarks only relate to new security issues that would augment it.

Already in the present chapter we have tried to emphasize the extreme tenuousness of the relation between those who supply the funds for new investment and those who discover the opportunities. Furthermore, we have stressed the point that new capital investment is inevitably tinged with uncertainties in an amorphous economic system. Investment being inherently speculative, one might argue that the insistence upon full disclosure might tend to emphasize to prospective security buyers the risks that attend commitment to a new issue. Most certainly such risks do exist, but *from the point of view of maintaining a high level of real investment* one might question whether it is socially wise to emphasize them continually to those who will assume them. It would seem to be true that more than a dash of optimism is essential to main-

"The Federal Securities Act, 1933-1936," *Journal of Political Economy*, Vol. 46 (1938), pp. 52-96; MacChesney, B. and O'Brien, R. H., "Full Disclosure under the Securities Act," *Law and Contemporary Problems*, Vol. 4 (1937), pp. 133-153; MacChesney, B., "Further Developments in 'Disclosure' under the Securities Act," *Illinois Law Review*, Vol. 33 (1938), pp. 145-169. The first half of Volume 4 of *Law and Contemporary Problems* is a symposium on "Three Years of the Securities Act."

12 For instance, it has been estimated that for 1929 in the United States real investment issues were only about 25 per cent of the total new issues. See the interesting study by Eddy, G. A., "Security Issues and Real Investment in 1929," *The Review of Economic Statistics*, May, 1937, pp. 79-91.

tain real investment at a high level. A person thoroughly cognizant of the risks and uncertainties attendant upon investment and fully aware of the losses suffered by security owners in times past would be likely to conclude, if he were rational and had no zest for risk-taking *per se*, that the prospective gains were more than outweighed by the probable losses. If such an attitude were to become general because the risks of investment were always stressed, the net result would be a decline in real investment or its restriction to "safe" commitments guaranteeing small returns. The social consequences in terms of reduced employment and a diminution in aggregate real income could be extremely serious.[13]

If there be any merit in the contentions in the foregoing paragraphs it is quite apparent that we are faced with a dilemma. It is not open to dispute that honesty in the flotation and sale of new securities is a desirable objective for which society can afford to pay a price. On the other hand a high level of real investment seems to be essential to a high level of employment which will permit a high level of real income. How far can we afford to insist upon complete disclosure if we recognize that "full disclosure" may have a deterrent effect upon aggregate real investment? It would seem to the writer that there are competing objectives here that might well be recognized. How far a capitalistic economy ought to sacrifice one to the other is certainly debatable and no formula can provide a ready answer. As to what "society" as a whole wants or in some ultimate sense ought to have, one person's guess is perhaps almost as good as another's. All that we

[13] The point sought for above may possibly be made clearer by an admittedly imperfect analogy. One might raise the question of the probable effects upon the marriage rate throughout society if before a marriage could occur there had to be "full disclosure" by both parties concerning their previous actions and behavior. Now it is doubtless true that in many instances such full disclosure would prevent imprudent marriages. On the other hand, it is at least conceivable that a requirement of "full disclosure" would also have the effect of forestalling an even greater number of marriages which would turn out successfully. The parties would be in a sense "warned off" by having certain facts brought forcibly to their attention. If one accepts the view that a high marriage rate is desirable he might well hesitate to urge the desirability of a "full disclosure" provision in order to prevent injudicious marriages even though there seem to be a large number of the latter annually. In the writer's opinion, the similarities between marriage and capital investment are probably greater than might at first appear. A certain irrational optimism is perhaps a prerequisite to both.

would urge is that, in part, "full disclosure" and a large volume of real investment are not wholly harmonious objectives.[14]

We must not be misunderstood as attempting to prove too much however. While we have argued that an insistence upon full disclosure may have the effect of reducing aggregate investment, we would certainly not insist that this is the primary reason why real investment on private account—i.e., excluding public works, armament expenditures, etc.—has not revived substantially since the great depression. Other difficulties of a political and social character are certainly much more important. All we would suggest is that pushing full disclosure with a vigorous hand may have some repercussions upon the volume of real investment.[15]

3. *Profits and real investment.* The basic factor in the refusal of long-term private investment to revive since the depression of 1932 is doubtless the gloomy expectations that have prevailed concerning the prospective profits from investment. Just why such gloomy anticipations should persist is of course the really interesting side of the problem, and a complete explanation would have to take account of innumerable political and social changes as well as the more strictly economic developments of recent years. On the economic side, however, some thoughtful students are coming around to the view that the opportunities for further capital investment which will yield substantial returns are rapidly disappearing because most highly developed capitalistic economies are already well equipped with capital goods. Mr. Keynes is probably the outstanding proponent of this view; but he is by no means

[14] My colleague, Professor Calkins, has urged the following argument in objection to our remarks in the present section. While it might be true that full disclosure has the short-run effect of reducing aggregate investment in the whole economy by emphasizing the risks of security purchases, none the less this would tend to pass away after persons had become "adjusted" to the newer forms of prospectus. Moreover, there are limits to how far persons can satisfy their disposition to hold idle balances as opposed to making investment commitments. The first point is certainly a possibility that must not be overlooked. As to the second, it is true that there are limits to how far persons can satisfy their liquidity preferences in any given situation, but, on the other hand, their individual efforts to hold more bank balances than the monetary authority is willing to allow may produce a deflationary situation that may become cumulative.

[15] It is worth observing that the refusal of long-term private investment to revive is not peculiar to the United States. Other countries in which there has been no corresponding new legislation affecting the capital markets have also experienced the same phenomenon.

alone. Just what important technological improvements the immediate future holds in store which would offset any tendency for investment opportunities to decline, no one knows of course. It is worth remembering, however, that the notion that most of the really significant inventions have already occurred is one that has appeared and past away many times since the advent of the industrial revolution. While this fact proves nothing about what is likely to occur in the proximate future it does suggest that our anticipations on such questions are quite unreliable.

Even if we accept the view that significant technological changes are not likely or in any case are not to be relied upon, it does not necessarily follow that investment opportunities are in for a secular decline towards more and more unattractive levels. A very large proportion of the world's population at present subsists at an unbelievably low standard of living. In these regions the marginal efficiency of capital investment from either the private or public point of view continues at a high level. Capital investment in such areas, in other words, would yield substantial returns to investors and raise the standards of living of the resident populations. As everyone knows, however, there are at present almost insuperable barriers standing in the way of a revival of international long-term investment on private account. Political upheavals, uncertain exchange rates, blocked balances, foreign exchange controls, import restrictions and export subsidies, the expropriation of foreign investments already made, all these and other factors certainly stand in the way of any immediate revival of international long-term investment. While it is possible that the next few years may witness the gradual disappearance of these obstacles to international investment it must be candidly admitted that at the time of writing (Spring, 1939) the prospects are far from encouraging. If the next few years do not see some restoration of order and tranquillity in international relations sufficient to permit a restoration of international lending on a substantial scale, then highly developed capitalistic economies may find that the domestic opportunities for capital investment are insufficient to maintain a high level of employment. What consequences may accompany conditions of chronic underemployment in these countries is surely anyone's guess.

REFERENCES: CHAPTER XV

BAKER, J. C.—*Executive Salaries and Bonus Plans*, New York and London: McGraw-Hill, 1938.

BLUM, J. W.—"The Federal Securities Act, 1933-1936," *Journal of Political Economy*, Vol. 46 (1938).

BURNS, ARTHUR R.—*The Decline of Competition*, New York and London: McGraw-Hill, 1936.

DENNISON, H. S., and GALBRAITH, J. K.—*Modern Competition and Business Policy*, New York: Oxford, 1938.

EDDY, G. A.—"Security Issues and Real Investment in 1929," *The Review of Economic Statistics*, May, 1937.

MACCHESNEY, B.—"Further Developments in 'Disclosure' under the Securities Act," *Illinois Law Review*, Vol. 33 (1938).

MACCHESNEY, B., and O'BRIEN, R. H.—"Full Disclosure under the Securities Act," *Law and Contemporary Problems*, Vol. 4 (1937).

LIST OF WORKS CITED

1. ABBOTT, C. C.—*The Rise of the Business Corporation*, Ann Arbor, Mich.: Edwards Bros., 1936.
2. ARTHUR, H. B.—"Inventory Profits in the Business Cycle," *American Economic Review*, Vol. 28 (1938).
3. BAKER, J. C.—"Executive Compensation Payments by Large and Small Industrial Concerns," *Quarterly Journal of Economics*, Vol. 53 (1939).
4. BAKER, J. C.—*Executive Salaries and Bonus Plans*, New York and London: McGraw-Hill Book Company, 1938.
5. BALLENTINE, H. W.—*Private Corporations*, Chicago: Callaghan, 1927.
6. BALOGH, T.—"The National Economy of Germany," *Economic Journal*, Vol. 48 (1938).
7. BARRETT, E. B.—" 'Fair Plan' under Section 77B, Applicability of the Boyd Case," *Michigan Law Review*, Vol. 34.
8. BATSON, H. E.—"The Economic Concept of a Public Utility," *Economica*, November, 1933.
9. BERLE, A. A.—*Cases and Materials on Corporation Finance*, St. Paul, Minn.: West Publishing Co., 1930.
10. BERLE, A. A.—*Studies in the Law of Corporation Finance*, Chicago: Callaghan and Co., 1928.
11. BERLE, A. A., and MEANS, G. C.—*The Modern Corporation and Private Property*, New York: Macmillan Company, 1932.
12. BLANDI, J. G.—*Maryland Business Corporation, 1783-1852*, Baltimore: Johns Hopkins, 1934.
13. BLUM, J. W.—"The Federal Securities Act, 1933-1936," *Journal of Political Economy*, Vol. 46 (1938).
14. BONBRIGHT, J. C.—*The Valuation of Property*, Vol. II, New York and London: McGraw-Hill Book Company, 1937.
15. BONBRIGHT, J. C., and BERGERMANN, M. M.—"Two Rival Theories of Priority Rights," *Columbia Law Review*, Vol. 28.
16. BREIT, M.—"Ein Beitrag zur Theorie des Geld- und Kapitalmarktes," *Zeitschrift für Nationalökonomie*, Band VI, Heft 5.
17. BRETHERTON, R. F.—"Note on the Law of Diminishing Elasticity of Demand," *Economic Journal*, Vol. 47 (1937).
18. BUCHANAN, N. S.—"A Reconsideration of the Cobweb Theorem," *Journal of Political Economy*, Vol. 47 (1939).
19. BUCHANAN, N. S.—"Certain Aspects of Utility Service Contracts," *Journal of Business of the University of Chicago*, Vol. 7 (1934).

20. BUCHANAN, N. S.—"The Origin and Development of the Public Utility Holding Company," *Journal of Political Economy*, Vol. 44, 1936.

21. BUCHANAN, N. S.—"The Public Utility Holding Company Problem," *California Law Review*, Vol. 25 (1937).

22. BUCKLAND, W. W.—*Elementary Principles of the Roman Private Law*, Cambridge, Eng.: Cambridge University, 1912.

23. BURNS, ARTHUR R.—*The Decline of Competition*, New York and London: McGraw-Hill Book Co., 1936.

24. BURTCHETT, F. F.—*Corporation Finance*, New York: Harpers, 1934.

25. CANNING, J. B.—"A Certain Erratic Tendency in Accountants' Income Procedure," *Econometrica*, Vol. I (1933).

26. CANNING, J. B.—*The Economics of Accountancy*, New York: Ronald Press, 1929.

27. CHAMBERLIN, E. H.—*The Theory of Monopolistic Competition*, Cambridge, Mass.: Harvard University Press, 3rd ed., 1938.

28. CLARK, J. M.—*Strategic Factors in Business Cycles*, New York: National Bureau of Economic Research, 1934.

29. COASE, R. H.—"The Nature of the Firm," *Economica*, August, 1937.

30. DANIELS, M. B.—*Corporation Financial Statements*, Ann Arbor, Mich.: University of Michigan, 1934.

31. DAVENPORT, D. H., and SCOTT, F. V.—*An Index to Business Indices*, Chicago: Business Publications, 1937.

32. DAVIS, J. S.—*Essays in the Earlier History of American Corporations*, Cambridge, Mass.: Harvard University Press, 1917.

33. Delaware, *Report of the Department of State for the Year 1936*.

34. DENNISON, H. S., and GALBRAITH, J. K.—*Modern Competition and Business Policy*, New York: Oxford Press, 1938.

35. DEWING, A. S.—*Corporation Securities*, New York: Ronald Press, 1934.

36. DEWING, A. S.—*Financial Policy of Corporations*, New York: Ronald Press, 1934.

37. DOBB, MAURICE—*Capitalist Enterprise and Social Progress*, London: Routledge, 1925.

38. DODD, D. L.—*Stock Watering*, New York: Columbia, 1930.

39. DODD, E. M., JR.—"The Securities and Exchange Commission's Reform Program for Bankruptcy Reorganizations," *Columbia Law Review*, Vol. 38.

40. DRINKER, H. S.—"The Pre-Emptive Right of Shareholders to Subscribe to New Shares," *Harvard Law Review*, Vol. 43 (1930).

41. Du Bois, A. B.—*The English Business Company after the Bubble Act, 1720-1800*, New York: Commonwealth, 1938.

42. Ebersole, J. F., Burr, S. S., and Peterson, G. M.—"Income Forecasting by the Use of Statistics of Income Data," *Review of Economic Statistics*, Vol. 11 (1929).

43. Eddy, G. A.—"Security Issues and Real Investment in 1929," *The Review of Economic Statistics*, Vol. 19 (1937).

44. Epstein, R. C., and Clark, F. M.—*A Source Book for the Study of Industrial Profits*, U. S. Department of Commerce, Washington, 1932.

45. Epstein, R. C.—*Industrial Profits in the United States*, New York: National Bureau of Economic Research, 1934.

46. Evans, G. H., Jr.—*British Corporation Finance, 1775-1850: a study of preference shares*, Baltimore: Johns Hopkins, 1936.

47. Evans, G. H., Jr.—"The Early History of Preferred Stock in the United States," *American Economic Review*, Vol. 19 (1929).

48. Fabricant, S.—*Studies in Income and Wealth*, New York: National Bureau of Economic Research, 1937.

49. Field, W. J.—"Some Uses of Holding Companies," *Journal of Land and Public Utility Economics*, Vol. 8.

50. Finletter, T. K.—*Principles of Corporate Reorganization in Bankruptcy*, Charlottesville, Va.: Michie, 1937.

51. Fjeld, E. I.—*Balance Sheet Classification and Terminology*, New York: Columbia, 1936.

52. Florence, P. S.—*The Logic of Industrial Organization*, London: Kegan, Paul, 1933.

53. Fortas, A.—"The Securities Act and Corporate Reorganizations," *Law and Contemporary Problems*, Vol. 4.

54. Foster, R. S.—"Conflicting Ideals for Reorganization," *Yale Law Journal*, Vol. 44.

55. Foulke, R. A.—*Behind the Scenes of Business*, New York: Dun and Bradstreet, Inc., 1937.

56. Frank, J.—"Some Realistic Reflections on Some Aspects of Corporate Reorganizations," *Virginia Law Review*, Vol. 19.

57. Fraser, L. M.—*Economic Thought and Language*, London: Black, 1937.

58. Frey, A. H.—"Shareholders' Pre-emptive Rights," *Yale Law Journal*, Vol. 38.

59. Garver, F. B., Boddy, F. M., and Nixon, A. J.—*The Location of Manufactures in the United States, 1899-1929*, Minneapolis: University of Minnesota, 1935.

60. Gerdes, John—*Corporate Reorganization under Section 77B of the Bankruptcy Act*, Chicago: Callaghan and Company, 1936.

61. GERSTENBERG, C. W.—*Financial Organization and Management*, New York: Prentice-Hall, Inc., 1934.

62. GLENN, G.—"The Basis of Federal Receivership," *Columbia Law Review*, Vol. 25.

63. GLENN, G.—*The Rights and Remedies of Creditors Respecting Their Debtors' Property*, Boston: Little, Brown, and Co., 1915.

64. GORDON, R. A.—"Stockholdings of Officers and Directors in American Industrial Corporations," *Quarterly Journal of Economics*, Vol. 50 (1936).

65. GOURRICH, P. P.—"Investment Banking Methods Prior to and Since the Securities Act of 1933," *Law and Contemporary Problems*, Vol. 4.

66. GRAHAM, B., and DODD, D. L.—*Security Analysis*, New York: McGraw-Hill Book Company, 1934.

67. GUTHMANN, H. G.—*Analysis of Financial Statements*, New York: Prentice-Hall, Inc., 1936.

68. HALLIS, F.—*Corporate Personality*, Oxford: Oxford Press, 1930.

69. HANNA, J.—*Cases and Materials on Creditors' Rights*, Chicago: Foundation Press, 1935.

70. HARROD, R. F.—*The Trade Cycle*, Oxford: Oxford Press, 1936.

71. HART, A. G.—"Anticipations, Business Planning, and the Cycle," *Quarterly Journal of Economics*, Vol. 51, pp. 273-297.

72. HARTZELL, E.—"Profits in the Steel Industry," *Accounting Review*, Vol. 9.

73. *Hearings on Investigation of Bankruptcy and Receivership Proceedings in United States Courts*, (pursuant to Senate Res. 78, 73rd Congress, 2nd Session) Washington: Government Printing Office, 1934.

74. HENDERSON, H. D.—"The Significance of the Rate of Interest," *Oxford Economic Papers*, No. 1 (1938).

75. HILLS, G. S.—"Model Corporation Act," *Harvard Law Review*, Vol. 48.

76. HOHFELD, W. H.—*Fundamental Legal Conceptions*, New Haven: Yale Press, 1923.

77. HUGHES, W. J.—*Federal Practice*, St. Paul, Minn.: West Publishing Company, 1931.

78. HUNT, B. C.—*The Development of the Business Corporation in England, 1800-1867*, Cambridge, Mass.: Harvard University Press, 1936.

79. KALDOR, N.—"The Equilibrium of the Firm," *Economic Journal*, Vol. 44, pp. 60-76.

80. KELLER, F. E., and CLARENBACH, F.—*Tax Systems of the World*, 7th Edition, Chicago: Commerce Clearing House, 1938.

81. KENDRICK, M. S.—*The Undistributed Profits Tax*, Washington: Brookings, 1937.
82. KEYNES, J. M.—*The General Theory of Employment, Interest and Money*. New York: Harcourt, Brace, 1936.
83. KNAUTH, O. W.—"The Place of Corporate Surplus in the National Income," *Journal of the American Statistical Association*, Vol. 18.
84. KNIGHT, F. H.—*Risk, Uncertainty, and Profit*, Boston: Houghton Mifflin, 1921.
85. LARCOM, R. C.—*The Delaware Corporation*, Baltimore: Johns Hopkins, 1937.
86. LATTY, E. R.—*Subsidiaries and Affiliated Corporations*, Chicago: Foundation Press, 1936.
87. LERNER, A. P.—"The Concept of Monopoly and the Measurement of Monopoly Power," *Review of Economic Studies*, Vol. 1.
88. LEVI, E. H.—"Corporate Reorganization and a Ministry of Justice," *Minnesota Law Review*, Vol. 23.
89. LYND, R. S. and H. M.—*Middletown*, New York: Harcourt, Brace, 1929.
90. LYON, H.—*Corporation Finance*, Cambridge, Mass.: Houghton Mifflin, 1916.
91. LYON, H.—*Corporations and their Financing*, New York, D. C. Heath, 1938.
92. McALLISTER, B. P.—"Lord Hale and Business Affected with a Public Interest," *Harvard Law Review*, Vol. 43.
93. MacCHESNEY, B.—"Further Developments in 'Disclosure' under the Securities Act," *Illinois Law Review*, Vol. 33.
94. MacCHESNEY, B., and O'BRIEN, R. H.—"Full Disclosure under the Securities Act," *Law and Contemporary Problems*, Vol. 4.
95. McCLELLAND, R. A., and FISHER, F. S.—*The Law of Corporate Mortgage Bond Issues*, Chicago: Callaghan and Company, 1937.
96. MAITLAND, F. W.—*Selected Essays* (ed. by Hazeltine, H. D., Tapsley, G., and Winfield, P. H.), Cambridge, Eng.: Cambridge University, 1936.
97. MAITLAND, F. W.—*Township and Borough*, Cambridge, Eng.: Cambridge University, 1898.
98. MARSHALL, ALFRED—*Principles of Economics*, London: Macmillan and Company, 8th edition, 1920.
99. MAY, G. O.—*Twenty-five Years of Accounting Responsibility*, New York: American Institute Publishing Co., 1936.

100. MEADE, J. E.—*An Introduction to Economic Analysis and Policy,* Oxford: Oxford Press, 1936.

101. MEADE, J. E., and ANDREWS, W. P. S.—"Summaries of Replies to Questions on Effects of Interest Rates," *Oxford Economic Papers,* No. 1 (1938).

102. MILLS, F. C.—*The Behavior of Prices,* New York: National Bureau of Economic Research, 1936.

103. MILLS, F. C.—"Changes in Prices, Manufacturing Costs and Industrial Productivity, 1929-1934," National Bureau of Economic Research, *Bulletin 53,* December 22, 1934.

104. MITCHELL, W. C.—"Business Cycles," *Encyclopedia of the Social Sciences,* Vol. 3.

105. MITCHELL, W. C., and BURNS, A. F.—"Production during the American Business Cycle of 1927-1933," National Bureau of Economic Research, *Bulletin 61* (1936).

106. MONTGOMERY, R. H.—*Auditing, Theory and Practice,* New York: Ronald Press, 1927.

107. MOSHER, W. E., and CRAWFORD, F. G.—*Public Utility Regulation,* New York and London: Harpers, 1933.

108. National Bureau of Economic Research, *Bulletin 50,* April 18, 1934.

109. National Bureau of Economic Research, "Changes in Prices, Manufacturing Costs and Industrial Productivity, 1929-1934," *Bulletin 53* (1934).

110. National Bureau of Economic Research, *Bulletin 55,* April 11, 1935.

111. New York, *Annual Report of the Secretary of State,* Legislative Document (1936), No. 44.

112. NOYES, C. R.—*The Institution of Property,* New York: Longmans, Green, 1936.

113. O'LEARY, P. M.—*Corporate Enterprise in Modern Economic Life,* New York: Harpers, 1933.

114. PATON, W. A.—*Corporate Profits as Shown by Audit Reports,* New York: National Bureau of Economic Research, 1935.

115. PAYNE, P. M.—*Plans of Corporate Reorganization,* Chicago: Foundation Press, 1934.

116. PLANT, A.—"Centralize or Decentralize," Plant, A. (ed.) *Some Modern Business Problems,* London: Longmans, Green, 1937.

117. POLLOCK, SIR F., and MAITLAND, F. W.—*The History of English Law,* Cambridge, Eng.: Cambridge University, 2nd Edition, 1898.

118. POTTER, H.—*An Historical Introduction to English Law,* London: Sweet and Maxwell, 1932.

119. *Proceedings* of the Second Dearborn Conference of Agriculture, Industry and Science; Dearborn, Michigan, 1936.

120. RADIN, MAX—*Handbook of Roman Law*, St. Paul, Minn.: West Publishing Company, 1927.

121. RADIN, MAX—"The Endless Problem of Corporate Personality," *Columbia Law Review*, Vol. 32.

122. *Recent Economic Changes*, New York: McGraw-Hill, 1929.

123. RIPLEY, W. Z.—*Main Street and Wall Street*, Boston: Little, Brown, 1927.

124. ROBERTSON, D. H.—*The Control of Industry*, New York: Harcourt, Brace, 1923.

125. ROBINSON, E. A. G.—"The Problem of Management and the Size of Firms," *Economic Journal*, Vol. 44.

126. ROBINSON, E. A. G.—*The Structure of Competitive Industry*, New York: Harcourt, Brace, 1932.

127. ROBINSON, G. H.—"The Public Utility Concept in American Law," *Harvard Law Review*, Vol. 41.

128. ROSENBERG, J. N.—"Corporate Reorganization and the Federal Court," *Columbia Law Review*, Vol. 17.

129. ROSENBERG, J. N.—"Phipps vs. Chicago, Rock Island & Pacific Ry. Co.," *Columbia Law Review*, Vol. 24.

130. ROSENBERG, J. N.—"The Ætna Explosives Case—A Milestone in Reorganization," *Columbia Law Review*, Vol. 20.

131. ROSENBERG, J. N., SWAINE, R. T., and WALKER, R.—*Corporate Reorganization and the Federal Court*, New York: Baker, Voorhis, 1924.

132. SALMOND, SIR JOHN—*Jurisprudence*, 8th edition, London: Sweet and Maxwell, 1930.

133. SCHUMPETER, J.—*The Theory of Economic Development*, Cambridge, Mass.: Harvard University Press, 1934.

134. Securities and Exchange Commission, *Report on the Study and Investigation of the Work, Activities, Personnel, and Functions of Protective and Reorganization Committees*, Washington (Government Printing Office), 1937, 1938.

135. SINGER, H. W.—"The Law of Diminishing Elasticity of Demand," *Economic Journal*, Vol. 48.

136. SLOAN, L. H., et al.—*Two Cycles of Corporation Profits*, New York: Harpers, 1936.

137. SMITH, G. C.—*An Outline for Market Surveys*, St. Louis, Mo.: The Industrial Club of St. Louis, 1930.

138. SMITH, HENRY—"Discontinuous Demand Curves and Monopolistic Competition," *Quarterly Journal of Economics*, Vol. 49.

139. SMITH, R. F., and WINAKOR, A. H.—"Changes in the Financial Structure of Unsuccessful Industrial Corporations," *University of Illinois Bulletin*, Vol. 32, 1935.

140. SRAFFA, P.—"The Laws of Return under Competitive Conditions," *Economic Journal*, Vol. 36.

141. *Statistical Abstract of the United States*, Washington: Government Printing Office, 1936.

142. STETSON, F. L., et al.—*Some Legal Phases of Corporate Financing, Reorganization and Regulation*, New York: Macmillan Co., 1917.

143. STEVENS, R. S.—*Handbook on the Law of Private Corporations*, St. Paul, Minn.: West Publishing Company, 1936.

144. STEVENS, W. H. S.—"Discretion of Directors in the Distribution of Non-cumulative Preferred Dividends," *Georgetown Law Review*, Vol. 24.

145. STEVENS, W. H. S.—*Railroad Sinking Funds and Funded Debt*, Washington (Interstate Commerce Commission, Bureau of Statistics), 1939.

146. STEVENS, W. H. S.—"Rights of Non-cumulative Preferred Shareholders," *Columbia Law Review*, Vol. 34.

147. STEVENS, W. H. S.—"Stockholders' Participation in Assets in Dissolution," *Journal of Business of the University of Chicago*, Vol. 10.

148. STEVENS, W. H. S.—"Stockholders' Participation in Profits," *Journal of Business of the University of Chicago*, Vol. 9.

149. STEVENS, W. H. S.—"Voting Rights of Capital Stock and Shareholders," *Journal of Business of the University of Chicago*, Vol. 11.

150. STEVENS, W. M.—*Financial Organization and Administration*, New York: American Book Co., 1934.

151. SWAINE, R. T.—" 'Democratization' of Corporate Reorganizations," *Columbia Law Review*, Vol. 38.

152. SWAINE, R. T.—"Reorganization of Corporations," in Ballantine, A. A. (ed.), *Some Legal Phases of Corporate Financing, Reorganization, and Regulation*, Chicago: Callaghan and Company, 1931.

153. SWAINE, R. T.—"Reorganization of Corporations: Certain Developments of the Last Decade," *Columbia Law Review*, Vol. 27.

154. SWAINE, R. T.—"Reorganization—the Next Step: A Reply to Mr. James N. Rosenberg," *Columbia Law Review*, Vol. 22.

155. SWANSTROM, L. D.—*Chapter X: Reorganization under the Federal Statute*, Chicago: Foundation Press, 1938.

156. SWEENEY, H. W.—*Stabilized Accounting*, New York and London: Harpers, 1936.

157. TODD, G.—"Some Aspects of Joint Stock Companies, 1844-1900," *Economic History Review*, Vol. 4.

158. TRACEY, J. E.—*Corporate Foreclosures, Receiverships and Reorganizations*, Chicago: Callaghan and Company, 1929.

159. United States Senate.—*United States Senate Report No. 365*, 73rd Congress, 2nd Session. Washington: United States Government Printing Office, 1934.

160. United States Senate.—Senate Document 92, 70th Congress, 1st Session: *Utility Corporations*, Washington: United States Government Printing Office.

161. United States Senate.—Senate Document 213, 69th Congress, 2nd Session. 1927. Washington: U. S. Government Printing Office.

162. Unsigned note.—"The 'Fair' Plan under Section 77B," *Columbia Law Review*, Vol. 35.

163. University of Illinois.—"A Test Analysis of Unsuccessful Industrial Companies," *University of Illinois Bulletin*, Vol. 27, No. 48, 1930.

164. VINER, JACOB.—"Cost Curves and Supply Curves," *Zeitschrift für Nationalökonomie*, Band III, Heft 1. (1932)

165. VON GIERKE, OTTO.—*Political Theories of the Middle Ages*, Cambridge University, 1900 (Translated by F. W. Maitland).

166. WALSH, W. F.—*Outlines of the History of English and American Law*, New York: New York University Press, 1924.

167. WALSH, W. F.—"The Development of the Title and Lien Theories of Mortgages," *New York University Law Quarterly Review*, Vol. 9.

168. WARRINGTON, W. E.—*The Nature and Extent of Losses to Bondholders in Corporate Reorganization and Liquidation, 1919-1928*, Philadelphia: University of Pennsylvania, 1936.

169. WATKINS, M. W.—"Large-Scale Production," *Encyclopedia of the Social Sciences*, Vol. 9.

170. WATKINS, M. W.—"Promotion," *Encyclopedia of the Social Sciences*, Vol. 12.

171. WEIDENHAMMER, R.—"Causes and Repercussions of the Faulty Investment of Corporate Savings," *American Economic Review*, Vol. 23.

172. WEINER, J. L.—"Theory of Anglo-American Dividend Law: American Statutes and Cases," *Columbia Law Review*, Vol. 29.

173. WEINER, J. L., and BONBRIGHT, J. C.—"Anglo-American Dividend Law: Surplus and Profit," *Columbia Law Review*, Vol. 30.

174. WIEDENFELD, K.—"Industrial Combination," *Encyclopedia of the Social Sciences*, Vol. 3.
175. WILBUR, D. E.—"A Study of the Policy of Dividend Stabilization," *Harvard Business Review*, Vol. 10.
176. WOOTTON, BARBARA, *Plan or No Plan*, London: Victor Gollancz Ltd., 1934.

GLOSSARY[1]

Average revenue curve: See demand curve.

Balance sheet equation: The basic assumption underlying the accounting technique in the sense that the "Net Worth" of an enterprise (or a person) is defined as the value of the assets *minus* the liabilities to outsiders; hence by transposition: Assets equals Liabilities *plus* Net Worth.

Degree of monopoly power: The degree to which an enterprise is able to exercise a control over the price of its product without its sales falling to zero or rising to infinity. In technical terms it could be defined as the ratio of price minus marginal cost over price. From this we can see that in pure competition (price equal to marginal cost) the ratio would be zero.

Demand curve: A curve showing the functional relationship between the quantity of the product purchased and its price under given conditions. The given conditions include buyers' schedules of preferences, their incomes, the prices of other products, and the time interval to which the curve relates. A demand curve always designates a "rate of flow" such as X units per day, week, month, etc.

Doctrine of comity: A legal principle according to which one sovereign authority recognizes as valid under its own laws certain acts performed under the laws of another sovereign power.

Elasticity of demand: For any demand curve the proportional relationship between changes in price and resulting variations in the quantities of the commodity purchased by buyers. Elasticity is perhaps most easily measured *via* the behavior of aggregate sales receipts as the price is varied. A demand curve is said to have an elasticity of unity when the aggregate expenditure on the commodity is a constant for all points on the curve, i.e., at all different prices. Elasticity greater than unity means that aggregate expenditure increases as the price of the product is reduced. Conversely if the aggregate expenditure decreases as the price is reduced the demand curve is said to have an elasticity less than unity. Any demand curve is likely to have different degrees of elasticity in its different segments, i.e., elasticity will not be constant throughout the curve.

Elasticity of substitution: This has reference to the degree to which, *ceteris paribus*, a change in the relative prices of two (or more) commodities (or factors of production) induces a consumer (or an entrepreneur) to alter his rates of consumption (or utilization) of

[1] Consult the Index for additional terms on which you may wish further elucidation.

the two (or more) commodities (or factors). Concretely if the price of factor A falls while the prices of all other factors remain unchanged, to what extent will an entrepreneur now substitute A for the other factors, B, C, D, etc.? The concept is difficult to define precisely in non-mathematical terms.

Elasticity of supply: The proportional relationship between changes in the quantity offered for sale and changes in price. If a given proportional increase in price calls forth an equal proportional increase in the quantity offered for sale the supply curve is said to have an elasticity of unity; if the increase in the quantity offered for sale is more than proportional (to the price increase) the supply curve is elastic; if less than proportional the supply curve is inelastic.

Judgment creditor: A creditor who has established legal recognition of his claim and is therefore entitled to take action in law for its collection, and subsequently in equity courts also if he does not obtain payment in full.

"Law" of diminishing elasticity of demand: A "law" attempting to relate changes in the elasticity of demand curves for the products of individual enterprises with changes in consumers' incomes. According to the "law" as consumers' incomes increase the elasticity of the demand curves for the products of the individual enterprises decreases and vice versa. The relation is perhaps over-dignified by the designation "law." See further, Ch. X, p. 273.

Liquidity preference: The disposition of enterprises or real persons with respect to the proportions in which they prefer to hold their assets in money balances (or very liquid assets) and other forms of a less liquid character. In general the preference for liquid assets is likely to increase as the rate of interest declines and as the prospect for lower rather than higher future commodity and asset prices increases; and vice versa. See further, Ch. X, sect. III.

Marginal cost curve: A curve depicting the *increments* in total cost associated with successive increments in output commencing with a rate of output of zero.

Marginal efficiency of an asset: That rate of discount which equates the prospective returns to be had from an additional unit of an asset with its current supply price. Alternatively stated, it is the prospective rate of return upon the cost of an additional unit of an asset. Necessarily it is based on estimates, not certainties.

Marginal principle: The principle of comparing increments of one thing with increments of another where the two are related in some causal fashion, e.g., increments of cost compared with increments of receipts. It becomes therefore the principle employed in problems of maximization.

Marginal revenue curve: A curve depicting the increments in total gross receipts accompanying successive (small) increments in the number of units sold. See further, Ch. VII, pp. 191 ff.

Production function: For any given product the physical relationship which holds between inputs of factors and outputs of product. Usually there is some unique combination which is an optimum, the technology of production being of course given. In a rough sense a cook's recipe book is a book of production functions relating to different foods and beverages. What combination of the factors of production will be most economically employed cannot be determined, of course, unless both the production function and factor prices are known. In other words, both the production functions and the relative prices of the factors of production must be known before the most economical combination of the factors can be specified.

Rate of output: By applying more or fewer variable factors of production to a given scale, i.e., combination of fixed factors, it is possible to increase or decrease the rate of output or volume of production. Increasing the rate of output means, *inter alia,* using the fixed factors of production more intensively.

Reference cycle: A statistical index of a composite character which is taken to represent fluctuations in "general business activity" and with which other indexes, single or composite, are compared with respect to amplitude and timing in their fluctuations.

Scale of production: That combination of certain of the factors of production, e.g., land, specialized capital goods, management, and a skeleton labor force to which are applied varying amounts of labor, materials, supplies, etc., to produce varying quantities of the finished product as a rate of output. From another point of view the scale of production is that combination of the factors which is unalterable over a given period and whose costs cannot be avoided or reduced. See further, Ch. VI, pp. 150 ff.

Supply curve: A curve portraying for given conditions what quantities of a commodity will be offered for sale at a whole schedule of prices, or alternatively, what prices must be offered if a whole schedule of quantities of the product is to be offered for sale. As with the demand curve "quantities" here means rates of flow per unit of time—day, week, month, etc.

INDEX OF NAMES

477

INDEX OF SUBJECTS

Failure, *Continued*
immediate cause of, 336
Fair plan in reorganization, 395
under Ch. X, 431, 434
under 77B, 424
under equity, 408
Financial plan, 170 ff.
and readjustment, 367 f.
conflicting interests in, 174
considerations affecting, 172
in expansion, 324 ff.
Foreign incorporation and corporations, 52 ff.
position of, 60
penalties for non-compliance with laws, 62
reasons for, 52
requirements to do business as, 61
Fortuities and business failure, 354
Fraudulent conveyance, 112, 243

Holding company
and expansion, 318
financial advantages of, 321

Income (*see also* Net income, Net returns)
accounting concept of, 210 ff.
computation of in promotion, 157
enterprise as a unit for computation of, 22
maximization of net, 181
treatment of durable assets in accounting, 213
Incompetence
and failure, 345 ff.
evidence of, 347
in financial judgment, 352
in use of working capital, 353
fixed assets, 350
meaning of, 345
Incorporation
certificate of, 46
cost of in different states, 57
foreign, 52 ff.
laws in different states, 52
process of, 45 ff.
professionalization of, 50
under general laws, 45 ff.
Integration, 307 ff.
Investment
and accounting reports, 228 f.
cyclical fluctuation in inducement to, 280 ff.
ethical aspects of, 455

Investment, *Continued*
in relation to dividend distribution, 234, 257
in reorganization, 375, 394, 405, 422
investigation of probable yield on in promotion, 146
limits to in new enterprise, 163
problem of maintaining, 452

Large corporation, 445 ff.
Lease, 313
Liquidation, 371 ff.
Liquidity
and business cycle, 284
in relation to working capital, 165

Marginal cost
and price policy, 227
concept of, 191
relation to average cost, 193
Marginal principle
in dividend distribution, 234 ff.
in expansion, 298 ff.
in promotion, 163
Marginal revenue
and price policy, 226 f.
derivation from demand curve, 196
Merger, 315
Money outlays
and working capital problem, 166
during an upswing, 272
downswing, 275, 358
Money receipts
and working capital problem, 166, 357
during an upswing, 272
downswing, 275, 257
cyclical variations in, 272, 274, 357, 361
Monopolistic competition
demand curve for firm under, 25
and price policy, 449
Monopoly, 25, 144

Net income
cyclical variations in reported, 276
in accounting and the volume of investment, 291
maximization of, 181
Net returns
and promotion, 145
maximization of, 179 ff.
meaning of, 180